Lincoln's Rise to Eloquence

NO

not for a broad audience
quite specialized - English dept
slashes!
plodding name! ironically

preface
into

corel yawn!

ev chapter begins "The pig..."

Lincoln's Rise to Eloquence

How He Gained the Presidential Nomination

D. LEIGH HENSON

UNIVERSITY OF
ILLINOIS PRESS
Urbana, Chicago, and Springfield

Frontispiece: President-elect Abraham Lincoln, November 25,
1860 (Photograph by Samuel G. Altschuler, Chicago, Library of
Congress, https://www.loc.gov/pictures/item/2005684966/)

Library of Congress Cataloging-in-Publication Data
Names: Henson, Darold Leigh, 1942- author.
Title: Lincoln's rise to eloquence : how he gained the presidential
    nomination / D. Leigh Henson.
Description: Urbana : University of Illinois Press, [2024] |
    Includes bibliographical references and index.
Identifiers: LCCN 2023056368 (print) | LCCN 2023056369
    (ebook) | ISBN 9780252045943 (cloth) | ISBN
    9780252088032 (paperback) | ISBN 9780252056925 (ebook)
Subjects: LCSH: Lincoln, Abraham, 1809–1865—Political career
    before 1861. | Lincoln, Abraham, 1809–1865—Oratory. |
    Republican Party (U.S. : 1854-) | Presidents—United States—
    Election—1860. | Political campaigns—United States—
    History—19th century. | Presidential candidates—United
    States—Biography. | Presidents—United States—Biography. |
    United States—Politics and government—1857–1861.
Classification: LCC E457.4 H46 2024 (print) | LCC E457.4
    (ebook) | DDC 973.7092 [B]—dc23/eng/20240606
LC record available at https://lccn.loc.gov/2023056368
LC ebook record available at https://lccn.loc.gov/2023056369

To my wife,
Patricia Leigh Steinke Hartman, MBA

Contents

Preface

Beginning in 1832 at the age of twenty-three, Abraham Lincoln advanced through two political careers to gain the US presidency in 1860. His experiences in politics, writing, and speaking were closely interrelated and mutually beneficial, with his compositions—speeches and other writings—driving his political advancement. This book tells the story of Lincoln's rhetorical growth that led the Republican Party to nominate him for president, explaining how he adapted fundamentals traced to classical rhetoric in various genres—sometimes creating original hybrids—to suit his political/rhetorical purposes in the decades prior to the Civil War.

The carefully composed address he gave at Cooper Union in New York City, February 27, 1860, and subsequent related speeches in the East so favorably impressed audiences and a wider reading public that the Republican Party nominated him as its presidential candidate in May of that year. His political/rhetorical advancement is remarkable because with less than a year of formal education, he learned how to adapt rhetorical skills to his evolving political activities and aims in troubled times. His physical qualities on the speaking platform and stump, including his peculiar gestures and rather high-pitched voice, are well known.[1] The substance, style, and significance of Lincoln's compositions are vastly more challenging to understand, and they have been analyzed by numerous biographers, historians, rhetoricians, and others. These writers have taken various approaches to the many works in the broad spectrum of Lincoln's rhetoric, with diverse results—often insightful but often limited and sometimes contradictory.[2] Yet approaches to Lincoln's rhetoric may be classified under just two perspectives: inclusive and exclusive.

Neither perspective can adequately explain Lincoln's rhetorical growth that enabled him to compose the Cooper Union address. In the inclusive perspective, Lincoln's compositions are just one element in accounts of his life and times. Biography in its traditional form is the genre that most often, but not always, treats Lincoln's rhetoric from the inclusive perspective, citing mostly his main compositions without much rhetorical analysis and without well accounting for them in an unfolding saga of political/rhetorical advancement. Some biographers lack the appropriate knowledge and skill necessary for intensive rhetorical/textual analysis, and the complexity of Lincoln's life does not afford enough space for biography to offer adequate rhetorical/textual analysis of his prepresidential compositions. Not every Lincoln biography even cites all of them. Lincoln biographers variously mention the political/rhetorical purposes and context of selected major compositions, perhaps summarize their main points, perhaps comment on their argumentation, perhaps quote one or more notable passages, and perhaps indicate contemporaneous responses, which tended to follow party lines. Biographers' critical commentary usually relates more to Lincoln's politics than to his rhetorical methods.[3]

The exclusive perspective offers detailed rhetorical analysis of one or more compositions, sometimes including minor ones and focusing on technical qualities. The exclusive perspective on Lincoln's rhetoric appears in specialized studies published most often in academic journals and sometimes books. Those studies provide close rhetorical/textual analysis and interpretation, discussing one or more of the subjects that Lincoln biography may only mention, especially genre, methods of argumentation, and literary techniques.[4] Publications with an exclusive perspective on Lincoln's compositions do not explain the full range of his prepresidential rhetorical experiences and their relationships, or account for his rhetorical growth.

As the only Lincoln rhetorical biography to date, this book attempts to surpass the limitations of previous approaches to his prepresidential, explicitly and implicitly, political writing by applying a full range of rhetorical fundamentals (identified below) to analyze and assess his evolving political/rhetorical purposes and methods in thirty-one main compositions (plus numerous lesser works) that account for his political struggle through the Cooper Union address: eleven from his first political career, twenty from his second. This book's central argument is that over time Lincoln developed a powerful and ethical rhetoric, gaining credibility (ethos) and political capital, by deploying rational (logos) and emotional (pathos) appeals through historical, legalistic, and moral argumentation, while sometimes using demagogic and satirical methods. Moral argumentation is the lifeblood of Lincoln's rhetoric that explains his rise to eloquence and that brought him the 1860 Republican presidential nomination and presidency, but the road to those achievements was tortuous. Lincoln's moral suasion, whether implicit or explicit, underpinned his policy arguments. William Lee Miller describes Lincoln as a "moral thinker" and "moral learner" and links his moral thought to his political activity, which served "not only his own possible rise and that of his party but also of worthy social purposes."[5]

Eloquent passages in Lincoln's prepresidential rhetoric show his rise to statesmanship, but his rhetoric also involved the use of elements inconsistent with statesmanship: demagoguery and satire. Lincoln biographer Reinhard H. Luthin allows, "There exists a bit of demagoguery in the most lofty of statesmen."[6] J. Justin Gustainis observes, "It does not necessarily follow that a speaker who uses demagogic rhetoric on a particular occasion is thus properly to be considered a demagogue."[7] The introduction explains that demagoguery and satire have been more clearly defined than eloquence.

Lincoln's main compositions blend moral suasion and controversial, sometimes demagogic elements—creating rhetorical tension. Lincoln spent his public life in a political culture marked by demagoguery, and many of his compositions were responses to the rhetoric of members of oppositional parties, revealing not only his handling of demagoguery but also his political beliefs and policies. Lincoln used demagogic methods more freely and crudely in his first political career—sometimes cruel personal attacks—than in his second. Lincoln's rhetoric often included satire—an implicitly moralistic method—of rivals' positions, policies, and personal qualities. Lincoln's moral sense concerned his beliefs about the greater good for the nation and what was right and fair for himself—his honor. Lincoln's moral argumentation was typically implicit in his first political career. In his second political career, moral argumentation—again, the key to his eloquence—was sometimes implicit but more often explicit, especially in his antislavery argumentation. He was skillful in addressing partisan audiences, but his compositions praised as eloquent reached beyond partisanship.

Vital to the story of Lincoln's rhetorical growth is how he responded to the demagoguery of his decades-long adversary/foil, Stephen A. Douglas. Lincoln first rebutted Douglas's rhetoric in the 1830s. In the 1850s Lincoln charged that Douglas's positions and policies would nationalize slavery. During the 1858 Senate race, Lincoln faced the question of how to deal with Douglas's fallacious claims and personal attacks, and Lincoln described their famous debates as a drama. Specifically, Lincoln had to decide whether or how to employ "turnabout is fair play" strategies that the public might view as abusive and thus threaten his principled ambition of seeking to earn public respect that he expressed in his first run for public office in 1832. Those strategies could also conflict with the need for self-respect that Lincoln first revealed in the mid-1840s as he competed for a congressional nomination. During and after the 1858 Senate race, Lincoln occasionally used controversial rhetorical methods, including personal attacks, while also using rational/moral argumentation to advance his positions and policies, and to refute Douglas's. In 1859 the rivals avoided face-to-face encounters, as Lincoln's main speeches continued to criticize Douglas's positions, policies, rhetoric, and moral character, with satire playing a major role in Lincoln's Cincinnati speech, his last major speech before the Cooper Union address.

The disparate and sometimes conflicting elements in Lincoln's rhetoric have resulted in antithetical views of its quality. Lincolnists often use the word *eloquent* in praising his most important compositions. The most common word his detractors use, often for the same compositions praised by others, is *demagogic*—a more condemnatory term even than *inarticulate*, an antonym for *eloquent*. Lincolnists describe some of his compositions or passages in them as eloquent without defining that quality. This book's introduction offers a working definition of eloquence and applies it throughout. Lincoln's critics may praise or condemn his compositions in their entirety or just passages, rhetorical methods, or language techniques.

Highly biased Lincoln detractors have made extensive efforts to show that his rhetoric proves he was an incorrigible demagogue. Most notably Edgar Lee Masters, Lerone J. Bennett Jr., and M.E. Bradford have presented lengthy arguments charging Lincoln with demagoguery throughout his public life, including the presidency.[8] Other, more objective Lincolnists have also identified demagogic elements in his rhetoric. Graham A. Peck, for example, observes that even in the Cooper Union address, Lincoln somewhat exaggerated the antislavery inclinations of the founders.[9] This book discusses Lincoln's use of the founders in numerous compositions, including the Cooper Union address. Lincoln's Democratic Party conspiracy accusation first presented in the 1858 House Divided speech also makes him vulnerable to the charge of demagoguery.

Abraham Lincoln did not gain distinction when he dabbled in poetry or delivered his first lectures—genres associated with creativity and originality— yet his ingenious compositions played a major role in his success as a politician and statesman. From the tradition of classical rhetoric—the work of ancient Greek and Roman rhetoricians—we have the term *invention* to designate the formulation of communicative purpose, creation of discourse content, and corresponding adaptation of other basic elements of communication. Classical rhetoric established the primary field of communication study that has been continually expanded and refined for centuries up to the present, including the early definition of rhetoric as the art of persuasion in three forms: political (deliberative), forensic (legalistic), and ceremonial (epideictic).[10] Today every academic field and profession applies fundamentals from classical rhetoric in generating, analyzing, interpreting, evaluating, and teaching spoken and written discourse.

Elements of classical rhetoric pervade Lincoln's compositions, and his use of those elements is surely attributable to more than common sense or intuition.

Yet the interior monologue of his composing/self-editing process, including whether his thinking used rhetorical or literary terms, has to remain obscure, for he made little comment on these matters. Also for that reason, we cannot know whether he understood that any elements of his writing and speaking originated in classical antiquity. Regardless, and most important, familiarity with those elements in his compositions is essential to understand and appreciate his political/rhetorical experiences, expertise, and evolution. This book's introduction further explains the principles and practices of classical rhetoric and the opportunities Lincoln had to learn them in his efforts to improve his communicative ability from childhood through adulthood, arguably the most important example of his ability to learn from experience. Benjamin P. Thomas regarded that ability as Lincoln's most significant quality: "The outstanding feature of Lincoln's life was his capacity for growth."[11]

This book presents systematic, detailed rhetorical/textual analysis and assessment of more Lincoln compositions than any other source, and those discussions include fresh insights but without the elaborate, technical explanations seen in some rhetorical studies of his individual compositions.[12] This book provides historical context and citations of selected critical commentary on Lincoln's compositions from contemporaneous and secondary sources to augment and give perspective to the rhetorical/textual analyses and assessments. Endnotes sometimes supply additional details, but a comprehensive review of published critical commentary is beyond the scope of this study.

This book serves multiple audiences from specialists to nonspecialists. Professional Lincolnists and rhetoricians, like all readers, will discover how Lincoln applied rhetorical fundamentals in devising messages to various kinds of audiences with increasing political advantage. This book will also appeal to wider audiences ranging from the generally well-educated reading public interested in Lincoln and his times to scholars, instructors, and advanced students in such diverse fields as history, political science, presidential studies, communications, journalism, and English studies.

A book on Lincoln's rhetoric has several benefits, as Don E. Fehrenbacher explains: "Among modern public leaders especially, important action is nearly always verbal. In the words of a Jefferson, a Napoleon, or a Churchill one finds not only the record but the substance of his principal deeds, as well as the clearest traces of his character. To study Abraham Lincoln, then, we must examine his words, and not only the words that he wrote but also those that he uttered, insofar as they are known."[13] Lincoln's compositions provide insight into his personality and character, and they help to define his distinctive political and literary achievements: "In the letters, speeches, and public papers of Abraham Lincoln, one finds the real man, but not the whole man. . . . The contours of Lincoln's character and career are plainly visible in his prose. . . . Most of that prose is strictly functional; to read it is to see him in action, pursuing practical results, rather than ultimate truth."[14] Yet this book shows that Lincoln's most important compositions aimed for practical results by presenting ultimate political truth.

This book will also aid readers' ability to navigate other Lincoln studies. Given the significance of classical rhetoric as the foundation of communication as a field of study, those who publish about Lincoln's discourse consciously or intuitively apply fundamentals of rhetoric, and readers—especially students— can use the principles of classical rhetoric as a lens to gain insights into those publications.

Acknowledgments

This book emerges from a journey that has taken me along career paths intersecting the study, teaching, and writing about literature and its pedagogy, rhetoric and composition, and technical and marketing communication. In the last few years, I have taken new trails, reaching successive plateaus of research and publication about my hometown, Lincoln, Illinois—the first Lincoln namesake town—its famous native-son editor/author, William Maxwell, and the rhetoric of Abraham Lincoln. I grew up two blocks from the site of the Postville Courthouse, where Abraham Lincoln practiced law (1840–1847). My formative years in Lincoln implicitly set the compass for this long journey. The following summary recognizes some of the most important people who influenced this journey, with apology to anyone I have overlooked.

In 1961 I moved from my hometown to attend Illinois State University, then for thirty years to teach high school English at Pekin, Illinois, and next to Missouri State University, where for fourteen years I taught and published on the theory, practice, and pedagogy of technical and marketing communication. Throughout my teaching careers, I often returned to my hometown to visit family and friends, always with the shadowy memory of some of Abraham Lincoln's activities there. By the late 1990s I had gained tenure at Missouri State, and with that security I had the time to reflect on how growing up in the first Lincoln namesake town and attending Lincoln College—the first Lincoln namesake college—my freshman year had influenced my personal life, education, and careers.

Then, Abraham Lincoln stepped out of the shadows. He became a central subject of the community history website of the first Lincoln namesake town, which I published in 2003 and have continually expanded. That website includes stories of the Lincoln legend I heard from Lincoln buff E.H. Lukenbill, the Logan County Superintendent of Public Instruction, when he visited classes I attended at Jefferson School through sixth grade. During those years my mother, the late Jane Wilson Henson, told me about Mr. Lincoln's law practice at Postville Courthouse. That site was a neighborhood playground before and after the 1953 courthouse replica was built. I attended its dedication as a student in Principal Bernadine Jones's sixth-grade class, witnessing the appearance of Governor William G. Stratton—a true Lincoln buff, as I discovered years later. During family picnics at nearby Postville Park, my mother told me about Mr. Lincoln playing sports there when court recessed. My hometown history website led to my research and publication about the political speeches Mr. Lincoln had given there in the 1850s.

That online history also includes information about the work of James T. Hickey, former curator of the Henry Horner Lincoln Collection in the Illinois State Historical Library (now the Abraham Lincoln Presidential Library and Museum) and author of many essays reporting his Lincoln research. As a freshman at Lincoln College in 1960–1961, I enjoyed his two-semester course in Lincoln literature. I never forgot the charming pleasure he expressed for the study of Abraham Lincoln, and that memory has been a motivating factor for my fun work of researching Lincoln's discourse in retirement.

In 2008, as an honorary member of the Abraham Lincoln Bicentennial Commission of Lincoln, Illinois, I researched and wrote the play script used for the reenactment of Lincoln's political rally and stump speech he gave on the steps of the Logan County Courthouse on October 16, 1858, the day after the last Lincoln-Douglas debate. I also proposed a statue of Lincoln and historical marker to commemorate that rally-speech, and they were erected in 2015. I am grateful to the civic leaders who helped to accomplish the reenactment as well as the statue and marker installation, including friends Wanda Lee Rohlfs; the late, lamented Lincolnist, Paul J. Beaver, professor emeritus of history at Lincoln College; and Ron J. Keller, then associate professor of history and political science at Lincoln College, and in 2023 the director of the Lincoln Heritage Museum.

I am grateful to many others from my earlier years who helped and encouraged my research and writing, especially Florence Molen, Dr. Stanley Renner, Dr. Daniel W. Stowell, Dr. Joseph Morris Webb, Dr. Kristene Sutliff, Richard E. Hart, William Furry, Richard Sumrall, David and Patrick Doolin, Bill Gossett, Geoff Ladd, and Mike Starasta. I thank my children, Kendra L. Henson, Brandon L. Henson, and their spouses for sharing interest in my hometown roots and for supporting my professional activities.

Since my retirement from Missouri State University in 2008, I have pursued several projects relating to the heritage and rhetoric of Abraham Lincoln. In 2011 I published *The Town Abraham Lincoln Warned: The Living Namesake Heritage of Lincoln, Illinois*, and several Lincolnists and historians provided suggestions and testimonials for that project, including Dr. Thomas F. Schwartz, Dr. Wayne C. Temple, Dr. Robert M. McColley, and Paul J. Beaver. Their support encouraged my further research on Lincoln's compositions. I have also been encouraged in this work by the interest in it often expressed by fellow native Lincolnite and author, James A. Knecht, justice of the Illinois Fourth District Appellate Court.

In 2014 I published "Classical Rhetoric as a Lens for Reading the Key Speeches of Lincoln's Political Rise, 1852–1856" in the *Journal of the Abraham Lincoln Association*, with critiques from peer reviewers and guidance from editors Dr. Bryon Andreasen and Dr. Christian McWhirter.

In 2017 I published *Inventing Lincoln: Approaches to His Rhetoric*. This work explains and critiques how Lincoln's speeches and other compositions have been treated in biographies—twenty-one, from 1872 to 2016—and studies of discourse analysis—thirty-six, from 1900 to 2015: five books and thirty-one book chapters or essays published in peer-reviewed journals largely unfamiliar to the general public. Lincolnists' fields of expertise, values, and beliefs affect the choice of his speeches and other compositions they write about and every aspect of treating them: contextualizing, analyzing, summarizing, explicating, quoting, paraphrasing, and assessing. In effect, all techniques of rendering the meaning of a text and judging it are interpretive. Through their various approaches to Lincoln's compositions, his interpreters are immensely responsible for inventing him—shaping the world's beliefs about Lincoln the man, Lincoln the politician, and Lincoln the statesman.

I am grateful to Dr. John M. Barr, Harold Holzer, and Dr. David Zarefsky for reviewing a draft of *Inventing Lincoln*. The comments and suggestions I received in that process enabled me to make revisions and additions that strengthened this project. My devoted, beloved wife, Patricia L. "Pat" Hartman, MBA, Boston University, has helped immeasurably through her sound advice, patient encouragement, and skill in content editing, copyediting, and indexing. I am grateful to Michael Stowe, former senior instructor at Missouri State University, for promptly responding to my sporadic calls for help in using software.

I have recently published articles in *The Lincoln Herald* and *Lincoln Lore*, and *Lincoln's Rise to Eloquence: How He Gained the Presidential Nomination* is the capstone of my academic life. For it I am most grateful to Alison Syring, acquisitions editor at the University of Illinois Press. She saw promise in an early rough draft and obtained excellent peer reviewers. Throughout a lengthy revision process, her skillful guidance and encouragement have been invaluable. I thank other staff members of the University of Illinois Press for their expertise in accomplishing this project. I am deeply indebted to two anonymous reviewers and Dr. Michael Burlingame: their critiques shaped and refined this work. Pat Hartman, my devoted wife, as always has assisted with continuous encouragement and numerous, tedious technical tasks. Despite the extensive collaboration that has brought this work to publication, I am solely responsible for its shortcomings.

Lincoln's Rise
to Eloquence

Introduction

This book's account of Lincoln's prepresidential political/rhetorical growth and achievement develops chronologically, featuring detailed rhetorical/textual analysis of his most important compositions. Those analyses take a systematic, topical approach, beginning with historical/biographical context and critical commentary on selected secondary sources to introduce the analyses, which then variously apply these topics: political/rhetorical purpose, genre, structure, content development (including satire when present), and style. Reporting on minor compositions fleshes out the story. Lincoln's compositions illustrate consistency and versatility, and some are milestones in his rhetorical evolution. This introduction presents information about rhetoric as a field of study, opportunities Lincoln had to learn rhetorical basics, and his political beliefs and aims. This background will help readers access the chapters.

Lincoln's compositions require understanding the term *rhetoric*, but that term is problematic. *Rhetoric* or *rhetorical* may refer to just speaking (oratory) or to the manner of delivering a speech or to language usage. Frequently the terms are negative, referring to someone manipulating the audience through unreliable facts, fallacious and misleading argumentation, or incendiary language. Rhetoricians Andrew King and Jim A. Kuypers lament the entrenched, pejorative usage of the word *rhetoric*: "Why it is not an honored term remains a mystery. Despite our professed best efforts the derogatory definition of rhetoric as insincere words and inflated style remains the predominant usage both inside and beyond the academy."[1] In fact, these negative meanings associated with the word *rhetoric,* whether in Lincoln studies or elsewhere, obscure the original definition of rhetoric in western civilization as "the art or the discipline that deals with the use of discourse, either spoken or written, to inform or persuade or motivate an audience, whether that audience is made up of one person or a group of persons."[2]

This book maintains that the effectiveness of Lincoln's rhetoric, especially the eloquent passages, was vital to his success as a politician and statesman. His rhetoric served his political purposes: to get elected, to shape and advance Whig Party positions and policies, to promote Whig presidential candidates and the first Republican Party presidential candidate (John C. Frémont), to formulate and promote Republican positions and policies, and to build its base through coalitions. As a Whig and later as a Republican Party leader and spokesman, he also sought to mold public opinion.

An overview of classical rhetoric provides background for the rhetorical/ textual analyses and interpretations in this study, beginning with its main components: communicative purpose, audience analysis, invention (content development, including argumentation and adaptation of other rhetorical elements), arrangement (organization/structural design), style (language), memory, and delivery.[3] Principles of classical rhetoric originally pertained to oratory but for centuries have been applied to many forms of writing. Contemporary rhetoricians Edward P.J. Corbett and Robert J. Connors observe that nineteenth-century rhetoric emphasized writing more than speaking and that "the rhetoric of writing does have many roots in classical rhetoric."[4]

Invention in legal and political compositions—the kinds most important to Lincoln's prepresidential careers—concerns effective argumentation, but invention also more broadly requires integrating all rhetorical strategies and techniques, including language. Argumentation makes appeals to logic (logos), emotions (pathos), and the communicator's credibility (ethos). The appeal to logic, often called the rational appeal, involves the use of artistic and nonartistic proofs. Artistic proofs consist of modes of reasoning, and nonartistic proofs derive from such sources as laws and testimonials.[5] Close reasoning with facts obtained through historical research characterizes Lincoln's political argumentation. Among the documents vital to Lincoln's argumentation were the Ordinance of 1787, the Declaration of Independence, and the Constitution. Style, according to classical rhetoric, whether plain or flowery, requires competent grammar and vocabulary. Direct, plain phrasing characterizes Lincoln's mature style, and he often clarified and enhanced his points with figurative language relating to common life.

In creating his legal and political compositions, Lincoln needed to devise and develop arguments in a coherent structure with appropriate language for diverse kinds of audiences. In examining the rhetorical elements of Lincoln's political compositions, this study pays close attention to structural design, because the sequence of his content development yields insight into the arguments he adapted for various purposes and audiences. Understanding structural design in classical rhetoric helps us understand Lincoln's use of it. That design consists of six elements: the introduction (exordium), a statement of the facts of a subject in question (narration), the outline of the main points in the speaker's case (division), the proof (confirmation), a refutation of the opposition (confutation), and the conclusion (peroration). The present study finds that two of Lincoln's major compositions are textbook examples of structural design based on the preceding sequence of elements. Yet this sequence is not meant to be a rigid formula, and the adaptation of these concepts allows for flexible arrangement, especially in the body of a work depending on a particular communicative purpose and audience.[6] Many of Lincoln's compositions examined here demonstrate such flexibility.

Sources of Classical Rhetoric
That May Have Influenced Lincoln

Lincoln, an eager learner from the beginning, would have encountered fundamentals of classical rhetoric in his early life. The tradition of classical rhetoric was a major influence on the work of nineteenth-century, Anglo-American rhetoricians, and some of the textbooks and anthologies that Lincoln is known to have read (or may have read) afforded him the opportunity to learn about classical rhetoric in his formative years.[7]

During Lincoln's childhood and teens in Indiana, he would have become familiar with at least two books that had information relating to classical rhetoric: William Scott's *Lessons in Elocution* (1823) and Lindley Murray's *English Reader* (1799), which included readings from such Enlightenment thinkers as David Hume, who influenced the writers of the American Declaration of Independence.[8] Nearly half of the readings in Murray's *English Reader* are borrowed from Hugh Blair's *Lectures on Rhetoric and Belles Lettres* (1783). Blair's writing testified to the value of literature and the importance of a plain writing style. Robert Bray notes that selections from Blair included in the *English Reader* illustrate the principles of "purity, propriety, and perspicuity," and Bray suggests those selections would have interested Lincoln. "Murray evidently regarded Blair as the perfect model of high moral seriousness propelled by a fine, clear style. All of the essays were didactic yet never bigoted and for the most part unsullied by self-righteousness."[9] William H. Herndon wrote that "Mr. Lincoln told me in later years that Murray's *English Reader* was the best schoolbook ever put into the hands of an American youth."[10] William Lee Miller explains that such works as the *English Reader* presented rhetoric as a rigorous intellectual and moral inquiry: "Rhetoric as a classical field had a closer connection to ethics than a modern mind might imagine. So it was not an anomaly for these editors putting together readers in 'elocution' and 'rhetoric' that would be perused by a young Indiana reader to include explicit and implicit treatments of moral life."[11]

Murray's work emphasized the importance of reading aloud to an audience, and Bray suggests that "a pupil such as Lincoln, almost never in school, could use the *English Reader* as a means of self-tutelage. And he probably did just that. Murray's introduction presents nine categories of voice training." Bray claims that as Lincoln "read in and out of school, silently in solitude, 'publicly' to his peers, he began to write from his reading—a lifelong habit."[12] Murray's book promoted the study of models of composition, including selections from classical times. Throughout its history, the pedagogy of classical rhetoric included copying and imitating models.[13] Biographers have cited Lincoln's stepmother's testimony that during his childhood he learned about language by copying material from books he read.

Nineteenth-century American education taught that grammar, rhetoric, logic, and morality were interrelated; and Lincoln may have known about the close relationship among these elements through his study of Kirkham's *English Grammar in Familiar Lectures* at New Salem, whose model sentences expressed moral principles. It follows that a Lincoln motivated to study one of these elements would also be interested in the others and their interrelationship.

Whether Lincoln read Blair's *Lectures* at New Salem is uncertain. Colonel Matthew Rogers lived just a few miles outside New Salem, and his family had a relatively large library, which included Blair's *Lectures* (2 vols.). James T. Hickey suggests that Lincoln borrowed from Rogers's library.[14] Bray, however, concludes it is quite unlikely that Lincoln read Blair's *Lectures* as a separate work. Bray cites Henry B. Rankin's testimony that Blair's *Lectures* was "one of Lincoln's favorite books," but Bray admonishes that Rankin "is never a reliable informant on Lincoln."[15] Douglas L. Wilson notes: "Except for the passages on rhetoric in the textbooks he read as a young man, it is doubtful that Lincoln ever studied the art of persuasion as a formal discipline or read Aristotle's *Rhetoric*."[16] But as Ronald C. White Jr. has observed, "Lincoln's rhetoric embodies the principles of the ancient Greek philosopher" (Aristotle).[17] In 1939 Roy P. Basler averred, "An examination of some of the textbooks which Lincoln used as a boy reveals that he probably had a more thorough training in rhetoric than the average college graduate of the present."[18]

David Zarefsky comments on Lincoln's self-directed learning process, observing that Lincoln "studied models. . . . Lincoln probably thought about rhetoric. . . . Lincoln's implicit theory [as suggested by the 1842 Temperance address] reaches back to the classical understanding of rhetoric as the discovery of available means of persuasion. His concern was not with artistry in itself but with making his message acceptable to his audience."[19] Zarefsky maintains that Lincoln "acquainted himself with some of the exemplars of the time . . . , [including] Jonathan Elliott's collection of debates on the US Constitution . . . and 'very likely' also the collected speeches of William Henry Seward, Joshua Giddings, and Theodore Parker, and it is 'somewhat likely' that he read those of Patrick Henry."[20]

Lincoln's first speech most significantly reflecting the adaptation of classical rhetoric is the 1839 Speech on the Subtreasury. The elements of classical rhetoric are so explicit and extensive in this speech—especially its organization and use of refutation—that Lincoln must have used them consciously, not intuitively, regardless of whether he knew of their origin in classical antiquity. Thus, an interesting and important question arises as to a derivative source of classical rhetoric for this speech. Regardless of whether Lincoln read Blair's *Lectures* as a separate work apart from its material in Murray's *English Reader*, it is worth noting that *Lectures* contains two chapters on organizational strategy based on classical rhetoric, but that information does not correspond well to the organization of the Subtreasury speech, and Blair has nothing whatsoever to say about refutation.[21]

A more likely source of classical rhetoric influencing Lincoln was the rhetoric of the Whig Senator Daniel Webster. Unlike Henry Clay, whose Whig rhetoric Lincoln also admired, Webster received advanced formal education, which included work in classical rhetoric.[22] According to Michael Burlingame, in 1837 Lincoln heard Webster speak in Springfield. Lincoln as an aspiring Whig had reason to pay attention to Webster's speeches in the 1830s while serving in the Illinois legislature, for Webster delivered major speeches on the National Bank (1832, 1834), the currency (1837), and the subtreasury (1839).[23] Those speeches were published in the *National Intelligencer* and the *Congressional Globe* for national distribution, and Lincoln said he read those publications.[24] They circulated in the Illinois state capitals of Vandalia and Springfield in the 1830s. Webster's economic interests "centered on banking and currency questions."[25]

Lincoln would have been motivated to read Webster's speeches as policy statements from one of his party's leaders on economic questions, and Lincoln's interest in self-education would have encouraged him to learn from Webster's rhetorical methods as well. Webster's 1837 Speech on the Currency and 1838 Second Speech on the Subtreasury Bill may have influenced Lincoln's 1839 Speech on the Subtreasury. Webster's 1837 Speech on the Currency uses a structural design from classical oratory, and Lincoln's 1839 Subtreasury speech is the first instance in which he uses a similar structure: both speeches employ early sections featuring much "statement of facts" material followed by sections first affirming "propositions" and then refuting major arguments of the opposition. In effect, Lincoln's 1839 Subtreasury speech is a textbook example of political (deliberative) discourse derived from classical rhetoric, as explained further in chapter 1.

Webster's 1837 speech and Lincoln's 1839 speech both argue that the federal government should solve the country's current financial crisis. Lincoln's speech echoes Webster's argument that the federal government has a "duty" to provide a currency that serves not only the government but also the interests of business and individuals. Webster and Lincoln maintained that the Constitution places this responsibility on Congress, not the executive branch. According to Webster and Lincoln, a national banking system is better suited to meet those needs than the subtreasury system proposed by the administration of President Martin Van Buren. Webster's and Lincoln's speeches maintain that historical precedent vindicates a national banking system and that such a system is constitutional. A direct, plain style characterizes the bulk of both speeches, including language to forecast and mark other transitions. Both use figurative language selectively, and both display flowery language in their perorations.

During his two years in Congress (1847–49), Lincoln met Webster, socialized at his Saturday breakfasts, and became more familiar with his discourse. According to Michael Burlingame, Lincoln "greatly admired Webster's speeches, which he predicted 'will be read forever.'"[26] Lincoln's celebrated 1854 Peoria speech employs a structure that closely parallels a speech by Daniel Webster, being another textbook example of classical rhetoric, as explained in chapter 4. Burlingame observes that Lincoln's 1856 Lost speech at Bloomington quotes from Webster's famous 1830 Second Reply to Senator Robert Y. Hayne: "Liberty and Union, now and forever, one and inseparable."[27] Burlingame further notes that the beginning of Lincoln's 1858 House Divided speech paraphrases the first sentence of that Webster speech.[28]

Lincoln's opportunities to learn about rhetoric continued beyond his time in the Illinois legislature. In the 1840s he may have learned about rhetoric from reading the speeches of his first law partner, John T. Stuart, who was also a Whig colleague elected to the US Congress. Stuart had earned a liberal arts degree and would thus have studied classical rhetoric. Lincoln's 1852 Eulogy on Henry Clay suggests familiarity with Clay's rhetoric: "Mr. Clay's eloquence did not consist, as many fine specimens of eloquence does [do], of types and figures [of speech]—of antithesis, and elegant arrangement."[29] Lincoln employed these very qualities in his rhetoric. Some of Lincoln's contemporaries, including William H. Herndon, Henry Clay Whitney, and John T. Stuart, recalled that in the early 1850s Lincoln had been studying the related subject of logic in the form of Euclid's *Elements of Geometry*.[30]

Lincoln became a student of the rhetorical process. Douglas L. Wilson has cited sources that testify Lincoln carefully, thoughtfully planned, composed, and revised.[31] Other Lincoln biographers have observed that in his writing process, he sometimes read drafts to political friends or provided written copies to solicit feedback. The best-known example of his rejection of feedback was his resolve to deliver the House Divided speech as he had planned but contrary to the advice of political friends, and the best-known example of accepting advice was his decision to use some of William Seward's suggestions in revising the conclusion of the First Inaugural Address.

Demagoguery, Eloquence, Satire, and Moral Argumentation

Questions of demagoguery, eloquence, satire, and moral argumentation in Lincoln's rhetoric concern how he created messages with appeals to reason (logos), emotion (pathos), and credibility (ethos). These appeals are closely interrelated, and the present study considers how Lincoln used them in concert, with emphasis on his efforts to gain credibility through rational and moral argumentation. Corbett and Connors write that "the ethical appeal can be the most effective kind of appeal; even the cleverest and soundest appeal to reason could fall on deaf ears if the audience reacted unfavorably to the speaker's character."[32] Credibility derives from a speaker/writer's reputation and in a given composition can be sought through rational and emotional appeals. Conversely, a speaker/writer's attempts to gain credibility or elicit approval of arguments could falter if an audience detected such demagoguery as fallacious argumentation. Many Lincolnists praise some of his compositions or parts of them as eloquent, but this praise usually reflects implicit notions, not stated criteria of what defines eloquence.

Demagoguery and satire are more clearly defined concepts than eloquence, and satire is a technique sometimes associated with demagoguery, for example, personal attacks, but not with eloquence. J. Justin Gustainis defines a demagogue as an opportunist mainly concerned with gaining and exercising power by suppressing a community (or component of a community) in a shared crisis, which the demagogue purports to resolve and thereby become a "savior."[33] According to Gustainis, the rhetorical techniques of demagoguery are personalized appeal, political pageantry, personal (ad hominem) attacks, fallacious argumentation, anti-intellectualism, and emotional appeals. Corbett and Connors similarly define demagoguery as the "exploitation of specious arguments . . . and rank emotional appeals to gain personal advantage rather than to promote public welfare."[34] Corbett and Connors identify various kinds of fallacies that constitute specious argumentation, including half-truths, factual errors, either/or options, unjustified personal attacks, appealing to the emotions and prejudices of the public in order to divert them from rational thought about important political issues (ad populum), faulty analogy, and the red herring.[35] These rhetoricians point out that effective persuasion results from a combination of rational and emotional appeals and that the ethical quality of suasion is what matters.

Gustainis notes that demagoguery can surface in a democracy because rhetorical abuse requires free speech. Lincoln lived during a time of increasing slavery agitation—a fearful time, thus conducive to demagoguery. Like many Americans, Lincoln and Stephen A. Douglas tried to mitigate this agitation through political action and rhetoric. As a US senator, Douglas was instrumental in the design and passage of both the Compromise of 1850 and the 1854 Kansas-Nebraska Act. The national firestorm over that 1854 legislation motivated Lincoln to return to politics and oppose its key principle of popular sovereignty—allowing local governments in new territories to decide for or against slavery.

Both politicians then faced career crises. Douglas had to defend popular sovereignty and his opposition to the proslavery Lecompton Constitution in Kansas despite the support of it from fellow Democrat President James Buchanan. Lincoln had to defend his opposition to slavery extension, the accusation that the Republican Party and he were radical abolitionists in favor of disunion, and the threat that his party would embrace Douglas for his opposition to the Lecompton Constitution. Rhetoric was the main weapon Lincoln and Douglas used against one another, reflecting and provoking partisan divisions.

Lincolnists variously cite passages or entire compositions as eloquent without much explanation, sometimes vaguely characterizing his eloquence as "soaring language." Dictionary definitions of eloquence are too ambiguous for practical application. The online Merriam-Webster's dictionary defines eloquence as "1: discourse marked by force and persuasiveness, also the art or power of using such discourse; 2: the quality of forceful or persuasive expressiveness."[36] The problem here is the failure to state that persuasion must serve a good cause. Eloquent rhetoric uses cogent moral argumentation and emotive language to inspire belief in a cause for social justice or human rights, or action to achieve them. The only primary source passages in this book labeled as eloquent are ones that comply with this definition. This book considers how Lincoln combines the three appeals to reach for eloquence in his prepresidential compositions, with attention to whether entire compositions ought to be referred to as eloquent and what language techniques characterize those passages commonly referred to as eloquent, including emotional appeals. Lincoln studies have emphasized the rational appeal of his historical, legalistic, and moral argumentation with less attention to his appeals to his credibility and emotions.

Lincoln sometimes used satire—humorous criticism—to enhance direct or indirect moral argumentation and sharpen refutation. Satire had emerged from classical antiquity as a literary genre, and like other writers before and after him, Lincoln used satire as a rhetorical method. From its origin, satire was based on the principle that for improvement in the human condition to occur, people must first learn to laugh at imperfections, especially in flawed social/political constructions and human nature itself.[37] From the beginning to end of his prepresidential political life, Lincoln often exaggerated with verbal and situational irony for satirical effect, with both sarcasm (Juvenalian satire) and lighter diminution (Horatian satire): "Lincoln combined modesty

√ monographic

and attack, consistently engaging in strategic self-deprecation to deprecate his opponents, their policies, and their arguments, thus refiguring satiric discourse as political discourse (and vice versa). At the same time, he astutely deflected his opponents' criticisms of him by admitting, embracing, and, sometimes, preemptively initiating those criticisms."[38] Lincoln's most significant targets were the positions, policies, rhetoric, and alleged moral turpitude of his chief rival, Stephen A. Douglas. Lincoln's typical criticism of Douglas took the form of serious, thorough refutation of his arguments, with occasional, satirical riffs on them and jabs at his demagogic methods and personal qualities. Lincoln's extended satire of Douglas in the 1859 Cincinnati speech is his most significant use of that mode.

Lincoln's moral argumentation was shaped by his beliefs about the greater social good. He held some of those beliefs consistently throughout his public life, and other beliefs about the welfare of society evolved as the political/ rhetorical development of his second political career increasingly hinged on antislavery argumentation. Throughout Lincoln's rhetorical growth his major compositions synthesize policy affirmation, implicit or explicit moral argumentation, lawyerly refutation, and demagogic and satirical elements.

Lincoln's Greater Good

History attributes Lincoln's most noble achievements to the Emancipation Proclamation and saving the Union for a "new birth of freedom." Lincoln said he had always been opposed to slavery, but his political activity against it was not a priority until 1854, when the threat of its extension compelled him to reenter the political arena. Yet Lincoln retained the Whig values he adopted in his first political career. Lincoln's 1859 autobiography said he was "always a Whig in politics," and Whig policies reveal what Lincoln considered the greater good in his first political career. In the early 1830s the Whig Party formed around Henry Clay's "American system" partly as a reaction to the corruption of Andrew Jackson's Democratic administration. Lincoln's 1832 announcement of his first run for the Illinois legislature indicated he aligned himself with Whig priorities.

William Lee Miller points out that Lincoln might have been expected to run as a Democrat because his jobs at New Salem as postmaster and deputy land surveyor were political appointments "controlled by Democrats." Miller speculates on the origin of Lincoln's interest in Henry Clay's politics: "In Indiana Colonel Jones let the young Abraham, while he worked in Jones's store in Gentryville, read the *Louisville Journal* and the *Missouri Republican*, both of which were strongly anti-Jackson and pro-Clay papers. Dennis Hanks would say years later that it was Colonel Jones who made Abe a Whig. Hanks also said that Abe liked Henry Clay's speeches. Lincoln, this young man of many words, liked the articulate Clay rather than the inarticulate man of action, Andrew Jackson. Clay, moreover, was young, a charmer, and from Kentucky."[39] Miller writes that Lincoln's early political decision was also a moral decision: Lincoln chose between parties with "competing notions of social goods." The Democratic Party advocated decentralized government, whereas Whigs believed in a tariff, a national banking system to develop a uniform currency, distributing profits from the sale of federal lands to state governments, and government support for "internal improvements" (rivers, canals, roads, and railroads).

Whigs' belief in social and economic improvement stemmed from valuing self-improvement, especially through education and other culture-building activity. Louise Stevenson describes the appeal of Whig values and beliefs to the young, idealistic Lincoln: "Whiggery stood for the triumph of the cosmopolitan and national over the provincial and local, of rational order over irrational spontaneity, of school-based learning over traditional folkways and customs, and of self-control over self-expression."[40] Lincoln's self-education was the key to his intellectual and rhetorical growth as well as his economic, social upward mobility. Robert Kelley graphically contrasts the life Lincoln was born into with the one he created for himself: "In a hard-drinking frontier society Lincoln avoided alcohol and counseled temperance. Surrounded by cigars and spittoons, he did not smoke or chew. In a violent society obsessed with guns, he would not even use them to hunt. Believing that only those who paid taxes should vote, he opposed universal manhood suffrage. In an aggressively male society, he advocated votes for women. Abraham Lincoln was a Whig, one must conclude, because he preferred what Whigs believed to be a more civilized way of life."[41]

David Herbert Donald speculates on how Lincoln interpreted the significance of Whig values and beliefs for the future of his country: "To Lincoln it embodied the promise of American life. Economically it stood for growth, for development, for progress. Clay's American System sought to link the manufacturing of the Northeast with the grain production of the West and the cotton and tobacco crops of the South, so that the nation's economy would become one vast interdependent web. When economic interests worked together, so would political interests, and sectional rivalries would be forgotten in a powerful American nationalism. Class antagonisms would also be erased."[42]

Lincolnists often write that in his first political career he was a staunch partisan workhorse. In the Illinois legislature he spoke and wrote in support of bills to implement his party's policies. Donald offers critical commentary on those compositions: "Lincoln closely followed the national Whig party line, which he sometimes seemed to echo rather than to understand."[43] Donald thus suggests that Lincoln merely voiced Whig policy, and his intensive partisan work observed by many other Lincolnists implies that he was limited to that role. Lincoln's Whig activity in the Illinois legislature and Congress suggests that his promotion of his party's positions and policies were opportunities to influence their development: "Lincoln helped codify, institutionalize, and perpetuate his party's policy stances."[44] As president, Lincoln signed bills whose purposes embodied principles that he first embraced as a Whig: notably, the 1862 Morrill Land-Grant Colleges Act, the Pacific Railway Acts of 1862 and 1864, and legislation that expanded the national banking system and tariffs.

By 1856 Lincoln had left the failing Whig Party to join and help develop the Republican Party, first at the state level and then at the national level. Republicans were committed first to preventing slavery extension, then to the gradual elimination of slavery. This book shows how Lincoln created compositions to shape and promote Whig and Republican positions, to influence public opinion, and to fulfill his political ambition with honor but without self-glorification.

PART I

Articulate Whig Stalwart

Entering the Illinois Political Arena and Confronting Stephen A. Douglas (1832–1842)

> I can say for one that I have no other [ambition] so great as that of being truly esteemed of my fellow men, by rendering myself worthy of their esteem.
>
> —Lincoln, announcement to run for first political office, 1832

The epigraph shows a moral principle of striving to earn public respect that must have functioned like a conscience in Lincoln's political/rhetorical thinking throughout his public life. As a youth and young adult, Lincoln became well known in local communities for impromptu speeches mixing serious and humorous elements, but he discovered that becoming a popular speaker did not gain him the kind of respect he prized, so he decided to pursue a career as a politician, not a humorist. Certain compositions of Lincoln's first political career included qualities revealing the rhetorical tension seen in his most significant prepresidential rhetoric: the paradoxical combination of moral suasion and controversial methods, especially personal attacks.

Beginning to Find a Political Purpose and Voice

Lincoln's earliest speaking experiences surely gave him the pleasure of exciting an audience. As a teenager in Indiana, "after hearing sermons or speeches, Lincoln repeated them nearly verbatim to his friends, mimicking the gestures and accent of the speaker. Often he would return from church, mount a box in the middle of the cabin, and replicate the service. He would do the same outdoors, climbing on a stump and inviting friends to hear him deliver sermons or political speeches."[1] In Indiana Lincoln also kept a copybook of passages he liked, and he wrote letters for neighbors.

Lincoln's speaking experience in the decade following his move to New Salem taught him the power of mixing serious and humorous elements in political rhetoric. At New Salem he gained local celebrity owing to his funny, sometimes bawdy, jokes and stories. There Lincoln also participated in a debating society, along with his tutor, Mentor Graham, increasing his speaking skill and reputation: "The backwoods society was tackling vital questions these days," and the participants "were no longer pooh-poohed when they talked of Henry Clay, running for the legislature, sober days and nights, and responsibility to God."[2] Lincoln had a fondness for mocking: "A strain of irreverence remained with Lincoln all his life."[3] Lincoln's popularity prompted his friends to suggest he run for public office. As he decided to run for the state legislature, he increased his communicative ability by reading newspapers to understand current events and by composing legal documents for local residents.

During this first period of Lincoln's professional life, he began a legal career with senior partners who gave him opportunities to learn political and rhetorical skills. His first two law partners and he shared an interest in politics and holding public office. Lincoln worked with John T. Stuart, from 1837 to 1841, before partnering with Stephen T. Logan, from 1841 to 1843. Lincoln and Stuart had served together in the Black Hawk War, and in the Illinois House of Representatives they were members of the legendary group from Sangamon County called the Long Nine (each was over six feet tall). Stuart, only two years older than Lincoln, had a college education in liberal arts that would have included the study of classical rhetoric and grammar. Lincoln may have observed the process and product of Stuart's political compositions during their mutual time in the Illinois legislature. Lincoln must have witnessed Stuart's skill in refutation, which became one of Lincoln's most effective methods of argumentation. Logan taught Lincoln the importance of thorough preparation and negotiated settlement. Lincoln adapted the need for careful preparation to his political compositions, whose rhetorical quality benefited from argumentation based on legal and historical research.

Lincoln was elected to four two-year, consecutive terms in the Illinois House of Representatives; and during this time he participated in local, state, and national campaigns as a Whig. Lincoln's eight years in the Illinois House (1834–1842) provided ample opportunities for him to leave his mark as a public servant. He composed resolutions and bills, but more important for his future political success was his experience in composing speeches delivered to the legislature, engaging in political debates, speaking on the stump, and writing public and private letters.[4] He spoke in rural settings, villages, and cities, and began to get his messages distributed in handbills and newspapers.

Lincoln's earliest political compositions show signs of potential for eloquence, but they are faint. Michael Burlingame points to the very limited success Lincoln had in the Illinois legislature: "Lincoln's greatness as a moral statesman in years to come would have been hard to predict based on his legislative record, which showed him to be likable and clever, but little more. . . . By the age of 32, Lincoln had proved himself to be an ambitious, gifted partisan but exhibited few signs of true statesmanship."[5] Besides elements of classical rhetoric seen throughout Lincoln's political/rhetorical growth, his compositions of this period express political positions and policies with implicit moral appeal. Yet his use of such demagogic techniques as exaggeration, withholding negative information, and personal attacks obscured his potential for eloquence and statesmanship.

Lincoln's major speeches in the Illinois legislature defined, defended, and promoted Whig positions and policies as socially beneficial while criticizing corresponding Democratic Party positions and policies, and some of their proponents. Sometimes Lincoln faulted opponents' politics, sometimes their personal qualities, including their moral character. The moral appeal of Lincoln's political rhetoric in this period often took the form of satire, sometimes sarcastic, sometimes light. In fact, Lincoln's use of personal attacks is a defining component of his political/rhetorical experience, and he employed them in various genres ranging from published anonymous and pseudonymous letters to private letters, legislative speeches, campaign and debate speeches, and lectures.

Within a year after moving to New Salem, Lincoln announced his first run for public office, showing that he aspired to be more than a village notable. In March 1832 Lincoln published an 1,800-word announcement of his candidacy in the Springfield *Sangamo Journal*, as he sought to introduce himself to the citizens of Sangamon County, then much larger than now. This announcement may also have been distributed as a handbill. His announcement came only one month before the outbreak of the Black Hawk War. Lincoln volunteered to serve in that war, along with other locals, who elected him captain. His return to New Salem in August just before the election left him little time to campaign.

Lincoln's campaign announcement began his lifelong support for one of the central goals of the Whig Party: to legislate for "internal improvements," including new roads, railroads, canals, and improved stream navigation. Whig values aiming to improve society formed the implicit moral good that underpinned Lincoln's political beliefs throughout his prepresidential political life, as indicated by his 1859 autobiographical testimony that he was "always a Whig in politics."[6] A leading Illinois Democrat contemporary of Lincoln who supported legislation for internal improvements was the person Lincoln would politically and rhetorically wrestle until 1860—Stephen A. Douglas.

There is almost no extant scholarship on the genre of campaign announcements, and Lincoln's could serve as a model: advocating a policy position and committing to public service. This announcement shows some of the qualities that would appear in his discourse throughout his public life, including directness, a sincere voice, and an implicit moral purpose of working to improve social conditions. Lincoln's most important compositions typically reflect the aphorism of trying to do well by doing good. He opened the announcement of his candidacy with a statement of rhetorical purpose: "to make known . . . my sentiments with regard to local affairs," and the structure, development, and style of this announcement reflect a surprisingly high level of clarity and skill for someone with less than a year of formal education.

Lincoln devoted the first half of his candidacy declaration to explaining his recommendations for navigational improvement of the Sangamon River. New Salem was located on the banks of this river, a tributary of the Illinois River, and the story of how Lincoln first saw New Salem in 1831 when he engineered the release of a stranded flatboat from a mill dam on the Sangamon is legendary. Improving transportation to the Illinois River, a tributary of the Mississippi River, would appeal to farmers because it would better enable them to move surplus products to the lucrative markets of New Orleans. Lincoln describes methods of straightening the Sangamon River channel to speed the movement of floating timber: turf clearing, damming, and cutting new channels through sharp bends. He provides no cost estimates while committing to support legislation for improving navigation on the Sangamon.

The remainder of the body of the campaign announcement consists of separate paragraphs, respectively, to supporting stricter laws against usury, for education, and for reviewing all existing laws. Lincoln asserts that education is "the most important subject which we as a people can be engaged in." He admits he has no particular "plan or system respecting it" but maintains that citizens need to be literate so they can read history and thus "duly appreciate the value of free institutions." The ability to read scripture, he maintains, is necessary to promoting "morality, sobriety, enterprise and industry."

The conclusion reveals personal qualities that would hold true throughout Lincoln's public life. First, he describes an ambition for distinction based on public service: "I can say for one that I have no other [ambition] so great as that of being truly esteemed of my fellow men, by rendering myself worthy of their esteem."[7] Second, he adopts a sincere, modest tone: "I was born and have ever remained in the most humble walks of life. I have no wealthy or popular relations to recommend me. My case is thrown exclusively upon the independent voters of this country." The common-man persona that Lincoln projected throughout his public life reflected his humble origins but concealed his resolute ambition. Third, he expresses stoicism: "But if the good people in their wisdom shall see fit to keep me in the background, I have been too familiar with disappointments to be very chagrined." Such an attitude would serve Lincoln well through future personal tragedies and political setbacks. Lincoln's announcement gains clarity and readability through varied sentence structure and a vocabulary that is plain, without being colloquial. Lincoln was learning to distinguish between informal and formal uses of language, depending on communicative purpose, audience, and genre.

Mentor Graham's biographers observe that "Lincoln and Graham had worked the wording of the announcement over and over and with John McNeil had argued out every phrase," including the need to avoid inappropriate, colloquial language.[8] Graham's biographers cite Lincoln's testimony as to the sources that influenced his announcement: "Lincoln read attentively the *Louisville Journal*, the *Missouri Republican*, and other papers. His textbook was the *Journal*. He was a regular subscriber to it."[9] The word *Whig* does not appear in his announcement, but his explanations of policy clearly reflect alignment with the principles embraced by this party as it began to emerge.

Lincoln gave his first campaign speech at Pappsville about a dozen miles southwest of New Salem, famously remarking that "I am humble Abraham Lincoln. I have been solicited by many friends to become a candidate for the legislature. My politics are short and sweet, like the old woman's dance. I am in favor of a national bank. I am in favor of the internal-improvement system and a high protective tariff," but he made no mention of usury laws or education.[10] Lincoln was not widely known in the expansive Sangamon County and was defeated, but his popularity in New Salem, where he gained a large majority of the vote, showed promise.

Writing and Speaking on Policy and during Campaigns (1834–1842)

Lincoln's legislative and campaign compositions are so closely interrelated that separating them would fragment the narrative. In 1834, when Lincoln again ran for the state legislature, he did not write a platform because he felt that the printed announcement of his first run had not yielded many votes. Rather, he decided to rely on stump speeches and personal visits (today called retail politics): "Lincoln's personal qualities appealed to the voters, especially his geniality and humor, both of which were highly prized by frontiersmen, and he was gifted in the art of calling on people in their homes."[11] He received the second highest number of votes of the four elected candidates, and Stuart was fourth.[12] As a freshman member of the Illinois General Assembly in Vandalia, Lincoln took little action to accomplish the initiatives he proposed in his 1832 campaign platform. He made no formal speeches and only a few remarks on bills, but he quickly became known for his writing ability, and his peers solicited him to write bills and committee reports. He had, however, learned about the legislative process and observed lawyers, judges, and political operatives, in addition to legislators.

One of the political operatives Lincoln observed in Vandalia was Stephen A. Douglas. Douglas's activity there provides insight into the character of a man who would be Lincoln's main political rival for thirty years and play an essential role in Lincoln's rhetorical experiences and growth. Douglas had been invited to Vandalia by John Wyatt, a Democratic legislator from Jacksonville, where Douglas was establishing himself as a lawyer and politician. Wyatt resented John J. Hardin, a Jacksonville lawyer, local celebrity, and former Democrat turned Whig. Hardin was also the state's attorney from the First Judicial District. Wyatt begrudged Hardin because he had worked to defeat some of the Democrats who had supported him for state's attorney. Wyatt agreed with Douglas's proposed revenge plot to devise a bill shifting the power of choosing state's attorneys from the governor to the legislature. The bill passed, and subsequently in a close vote in the legislature, Douglas defeated Hardin for state's attorney from the First Judicial District. Lincoln voted against the bill. Douglas engaged in other self-serving intrigues in Jacksonville and Vandalia.[13] Sometimes cited in Lincoln lore is the claim that Lincoln's observation of Douglas in Vandalia led Lincoln to quip, "He's the least man I ever saw." Douglas was five feet four inches tall, a foot shorter than Lincoln, and whether true or not, the jab sounds like Lincoln.

During his first legislative term Lincoln wrote anonymous, partisan commentary for the *Sangamo Journal*: "Although Lincoln's journalism is not easy to identify with certainty, dozens of pieces from the 1830s seem clearly to be his [pro-Whig] handiwork, including dispatches from an unnamed Whig member of the legislature. At first those dispatches simply offered terse accounts of legislative activity; in time, they grew longer and more partisan."[14]

Encouraged by his early experience as an elected official, Lincoln in June 1836 published a brief announcement in the *Sangamo Journal* of his candidacy for reelection to the Illinois House. Lincoln's 200-word, 1836 candidacy announcement is 1,600 words shorter than his 1832 announcement. Repeating support for internal improvements, the 1836 announcement calls for the proceeds of the sale of public lands to go to the states for canal and railroad construction. Such a policy would avoid the need to borrow money and would gain interest earnings. His support for extending the vote to women is an example of the independent thinking and support for social justice seen throughout his public life.

During the 1836 campaign Lincoln became an aggressive Whig critic of Democrats, and he seasoned his political rhetoric with satire. Lincoln reveled in the biting personal attacks that were then commonplace.[15] His stump speaking followed the pattern of the times, with emphasis on stories that made opponents look foolish, and he became unequaled in this genre: "a form of cruelty that reflected his primitive background."[16] Lincoln, however, could adapt to other kinds of audience; for example, he could be more "dignified" when speaking to an audience of men and women than when he spoke to an all-male gathering.[17] Besides stump and debate speeches, Lincoln composed anonymous and pseudonymous attack letters targeting Democrats, and they were published in the Whig *Sangamo Journal*. For example, in letters signed by Johnny Blubberhead, Lincoln ridiculed several Democratic leaders and the editor of a Springfield Democratic newspaper. Those kinds of letters used a mock dialect, a technique for which he became well known in both speaking and writing.[18]

In the 1836 campaign Lincoln spoke not just in remote areas, as he had before, but in villages and towns. During a July debate at Springfield, Lincoln humiliated George Forquer, a former Whig newly turned Democrat, who enjoyed the spoils of political office and whose modern Springfield home featured a lightning rod. Listening to Forquer's personal attack on him, Lincoln silently bristled before replying: "I am not so young in years as I am in the tricks and trades of a politician; but live long, or die young, I would rather die now, than, like the gentleman change my politics, and simultaneous with the change, receive an office worth three thousand dollars per year, and then have to erect a lightning-rod over my house, to protect a guilty conscience from an offended God."[19]

Personal attacks invited retaliation, which in those days meant the possibility of violence. Awareness of these dangers surely explains why Lincoln invented fictional Democratic spokesmen. Their ironic observations ridiculed their party's convention and patronage systems and support for voting rights for black people, including Democratic president Martin Van Buren's alleged endorsement. In June 1836 the *Sangamo Journal* published a pseudonymous letter by a black person that Michael Burlingame says Lincoln likely wrote and that alleged Van Buren's support for black voting rights and black people's favoritism for Van Buren in kind. The letter illustrates Lincoln's ability to mimic dialect for political effect:

> Oh hush, ha, he, ho! Youd split your sides laffin to hear Capun [Democrat John C. Calhoun, US vice-president, 1825–1832] tell how much Wanjuren [Van Buren] is goin to do for de nigger—de ways deys goin for him, man— oh, hush! and dat man who used to buse old Jackson so, case as how he was gainst the niggers voting—ah, law! de way he roots for Wanjuren now is sorter singular—he look precisely like a pig off in a Corn Field—wid one ear marked, so he massa know 'em. De way de niggers is goin for him now, oh hush![20]

In this race-baiting vein Lincoln was echoing Illinois Whig strategy evident in its House legislative maneuvering "to embarrass Van Buren and his supporters . . . for implicitly endorsing black voting rights."[21] Burlingame maintains that "this line of attack was unfair, for Van Buren disliked slavery but believed it should be dealt with on the state and local level, not by the federal government."[22] Lincoln's Whig partisan participation in this demagoguery did not necessarily correspond to his personal views on the related subject of slavery, as seen in his 1837 coauthored Protest in Illinois Legislature on Slavery.

Lincoln's debate and stump speech performances in this campaign targeted the Democratic Party, not just its leaders. In the 1836 campaign both Whigs and Democrats praised Lincoln for delivering memorable messages owing to his amusing anecdotes and plain, conversational language. Those performances increased his political reputation. On August 1, 1836, Lincoln received the most votes among seventeen contestants from Sangamon County, and he subsequently became a leading Whig in and out of the legislature. In the 1836–37 legislative session Lincoln and the other Long Niners labored to move the state capital from Vandalia to the more centrally located Springfield and to promote internal improvements. Whigs nationwide favored bank financing of internal improvements.

On January 11, 1837, in the Illinois legislature, Lincoln delivered a speech in response to Illinois House Democratic Usher F. Linder's call to investigate the Illinois State Bank. Democrats at all levels of government, adhering to policies of the Jackson and Van Buren administrations, opposed banks as unconstitutional and as un-American for allegedly creating a wealthy class. The Illinois State Bank's funding of speculative projects included some involving internal improvements, so Lincoln adhered to the Whig position of supporting the Illinois State Bank, at Springfield. An investigation of that institution could have destroyed it and undercut the Long Nine's efforts to move the capital to Springfield.[23]

Lincoln's State Bank speech was his first important legislative speech, thus serving as a benchmark of his skill in political rhetoric. The State Bank speech has prompted conflicting commentary, which suggests the need for reexamination. Illinois congressman, senator, and historian Paul Simon, noting that Lincoln's State Bank speech was his first published speech, describes it as "eloquent," but Simon does not explain the rhetorical qualities that justify that praise.[24] David Herbert Donald is far less kind, citing the speech's weaknesses, including its fallacious argumentation: "A clumsy, poorly organized effort, it was in part an *ad hominem* attack on Linder's haughty airs and entangled rhetoric. . . . Clearly not at home in discussing the economic issues involved in banking, Lincoln resorted to demagogy."[25] Burlingame calls this speech "somewhat demagogic": "In this partisan speech Lincoln did not forthrightly address all the criticisms of the bank. . . . Lincoln was also disingenuous in alleging that the bank had met its legal requirements to redeem its notes in specie."[26] Olivier Fraysse also cites withholding negative information as one of this speech's demagogic tactics: Lincoln failed to mention that Whig capitalists may have swindled Democratic capitalists.[27]

Lincoln's 3,700-word State Bank speech was better planned and crafted than critics have acknowledged, for they have underemphasized its implied moral stance and its careful structure and development. This speech reveals Lincoln as a combative politician who wanted to serve as a Whig spokesman and who was not intimidated by an ambitious, well-spoken opponent. Despite the melancholy he expressed in a letter during this period, he must have seen this speech as an opportunity to increase his political capital through a rhetorical challenge to the impressive Linder. The speech consists of five sections: introduction, refutation of resolutions, refutation of insinuations against the bank, legality of the bank's policies and procedures, and conclusion. The early and lengthy refutations show Lincoln's ability to get directly to his purpose and develop it thoroughly. Those refutations feature legalistic argumentation with implied moral appeal for a policy to benefit society, with personal attacks against Linder threaded into the argumentation.

Lincoln's introduction asserts his opposition to Linder's resolutions but quickly uses self-deprecating humor and personal satire of Linder to create a receptive mood in the audience. Undoubtedly Lincoln learned the appeal of humor from his participation in rural storytelling gatherings with friends and neighbors, and speaking extemporaneously on the stump. Lincoln says he protests because he is confident Linder would not waste "ammunition" on such "small game" as himself. Lincoln understood that one of the targets in the tradition of personal satire is pomposity, and he further satirizes Linder for alleged arrogance and pretentious prose: "In one faculty, at least, there can be no dispute of the gentleman's superiority over me, and most other men; and that is, the faculty of entangling a subject, so that neither himself, or [sic] any other man, can find head or tail to it."[28] This sarcasm shows Lincoln knew how to deliver a punch line. He complains that half of Linder's speech defending his resolutions is about subjects other than the resolutions. Lincoln also complains that Linder's resolutions insinuate the bank's unconstitutionality—a charge that Lincoln says the Illinois Supreme Court had denied.

In the tradition of classical rhetoric, the first sentence of section two forecasts the direction of Lincoln's speech: he will "now proceed to the resolutions." Forecasting strengthens clarity of organization and coherence, especially important qualities in a lengthy speech.[29] Lincoln says that the thousands of dollars it would cost to enact Linder's resolutions leading to an investigation of stock availability would be a waste of taxpayer money. Lincoln acknowledges that the Illinois State Bank has connections with banks in other states but denies the illegality or injustice of these business relationships. Lincoln defends the Illinois State Bank's administrators' right to enact bylaws that would require its employees to maintain "secrecy," just another word for confidentiality.

Lincoln then attacks several "insinuations" in the resolutions as "silly" and unworthy except that they allege *great injury of the people at large.*" This section has some of the most impassioned, direct language of the speech, including the use of rhetorical questions, repetition, parallelism, figurative language, and hyperbole. Lincoln flatly denies the bank exploits Illinoisans: "I make the assertion boldly, and without fear of contradiction, that no man, who does not hold an office, or does not aspire to one, has ever found any fault of the bank."[30] The section on insinuations ends with rejection of allegations of bank usury and bank refusal to pay by specie. Lincoln argues that a committee of inquiry would have no authority to redress any victim of usury and unleashes a sarcastic, personal attack on Linder: "Does not the gentleman from Coles [County] know, that there is a statute standing in full force, making it highly penal, for an individual to loan money at a higher rate of interest than twelve per cent? If he does not he is too ignorant to be placed at the head of the committee which the resolutions propose, and if he does, his neglect to mention it, shows him to be too uncandid to merit the respect or confidence of anyone."[31] The charge of the bank's refusal of specie payment is false, he argues, because no one has sued for damages as provided by the bank's charter.

With moral appeal Lincoln then briefly addresses what he says would be the proposed commission of inquiry's "principal object"—to "ferret out, a mass of corruption, supposed to have been committed by the commissioners who apportioned the stock of the bank." Lincoln contends that any committee of inquiry would be just as susceptible to corruption as the bank commissioners might be, and this scorn provoked Linder to interrupt, demanding that the session chairman call Lincoln out of order. After the chairman refused, Linder appealed to the House but quickly withdrew. He was willing for Lincoln to continue because in so doing he thought Lincoln "would break his own neck." Lincoln quickly retorts, "Another *gracious condescension*." Lincoln asserts that the bank commissioners would be less likely to be corrupted than any several chosen from the House for the committee of inquiry, even if they were "headed and led on by 'decided superiority'"—another poke at Linder.

Lincoln disingenuously claims that he is "by no means the special advocate of the Bank." He denies the legality of the proposed resolutions and accuses Linder of being inconsistent in his legislative actions. Lincoln favors bank examination when proper but denies the proposed resolutions make such a case. The final section emphasizes that the proposed committee of inquiry would be illegal, and he stretches the point when he connects the formation of such a committee to "that lawless and mobocratic spirit . . . which is already abroad in the land; and is spreading with rapid and fearful impetuosity, to the ultimate overthrow of every institution, or even moral principle, in which persons and property have hitherto found security." This hyperbolic language is fearmongering, and Lincoln would develop the mobocratic theme more appropriately a little more than a year later in his better-known 1838 Lyceum lecture.

The State Bank speech forcefully closes with a series of rhetorical questions followed by assertions that the proposed committee of inquiry would be a waste of money, for it could do no good but cause great harm by damaging the bank's credit. The stockholders are rich men who would not be significantly affected, but depreciated specie would hurt the farmer and mechanic. In effect, government financial matters have social consequences and thus a moral dimension. Paul Simon reported that Lincoln's State Bank speech did not receive a majority endorsement in the House and that shortly after the speech, a resolution passed in the state senate calling for investigation of the state banks at Springfield and Shawneetown. The investigation failed to produce any change in policy. The legislature soon authorized the Springfield State Bank to purchase $100,000 worth of additional stock.[32]

On March 3, 1837, Lincoln and fellow Springfield Whig lawyer and colleague in the Illinois General Assembly Dan Stone issued a 148-word resolution known as the Protest in Illinois Legislature on Slavery. Its brevity notwithstanding, this composition asserts one of Lincoln's most significant implied moral positions during his eight years in the Illinois legislature. Lincoln and Stone were objecting to the anti-abolitionist resolutions passed in the Illinois legislature several weeks earlier, with a large majority. Lincoln and Stone voted against those resolutions; Stephen A. Douglas, for them. The Lincoln-Stone protest is legalistic in content and structure but features plain language, not legalese.[33] The protest declares a middle-ground position: "that the institution of slavery is founded on both injustice and bad policy; but that the promulgation of abolition doctrines tends rather to increase than to abate its evils."

This protest condemns slavery but does not develop with moral argumentation. The protest also says the authors believe Congress "has no power, under the Constitution, to interfere with the institution of slavery in the different states" but has the power to abolish slavery in the District of Columbia if requested by its citizens.[34] Lincoln adhered to these positions in his most important, later political discourse, but his objections to slavery and its extension would famously emphasize moral argumentation supported by interpretations of such founding documents as the Declaration of Independence and the Constitution. Some Lincolnists have maintained that Lincoln exaggerated the founders' antislavery intentions.[35]

In this period Lincoln began earnest political competition with Stephen A. Douglas, including Lincoln's moral criticism of his rival that would come to a head during Lincoln's second political career in the 1850s. At the beginning of this competition Lincoln was just as eager to attack Douglas's character as his politics. In 1838, as Lincoln campaigned for reelection and for John T. Stuart's election to Congress, Lincoln criticized Douglas, Stuart's opponent, beginning in January when Lincoln attacked him in a series of pseudonymous letters in the *Sangamo Journal*. The previous December Lincoln had added a snide PS about Douglas to a personal letter: "We have adopted it as part of our policy here, to never speak of Douglass [Douglas originally spelled his name with two "s"es] at all. Isn't that the best mode of treating so small a matter?"[36] Yet the 1838 winter pseudonymous letters show that Lincoln viewed Douglas as a sizable political target who deserved criticism, without revealing the source.

These letters were allegedly written by disgruntled Democrats, arguing that Douglas was unfit for public office. Specifically, the letters charged that he was corrupt in scheming to gain his party's nomination and incompetent for advocating banking policies based exclusively on specie payment and granting excessive power to the legislature. Douglas was outraged, asserting that "my *private* and *moral*, as well as public and political character [has] been assailed in a manner calculated to destroy my standing as a man and a citizen."[37]

On February 28, 1838, the Illinois legislature passed a bill that moved the state capital from Vandalia to Springfield, bypassing other communities that had fought for this prize, including Alton, Jacksonville, Peoria, and Decatur. The Long Nine had accomplished one of its main goals, with Lincoln as the ramrod, but the move has been controversial. Critics have cited the group and thus Lincoln for logrolling—that is, marshalling support for the move in exchange for votes to pass internal improvements legislation.[38]

The election to decide the 1838 race between Stuart and Douglas took place in August, but the outcome was not known until later that fall. Stuart won by thirty-six votes. Responding to rumors of Whig vote tampering, Douglas worked until nearly the end of 1839 to try to get a recount. Stuart would not agree to it, but Lincoln did: "This was clearly an important matter to Lincoln. He suggested that political friends be solicited to help with the investigation and to expand it, appoint precinct committeemen to help where they thought it advisable."[39] From this experience Lincoln and Douglas surely were coming to know and respect one another's talents and tenacity.

When the Illinois legislature convened in December 1838, Lincoln more actively promoted Whig policy for better government and the greater good than he had previously. For example, he proposed that the state purchase twenty million acres of federal land within its boundaries at a low cost and sell it at a high enough rate to retire the state's debt. The legislature passed resolutions in support of this proposal, but Congress took no action. Paul Simon's comment on this proposal places it in the context of Lincoln's other legislative activity: This initiative "is one of the few examples of Lincoln's showing original thinking and leadership in the sense of introducing legislation of more than local interest. His role was not particularly creative in this or in any other session. His leadership was mostly in reaction to legislation introduced by others, by amendment to these proposals, and in the ability to get along with his colleagues and to sense what they would support and would not support."[40] Lincoln also favored reforming property tax laws so that the tax burden was not limited to out-of-state property owners and so that owners of highly valued property would pay more taxes. Lincoln paradoxically continued to support internal improvements while feeling a moral obligation to reduce the public indebtedness they incurred.

The subject of slavery surfaced in the 1839 winter session of the Illinois legislature, and Lincoln's voting record on several related resolutions gave no hint of his later moral stance against slavery. In January the legislature considered a resolution denouncing the governor of Maine for not extraditing men from Georgia who aided runaway slaves and another resolution calling for noninterference with slavery in existing states. Lincoln initially agreed with the resolutions but decided that "he wanted more time for deliberation" and moved for postponement.[41] In February Lincoln voted with the majority that defeated resolutions calling for Congress to ignore abolitionist pleas to eliminate slavery in the nation's capital and Western territories, and slave trading in the United States.

In November 1839, during the first of a series of debates between Whig and Democratic orators that Lincoln helped to arrange, he debated Douglas concerning the Bank of the United States. Lincoln condemned the presidential administration's subtreasury plan as "a scheme of fraud and corruption." One of Lincoln's friends said he faltered against Douglas. Apparently this weak performance spurred Lincoln to strengthen his bank defense, and this effort paid off on two occasions in December during the second debate series. Douglas cleverly arranged for Lincoln to speak on the final night of the series, the day after Christmas Day, when attendance would be poor. Lincoln spoke on schedule in the capitol, delivering an 8,900-word speech. Lincoln's same friend who noted his weak performance in November said he did much better in the Subtreasury speech.[42]

Lincoln scholars have cited strengths and weaknesses in the Subtreasury speech, but they have underreported its merits. The purpose, content, structure, and style of this speech show that Lincoln had carefully composed it not just for the listening audience but also for a wider, well-educated reading audience. The rhetorical qualities of Lincoln's speeches on the state bank and subtreasury are strikingly different. Burlingame has nothing positive to say about the State Bank speech, while he sees both positive and negative qualities in the Subtreasury speech. He writes that it was "such a powerful address that it became the Illinois Whig Party's textbook for 1840," describing it as "a sober analysis of President Van Buren's independent subtreasury scheme for government funds, a deflationary plan." Yet, "rhetorical bombast marred this speech."[43] Douglas L. Wilson offers general praise for this speech, describing it as "tightly focused, methodical, and closely reasoned. . . . In the Subtreasury speech one begins to hear, in the tone and choice of language, a harbinger of the distinctive voice of the writer to come."[44] Wilson does not further explain Lincoln's rhetorical methods. This speech has a formality appropriate for a printed message, and it reveals a more advanced level of rhetorical knowledge and skill than his previous speeches. This speech is a textbook example of a political composition, with elements stemming from classical rhetoric.

Lincoln surely realized that this subject of national significance was an opportunity for him to influence his party's financial policy at the state level, reach for publicity at the national level, and increase his political reputation. In this speech Lincoln took advantage of an occasion to attack Douglas: the refutation toward the end of the speech demeans his politics, rhetoric, and personal qualities. Suggesting the careful preparation of this speech, Joshua Speed, in a reminiscent account, wrote that Lincoln delivered it "without manuscript or notes."[45] The speech is so well researched and so well written that he must have drafted it in advance and memorized it, as he often did later with important speeches. Lincoln used his research on the history of the subtreasury throughout the speech, and most likely he took advantage of the newly established Illinois State Library for this purpose, as he would continue to do throughout his time in Springfield.[46]

The speech indicates that Lincoln had increased his knowledge of the national government's financial problems since giving his State Bank speech. As explained in this book's introduction and as this speech suggests, Lincoln was influenced by the content, not just the style, of the speeches of Senator Daniel Webster, the Whig party leader and chief spokesman for that party's positions on the national economy.[47] Certainly Lincoln was proud of his Subtreasury speech, describing it to John T. Stuart as "a big speech."[48]

One of the most important and revealing qualities of the Subtreasury speech is the use of a formal structure (arrangement/organization) related to deliberative (political) discourse in classical rhetoric. The main elements in this structure are an introduction (exordium), which tells the audience about the subject and purpose and tries to "dispose the audience to be receptive"; a statement of the facts of an issue in question (narration); the outline of the main points in the speaker's case (division); a body section with about equal amounts of the proof (confirmation) and refutation of the opposition (confutation); and the conclusion (peroration). Blending confirmation and refutation demonstrates a principle of classical rhetoric that allows for flexible arrangement in the body of a work depending on a particular communicative purpose and audience.[49]

With the Subtreasury speech Lincoln delivers his best performance in the Illinois legislature, defining and promoting Whig policy to create good government through fiscal responsibility. As Lincoln delineates the virtues of his party's financial system and attacks the opposition's policy and rhetoric, he speaks with a moral voice. He begins without blaming his opponents, especially the wily Douglas, for the small audience, as he had reason to. Rather, Lincoln is implicitly solicitous, using humility to express the fear that those in attendance are there only "to spare me of mortification" and that he may be unable to overcome his "dampened spirits" that evening. He asserts that during this series of debates, Democrats have ignored Whig calls for discussions based on "fact and argument": "I now propose, in my humble way, to urge those arguments again; at the same time, begging the audience to mark well the positions I shall take, and the proof I shall offer to sustain them, and that they will not again permit Mr. Douglass or his friends, to escape the force of them, by a round and groundless assertion, that we 'dare not meet them in argument.'"[50] As Lincoln develops his arguments throughout the speech, he often provides historical background (statement of facts).

Next, in a short division section of four sentences, Lincoln does not forecast all the sections in the body, but he states the three "propositions" to be developed in the first body section. His thesis is that the Democrats' subtreasury would "injuriously affect the community by its operation of the circulating medium; it will be a more expensive fiscal agent" than the National Bank; and "it will be a less secure depository of the public money." Throughout the speech Lincoln uses transitional language that summarizes preceding content and forecasts a succeeding topic.

The first body section exemplifies what would become Lincoln's lawyerly skill of assimilating arguments for a position or policy and against opposing positions and policy. Refutation in this speech criticizes established arguments (prolepsis) and anticipates objections from the opposition (procatalepsis). In this section, soon after Lincoln begins a statement-of-facts review of the National Bank's history, he asserts that the bank's policy of collecting and loaning revenues is more advantageous than the proposed subtreasury's policy of hoarding received revenue, which "robs the people of the use of it, while the government does not itself need it, and while the money is performing no nobler office than that of rusting in iron boxes." Reduced circulating money harms both debtors, who have to sacrifice property to pay creditors, and creditors, whose loans are not repaid.

Lincoln contends that reducing the amount of circulating money will bring "permanent hardship" to both states and territories. He predicts that with less money in circulation, wages will be reduced, and people will have less money to buy public land. Lincoln finishes developing his first proposition by refuting the often-used argument (prolepsis) that revenue under the proposed subtreasury policy "will not lie idle in the vaults of the Treasury; and, farther [sic], that a national bank produces greater derangement in the currency, by a system of contractions and expansions than the subtreasury would produce in any way." The history of the National Bank, Lincoln maintains, shows that for twenty years it annually paid the federal government "for the privilege of using the public money between the times of its collection and disbursement." Lincoln maintains that a national bank would fulfill its duty to provide "a sound and uniform currency."[51]

Then Lincoln demonstrates his second proposition: that the National Bank has proved less expensive to administer than the proposed subtreasury would. Lincoln's rational/moral appeal of logical deduction by historical precedent carries a patriotic, emotional appeal. Citing cost estimates from two sources, Lincoln concludes that the subtreasury policy would cost $405,000 more annually than the National Bank system. This amount "is sufficient to pay the pensions of more than 4,000 Revolutionary Soldiers, or to purchase a 40-acre tract of Government land, for each one of more than 8,000 poor families."

The third proposition emphasizes the moral appeal that a national bank is less vulnerable to corruption than a subtreasury, which would require various federal agencies to have possession of revenues between collection and disbursement. Lincoln names several officials of these agencies who were found guilty of major "defalcations" involving hundreds of thousands of dollars. In contrast, in its forty-year history, the National Bank processed almost $500,000 without losing "one dollar, nor one cent" to embezzlement. He says the banking system avoided the problem of the subtreasury policy of allowing too much money to remain too long in the hands of individual managers. Lincoln admits that dishonest people might be employed in either system, but he argues that the subtreasury affords a more tempting system for its managers to give in to self-interest and theft: "that the Sub-Treasurer will prefer opulent knavery in a foreign land, to honest poverty at home."

Another virtue Lincoln associates with a national bank is fidelity, because without faithful commitment to its mission, the bank would lose its charter. Lincoln rejects the argument that the "Penitentiary Department" provision of the subtreasury proposal will prevent theft. Neither will imprisonment restore lost funds "any more than the hanging of a murderer restores his victim to life." Lincoln denies that Democrats will be able to refute his three propositions, and he even goes so far as to speculate that Senator John C. Calhoun will not even attempt to dispute the proposition that administering a subtreasury would be more costly than administering a national bank.

Lincoln next launches into a lengthy refutation of the argument that the National Bank is unconstitutional and of the arguments presented by Democrats Josiah Lamborn and Stephen A. Douglas. Lincoln maintains that the founders and congressional legislation have endorsed a national bank.[52] Lincoln concedes that the Constitution does not specifically authorize a national bank or the subtreasury, but he maintains that some kind of "fiscal agent" is "necessary and proper," so a choice ought to be made, and Congress, with the constitutional authority to pass laws, has the power to enact a national bank charter.

The last forty percent of this speech refutes other Democratic arguments he has heard in preceding sessions, with particular attention to Douglas's rhetoric. Lincoln admits that all relevant presidential administrations have made "errors" concerning "public expenditures," but he contends that the greatest errors have occurred in the Democratic Jackson and Van Buren administrations. Lincoln says if Democrats can prove otherwise, "we call off the dogs." Before proceeding, he names the sources (nonartistic proofs) that will support his arguments: the "annual reports, made by all the Secretaries of the Treasury from the establishment of the Government down to the close of the year 1838." Citing specific government sources, Lincoln says that expenditures for the decade of the Jackson and Van Buren administrations were greater than all of the first four administrations. Lincoln denies Democrats' accusation that Whigs have been guilty of extravagant expenditures, and he attacks the "excuses" Douglas has made in defending the 1838 expenditures of the Van Buren administration by exposing factual errors, sometimes petty, in a litany of Douglas's statements. Those errors angered Lincoln, whose response ended in a carefully crafted, lengthy (periodic) sentence, with its repeated clause of denial (epiphora), as a scathing indictment of Douglas's demagoguery:

> Those who heard Mr. Douglas, recollect that he indulged himself in a contemptuous expression of pity for me. "Now he's got me," thought I. But when he went on to say that five millions of the expenditure of 1838, were payments of the French indemnities, *which I knew to be untrue*; that five millions had been for the Post Office, *which I knew to be untrue*; that ten millions had been for the Maine boundary war, *which I knew to be untrue, but supremely ridiculous also*, and when I saw that he was stupid enough to hope, that I would permit such groundless and audacious assertions to go unexposed, I readily consented, that on the score both of veracity and sagacity, the audience should judge whether he or I were the more deserving of the world's contempt.[53]

During his competition with Douglas in the 1850s, Lincoln would again accuse him of lying.

Lincoln's language in this speech is direct and clear. Despite the speech's legalistic argumentation, there is almost no legal jargon. The language is mostly commonplace, but some of it reveals that his ongoing self-education was yielding a mature vocabulary especially appropriate for reading audiences, for example: *mortification, derangement, defalcations, peculations, adroit, contingent, nabob, appropriated, contemptuous,* and *fallacious*. Lincoln also used sparingly but effectively colloquial, metaphoric expression, for example: "call off the dogs," "by-gone times," "lying idle in their hands," "to use a homely phrase, cut its own fodder," and "why build a cage if they expect to catch no birds?" The only part of this speech that departs from these language traits is the florid style of the conclusion (peroration). Some of Lincoln's contemporaries saturated their speeches with overblown language, but Lincoln used it mainly in conclusions (both plain and flowery language were in the tradition of classical rhetoric). Lincoln's conclusion states a commitment to purpose, with exaggerated emotional and ethical appeals:

> If ever I feel the soul within me elevate and expand to those dimensions not wholly unworthy of its Almighty Architect, it is when I contemplate the cause of my country, deserted by all the world beside, and I standing up boldly and alone and hurling defiance at her victorious oppressors. Here, without contemplating consequences, before High Heaven, and in the face of the world, I swear eternal fidelity to the just cause, as I deem it, of the land of my life, my liberty and my love. . . . Let none faulter, who thinks he is right, and we may succeed. But, if after all, we shall fail, be it so. We still have the proud consolation of saying to our consciences, and to the departed shade of our country's freedom, that the cause approved of our judgment, and adored of our hearts, in disaster, in chains, in torture, in death, we NEVER faultered in defending.[54]

The impassioned, self-righteous language of the conclusion is so overreaching for a speech about the technical pros and cons of government financial systems that it reads like a parody. From another perspective, the florid language reflects Lincoln's pride in championing a Whig cause with a well-researched, well-written composition.

The main qualities of this speech—its political/rhetorical purposes, content, structure, and style—show that Lincoln combined the personal attacks common in stump speeches with the more extensive, formal discussion of policy required by speeches in the legislature. In the Subtreasury speech Lincoln may have reserved his scornful remarks about Douglas for near the end of the speech to give them impact.

The Subtreasury speech demonstrates a promising capacity for political discourse. Through logical argumentation using historical and legal precedents, Lincoln undermines the credibility of Democratic policies and leaders for achieving economic and social stability and progress, and the result is an implicit moral appeal for his party and himself. This speech appeared in Whig newspapers in Springfield and Quincy and was printed as a pamphlet, which Basler notes "received wide distribution during the ensuing campaign" (the presidential campaign of 1840).[55]

The Subtreasury speech marks Lincoln's first major use of the founders, the Declaration of Independence, and the Constitution—nonartistic proofs that he would draw upon throughout his public life. In his first political career, the founding document Lincoln most often invoked was the Constitution. Brian R. Dirck cites the tradition of constitutional interpretation that Lincoln had adopted to support his defense of the bank: "Lincoln was very much a Hamiltonian, broad constructionist in his interpretation of the US Constitution. He saw the Constitution less a limiter on national government action, and more as a catalyst for necessary economic development."[56] Yet, Lincoln "respected the rule of law and the limitations placed by the Constitution's legal and political system on people's actions. Lincoln wanted an energetic but not a dangerous government, and he wanted a flexible but not an infinitely malleable Constitution."[57]

In 1839 and 1840 Lincoln, while maintaining his law practice, campaigned for reelection, and he guided the Illinois campaign for the Whig presidential candidate, William Henry Harrison. Lincoln's campaign trail took him throughout the Eighth Judicial Circuit and into southern Illinois, and during this campaign he again crossed rhetorical swords with Douglas.

From November 1839 to late March 1840, Lincoln wrote private letters mostly about politics, and he wrote eight letters to John T. Stuart. These letters, just two or three short paragraphs each, are examples of the kind of private letters he would write to political friends in future campaigns. The subject matter, tone, and style of these letters to Stuart are businesslike, with only a few references to their law practice and personal/family matters. These letters provide news about the state legislature and politics, with several references to Douglas, including the anecdote of the April 1840 infamous street brawl between Douglas and Simeon Francis, editor of the pro-Whig *Sangamo Journal*. Lincoln requested Stuart to help him with his campaign work, as seen in the letter of January 20: "Be sure to send me as many copies of the life of Harrison, as you can spare from other uses. Be *verry* [sic] sure to procure and send me the Senate Journal of New York of September 1814. I have a newspaper article which says that that document proves that Van Buren voted against raisin[g] troops in the last war. And, in general, send me everything you think will be a good 'war-club.'"[58] Whenever possible Lincoln mined printed sources for use in his compositions.

By 1840 Lincoln excelled in speaking on the stump, mixing logical argumentation with stories and jokes. According to one eyewitness, Lincoln could tell off-color stories in a manner that "gave no offense even to refined and cultured people," eliciting "loud bursts of laughter and applause."[59] Burlingame, however, notes that in this campaign, "the few extant examples of Lincoln's speeches show that he indulged in the same race-baiting that he had so freely employed four years earlier."[60]

In March, during one of Lincoln's debate encounters with Douglas, Lincoln held up a copy of William H. Holland's biography of Democratic President Martin Van Buren that claimed he supported limited black suffrage, and that reference so angered Douglas that he "seized the volume, damned it, and flung it out into the audience."[61] This incident illustrates Lincoln's skill in using printed material to catch an opponent in a contradiction.

Sometimes Lincoln's personal attacks backfired, for example, in the July 1840 incident known as "the skinning of Thomas." In a public harangue,

Lincoln mimicked Democrat Judge Jesse B. Thomas so cruelly that he left the scene in tears, and the Democratic press berated Lincoln so effectively that he apologized to Thomas. At Belleville Lincoln cited the low sale price of a horse as an example of the effects of Democratic policies, but he realized he made an embarrassing gaffe when the owner of the horse pointed out that the price was low because the horse had only one eye. At other speeches audience members chided him for demagogic tactics and anecdotes that fell flat.

In August 1840 Lincoln was reelected to a fourth and final term in the Illinois legislature and was almost elected speaker of the House. In November Harrison won the presidency, carrying Illinois decisively, to Lincoln's gratification. In his final legislative term Lincoln was entangled in the web of intensified partisan wrangling as he worked to sustain the state bank. Lincoln continued to write anonymous, satirical letters published in the *Sangamo Journal*, but he gave no major speeches. He did not run for reelection, perhaps because as an ambitious, rising Illinois Whig, he was thinking about running for Congress. His pursuit of that goal, however, became complicated owing to intraparty rivalry. Douglas was elected to the US House of Representatives in 1843, the year that Lincoln failed to get his party's congressional nomination.

Lecturing with Political and Moral Themes

On January 27, 1838, during his reelection campaign and disputes with Douglas, Lincoln delivered a political lecture, "The Perpetuation of Our Political Institutions," to the Young Men's Lyceum of Springfield. In this address Lincoln circumvented the Lyceum rules prohibiting political rhetoric by offering political principles without stating partisan positions. This 3,575-word address has elicited some of the most diverse commentary on Lincoln's compositions of this period, especially on the "towering genius" figure, which targets Douglas, as explained below. Critical commentary on the Lyceum address fails to reveal the incremental problem-solution structure that contributes to its power. Douglas L. Wilson cites Thomas F. Schwartz's view that Lincoln chose a nonpartisan subject for this speech to offset the partisan politics he had been embroiled in.[62] Yet, according to Burlingame, the Lyceum address is suffused with politics: criticism of the Democratic Party, racism, anti-abolitionists, and Douglas.[63] Burlingame also maintains that this address "offers sympathy for blacks and abolitionists in addition to its condemnation of mob action." Harry V. Jaffa regards the Lyceum address as an original discussion of political power, leadership, and legacy.[64] John Channing Briggs discusses this address as a critique of Van Buren's and Jackson's principles conceived to "perpetuate" the nation's representative government in the face of inevitable challenges.[65]

In the Lyceum address, just before he turned twenty-nine, Lincoln probes the challenge of sustaining self-government after the initial success of the founders' generation and in the face of the current, increasing lawlessness. Qualities of this speech characterize Lincoln's most significant prepresidential writing, including a moral perspective on a subject of national importance, problem-solution structure and development, and criticism of political opposition that reveals Lincoln's views. The Lyceum address develops through two, closely related cycles of problem analysis and solution. This structure is logical and coherent because the second problem-solution stems from the first.

In the first cycle Lincoln describes the contemporary problem of social instability that he calls the "mobocratic spirit," a matter of national importance of particular concern to the Whigs.[66] Lincoln describes this problem as the "increasing disregard for law which pervades the country; the growing disposition to substitute the wild and furious passions, in lieu of the sober judgment of Courts; and the worse than savage mobs, for the executive ministers of justice." Mob violence, Lincoln says, leads to disillusionment in the populace, government breakdown, and anarchy; but this fate can be prevented if citizens will obey the law, adhere to the legislative process that allows for repeal, and teach these values as "the political religion of the nation." Lincoln does not explicitly link social unrest to slavery and abolition, but his audience would have because he describes the lynching in St. Louis of a black man who had murdered two white men and the murder by a mob of the abolitionist newspaper editor Elijah Lovejoy at Alton, Illinois, just a few weeks before the Lyceum address. Burlingame points out Lincoln's courage in expressing sympathy toward a black murderer of white people and an abolitionist in a negrophobic region.

Lincoln identifies a future leader's egomania as another potential threat to "our political institutions," arguing that ambition can be so strong in some politicians that they are not content with the rewards of conventional public service. Anticipating a national crisis, Lincoln fears "the towering genius" that "burns for distinction; and, if possible, it will have it, whether at the expense of emancipating slaves, or enslaving freemen." The appearance of such a person will test the "political religion" of the nation: "It will require the people to be united with each other, attached to the government and laws, and generally intelligent, to successfully frustrate his designs." The antidote for the potential threat of the "towering genius" is an enlightened citizenry. In the peroration Lincoln uses the conventional flourish, including metaphoric language and sentences with parallelism and repetition to emphasize this point:

> It [passion] will in future be our enemy. Reason, cold, calculating, unimpassioned reason, must furnish all the materials for our future support and defence. Let those [materials] be moulded into general intelligence, [sound] morality and, in particular, a reverence for the Constitution and laws; and, that we improved to the last; that we remained free to the last; that we revered his name to the last; [tha]t, during his long sleep, we permitted no

hostile foot to pass over or desecrate [his] resting place; shall be that which to le[arn the last] trump shall awaken our WASH[INGTON. Upon these] let the proud fabric of freedom r[est, as the] rock of its basis; and as truly as has been said of the only greater institution, "the gates of hell shall not prevail against it."[67]

This hyperbolic language expresses a passionate commitment to foundational principles that Lincoln finds threatened by mob rule. The perceived problem is hypothetical, and the solution deriving from applied rationality is vague. Yet in that solution are two values that would be central to Lincoln's future political discourse: morality and "reverence for the Constitution." Lincoln advocates for an enlightened citizenry supporting the rule of law as the key to preventing a potential malevolent dictator from gaining public office. Lincoln does not say who is responsible for teaching these principles. The "towering genius" represents the antithesis of an ideal political leader, as Jaffa explains: "The task of a leader is to find the point of coincidence between the moral demands which are dear to the men he would lead and their self-interests, and to turn this, not only against the unjust self-interests of others, but against the unjust self-interests of his own followers."[68]

The "towering genius" dictator portrayed in the Lyceum address has led to various interpretations relating to Lincoln's ambition.[69] Some historians have argued that Lincoln had himself in mind as a potential dictator, and some have debated whether Lincoln abused his constitutional powers as president during the Civil War when he suspended habeas corpus. Among the earliest proponents of this view is Edmund Wilson, who wrote: "It is evident that Lincoln has projected himself into the role against which he is warning them."[70] Jaffa cites this view.[71] In contrast, Burlingame asserts: "Clearly, the 'towering genius' was Douglas, the man whom the flatterer in 'Conservative No. 2' [a pseudonymous letter in the *Sangamo Journal* attributed to Lincoln] called 'a towering genius.' (This was probably a slighting reference to Douglas's diminutive stature—5 feet 4 inches—which Lincoln in December 1837 had alluded to.)"[72] Lincoln risked criticism with this veiled disparagement of Douglas in a speech that was supposed to exclude partisanship. Burlingame's praise for this speech relates to its implied moral appeal: "Despite its banality, Lincoln's address offered beneath the surface a bold commentary on slavery and race, couched so as to give little offense but nevertheless designed to prick the conscience of his audience."[73]

The style of the Lyceum address is more complex than Lincolnists have acknowledged. Douglas L. Wilson argues that the Lyceum address was "designed in part to show that he [Lincoln] was capable of the florid style of oratory then in vogue."[74] Burlingame says that Lincoln "may have been imitating the flamboyant oratorical style of Daniel Webster, whom he had heard speak a few months earlier in Springfield."[75] Some of Lincoln's language does use hyperbole, for example, a description of mob action: hanging went from "gamblers to Negroes, from Negroes to white citizens, and from these to strangers; till, dead men were seen literally dangling from the boughs of trees upon every road side; and in numbers almost sufficient, to rival the native Spanish moss of the country, as a drapery of the forest." Yet much of this speech is written in the plain English style that marks Lincoln's mature writing. For example, he uses unadorned language to describe an incident with implicit moral and emotional appeal: "A mulatto man, by the name of McIntosh, was seized in the street, dragged to the suburbs of the city, chained to a tree, and actually burned to death; and all within a single hour from the time he had been a freeman, attending to his own business, and at peace with the world. Such are the effects of mob law."[76] Here the vocabulary is commonplace, and nouns and action verbs precisely convey the meaning, with few modifiers.

Throughout the 1838 campaign Lincoln continued to criticize Douglas in debates and stump speeches. Douglas's 1838 campaign activity revealed his talent for ingratiating himself to immigrants to solicit their votes. Douglas, whose ancestry was Scottish, told Irish immigrants working as canal laborers in northern Illinois that he was of their descent, and Douglas claimed they cheered him for it. Douglas told others, including journalists, that his fabrication was justified if it contributed to his victory. Douglas did carry the canal counties. Douglas biographer Reg Ankrom comments on the significance of this fabrication: "The distortion of facts when they seemed harmless but useful for his own purposes was becoming more and more characteristic of Douglas. There were some in his adopted hometown of Jacksonville who believed his success as a lawyer 'lay in his utter indifference to the line that separates truth from falsehood. If he could but win he did not hesitate about the means.'"[77] Douglas's rhetoric played a major part in growing his political power, and that rhetoric would depend heavily on demagogic methods. In the 1850s Lincoln would contend mightily with them.

The invited address Lincoln delivered to the Springfield Washington Temperance Society on February 22, 1842, expresses a moral appeal for patient, sympathetic understanding of the problem of intemperance. The society consisted mainly of reformed alcoholics, and Lincoln urged them not to use the harsh condemnation of enablers and victims of this disease as other reformers had done, but rather to empathize with them and employ "kind, unassuming persuasion."[78] Some of the churchgoers in the audience were offended by Lincoln's unorthodox, forbearing attitude toward the alcoholic sinners.[79] Burlingame observes that this address "implicitly chides abolitionists for their stridency while explicitly addressing only temperance reformers." Douglas L. Wilson notes: "Like the Lyceum address of 1838, Lincoln's temperance speech ends with an emphasis on rationality with moral underpinning as the solution to society's problems."[80] Lincoln's approach to the problem of intemperance encapsulates an essential component of the ethos that would drive his political/rhetorical rise: emphasizing moral suasion through rational appeal to reach for credibility.

In 1841 Lincoln ended his law partnership with John T. Stuart and became the junior law partner of Stephen T. Logan. On November 4, 1842, Lincoln and Mary Todd were married after a troubled courtship. Stephen A. Douglas had been one of his rivals for her hand.

Conclusion

Lincoln's compositions during his time in the Illinois legislature show that he adapted rhetorical methods to his political purposes for audiences in both formal and informal settings. Writing carefully for various purposes and audiences in several genres, Lincoln formulated and promoted Whig policy to foster economic and social progress, and his rhetoric enabled him to advance from a political novice to a state party leader. Some of his compositions of this period feature qualities that would characterize his most important prepresidential rhetoric. For example, his 1837 slavery protest reveals his ability to think for himself on a complicated, controversial issue, and he would never abandon his self-confidence or deviate from his antislavery stance. His 1839 Subtreasury speech is a textbook example of principles and methods originating in classical rhetoric, and this speech demonstrates the scrupulous argumentation, including lawyerly refutation, thoughtful structure, and skillful language typically seen in his future, forceful public-affairs rhetoric.

Another aspect of Lincoln's early rhetoric seen in subsequent compositions is the paradoxical combination of moralistic and demagogic elements. Lincoln's advocation of Whig policies for the greater good of society carried implicit moral appeal, but he was capable of articulating those policies with such demagogic methods as withholding negative information and racist expressions. A central method of Lincoln's advocation of Whig policies was criticism of Democratic policies, and he sometimes satirized them and the rhetoric and personal qualities of opponents, for example, his treatment of Usher F. Linder and Stephen A. Douglas in legislative speeches. Lincoln's criticism of them was moderate, but his personal attacks in less formal situations could be harsh, for example, his sarcastic treatment of George Forquer and Jesse B. Thomas.

Lincoln's political work during his time in the Illinois legislature fueled his ambition, and in 1843 he ran for Congress, perhaps prodded by his wife. That run surely took more time and effort than he expected, but his writing ability proved indispensable to his ultimate success. By the time Lincoln ran for Congress, he surely had discovered that using demagoguery could be risky. As he courted Mary Todd in mid-1842, he admitted to writing the second of three letters signed "Aunt Rebecca" that were personal attacks on the Democratic leader James Shields. Outraged, Shields challenged Lincoln to a duel, and it was averted only at the last minute. Lincoln always regretted this incident, and he would never again write such letters. Yet satire became part of Lincoln's rhetorical stock-in-trade, and an interesting question arises over what might happen if Lincoln would incorporate sarcastic personal attacks in formal compositions.

2

Writing Himself into Congress (1843–1847)

Let the pith of the whole argument be
"turnabout is fair play."
—Lincoln, Letter to Benjamin F. James, 1845

The epigraph expresses Lincoln's moral stance that his party's aspiring rivals should take turns as candidates for Congress, and Lincoln would appeal to fairness often in his subsequent political rhetoric. Lincoln's first announcement to run for public office (1832) said that he sought the esteem of fellow citizens, and his pro-Whig rhetoric during his Illinois legislative years was at the heart of his attempt to reach that goal. From 1843 to 1846 Lincoln labored to gain his party's congressional nomination, and he relied heavily on his writing ability in that pursuit. In the course of events, he realized that while he sought others' respect, he needed to guard his self-esteem. To do so, he applied a "turnabout is fair play" argument on several occasions, and that strategy was effective in helping him secure the congressional nomination. The need to protect his self-esteem would play an important role in the mixture of principled argumentation and controversial methods in Lincoln's rhetoric during his competition with Stephen A. Douglas in the 1850s.

Writing to Shape and Promote Whig Policy

On March 1, 1843, Lincoln took a party leadership role by composing the Illinois Whig platform, a series of resolutions, in advance of the party's district convention in May, which would choose its congressional candidate. This platform reflected national Whig economic policies. Lincoln began by proposing a tariff on "imported goods," claiming it would pay the "necessary expenditures" of the federal government and would be "so adjusted as to protect American industry."[1] He advocated a national bank and "the distribution of the proceeds of the sale of public lands upon the principles of [Henry] Clay's bill."[2] Lincoln also recommended replacing primaries with conventions in the seven districts, "each to nominate one candidate for Congress and one delegate to a national convention for the purpose of nominating candidates for president and vice president."

Three days after Lincoln wrote the Illinois Whig platform, he co-authored a Whig campaign circular. It elaborates on the platform, demonstrating that Lincoln had a hand in shaping Whig policy as well as promoting it. In this circular Lincoln directs criticism mostly against policy failures, both Democratic and Whig, and against individuals to a lesser extent, and his occasional sarcasm and hyperbole add emotional appeal to its overall rational tone.

This printed composition features some of the qualities of Lincoln's political speeches; in fact, its title is Address to the People of Illinois. This composition exemplifies his use of the classical pattern of developing an argument to support a proposition, explaining its rationale, and citing examples. The circular of 3,460 words uses a structure based on the sequence in which the seven resolutions were passed, beginning with those subjects of national importance and then those of importance to Illinois. Lincoln discusses the Whig resolutions as solutions to problems. The logical structure and development of this circular emphasize rational appeal, with forecasting language transitioning from one subject to another and strengthening its coherence. The first four resolutions concern subjects of national significance: a pro-tariff position, opposition to direct taxation, and support for a national bank and the Land Bill of the venerable Henry Clay. Lincoln may have reserved discussion of the remaining three resolutions for last because they directly concerned strengthening the organization and power of the Illinois Whig Party, as Lincoln aspired to strengthen his reputation as a member.

Lincoln's fifth resolution calls for each district to choose a congressional candidate "regardless of the chances of success." In plain language he argues for a Whig convention system rather than allowing numerous candidates to run in the same election, to avoid giving the advantage to Democrats: "Our political identity is partially frittered away and lost. And again, those who are thus elected by our aid, ever become our bitterest prosecutors"[3] (persecutors). He then concludes with the rational and emotional appeal of an implied moral argument expressed with hyperbole: "During the last summer the whole state was covered with pamphlet editions of misrepresentations against us, methodized into chapters and verses, written by two of these same men, Reynolds and Young; in which they did not stop at charging us with error merely, but roundly denounced us as the designing enemies of human liberty itself. If it be the will of Heaven that such men shall politically live, be it so, but never, never again permit them to draw a particle of their substance from us."[4]

In support of the sixth resolution, Lincoln says that, regardless of any ethical issue with the convention system, it "is madness in us not to defend ourselves with it." He cites the history of the Illinois Whig Party showing that without party unity behind one of its particular candidates, the split vote enabled Democratic candidates to win although their party membership had not increased. Lincoln's language drives home his point not through hyperbole but through a series of direct, incisive phrases in answer to a rhetorical question, adding impact. The numerical details Lincoln cites indicate he has studied his party's state predicament: "The election came, [and] what was the result? The Governor beaten, the Whig vote being decreased many thousands since 1840. . . . Beaten almost everywhere for members of the legislature. Tazewell, with her four hundred Whig majority, sending a delegation half Democratic. Vermilion, with her five hundred, doing the same. Coles with her four hundred, sending two out of three." Near the end of his plea for adopting the convention system, Lincoln quotes the aphoristic line that would mark his famous 1858 speech accepting his party's nomination for the US Senate: "A house divided against itself cannot stand" (perhaps his first use of that metaphor).

Lincoln's conclusion laments that Democrats have won elections at the national level after the sweeping Whig victories of 1840 because "tens of thousands [of Whigs] . . . have not voted at all." He says that President Harrison's sudden death prevented the fulfillment of the Whigs' agenda because the succeeding Tyler administration allowed the Democrats to obstruct it and make false charges against the Whigs. He then exhorts readers to action in the next presidential election: "We declare it to be our solemn conviction, that the Whigs are always a majority of this nation; and that to make them always successful, needs but to get them all to the polls, and [to] vote unitedly. This is the great desideratum. Let us make every effort to attain it." This exhortation expresses Lincoln's aspiration of party leadership.

Writing and Stumping to Gain the Whig Congressional Nomination

Early in 1843, when Lincoln began to seek a congressional nomination, he encountered worthy competitors, including the charismatic Edward D. Baker. Lincoln admired him so much that in 1846 Lincoln named his second son Edward Baker. Another rival, John J. Hardin, was a lawyer, fellow veteran of the Black Hawk War, and three-term member of the Illinois General Assembly. Lincoln also admired Hardin. Chosen by the Sangamon County Whigs as a delegate to its 1843 district convention at Pekin, Lincoln was expected to vote for Baker as their party's congressional candidate, but Hardin was chosen. Lincoln believed that an understanding emerged from the Pekin convention (known as the Pekin Agreement) that an elected candidate would serve only one term, and a successive candidate would be chosen on a rotation basis. Hardin served one term in Congress (1843–1845) and deferred to Baker in the 1844 competition. Thus, Lincoln hoped to be his party's candidate in 1846.

Throughout 1843 Lincoln gave few speeches, devoting much time to his law practice, but in December his political activity increased when he was selected as one of nine presidential electors to his party's 1844 state convention. Springfield Whigs were urging Lincoln to run for governor, but he declined because he was determined to get to Congress and because no Whig stood a chance of winning a statewide office in a predominantly Democratic state like Illinois. In pursuit of his congressional aspiration, Lincoln continued to build his reputation as a reliable party workhorse. Beginning in January 1844 he faithfully campaigned for the Whig presidential candidate, Henry Clay.

In the 1844 campaign Lincoln typically argued for the tariff and a national bank in stump speeches and debates. No text of these speeches is extant, and newspaper accounts are biased and sketchy. For example, the Democratic *Illinois State Register* in critiquing Lincoln's defense of the tariff on March 1 at Sugar Creek reported that he "attempted to make the farmer believe that the high pressure tariff made everything they bought cheaper, but said also he could not tell the reason."[5] Regarding a series of debates in Springfield later that month, the *Register*'s report on what Lincoln said about the tariff consisted of brief descriptions: first, that he "promised to forfeit his 'ears' and his 'legs' if he did not demonstrate that protected articles have been cheaper since the late tariff than before" and second, that he "very candidly acknowledged his inability to prove that the tariff had anything to do with the late low prices throughout this country and Europe."[6] This Democratic newspaper report closed with uncommonly even-handed analysis of the debaters: "The discussion has been well attended, and we readily accord Mr. Calhoun due praise for making most of a bad cause. The efforts of Mr. Lincoln were distinguished for ability, and in all candor we must say that we did not discover a single position raised by Mr. Calhoun that he did not entirely demolish."[7]

According to Burlingame, a pseudonymous article in the *Sangamo Journal* early in the campaign was probably written by Lincoln so he could give his views on the tariff. The article features imaginary dialogue (prosopopoeia) in which Lancaster (a fictional Whig character) speaks for Lincoln, illustrating the adaptation of a literary technique for political purpose that he surely also used in stump speaking:

> Protective tariffs did not unfairly burden "the poor farmer," Lancaster argued, because all "manufactured articles were sold as low and many lower after [the enactment of the 1842 tariff] than they were before. . . . " Lancaster insisted that " . . . *our revenue is paid entirely by the foreign manufacturers*; except perhaps occasionally some of our Fops and Dandies may be inclined to show off with a London Coat, a Paris pair of boots, or ornament his table with a set of *English knives and forks*, or his parlour with an European carpet. . . . American manufacturers of broadcloth would benefit from a

35 percent tariff, but farmers would also benefit from that protection, for the manufacturers paid for wool and lard oil, which the farmers produced, and paid wages to workers, who spent three-quarters of their income on goods produced by farmers.[8]

Lincoln was arguing with common-sense logic and a mixture of plain and loaded language.

Even before Lincoln gained his party's congressional nomination in 1846, he was attempting to influence how his party might solve problems at the national level. In June he confronted the problem of nativist agitation over increased immigration involving anti-Catholic rioting and bloodshed in Philadelphia. At a Springfield public meeting Lincoln offered resolutions in which he denied Whig Party responsibility for those riots, as some had charged. The resolutions presented a fair-minded policy toward naturalization: "Foreigners should be put to some reasonable test of fidelity to our country and its institutions and should first dwell among us a reasonable time to become generally acquainted with the nature of those institutions[,] and consistent with these requisites, naturalization laws should be so framed as to render admission to citizenship under them as convenient, cheap, and expeditious as possible."[9] Lincoln also asserted that the constitutional "rights of conscience" were "most sacred and inviolable." The pro-Democratic *Illinois State Register* said Lincoln's resolutions were heartfelt but did not reflect the views of other Whigs.

Lincoln wrote the resolutions for a Whig convention at Peoria that endorsed Henry Clay as the Whig presidential candidate and prioritized the party's policies. Most important was a tariff. Next was "the plan of distributing the proceeds of the public lands among several states," an accurate documentation of those transactions, and the establishment of a sound currency. Lincoln concluded with sensible policy proposals: "The practical restriction of the veto power, so that it may not be wielded to the centralization of all power in the hands of a corrupt and despotic executive; the limitation of the presidential office to one term . . . ; and reform of all those abuses which have sprung out of the corrupt use of the power of appointments." Lincoln concluded the campaign of 1844 by speaking in Indiana for several days just before the November election, including a one-hour speech about the tariff at Rockport.

Lincoln's 1844 stump speeches and debate speeches with the able Illinois Democrat John Calhoun enhanced Lincoln's political/rhetorical experience and reputation as a Whig spokesman. Burlingame says the historical record supports David Davis's 1844 observation that Lincoln was the leading stump speaker in Illinois at the time.[10] The tariff continued to interest Lincoln throughout his political careers, and this chapter later discusses material for a speech on this subject that he may have been planning as a congressman. Henry Clay lost the 1844 election to James Polk, and in an 1845 letter Lincoln blamed "Whig abolitionists of New York," who refused to vote for Clay. Third-party voting for James G. Birney, an abolitionist there, took enough votes away from Clay to throw the state and the country to James K. Polk.[11] Abolitionism would concern Lincoln throughout the rest of his public life.

Writing to Run for Congress Based on Moral Principle

Following the 1843 Pekin Agreement, Lincoln assumed he would become the 1846 Whig candidate for Congress from his district after the terms of Hardin and Baker, but in the fall of 1845 Lincoln anticipated Hardin's reneging. Thus, as Lincoln traveled the circuit late that fall, he began to solicit support for his candidacy, and he cast his net widely. Recalling that Clay may have lost the 1844 presidential election because New York abolitionists refused to vote for him, Lincoln apparently sought to avoid a similar problem of losing votes from those he thought might withhold their support. In October 1845 he wrote to Williamson Durley of Hennepin in Putnam County, north of Peoria, observing that Durley and others in that county did not call themselves abolitionists but Liberty-men. Lincoln notes that Liberty-men were opposed to the annexation of Texas and speculates that if they had helped to elect Clay president, Texas would not have been annexed. Lincoln rejects the reasoning he was told as to why the Liberty-men failed to vote for Clay. In Lincoln's analysis, "if by your votes you could have prevented the *extension*, &c. of slavery, would it not have been *good* and not *evil* so to have used your votes, even though it involved the casting of them for a slaveholder? By the *fruit* the tree is to be known. An *evil* tree cannot bring forth *good* fruit. If the fruit of electing Mr. Clay would have been to prevent the extension of slavery, could the act of electing have been *evil*?"[12]

Lincoln further explains that he did not believe annexing Texas would "augment the evil of slavery," except that some slaves sent to Texas may have otherwise been freed. He asserts that "we" should not do anything "directly or indirectly, to prevent slavery from dying a natural death. . . . " Lincoln tells Durley that his views could be shared with others in Morgan County. Hardin, in competition with Lincoln for their party's nomination, denied that he had acquiesced in the Pekin Agreement. Hardin also tried to undermine Lincoln and Baker's friendship, and Hardin urged replacement of the convention system with a primary election. In trying to gain his party's nomination and maintain its harmony, Lincoln corresponded with Hardin.

Well aware of the potential of the press, Lincoln sought endorsement of the Pekin Agreement from Whig editors in the district, embarking on his most vigorous letter writing to date. He began dictating letters to a legal assistant who then suggested sending a form letter. Lincoln refused to use a form letter because he knew the value of personalizing his message. All of Lincoln's letters, to friend and foe alike, are succinct and deferential. In his 1845–1846 letters Lincoln sought cooperation in advancing his chances to become the district's congressional candidate, but he also wanted to avoid conflict and maintain cordial relations for party unity. These letters reveal Lincoln as a skillful political analyst, strategist, and self-promoter.

Counting on support from his home county of Sangamon and surrounding counties, he calculated that he could secure the nomination with additional votes of the six delegates from three northern counties of the district, including Tazewell County, where Pekin was the seat. Thus, on January 7, 1846, Lincoln wrote a letter to ask for help from one of his best political allies just north of Peoria at Lacon in Marshall County: Dr. Robert Boal, a physician, Whig leader, and state senator. The letter's introduction identifies Hardin's push for the nomination. The second paragraph precisely states the rational/ethical appeal of Lincoln's case:

> If Hardin and I stood equal—that is, if *neither* of us had been to congress, or if we *both* had—it would only accord with what I have always done, for the sake of peace, to give way to him; and I expect I should do it. That I *can* voluntarily postpone my pretentions, when they are no more than equal to those to which they are postponed, you have yourself seen. But to yield to Hardin under present circumstances seems to me as nothing else than yielding to one who would gladly sacrifice me altogether. This I would rather not submit to.[13]

Lincoln compliments Hardin, describing him as "talented" and "energetic," but cleverly suggests Hardin is not without self-interest by describing him as "*usually* generous" (emphasis mine). Lincoln strongly closes, using a common expression: "You know that my only argument is that 'turnabout is fair play.' This he, practically at least, denies." The fair-play tagline summarizes Lincoln's argument that ethical protocol should disqualify Hardin from receiving another Whig congressional nomination at that time, and Lincoln used this plea often in other communication. Lincoln then asks for names of Boal's "Whig neighbors" so Lincoln can write to them. Lincoln emphasizes the importance of Boal's cooperation: "My reliance for a fair shake (and I want nothing more) in your county is chiefly on you, because of your position and standing, and because I am acquainted with so few others." Lincoln assures Boal that their communication is confidential.

Most of Lincoln's correspondence in this campaign was with the influential Benjamin F. James, editor of the *Tazewell Whig* and chairman of the Whig District Central Committee. From November 1845 to February 9, 1846, Lincoln sent seven letters to James, who endorsed Lincoln in a December issue of the *Tazewell Whig*. In the second letter of this series, Lincoln emphasized that he did not scheme to push for Hardin as governor in order to promote his own run for Congress. In the third letter to James, Lincoln estimated his votes county by county, asking James to help gain the northern counties for him but without denigrating Hardin: "Let the pith of the whole argument be turnabout is fair play.'"

In subsequent letters to James, Lincoln expressed his ongoing anxiety about the northern counties and asked to be kept informed about his chances there. He also asked James to use his paper to endorse the convention system after Hardin sought to have it replaced with a primary election that would work more to his advantage than to Lincoln's. In his final letter of this series, Lincoln told James that an article in the Morgan County *Journal* deliberately misrepresented him on a technicality of voting procedures, requesting James to share the facts with friends but not to publish on the matter to avoid unnecessary agitation within the party: "It will be just all we can do, to keep out of a quarrel—and I am resolved to do my part to keep peace."[14]

The sense of fairness and sincere desire for harmony within the Whig Party are evident in the two letters Lincoln wrote to Hardin in the winter of 1846. On January 19 Lincoln wrote Hardin to endorse the use of the convention system to choose candidates, rather than the "old system" that Hardin and many other Whigs preferred, in which any Whig could run for any office. The Democratic Party had adopted the convention system earlier than the Whigs and had benefited because it enabled them to "unite on one candidate while Whig support was divided among several."[15] Lincoln protested that not using the convention system gave Hardin the advantage of name recognition owing to his congressional term, but if the "old system" is to be used, Lincoln called for "a more accurate and just appointment of delegates, or representative votes, to the constituent body, than exists by the old, and which you propose to retain in your new plan."[16] Regardless, Lincoln's tone is conciliatory, and he promised to "keep cool' under all circumstances." The intricacies of Hardin and Lincoln's correspondence are worth following, for they reveal Lincoln as a shrewd but ethical politician.

Lincoln's longer, 2,650-word letter to Hardin of February 7, 1846, is an early example of Lincoln's rhetorical methods of refuting a political rival—later adapted against his greatest political adversary, Stephen A. Douglas. Lincoln was provoked by an article critical of him published in the Morgan County *Journal* that Lincoln says has material only Hardin could have provided. Lincoln's letter to Hardin of February 7 explicitly addresses a letter Hardin had written to Lincoln regarding their competition for their party's congressional nomination. The purpose of Lincoln's February letter was to correct factual errors in Hardin's earlier letter, and in setting the record straight, Lincoln wanted to avoid hard feelings for the sake of party unity and to bolster his reputation as an honorable rival. In composing his February letter Lincoln thus faced a difficult challenge. In some places his sentences, although clear, are grammatically complex as he tries to untangle misconceptions. In some places his emphatic denials are verbose.

Lincoln's refutation of Hardin's letter uses a litigious, point-by-point strategy leading to moral appeal. In fact, such legalistic words as *charge, witnesses, justice, injustice, convict,* and *conviction* are distributed throughout. This metaphoric language is appropriate for emphasizing the often-stated theme of Lincoln's letter that he seeks fairness on all aspects of his political activity in pursuing his party's nomination. As in a legal proceeding, Lincoln quotes from Hardin's letter on each point of contention. The first point Lincoln addresses is Hardin's complaint that the "manner" of Lincoln's efforts to run has been "improper." Lincoln also denies he has sought to suppress a party member "but only that he should not *himself* be a candidate out of his turn."[17] Lincoln also denies that his argument of "turnabout is fair play" is a rejection of the people's right to choose a nominee.

Lincoln tries to sort out tedious details of claims and counterclaims among Baker, Hardin, and himself over what they said or did not say about their interest in running for Congress. Lincoln says that in withdrawing from the race, Baker has wished him well, but Lincoln has no knowledge that Baker has urged others to support him over Hardin. Lincoln asks Hardin if he has heard of or seen any letters possessed by his friends in which Baker has expressed opposition to Hardin. Lincoln denies that he urged other Whigs to nominate Hardin for governor as a way of diverting him from the congressional race. Lincoln rejects the "imputation that I *procured*, or *winked* at, or in some way directly or indirectly, had a hand in, the nominating of you for governor, and the imputation is to the utmost hair-breadth of it, unjust." Lincoln says when he heard about this insinuation, he went to the *Sangamo Journal*, which had already prepared a clarification since published and "seen by you, I suppose."

Lincoln writes that his friends are the ones who insist on Hardin's compliance with the Pekin Agreement and that Lincoln's rationale for seeking the congressional nomination is related but different: "I have said that 'turnabout is fair play'; but this I have said just as I would, if that resolution had never been thought of. . . . I repeat, I desire nothing from the Pekin convention. If I am not, (in services done the party, and in capacity to serve in the future), near enough your equal, when added to the fact of your having had a turn, to entitle me to the nomination, I scorn it on any and all other grounds."[18]

This claim somewhat contradicts Lincoln's letter to Dr. Boal in the preceding month that cited the Pekin Agreement as an argument for Hardin to yield to Lincoln as the Whig candidate succeeding Baker. Of course, the letters to Boal and Hardin were private, giving Lincoln cover. Lincoln must have felt that his "turnabout is fair play" argument did not require an agreed, formal arrangement, but it did require shared ethics. Next Lincoln addresses Hardin's complaint that rivalry for their party's congressional nomination weakens its unity. Lincoln's rhetorical questions directly insinuate that Hardin is the problem: "Who are most responsible for these struggles, those who are willing to live and let live, or those who are resolved at all hazards, to take care of 'number one'?" Lincoln says some of his own supporters helped elect Hardin to Congress and that party unity will not be served if they cannot now support their preference: "Is it natural that they shall be greatly pleased at hearing what they helped to build up, turned into an argument, for keeping their own favorite down . . . ? Is it by such exclusiveness that you think a party will gain strength?" Lincoln thus associates fair play with party unity.

Lincoln closes his case by boldly charging Hardin with hypocrisy, turning the tables on him by quoting his letter accusing Lincoln of it—an early example of the blunt rhetoric that Lincoln would later use against Douglas: "For it is mortifying to discover that those with whom I have long acted and from whom I expected a different course, have considered it all fair to prevent my nomination to congress." Lincoln expresses anger over the irony of the one who calls for fair play being called a hypocrite: "Feeling, as I do, the utter injustice of these imputations, it is somewhat difficult to be patient under them—yet I content myself with saying that if there is cause for mortification anywhere, it is in the readiness with which you believe, and make such charges, against one with whom you truly say you have long acted; and in whose conduct, you have heretofore marked nothing as dishonorable." Yet the final sentence of Lincoln's letter is a tempered request for Hardin to reconsider: "I believe you do not mean to be unjust, or ungenerous; and I, therefore am slow to believe that you will not yet think better and think differently of this matter."[19]

In mid-February Hardin withdrew from consideration but maintained he had not interpreted the Pekin Agreement as Lincoln had. Hardin's Whig supporters from Morgan County and its seat of Jacksonville (Hardin's hometown, just thirty-six miles west of Springfield) "continued, however, to rebel against the convention system of nominating candidates which their favorite son, John J. Hardin, opposed"; and the conflict between Lincoln's and Hardin's supporters was the subject of a conciliatory letter Lincoln wrote in April to James Berdan, a Jacksonville Whig lawyer. This letter shows an early example of Lincoln's ability not to hold grudges but to plead for party unity. The letter also reveals Lincoln's understanding of the importance of face-to-face dialogue, not just written communication, to work out differences: "Previous to Genl. Hardin's withdrawal, some of his friends and some of mine, had become a little warm; and I felt, and meant to say, that for them now to meet face to face and converse together, was the best way to efface any remnant of unpleasant feeling."[20] In 1847 Hardin was killed during the Mexican War in the Battle of Buena Vista, and in April of that year the resolutions that Congressman Lincoln introduced at a meeting to commemorate the soldiers who had fought and died in that battle cited "Co. J.J. HARDIN."

After Lincoln gained his party's nomination for Congress in May 1846, he spoke often throughout his congressional district, but the historical record of his speeches is scant. A report in the *Illinois Gazette* at Lacon said that the main subject of a speech he gave there in mid-July was the tariff, and other subjects were the Mexican War, Texas annexation, and the Oregon territory.[21] In response to rumors being spread of his "infidelity" in a "whispering campaign" by his Democratic opponent Peter Cartwright, on July 31 Lincoln tried to refute Cartwright's accusation that he was a religious skeptic by releasing a two-paragraph "Handbill Replying to Charges of Infidelity." Lincoln denies that he is "an open scoffer of Christianity" and says that he has "never denied the truth of the Scriptures," nor has he ever spoken disrespectfully "of religion in general, or of any denomination of Christians in particular." He allows he had sometimes argued for his belief in a fatalistic "Doctrine of Necessity" but "never publicly." He ends by saying that he could never vote for anyone he might know to be "an open enemy of, and scoffer at, religion" or who would otherwise "insult the feelings, and injure the morals, of the community in which he may live."[22] Richard Carwardine writes that this statement shows Lincoln "recognized both the social grip of religion and the duty of politicians to respect the religious sensibilities of voters."[23]

Several Lincolnists have justifiably faulted his response to Cartwright. For example, William C. Harris points out that residents of New Salem contradicted Lincoln's claim that he never denied the truth of the Scriptures.[24] Allen C. Guelzo describes Lincoln's response as "somewhat disingenuous," and Guelzo discusses how the religious/moral implications of the Cartwright-Lincoln dispute may have resonated with certain Protestant denominations of that time: "If Lincoln's 'necessity' horrified Methodists like Cartwright, then by way of reply, Lincoln was indirectly suggesting that Cartwright's free-willism horrified a good many righteous Presbyterians and Congregationalists."[25] Burlingame says the contemporaries who faulted Lincoln's logic were justified: "Lincoln seemed to make two different claims: that he never believed in infidel doctrines, and that he never publicly espoused them. If the former were true, the latter would be superfluous; if the former were untrue, the latter would be irrelevant. Moreover, his reference to the doctrine of necessity was a dodge, for he was accused of infidelity, not fatalism."[26]

How much good this handbill did Lincoln is questionable, for the election was held on August 3, just days after the handbill was issued. Lincoln won the election by more than 1,200 votes, but Cartwright's whispering campaign had cost Lincoln votes in the northern counties, where he was least known. On

August 11, Lincoln wrote a five-paragraph letter to Allen N. Ford, editor of the *Illinois Gazette*, requesting publication of his handbill in that newspaper. Roy P. Basler suggests Lincoln was thinking about his reputation for possible future political activity. The letter to Ford and the handbill appeared in the *Illinois Gazette* on August 15, and the letter provides insight into the historical-rhetorical context of the issue of religion for Lincoln in this campaign and into his view of the relationship between rational and ethical appeals. Lincoln notes that before his speaking campaign in the northern counties in the second half of July, he learned of Cartwright's charge of infidelity in the Jacksonville area, and Lincoln says he immediately "wrote a contradiction of it," sending it to the local press there and leaving publication to the editor's discretion. This message was not published there and then. After hearing of Cartwright's whispering campaign in the northern counties toward the end of July, Lincoln says his opponent was not playing fair because "he knew I could not contradict him, either in person or by letter before the election." Lincoln doubted those rumors were heard by very many citizens but decided to publish "the little hand-bill" as a precaution.

When the election returns showed Lincoln's weak support in the northern counties, he became convinced that Cartwright "has succeeded in deceiving some honest men there" and thus requested Ford to publish the handbill with the implication of setting the record straight. Lincoln also complained about a Mr. Woolard, a citizen in Henry County, whose negative views of Lincoln were published in the *Illinois Gazette* as reported by a correspondent in that county. Lincoln believed Cartwright had poisoned Woolard against him and that Woolard's attack on Lincoln's character was unjustified because they were personally unacquainted. Lincoln used a maxim, a technique from classical rhetoric, to emphasize the need to form opinion based on fact: "He who makes an assertion without knowing whether it is true or false, is guilty of falsehood."[27]

Researching and Writing to Prepare for Congress

Lincoln was elected in August 1846, but his congressional term did not begin until December 1847. In a letter to Joshua Speed just three weeks after the election, Lincoln commented only briefly about his success: "Being elected to Congress, though I am very grateful to our friends, for having done it, has not pleased me as much as I expected." During the months before Lincoln began his congressional term, he had no need to give political speeches or write public or private letters with political purposes, but compositions Lincoln wrote after his election show that he was thinking about such Whig policy subjects as internal improvements and tariffs, and he probably thought he would champion them in Congress.

At the end of June Lincoln co-authored a 1,300-word, nonpolitical Open Letter on the Springfield and Alton Railroad, addressing it to the people of Sangamon County. This letter illustrates Lincoln's ability to collaborate, a quality that would help him advance in the political world, and the letter testifies to Lincoln's commitment to internal improvements and thus Whig policy. Two other signatories of this letter were John T. Stuart, who was Lincoln's former law partner and Whig veteran member of the Illinois House of Representatives, and Democrat John Calhoun, Lincoln's debate rival. The letter begins with the question of whether citizens should invest in railroad stock to extend the Alton Railroad from St. Louis to Springfield. Lincoln develops this letter as a problem-solution/recommendation report. The first two paragraphs describe two challenges. One is that investments from "Eastern capitalists" must be secured for the railroad to be built, and the second challenge is that local citizens "must stake something of our own in the enterprise, to convince them [eastern investors] that we believe it will succeed."[28] Lincoln argues that this construction project would be a good investment.

Lincoln advances his argument with facts and figures gained through research. He specifies stock price, construction feasibility based on communication he had with an engineer, estimated investment amount needed for construction, gross income needed for investment payback, estimated costs of dry goods, and estimated stockholder profits ranging from 9% to 28%. Lincoln says eventually a railroad will be built to connect eastern cities to the Mississippi River, so a St. Louis-Springfield rail connection presents an opportunity: "If we complete, or even begin our road first, it will attract the other, and so become, not merely a local improvement, but a link in one of a great national character, retaining all its local benefits, and superadding many from its general connection."[29] Lincoln closes by citing amounts already invested by "some four hundred farmers, mechanics, merchants, and members of all classes" from five counties as precedent to motivate others to subscribe to the stock.

In early August Lincoln was a member of a committee that published a lengthy progress report in the *Sangamo Journal* describing construction activities and plans of several railroads that would play roles in connecting eastern cities with the Mississippi River. The report repeated the need for eastern investment in Illinois railroads to accomplish this connection.[30] Later, Lincoln would devote one of his few speeches in Congress to the need for building infrastructure, and one of his arguments would be that improvements can benefit others beyond the local level.

As Lincoln anticipated entering Congress, he knew the importance of communication, and one of the other possible subjects of concern to Whigs that he might write and speak about was the protective tariff. It had been a subject he had often spoken about, perhaps more than any other. Before Lincoln reached

Washington, he had continued research and composed a 2,038-word exploratory essay about the tariff that went beyond his previous ideas.[31] Known as Fragments of a Tariff Discussion, this composition consists of a sequential list of topics for a potential speech and paragraphs indicating his efforts to work out his thinking on the subject. These fragments are significant because they are an early example of Lincoln's ability to combine research and exploratory writing about a subject of national importance.

In Congress, however, Lincoln did not find circumstances favorable to giving a speech on the tariff. The Polk administration's Walker Tariff, passed in 1846, favored free trade and began to allow increased American farm exports and prosperity, and these developments undermined Lincoln's rationale for a higher tariff. Gabor S. Boritt observes, "Lincoln found even his Whig colleagues mostly unreceptive to tariff discussions."[32] Developing his views on the tariff presented Lincoln with one of his most difficult intellectual challenges, and the tariff fragments represent a form of private brainstorming that Lincoln would continue to use to create and phrase arguments that he could draw upon to develop his communication.

Because Lincoln did not deliver a tariff speech in Congress or publish anything about this subject during that period, the Lincoln literature offers little discussion on his Fragments of a Tariff Discussion. This writing is important because it expresses Lincoln's sense of the moral value of labor that he would later use in antislavery argumentation. The tariff fragments include a biblical quotation that Burlingame notes Lincoln would sometimes use later: "In the early days of the world, the Almighty said to the first of our race 'In the sweat of thy face shalt thou eat bread,' and since then, if we except the light and the air of heaven, no good thing has been, or can be enjoyed by us, without having first cost labor." In the tariff fragments Lincoln says nothing explicitly about free labor vs. slavery, but biographer Fred Kaplan suggests Lincoln at this time may have been reluctant to speak out: "It was hardly, in these terms, a safe subject for a freshman congressman, and this may have been the reason why he chose not to speak on the tariff during his two years as a congressman."[33]

Other aspects of Lincoln's tariff fragments afford further insight into his process of organizing and developing ideas, including the use of elements originating in classical rhetoric. The fragments consist of four discrete components in the following order: 1. a cryptic outline of a speech, 2. three paragraphs on "the true effect of duties [tariffs] upon prices," 3. three paragraphs on buying and selling, and 4. eight paragraphs synthesizing ideas of the preceding components. Kaplan praises the clarity, coherence, and style of the tariff fragments: "Repetition of key words for contrast and emphasis, preciseness of diction, lucidity of phrasing, colloquial sentence rhythms, quotation or allusion to familiar and resonating sources such as the Bible, the slight elevation into formality and a more literary style to raise the tone—all these characteristics of his later compositions are present."[34]

The rough outline begins with language that indicates the need for a policy decision affecting the country's future economy: "Whether the protective policy shall be abandoned, is now the question." Lincoln intends to show the "discussion and experience already had" demonstrated that the "question [is] now in greater dispute than ever." That is, he will use the classical technique of reviewing the history of the subject to define the problem. He will consider only a period of peace "to furnish a fair average under all other causes operating on prices—a period in which various modifications of higher and lower duties have occurred." The only other items in this outline are sentence fragments indicating he will consider only "protected articles" and only "the labor price." Thus, the outline is vague. The fourth component is complete and coherent enough to be considered an essay. The first paragraph of the essay does not define its scope, but the composition is especially coherent because of its logical development, forecasting, and other transitions.

In the tariff essay after the first sentence, with the biblical quotation as noted above, the opening paragraph continues with a fundamental proposition, and it is the basis for a central, moral objection he would make to slavery in his second political career: "And, inasmuch [as] most good things are produced by labour, it follows that [all] such things of right belong to those whose labour has produced them. But it has so happened in all ages of the world, that *some* have laboured, and *others* have, without labour, enjoyed a large proportion of the fruits. This is wrong and should not continue. To [secure] to each labourer the whole product of his labour, or as nearly as possible, is a most worthy object of any good government."[35] Considering this question requires analysis of economic activity, and Lincoln proceeds with a classical definition that divides "the habits of our whole species" into three classes: useful labor, useless labor, and idleness, with only the first category being "meritorious." The second and third categories are "heavy pensioners upon the first." Thus, the discussion proceeds with a classical technique of process description, that is, how to eliminate useless labor and idleness. Labor needed to import such materials as iron, cotton, and wool is useless because the US produces them. Imports require costs for transportation, insurance, and middle merchants, "*depressing* the price to the *producer*" and "enhancing it to the *consumer*."

Next is an elaborate example featuring respective costs of cotton grown in South Carolina and cotton cloth produced in Great Britain's Manchester. Both cotton grower and cloth producer who buy and sell their respective goods with one another suffer reduced profit. This extended example is easier to follow in print than it would be if heard in a speech. The implication is that a tariff would encourage domestic buying and selling, and reduce the stifling effects of "useless labor." The protective tariff would not be applied to such commodities as coffee that cannot be produced domestically.

Lincoln next discusses the economic prospects without a protective tariff. He describes American farmers buying foreign goods sold more cheaply than domestic goods because of the lower cost of foreign labor. This practice would put domestic manufacturers out of business, depriving farmers of a market for their produce and thus a source of income needed to purchase goods. Lincoln dramatizes these propositions through an elaborate dialogue (prosopopoeia) between a symbolic farmer and Vulcan, a symbolic manufacturer. The farmer complains to Vulcan that without a market the farmer will resort to subsistence farming only. Lincoln valorizes labor: "If at any time all *labour* should cease, and all existing provisions be equally divided among the people, at the end of a single year there would scarcely be one human being left alive—and all would perish by want of subsistence."[36]

Conclusion

In the mid-1840s, as Lincoln sought his Whig Party's congressional nomination, he was striving to become an important standard bearer at the state level by debating, stumping, and writing on his party's behalf. He was extending his efforts to shape and promote party policy as he did during his time in the Illinois legislature. As Lincoln sought a congressional nomination, he experienced intraparty rivalry and discovered the effectiveness of a rhetorical "turnabout is fair play" strategy. In using it, he could be mildly demagogic—disingenuous by playing up this kind of argument implicit in the Pekin Agreement to several correspondents and playing down that agreement to John J. Hardin. Lincoln was also somewhat demagogic in using questionable if not fallacious reasoning in the Handbill on Infidelity. In the 1850s Lincoln would employ modified "turnabout is fair play" strategies as he contended with Douglas, and in using these methods he sometimes blurred the line between moral and demagogic suasion.

As he prepared to enter Congress, Lincoln tried to identify political subjects of national significance, research them, and probe them in exploratory writing ("fragments"). His exploratory writing affords insight into his thinking/writing process and the importance he placed on cogency and coherence. In his tariff fragments Lincoln explained the people's right to enjoy the product of their own labor, and he repeatedly applied that moral position in antislavery argumentation during the 1850s. Before his congressional term Lincoln did not have a reason to address slavery because it was not yet a hot topic nationally. The few antislavery references in his rhetoric of the mid-1840s reveal that his attitude toward this problem had not changed since his time in the Illinois legislature. Lincoln's compositions of this period use biblical allusions that would have appealed to the religious/cultural background of his audience and that he would especially use later in his rivalry with Douglas.

Lincoln reported for the first session of the Thirtieth Congress in December 1847 as the only Whig congressman from Illinois. He must have then felt his self-confidence, sociability, knowledge of the law, political background, communicative experience, and ability to research, formulate, and articulate ideas well prepared him to advance in the political arena at the national level.

3

Writing and Speaking to Gain Distinction in Congress (1847–1849)

The point—the power to hurt—of all figures [of speech] consists in the truthfulness of their application.
—Lincoln, Speech on the Presidential Question, 1848

The epigraph expresses a moral principle that truth justifies painful criticism, and Lincoln never shied from that principle. In his single two-year congressional term, Lincoln expanded his work to define and promote national Whig positions and policy, including their implicit moral appeal, that he began in the Illinois legislature. His compositions during the Thirtieth Congress show that he was striving for national Whig leadership, and he increased his experience with rhetorical methods that he would adapt in his second political career. That experience included attacking the Democratic Party and its leaders, sometimes with moral criticism involving harsh and light satire in different compositions.

Advocating Whig Causes in the First Session

The ambitious, self-confident Lincoln wasted no time using his rhetorical talent to insert himself into national politics. When he began to serve in the US House of Representatives, the Mexican War was a controversial, hot political topic although the US was winning. As President Polk asked Congress for more money to conclude the war, he repeated his accusation that Mexico had started it. Such a self-serving pronouncement irritated many Whigs. Lincoln saw this situation as an opportunity to use his speaking and writing ability to enhance his party's appeal and his political reputation. Burlingame notes that in this period few House leaders were known for their oratorical powers.[1] According to David Herbert Donald, "Lincoln led the assault on Polk."[2]

On December 22, 1847, just three weeks after Lincoln took his seat in the Thirtieth Congress, he introduced seven resolutions in the House of Representatives challenging President Polk to justify his claim that Mexico started the war. Citing one of Polk's speeches and two of his annual messages to Congress, Lincoln phrased the resolutions as rhetorical questions that implied Polk would be unable to provide a factual basis for sending US troops to fight the Mexicans.

Lincoln sequenced the resolutions so that the most important ones were last, and despite the legalistic phrasing of the longer ones, each was clear, as seen, for example, in the fifth resolution asking for proof that the victims of the first bloodshed were US citizens: "Whether the *People* of that settlement [of first victims], or a *majority* of them, or *any* of them, had ever, previous to the bloodshed, mentioned in his [Polk's] messages, submitted themselves to the government or laws of Texas, or of the Unites States, by *consent*, or by *compulsion*, either by accepting office, or voting at elections, or paying taxes, or serving on juries, or having process served upon them, or in *any other way.*"[3] The final resolution asked whether Polk ordered the advancement of troops even "after General Zachary Taylor had, more than once, intimated to the War Department that, in his opinion, no such movement was necessary to the defence or protection of Texas."[4]

On January 5, a week before Lincoln spoke to the House at length about the Mexican War, he spoke there about postal contracts. Few Lincolnists mention the Postal Contracts speech. Burlingame sardonically notes that it "did not prove to be his magnum opus. It dealt with a government mail contract and was not a conspicuous success. He presented his argument in the form of a legal pleading."[5] In a letter to Herndon, a cautious Lincoln implied that the Postal Contracts speech was his way of testing the waters of addressing the House, and he said he would deliver another speech "in which I hope to succeed well enough to wish you to see it."[6] Despite the lackluster quality of the Postal Contracts speech, it reflects a serious policy effort. There is no extant text of the speech, but the report in the *Congressional Globe* is thorough enough to reveal its purpose, organization, and development.

This speech defends the postmaster general's rejection of a railroad company's demand for increased compensation to deliver mail from the US capital to Richmond, and the speech includes some of the qualities seen in Lincoln's more important political addresses: humor; legalistic, coherent argumentation informed by careful research; and a moral perspective. Lincoln cites several pertinent laws and acknowledges that legislative decisions require legal interpretation. He then explains calculations of transportation costs based on his research that account for his support of the postmaster general's positions, leading to his moral stance: "There is a principle involved; and if we once yield to a wrong principle, that concession will be the prolific source of endless mischief . . . claims equally unjust, and therefore I cannot vote to make the allowance."[7] Referring to the solution as "removing this evil," Lincoln says his position in committee is that payment for transportation should be based on "just and fair principles." He agrees the government should compensate the steamboat company for breaking its contract to transport the mail by river, and he cites the law saying the government cannot be sued.

On January 12, 1848, Lincoln gave an audacious speech on the Mexican War in which he excoriated President Polk for an unjustified war. The critical commentary on this major speech ranges from condemnation to praise, suggesting the need for reexamination.[8] Albert J. Beveridge implies that Lincoln's attack on Polk was demagogic for being "perilously close to pettifogging" (emphasizing petty details).[9] Some critics emphasize Lincoln's personal attack on Polk without relating it to an accusation of moral failure. A few writers note the speech's moral appeal, but they do not elaborate on how Lincoln tried to elicit that appeal through specific techniques.[10]

Lincoln's 4,300-word Mexican War speech was the most daring speech he had given to date. Within the hour he was allotted, he charged Democratic President Polk with two political/moral offenses: deceiving the American people over who had started the war and failing to provide leadership in concluding it. This speech indicates careful preparation, with a structure and argumentation using rational and emotional appeals to underpin his moral criticism: the speech is well organized and logically argued, with ample detail based on solid research, a characteristic of his major works. This anti-war speech has five parts: introduction, refutation of Polk's "propositions" or "evidence" (alleged facts from his speeches), discussion of the boundary between Texas and Mexico, criticism of Polk's failed leadership to end the war, and conclusion. Lincoln uses forecasting to mark transitions between all parts except the third and fourth, and transitions often appear within a part. Despite the demagoguery of personal attacks on the president, some of the language of the Mexican War speech suggests the eloquence of Lincoln's second political career.

Lincoln infuses his Mexican War speech with an underlying moral purpose developed with historical/legalistic argumentation pointing to unjustified US military action. The speech responds to Polk's attempt to conflate the call for additional military supplies with justification for the start of the war. Lincoln says he voted for his party's decision to supply troops, but he declares that he has not been motivated by partisanship alone. Rather, he believes that the war "was unnecessarily and unconstitutionally commenced by the President. I admit that such a vote should not be given, in mere party wantonness, and that the one given, is justly censurable, if it have no other, or better foundation. I am one of those who joined in that vote; and I did so under my best impression of the truth of the case," and the purpose of the speech is to show the truth about the war.[11] Lincoln asserts that Polk's claim of taking defensive action attempts to deceive.

Each successive section in the body of the speech builds on the preceding one. The first body section exposes errors in the president's argument that the war was a defensive action, blending historical review (statement of facts) and refutation. The validity of Polk's justification for the war depends on the Rio Grande as the boundary between Mexico and the United States. Lincoln says word-of-mouth claims supporting that position are invalid; neither does any government document verify that boundary claim. Lincoln cites the *Niles Register* by volume and page as the only possible official document where Polk could have read about any boundary agreements between the United States and Texas with Mexico, but that source does not call any of those agreements a treaty. Thus, when Polk does so, he has deliberately misrepresented the historical record.

Lincoln contends that the question of whether the United States engaged in a legal war hinges on which side possessed the part of the disputed land between the Rio Grande and Nueces River, where the fighting began. Lincoln at length discusses revolution as a means by which land may be legitimately acquired. (Michael Burlingame notes that Lincoln's statements on the right of a people to revolt "would return to haunt him thirteen years later when some Southern states left the Union."[12]) The argument Lincoln uses to challenge the president to produce evidence of United States possession of the land where the first blood was shed is both legalistic and moral. The repeated use of "let" as the main verb (anaphora), the allusion to Washington, which carries patriotic, emotional appeal, and the alliterative charge for Polk to "answer, fully, fairly, and candidly" apply impassioned language for a moral purpose. This language gives a glimpse of the eloquence for which Lincoln would later become famous: "Let him answer with *facts*, and not with arguments. Let him remember he sits where Washington sat, and so remembering, let him answer, as Washington would answer. As a nation *should* not, and the Almighty *will* not, be evaded, so let him attempt no evasion—no equivocation."[13]

Further, Polk must prove that in the place where the fighting began, "the inhabitants had submitted themselves to the civil authority of Texas, or of the United States." If Polk can satisfy these demands, "then I am with him for his justification." Lincoln also says he pursues the truth about the beginning of the war to help him decide future votes conscientiously. With biblical allusion he asserts that Polk's failure to answer will confirm suspicion that he "is deeply conscious of being in the wrong—that he feels the blood of this war, like the blood of Abel, is crying to Heaven against him." The following hyperbolic passage begins the harsh personal satire that detracts from the previous rational/moral appeal of legalistic argumentation, featuring a metaphor invoking the biblical evil serpent and ending with stunning personal attack: "by fixing the public gaze upon the exceeding brightness of military glory—that attractive rainbow, that rises in showers of blood—that serpent's eye, that charms to destroy—he plunged into it, and has swept, *on* and *on*, till, disappointed in his calculation of the ease with which Mexico might be subdued, he now finds himself, he knows not where. How like the half insane mumbling of a fever-dream, is the whole war part of his late message!"[14] The personal criticism extends into the last body section of the speech, which condemns Polk for his confusion over how to end the war.

Lincoln identifies several reasons Polk has alleged at various times to justify the war and what he would or would not require of Mexico in a peace treaty. In the beginning, according to Lincoln, Polk said the war was fought for "the national honor, security of the future, and everything but territorial indemnity." Yet presently Polk demands "full territorial indemnity for the expenses of the war. . . . He insists that the separate national existence of Mexico, shall be maintained; but he does not tell us how this can be done, after we shall have taken *all* her teritory [*sic*]."[15] Lincoln questions how the United States could possibly use the better, relatively uninhabited half. The same question applies to other, more inhabited areas. Lincoln sarcastically says, "I suppose no one will say we should kill the people, or drive them out, or make slaves of them, or even confiscate their property. How then can we make much out of this part of the territory? If the prosecution of the war has, in expenses, already equaled the better half of the country, how long it's [*sic*] future prosecution will be in equaling the less valuable half, is not a speculative question."

Polk has proposed first one way and then another as to how the Mexican government can be reorganized for the United States to gain a secure, peaceful settlement. Then Lincoln says the president is insane (an extreme accusation he would make about only one other politician, Stephen A. Douglas): Polk's "mind, tasked beyond it's [*sic*] power, is running hither and thither, like some tortured creature, on a burning surface, finding no position, on which it can settle down, and be at ease." Lincoln tones down his final statement: "As I have before said, he knows not where he is. He is bewildered."[16]

Lincoln took considerable risk in challenging the president, who might have been able to produce evidence to refute and humiliate him. Yet this speech is the first example of the confidence Lincoln had in his ability to research a national subject involving moral controversy, analyze the findings, and boldly adapt them in forceful rhetoric to a national audience. Lincoln designed this speech to have a strong impact: it begins with legalistic argumentation to express a moral position, develops with logical structure, and ends with a personal attack that reifies moral appeal. Lincoln apparently believed that the strength of his legalistic argumentation with moral and patriotic emotional appeal justified the ad hominem denigration as an effective way to close his case against the man who was both president and leader of the opposition party. Lincoln could have used a more rational tone to charge Polk with incompetence, avoiding rhetorical overkill.

Lincoln's Mexican War speech appeared in various newspapers in addition to the *Congressional Globe*. He hoped this speech would serve his political aspiration well, but the outcome surely disappointed him. Whether Polk knew of this speech is unclear, for he gave no known response. It is feasible that the president (and leader of his party) would think he had nothing to gain by acknowledging the existence of a freshman congressman of the opposition party. Lincoln knew his speech was troublesome for some. In writing to Herndon on February 1, he expressed concern about Herndon and others misunderstanding his war position, and Lincoln asked Herndon to read the speech "over again, sentence by sentence; and tell me honestly what you think of it."[17] In June Lincoln wrote Horace Greeley to complain that his paper, the *Tribune,* had reported the Nueces River as the national boundary—contrary to the Whigs' view that the boundary was somewhere in the inhabited valley between the Nueces and the Rio Grande. Lincoln said the *Tribune*'s misinformation benefited the Democrats, implying the need for a correction.[18]

Also on February 1, when Lincoln wrote Herndon, Stephen A. Douglas delivered his first speech as a US senator, and it may have been influenced by Lincoln's Mexican War speech. Douglas biographer Reg Ankrom assumes Douglas was familiar with Lincoln's speech: "Douglas fired back in a two-hour speech to address antiwar challenges, including Lincoln's, to the administration and war."[19] Robert W. Johannsen, an earlier Douglas biographer, observes that "the major part of his [Douglas's] argument dealt with the question of whether American blood had been shed on American soil in the spring of 1846, perhaps in part an answer to Abraham Lincoln's examination of the same question in the House of Representatives only two weeks before."[20] Johannsen writes that Douglas carefully prepared his speech. Lincoln had researched his subject, and perhaps Douglas also had or at least wanted to give that impression: "Surrounded by an array of books, he promised to 'state no fact for the accuracy of which I have not the most conclusive authority in the books before me.' His tone was scholarly, lacking the warmth and spontaneity which people had come to expect of him." Perhaps Douglas was trying to emulate Lincoln's use of historical research and tone, as Douglas would do in a more famous 1859 composition in *Harper's Magazine.*

Douglas rejected the Whigs' argument that Polk had ordered General Zachary Taylor to advance to the Rio Grande, and Douglas read from Taylor's dispatches to show that "the General himself had advised the move 'as a peace measure, calculated to facilitate and hasten the settlement of the boundary question . . . as a right and wise' move."[21] Douglas may also have had Lincoln's presidential support for Taylor in mind, as Johannsen writes: "Douglas could not resist sarcasm when he pointed out that the men who denounced the order [to advance given by Taylor] as bringing on the war were the same persons who were urging Taylor's election for the presidency." Douglas closes with an emotional appeal based on praise for the patriotism of the "many thousands" who volunteered to fight against Mexico.[22]

Johannsen does not critique the accuracy of Douglas's version of the question of the boundary and its role in the start of the Mexican War, but in fact the United States–Mexican border at the time was disputed.[23] Johannsen observes that several members of the House of Representatives were in the audience to hear Douglas's speech, but there is no indication that Lincoln was among them. The day after Douglas's speech, Lincoln sent a brief letter to Herndon, with high praise for a speech Lincoln heard by Congressman Alexander H. Stephens of Georgia. That letter has no mention of Douglas. Lincoln and Douglas differed over the Mexican War but did not become entangled over it as they would over slavery.

By May 1848 the United States had successfully brought the Mexican War to an end and consequently gained a large tract of land in the Southwest that led to the formation of new territories and eventually several states. The possibility of extending slavery into new territories prompted a national debate, affecting the 1848 presidential campaign. Lincoln became heavily involved in this campaign, and his rhetoric touched on the slavery question in ways that foreshadowed the views he would take in his second political career.

As early as the summer of 1847, Lincoln decided that Taylor, a hero of the Mexican War, had a better chance of becoming a successful Whig candidate for president than Henry Clay, and Lincoln favored Taylor even before the Whigs chose him as their presidential candidate in June 1848. Taylor was not attractive to some northern Whigs because he was a slave owner, and Taylor had seemed ambivalent about party alignment until he joined the Whigs in April. The Democratic presidential candidate was Senator Lewis Cass of Michigan. He had coined the term *popular sovereignty*, which meant allowing local residents to decide the question of allowing or disallowing slavery, rather than Congress.

Taylor had been coy about his views on political policy, and early in 1848 (possibly in March) Lincoln privately wrote an idealistic view of Taylor's political thinking: "Fragment: What General Taylor Ought to Say." In that three-paragraph exploratory writing, Lincoln has Taylor taking a stance against slavery agitation: "We [the United States] shall probably be under a sort of necessity of taking some teritory [*sic*]; but it is my desire that we shall not acquire any extending so far South, as to enlarge and agrivate [*sic*] the distracting question of slavery."[24] In Taylor, Lincoln saw a candidate who could attract a coalition of dissident Free Soil Democrats and other factions strong enough for Whigs to gain the White House. (A decade later Lincoln would use coalition building to develop the Republican Party at the state and national levels.) The Free Soil Party was exclusively concerned with preventing slavery extension in new territories, and its 1848 presidential nominee was Martin Van Buren. According to David Herbert Donald, Lincoln conceived of a strategy for Taylor to remain aloof from controversies that could divide the party.[25] Projecting himself as the prospective chief executive, Lincoln favored allowing Congress to take the lead in handling such matters as a national bank and a tariff: "Finally, were I president, I should desire the legislation of the country to rest with Congress, uninfluenced by the executive in it's [sic] origin or progress, and undisturbed by the veto unless in very special and clear cases."[26] This fragment further shows that as a freshman congressman Lincoln was capable of astute contemplation of national political policy.

By mid-1848 Lincoln had begun stumping for Taylor and corresponding with other Whigs to convince them to support their party's candidate. In this activity Lincoln would again criticize Polk. On June 10 in a speech at Wilmington, Delaware, Lincoln observed the Polk administration first denied that the United States fought Mexico to gain more territory for the purpose of extending slavery, but in the treaty negotiations Lincoln wonders, "Why is it that this government desires a large sum of money to gain more territory than will secure 'indemnity for the past and security for the future?'" Lincoln notes that the treaty Polk sent to the Senate for ratification sought $15,000,000 for that "additional territory," and he says this matter has "never been satisfactorily explained to him."[27] Most likely Lincoln was more concerned about the possibility of new territory being used to extend slavery than he was about the money.

On June 20 Lincoln delivered a major congressional speech on internal improvements, and he tied it to the campaign. Lincoln studies offer limited discussion of this speech. The only part of this speech David Herbert Donald refers to is Lincoln's rejection of a constitutional amendment to justify federal spending on internal improvements.[28] Without commenting on the speech's rhetorical methods, Burlingame suggests the timing of the speech was appropriate because with the war settled and Taylor's campaign begun, more attention could be given to advancing a component of Whig policy that had been overshadowed by the controversial war. Burlingame quotes a contemporary journalist who had praised Lincoln for his understanding of the subject and making it clear to his colleagues in the House.[29] Fred Kaplan provides a two-page summary but no rhetorical analysis.[30] William C. Harris dismisses this speech with the phrase "technical and uninspiring."[31] In several paragraphs William Lee Miller summarizes this speech, quoting from it but offering no critical commentary on its rhetoric.[32] The scant critical commentary on this speech invites a closer look.

Lincoln's 4,755-word Internal Improvements speech attempts to refine and advance a Whig economic policy for the greater good. The speech resembles a present-day recommendation report: it identifies a problem and argues for solutions, using a logical organization rooted in classical rhetoric: an introduction, which identifies arguments against internal improvements; a section attempting to refute those arguments; a section refuting Polk's claim of tonnage duties as a sufficient source of revenue for limited internal improvements; a rejection of Polk's proposal to amend the Constitution as a strategy for dealing with internal improvements; and a conclusion that presents not only a proposed policy but also a recommended procedure to implement it. In several refutation components of this speech, Lincoln first grants a limited validity to an opposing position before closing with his own argument, a favorite strategy he used in trials.

In 1848 Lincoln did not simply repeat arguments he gave in the Illinois legislature supporting internal improvements. Rather, in the introduction Lincoln notes that Polk recently sent Congress "what may properly be called an internal improvement veto message" and that the Democratic platform states that the federal programs of internal improvement would be unconstitutional. Lincoln then asserts: "This being the case, the question of improvements is verging to a final crisis; and the friends of the policy must now battle, and battle manfully, or surrender all."[33] In this speech Lincoln not only validates internal improvements as a timely election-year issue but also deals with the challenges of refuting Polk's rejection of internal improvements as a national policy and of solving the problem of defining such policy.

Most of the speech refutes arguments that federal internal improvements would cost too much, benefit only local areas, and be unconstitutional, and that they should be limited just to projects that could be paid for by "tonnage duties." Lincoln concedes that expenditures for internal improvements are too easily increased, but he maintains that Congress can "restrain this expansive tendency." He disputes Polk by citing the same historical record Polk had used to attack internal improvements: Polk mentioned the $200,000,000 that President Adams had sought for improvements, but Lincoln says in reality only $2,000,000 was spent, and he maintains that "authentic documents" verify this (but without specifying those documents). Lincoln also concedes, "There is some degree of truth" that the cost of such improvements is the responsibility of all, and the benefits are "local," but he then avers, "the converse is also true. Nothing is so local as to not be of some general benefit," and he cites the Illinois and Michigan Canal as an example. Transporting sugar from New Orleans through the canal to Buffalo, New York, cost less than the ocean route and enabled sellers to get more for their products and consumers to pay less.

In continuing his refutation, Lincoln uses a rational appeal that encompasses both moral principle and expediency. To the problem of unequal benefits, he urges federal and state cooperation: "I hope and believe, that if both the nation and the states would, in good faith, in their respective spheres, do what they could in the way of improvements, what of inequality might be produced in one place, might be compensated, and that the sum of the whole might not be very unequal."[34] He admits inequality of benefits cannot be totally eliminated, but in principled language he says that is no reason to reject a policy entirely: "There are few things *wholly* evil, or *wholly* good. Almost everything, especially of governmental policy, is an inseparable compound of the two; so that our best judgment of the preponderance between them is continually demanded. On this principle the president, his friends, and the world generally, act on most subjects. Why not apply it, then, upon this question?"[35] In refuting the charge that the Constitution does not authorize internal improvements, Lincoln cites two authoritative publications on constitutional law as testimony that such improvements are not disallowed. He acknowledges the constitutional question will need to be settled by the courts, but meanwhile he suggests following "expediency."

In the last section of the body, Lincoln strikes a blow against Polk's support for tonnage duties. Lincoln maintains that using tonnage duties collected from one harbor spent to improve some other harbor "would be an extremely aggravated form of that inequality which the president so much deprecates." Lincoln says it is out of the question to suppose that tonnage duties would be sufficient to fund any new improvements. With an anecdote that today might be seen as politically incorrect, he jokes, "The idea that we could, involves the same absurdity of the Irish bull about new boots—'I shall niver git em on' says Patrick 'till I wear em a day or two, and stretch em a little.'" Lincoln says Polk errs in calling for a constitutional amendment to authorize revenue for internal improvements "to enable congress to do what, in his opinion they ought not to do, if they could!" Additionally, "neither the president, nor any one [else], can possibly specify an improvement, which shall not be clearly liable to one or another of the objections he has urged on the score of expediency." Lincoln also insinuates that Polk is not being honest with "the people, or perhaps to himself" about the questionable logic of his position on internal improvements.

Lincoln closes the body of the speech by saying he does not believe the cause of internal improvements rises to the level of requiring a constitutional amendment, for conscientious expediency is sufficient to justify revenue for those kinds of projects. He asserts the insufficiency of the arguments against internal improvements and begins the conclusion with a modest flourish in the form of a quoted couplet: "Attempt the end, and never stand to doubt;/ Nothing so hard, but search will find it out."[36] For emphasis, he paraphrases the couplet in plain language: "Determine that the thing can and shall be done, and then we shall find the way."[37]

The two-paragraph conclusion discusses expedient solutions. First, Lincoln would exercise caution against trying to do too much, and he is opposed to borrowing money for internal improvements, indicating a hard lesson learned from the debt-ridden Whig internal improvements program in Illinois that he helped to enact and long supported. His recommended procedure is for each session of Congress to determine first how much can be spent on such projects and then which ones "*are* the most important." He calls for "statistics" as the basis for establishing correct priorities, implying the need for careful research to provide information about product surplus, place of consumption, and transportation that would determine financial support from the government.[38] Lincoln was ahead of his time for advocating data-based legislation.

Further, the statistical findings should be shared with states to help determine which projects would be most appropriate for various levels of government. Lincoln optimistically concludes that these measures would eventually reduce the inequality of economic ways and means throughout the country, avoid "extravagances," and contribute to national prosperity. The skillful rhetoric of this speech on a traditional, core Whig policy had the potential of favorably contributing to Lincoln's reputation in his party. Yet the appeal of this speech was limited because, with the 1848 presidential election approaching, slavery was becoming the dominant question in national politics, leading to conflict within the Whig Party. After Lincoln gave the speech, he provided a copy for publication in the *Congressional Globe* Appendix; and according to Roy P. Basler, a sentence was "written in the margin" indicating that Lincoln revised for publication, as he typically did for important later works.

Lincoln worked hard in and out of Congress for the election of Taylor. Some of the antislavery northern Whigs, distrustful of Taylor as a slave owner, collaborated with antislavery Democrats to form the Free Soil Party (its slogan was "free soil, free speech, free labor, and free men"). A cautious Lincoln remained loyal to the center of his party. On July 27, 1848, Lincoln gave a rousing campaign speech in the House of Representatives, after several other congressmen had made overtly political speeches there.

Lincoln's Speech on the Presidential Question is a mixture of defending Whig positions and General Taylor, and humorously attacking Democratic policy and Senator Lewis Cass, the Democratic presidential candidate. Lincoln studies contain various references to this speech, mostly to its passages of political and personal satire.[39] This speech is a rare opportunity to get a close look at the rhetoric of Lincoln's stump speeches, for most of them are known only through newspaper reports. This speech, a model stemwinder of the times, is more artistic than critics have realized: it is a combination of campaign argumentation and policy explication using formal reasoning with facts derived from research and informal appeal using anecdotes, satire, and colloquial language. Lincoln's stump speech rhetoric demonstrates that he had a talent for adapting literary techniques to political purpose.

In 1848 the Whigs did not have an official platform, so Lincoln's Speech on the Presidential Question provided him with another opportunity to influence his party's policy and its candidate's positions, and of course to advance his own credibility and political status. The structural design of this 6,791-word speech contributes much to its originality. Lincoln does not forecast the sections of the speech in an introduction, as he sometimes does in a more formal address. In this speech he typically expresses a logical connection between one section and another, creating coherence in a speech that sometimes alternates between serious and humorous sections. The pamphlet version features headings for the sections, and these headings clue readers in on what to expect. In accordance with the double context of a presidential campaign and a speech in the House of Representatives, Lincoln uses the first two sections to address serious concerns of the opposition: GEN. TAYLOR AND THE VETO AND TAYLOR ON MEASURES OF POLICY. These sections, composing about a third of the speech, are straightforward discussions without anecdotes.

The rest of the speech shifts between sections predominantly serious and humorous, and this quality helps to hold the attention of both Whigs and Democrats in such a lengthy speech. Sections three and four offer comic relief through political satire: first targeting the Democratic Party in OLD HORSES AND MILITARY COATTAILS and second, focusing on candidate Cass in MILITARY TAIL OF THE GREAT MICHIGANDER. The fifth section is a serious, fact-filled critique titled CASS ON THE WILMOT PROVISO (proposed legislation prohibiting slavery in new territories). The sixth section is more personal satire: CASS ON WORKING AND EATING. The seventh section is a serious mini-essay titled THE WHIGS AND THE [Mexican] WAR. The final section is political satire aimed at the Democratic Party: DIVIDED GANGS OF HOGS.

Lincoln's language shows awareness of the special context of this speech. In the first section he humorously chastises the Democrats for their hypocrisy in accusing Whigs of riding the coattails of their popular war-hero candidate: "Like a horde of hungry ticks you [Democrats] have stuck to the tail of the Hermitage lion [Andrew Jackson, another war hero] to the end of his life; and you are still sticking to it, and drawing a loathsome sustenance from it, after he is dead."[40] After Lincoln uses this colorful anecdote in language loaded with negative connotation, he tells the audience he realizes such language is not ordinarily appropriate in a congressional setting, but he defends its usage because another speaker, apparently a Democrat, has done so first: "I would not introduce this mode of discussion here; but I wish gentlemen on the other side to understand, that the use of degrading figures [of speech] is a game at which they may not find themselves able to take all the winnings. . . . The point—the power to hurt—of all figures, consists in the truthfulness of their application, and understanding this, you [Democrats] may well give it up. They are weapons which hit you, but miss us" (Whigs).[41] Lincoln's comment shows that he was mindful of language usage context and that making a personal attack made him vulnerable to criticism. In subsequent passages Lincoln uses other earthy anecdotes.

In the first section of his speech, Lincoln again advocates for presidential deference to Congress through restrained exercise of the veto. As testimony, Lincoln quotes Jefferson's statement that the presidential veto should not be used just because of a bill's controversy but should be applied only when legislators are "clearly misled by error, ambition, or [self] interest." Lincoln also quotes a public letter by Taylor that said the veto "should never be exercised except in cases of clear violation of the Constitution, or manifest haste, and want of consideration by Congress."

The second section explains Taylor's anticipated approach to key policy issues while criticizing Cass's alleged positions. Lincoln forecasts the development of this section through the sequence of the items in series: currency, tariff, internal improvements, and the Wilmot Proviso. Lincoln cites the same public letter by Taylor quoted earlier to indicate his willingness to let Congress decide on all of the issues except the Wilmot Proviso, and Lincoln uses the classical technique of imaginary dialogue (prosopopoeia) to dramatize this point. This passage is another example of Lincoln's use of a literary technique for political purpose: "The people say to Gen. Taylor . . . 'If you desire a bank, an alteration of the tariff, internal improvements, any, or all, I will not hinder you; if you do not desire them, I will not attempt to force them on you. Send up your members of Congress from the va[rious] districts, with opinions according to your own; and if they are for these measures, or any of them, I shall have nothing to oppose; if they are not for them, I shall not, by any appliances whatever, attempt to dragoon them into their adoption.'"[42]

Lincoln repeats for emphasis the Whigs' argument that Congress more accurately reflects the will of the people than a president's opinion does. Lincoln makes a play for the votes of some Democrats by pointing out that almost half of them in the audience support internal improvements, but that support would be lost if they elect Cass, who endorses the Democratic platform's opposition to them. Lincoln interrupts the discussion of internal improvements to make another appeal to antislavery Democrats based on likely differences between Taylor and Cass in their views of the Wilmot Proviso. According to Lincoln, Cass is more likely than Taylor to reject the Wilmot Proviso, "leading to new wars, new acquisitions of territory and still further extensions of slavery."

One of Lincoln's favorite methods of legalistic refutation is to charge contradiction and hypocrisy in an opponent, reducing the opponent's moral appeal and thereby elevating his own. Lincoln observes that Cass said he would support some internal improvements, but he has also said he fully endorsed the Democratic platform, which claims that internal improvements are unconstitutional. Lincoln says if Cass opposes "general" improvements, the only others he could possibly support would be "*particular* and *local*" ones. Lincoln complains: "Now this is taking the subject precisely by the wrong end. *Particularity*—expending the money of the *whole* people, for an object, which will benefit only a *portion* of them—is the greatest real objection to improvements, and has been so held by Gen. Jackson, Mr. Polk, and all others, I believe, till now." The Democrats attacked the Whigs for not having a platform, and Lincoln uses his closing remarks on internal improvements to defend his party's lack of a platform: he insinuates that the Democratic candidate will unquestioningly adhere to his party's platform, whereas the Whig candidate will allow Congress to enact the will of the people directly.

This difference leads into the next section, laced with anecdote, which refutes the Democrats' accusation that Whigs lack principles. Lincoln cites the Democrats' criticism that the Whigs "had turned Henry Clay [1844 Whig presidential candidate] out, like an old horse to root." Lincoln says the complaint is hypocritical because the Democrats had rejected Van Buren in 1844 despite the "large majority" of Democrats who had "instructed" delegates to the party's presidential convention to nominate him. Lincoln then discusses the Democrats' complaint that using the coattails of Taylor further shows the Whigs' lack of principle, which Lincoln refutes with a lengthy, hyperbolic anecdote about the Democrats' use of Jackson's coattails.

The coattail metaphor transitions to the next section in which Lincoln attacks the Democrats for portraying Cass as a military hero. Lincoln apparently had researched Cass's biographies, which Lincoln says have tended to exaggerate Cass's role as an aide to General William Henry Harrison at the 1812 decisive Battle of the Thames in Canada. Lincoln says the Democrats in 1840 claimed "Harrison [Whig president, 1841] was picking huckleberries two miles off while the battle was fought, I suppose it is a just conclusion with you, to say Cass was aiding Harrison to pick huckleberries." Lincoln then says Cass's military career reminds him of his own during the Black Hawk War, continuing the mockery: "If Gen. Cass went in advance of me in picking huckleberries, I guess I surpassed him in charges upon the wild onions. If he saw any live, fighting Indians, it was more than I did; but I had a good many bloody struggles with the musquetoes [*sic*]; and, although I never fainted from loss of blood, I can truly say I was often very hungry." The self-denigration softens the personal attack on Cass.

Lincoln expands the discussion of political principles by examining Cass on the Wilmot Proviso as "a specimen" of the Democratic candidate's character. Again, Lincoln's arguments benefit from his research, and this discussion cites a newspaper report of a speech by Cass and a published letter Cass wrote, with details of where Lincoln located these materials. With sarcasm, Lincoln uses these documents to show Cass was for the Wilmot Proviso in 1846 before he was against it in 1847. Lincoln mocks the Democrats' charge that Whigs are unprincipled: "Have no fears, gentlemen, of your candidate. However much you may be distressed about *our* candidate, you have all cause to be contented and happy with your own. If elected, he may not maintain all, or even any of his positions previously taken; but he will be sure to do whatever the party exigency, for the time being, may require."[43] Ironically, Lincoln faults Cass and his party for acting on expediency, but Lincoln used expediency as an argument for Whig policies, as noted earlier.

In the next, sixth section Lincoln further attacks Cass's character, satirizing him as greedy and possibly corrupt. Lincoln says Cass for seventeen years received salaries as governor of the Michigan Territory and ex-officio superintendent of Indian affairs. He also received funds from the US Treasury for "personal services, and personal expenses" relating to his administration of Indian affairs in the Michigan Territory and beyond its borders. Lincoln obviously put considerable effort into investigating government documents, for he enumerates all of this money in tedious detail and says he can find no evidence that Cass ever used expense funds to rent offices or hire staff or ever kept a record of expenditures. Lincoln feigns amazement that Cass could do multiple jobs in several places at the same time. Then Lincoln describes Cass's gluttony, in an application of personal satire for political purpose: "Mr. Speaker, we have all heard of the animal standing in doubt between two stacks of hay, and starving to death. The like of that would never happen to Gen. Cass; place the stacks a thousand miles apart, he would stand stock still midway between them, and eat them both at once; and the green grass along the line would be apt to suffer some too at the same time. By all means, make him President, gentlemen. He will feed you bounteously,—if—if there is any left after he shall have helped himself."[44] Clearly, Lincoln understood how to ridicule foibles and deliver a punch line—what Mark Twain called "the snapper."

The next-to-last section is a five-paragraph, reprised refutation of the Democrats' accusation that the Whigs "have always opposed the [Mexican] war." Lincoln reiterates the thesis of his speech on the war earlier in January. If opposing the war means saying it was "unnecessarily and unconstitutionally commenced by the President," then Whigs are opposed. Yet Lincoln says Whigs agreed with Democrats in supporting the nation by "the giving of our money and our blood." Lincoln names Whig politicians who served in the war, adding that sons of Clay and Webster were casualties. Members of both parties, he emphasizes, had served and sacrificed. Lincoln admonishes the Democrats that partisan bias misleads them into adopting Polk's view on the war.

Lincoln concludes with a humorous riff against the Democrats, introduced with a statement indicating that "with only three minutes left," he had to "throw out one whole bunch of my subject." Lincoln addresses the Democrats' complaint that Whigs are divided and that no one knows which faction Taylor will align himself with. Lincoln follows several sarcastic rhetorical questions about whether the Democratic Party includes dissenters with an earthy anecdote poking fun at the alleged strife among New York Democrats, another example of using folksy humor for political effect:

> I have heard some things from New York; and if they are true, one might well say of your party there, as a drunken fellow once said when he heard the reading of an indictment for hog-stealing. The clerk read on till he got to, and through the words "did steal, take, and carry away, ten boars, ten sows, ten shoats, and ten pigs" at which he exclaimed "Well, by golly, that is the most equally divided gang of hogs, I ever did hear of." If there is any *other* gang of hogs more equally divided than the democrats of New York are about this time, I have not heard of it.[45]

Burlingame says contemporary accounts of this speech indicate that his audience "laughed uproariously several times" and that both Whig and Democratic newspapers were complimentary. Undoubtedly this speech contributed to Lincoln's reputation as a wit, and Burlingame writes, "He was in fact the leading Whig wag in Congress."[46] Lincoln surely was gratified, but he aspired to be more than an entertainer.

Between Sessions, Writing and Speaking for Taylor's Election

When Congress adjourned in mid-August, Lincoln did not immediately return to Springfield but remained in the East for several weeks to handle communication for the Whig Executive Committee of Congress and to campaign for Taylor before returning to Illinois. On August 17 Lincoln franked a Whig circular letter, which solicited lists of names and addresses of Whigs' neighbors so that Whig pamphlets and congressional speeches could be sent to them. Lincoln wanted the circular's recipients to understand "the excellent results which have been and may be produced by this plan of operation" and the importance of prompt cooperation.

Lincoln understood the value of personalizing communication. The postscript of the circular identified the name of the individual providing the recipient's name and address, and Lincoln asked respondents to provide demographic information about people whose names would be supplied: "I would suggest that the names of the Whigs be distinguished from those of the more moderate of our opponents, and that the most active and influential Whigs be also designated from the general number." Lincoln also corresponded with Whigs in personal letters, soliciting news about the upcoming presidential election. He had written to every county in his home district, and "in answer I got the names of four against us and, eighty-three for us." Additionally, he looked carefully at the language of the letters he received: "The tone of the letters—free from despondency—full of hope—is what particularly encourages me. If a man is scared when he writes, I think I can detect it, when I see what he writes."[47] Lincoln's reading and writing skills enabled him to be ahead of his time as a political promoter, and he would effectively apply his communication savvy in his second political career in the 1850s.

No text is extant for the speeches of Lincoln's New England campaign, and newspaper accounts were typically partisan, with commentary on various rhetorical factors. Lincoln accepted an invitation to speak at the Massachusetts Whig convention at Worcester in mid-September. Most likely that invitation resulted from the favorable reputation he gained through party service, including his criticism of Polk and opposition to slavery extension. An account of that speech appeared in the pro-Whig *Boston Daily Advertiser*, so the report is highly favorable, praising Lincoln as "having a searching mind, and a cool judgment. He spoke in a clear and cool, and very eloquent manner, for an hour and a half." As noted previously, the tariff was a subject of Whig policy that Lincoln had yet to speak about in Congress, and Burlingame reports that Lincoln offered to speak about it to the Worcester convention but was advised to speak about "the Whig cause" more broadly and to take the Free Soilers into consideration. Lincoln begins his speech with a refutation of the complaint of the "LocoFocos" (Democrats) that Taylor is without principles. Lincoln argues that Taylor supports the traditional Whig "platform" of "resisting Executive influence" in favor of the "will of the people" (Congress).

Lincoln accepted diverse views within his party. According to the newspaper, Lincoln "examined the absurdity of an attempt to make a platform or creed for a national party, to all parts of which all must consent, when it was clearly the intention and the true philosophy of our government, that in Congress all opinions and principles should be represented, and that when the wisdom of all had been compared and united, the will of the majority should be carried out."[48] The final section attempts to convince antislavery Whigs to stay loyal. Lincoln admonishes that voting for Van Buren, the Free Soil Party candidate, would help elect Cass. Lincoln criticizes Free Soilers' ethics: "The 'Free Soil' men in claiming that the name indirectly attempted a deception by implying the Whigs were not Free Soil men" (opposed to slavery extension). He also criticizes the Free Soilers, including former Whigs, as sympathetic to the Polk administration that the beginning of the Mexican War was justified. Lincoln "declared that of all the parties asking the confidence of the country, this new one [Free Soil Party] had less of principle than any other." In contrast, he champions Whigs for their patriotic virtue. As reported in the *Boston*

Daily Advertiser, Lincoln praised them for "keeping up the character of the Union" and "keeping our fences where they are and cultivating our present possession, making it a garden, improving the morals and education of the people; devoting the administration to this purpose."[49] The appeal to public conscience was an ongoing theme in Lincoln's discourse.

The favorable response to this Worcester speech led Lincoln to speak in eight other Massachusetts communities. Lincoln spoke at Taunton, but again no text is extant, and Basler notes that the "account from the *Bristol County Democrat*, September 29, 1848, although politically unsympathetic, is the most extensive available." Just as the pro-Whig *Boston Daily Advertiser* began with a favorable account of Lincoln's speech at Worcester, including a flattering description of his delivery style, the anti-Whig *Bristol County Democrat* begins with a corresponding derogatory description: "The speaker was far inferior as a reasoner to others who hold the same views, but then he was more unscrupulous, more facetious and with his sneers he mixed up a good deal of humor. His awkward gesticulations, the ludicrous management of his voice, and the comical expressions of his countenance, all conspired to make his hearers laugh at the mere anticipation of the joke before it appeared."[50] This description of Lincoln's animated facial expressions, gestures, and humor reflects other eyewitness accounts of them.

On the campaign trail Lincoln may have played looser with facts than he did while speaking in the legislature. At Taunton "Lincoln criticized Van Buren for favoring the Mexican War and Texas annexation, though in fact the former president had opposed both."[51] The *Bristol County Democrat*'s report on Lincoln's speech at Taunton is a rhetorical/legalistic refutation, alleging inconsistencies, contradictions, and fallacies in his positions and arguments. Lincoln, says the paper, claims Taylor has principles on "the tariff, bank, and other questions of policy," but Taylor says he will answer questions about them "only after investigating them." The newspaper argues that Lincoln contradicted himself by admitting that Cass's Nicholson letter acknowledged that Congress had no right to "exclude slavery from any territory" but then maintaining that the Wilmot Proviso's denial of the right to take slaves into territories was constitutional.

The newspaper faults Lincoln's logic in presuming Taylor as a slaveholder who, after being elected president, would "do more to prevent the extension of slavery than any other man whom it is possible to elect. . . . It needs no argument to prove that the major proposition does not include the minor one and has nothing to do with it. But let that pass. The minor proposition asserts that General Taylor will do 'more' to prevent the extension of slavery than any other man it is possible to elect, and this assertion is made before the logician has even attempted to prove that General Taylor was opposed to the extension of slavery at all!"[52] That newspaper dismisses Lincoln's claim that Taylor would not veto the passage of the Wilmot Proviso (preventing the extension of slavery) because such a passage is unlikely: "The slave states are equal with the free states in the Senate and before the Proviso can pass that body one or two of the Southern senators must yield."

The newspaper mocks Lincoln's argument against voting for Martin Van Buren, the Free Soil Party's presidential candidate, because Van Buren would fail to carry the Electoral College. The conclusion of this report, confirming that it reflects the Free Soil wing of the Democratic Party, presents an uncanny prediction: "The abolition of slavery in the territory of the United States can never be accomplished unless the North is united. But the North cannot be united until old party lines are broken down. But these lines cannot be broken down unless every man is willing to sacrifice his attachments to minor questions and make opposition to slavery the leading idea; therefore, we have come out of the old pro-slavery parties and formed the United Party of the North."[53] Rather, that party would be named the Republican Party.

On October 5 Lincoln arrived by train at Chicago, speaking there for Taylor and subsequently elsewhere in Illinois until the November election, but none of those speech texts is extant. The most complete newspaper account of those speeches is the Springfield, pro-Democratic *Illinois State Register*'s report on Lincoln's debate with Democrat Murray McConnel in Jacksonville, October 21. McConnel contended that the antislavery Whigs would be better served by supporting the Free Soil candidate than Taylor. The newspaper reported Lincoln said that idea would be acceptable if there were not "other questions about which Taylor and Van Buren disagreed." When McConnel pressed Lincoln to specify those questions and "what Taylor is for and against, Lincoln could not answer, and was most palpably exposed before his friends." The newspaper also said Lincoln "crouched in silence" when McConnel asserted that Lincoln's denunciation of the Mexican War "misrepresented the wishes of the patriotic people of this district."[54] On November 1 Lincoln spoke at Lacon, and besides his often-expressed arguments for Taylor and against Cass and Van Buren, the *Illinois Gazette* reported that Lincoln used "the most scathing language" in blaming abolitionists for aiding in the election of Polk and upsetting the balance of power.[55] On November 7, 1848, Zachary Taylor was elected president.

During the first session of the Thirtieth Congress, ending August 14, 1848, antislavery members proposed bills relating to the extension of slavery in new territories and the status of slavery in the District of Columbia, where slaves were sold on the open market and where slaves had rioted. Lincoln generally voted for bills prohibiting slavery in the territories, but he typically kept quiet during official proceedings. According to Burlingame, Lincoln "may have avoided speaking on the slavery issue for fear of endangering party unity in a presidential election year."[56] Also, most likely his natural caution led him to want time to ponder these questions and formulate his political positions.

Finishing His Congressional Career
with Little Distinction

Lincoln became somewhat involved in the increasing controversy over slavery that developed in the second session of the Thirtieth Congress. At this time Lincoln's legislative activity foreshadowed some of the positions on slavery that he would pursue during his second political career in the 1850s and into the presidency. His earlier political rhetoric shows he considered the implicitly moral aspects of the subjects he wrote and spoke about, and as early as 1837, he had called slavery an "injustice," but he did not use moral argumentation during his limited antislavery activity in Congress.

Congressman Lincoln took a moderate position on antislavery bills for the capital, in contrast to the harsh rhetoric of both anti- and proslavery congressmen. Lincoln voted against legislation that would unduly antagonize southerners. Some southern congressmen were threatening disunion in response to inflammatory language in the preamble of a resolution by Congressman Daniel Gott of New York that would outlaw the slave trade in the capital, and Horace Greeley had written that preamble. Lincoln was among those who voted unsuccessfully to table Gott's resolution. Lincoln believed in the need to outlaw both the slave trade and slavery in the capital, but he was opposed to freeing slaves without compensating their owners. On January 10, 1849, Lincoln announced his intention to offer his own alternative to Gott's resolution.

Lincoln's 811-word Remarks and Resolution Concerning Abolition of Slavery in the District of Columbia consists of eight sections, each a single paragraph, with several consisting of just one long sentence. In this legalistic composition, sentences are typically lengthy, but they are well structured and phrased in clear, plain language. For example, Section 1 says in its entirety: "Be it enacted by the Senate and House of Representatives of the United States of America, in Congress assembled: That no person not now within the District of Columbia, nor now owned by any person or persons now resident within it, nor hereafter born within it, shall ever be held in slavery within said District."[57]

The remaining sections qualify the main proposition stated in the first section, and their logical sequence makes the document coherent. In prohibiting slavery in the District, Lincoln's proposal excluded "servants" of federal employees who were citizens of slaveholding states while those employees were in the capital on official business. Children born to slave mothers beginning in 1850 would be free, would "be reasonably supported and educated" by their mothers' owners, and would "owe reasonable service, as apprentices, to such owners, heirs and representatives" until they reach an age that Congress would determine "when they shall entirely be free." Local authorities would administer the process. Congress would compensate slave owners at values determined by a board consisting of the president, secretary of state, and secretary of the treasury. Local authorities would arrest and return fugitive slaves in the district. The proposal would be subject to approved vote by "free white male citizens above the age of twenty-one years" who have lived in the district at least a year prior to the vote.

At the time Lincoln made his proposal, he said he had obtained support from fifteen of the leading citizens of the district, but he never submitted the bill. In an 1860 interview with James Q. Howard, Lincoln explained that southern congressmen had met with some of his supporters, including the mayor of the district, and persuaded them to withdraw their support, so Lincoln "dropped the matter knowing that it was useless to prosecute the business at that time."[58]

Before Lincoln left Congress in March 1849 and returned home in April, the historical record indicates only one other instance in which he addressed the House. On February 13 he briefly spoke in defense of a bill granting public lands to states that would sell portions to fund such infrastructure projects as canals and railroads. His remarks are known through a report in the *Congressional Globe*. In the matter of pricing public land for sale, Lincoln advocated compromise between old states that wanted to keep it high and new states that wanted to reduce it as a way to foster infrastructure development.[59]

After Lincoln began his congressional campaign in 1843, he said he intended to serve a single term, and in 1849 he hoped that with the Whig Party in power, his congressional service would allow him to share in "the control of federal patronage in Illinois."[60] The plum of federal patronage appointments was the lucrative position of commissioner of the General Land Office at Washington. The appointment was expected to go to an Illinoisan. When Lincoln and other Illinois party leaders failed to agree on a candidate, Lincoln's friends encouraged him to apply, but initially he declined, to honor his support of another candidate. When he did become a candidate, he "pitched in frantically, requesting recommendations [by private letters] from anyone who might have influence at the federal capital."[61] In late June the position was awarded to Lincoln's rival. The Taylor administration "generally bungled patronage distributions," and "Lincoln's boldness in framing an antislavery bill may also have hurt his chances."[62] As always, Lincoln did not succumb to post-defeat depression or hold grudges that could harm relationships and complicate attaining future political goals.

In September 1849 Lincoln was a member of a committee appointed by Illinois Whig leaders, including his political allies Simeon Francis, editor of the pro-Whig *Illinois Journal*, and Judge David Davis, for the purpose of composing Resolutions of Sympathy with the Cause of Hungarian Freedom. Lincoln then was politically inactive, and in June of 1850 the *Illinois Journal* published a short letter by Lincoln to set the record straight that he would not run for the next session of Congress. He stated his preference for Whigs to hold a convention to select a candidate, and he was confident they would be able to choose one who could be elected "quite as easily as they could elect me."

Conclusion

In Congress Lincoln labored to strengthen his reputation as an articulate Whig stalwart by delivering partisan legislative speeches, speaking on the campaign trail, and composing campaign literature and private letters. As in the Illinois legislature, however, Lincoln did not distinguish himself on policy or legislation, and historians have held mixed views of his service as a congressman.[63] Lincoln's single term in Congress ended his first political career, and during that time he had not succeeded in gaining the public esteem he aspired to, as expressed in his first campaign announcement (1832). Yet Congressman Lincoln increased his experience with the rhetorical methods that he used during his time in the Illinois legislature. He expanded his experience in applying historical and legalistic argumentation to subjects of national political significance: the Mexican War speech refuted President Polk's alleged justification for invasion and combat with that nation, and the Internal Improvements speech presented a cogent case for a major Whig policy.

Congressman Lincoln also gained much experience with weaving satire into political argumentation. The target of Lincoln's harsh satire was President Polk, and the targets of Lincoln's tempered satire were the Democratic Party and Lewis Cass, the 1848 Democratic presidential candidate. Lincoln used research into the historical record to tar Polk and Cass as incompetent and morally unacceptable, and Lincoln positioned those attacks at the ends of speeches for emphasis. Lincoln's criticism of Polk in the Mexican War speech represented a more caustic version of the legalistic, implicitly moral rhetoric seen in the attacks he made earlier on Usher F. Linder and Stephen A. Douglas. Lincoln attributed Polk's ineptitude first to deception, then to mental confusion. The legalistic and bitter personal attacks on Polk in the Mexican War speech overshadow its moral appeal.

Lincoln had not criticized the Democratic Party for supporting Polk's role in the Mexican War. In fact, the words *Democrat* and *Democratic Party* do not appear in Lincoln's Mexican War speech, but Lincoln framed his attack on Cass with the criticism that the Democratic Party's endorsement of him conflicted with its platform. Lincoln also demeaned Democrats for exaggerating Cass's military accomplishments before lampooning him as inconsistent and entirely self-serving. While the hyperbole of Lincoln's attack on Polk was bitter, on Cass it was good natured. In both instances Lincoln used his literary writing ability to compose piercing political satire. Lincoln's criticism of Polk's and

Cass's characters, disapproval of slavery through support for Zachary Taylor as president, and Resolution Concerning Abolition of Slavery in the District of Columbia foreshadow the moral impetus that would drive Lincoln's second political career. Satire would play a major role in his renewed competition with Stephen A. Douglas in the 1850s.

Without a clear plan to continue in politics, Lincoln returned to Springfield and his law practice, where his avid reading of newspapers enabled him to keep up with political activity at the state and national levels. His law practice gave him opportunities to cultivate his plain-language writing style, and three speeches he composed before returning to national politics in 1854 demonstrate his continuing interest in politics, rhetoric, and slavery.

Before that return Lincoln had time to reflect on his political experience, and he may have pondered rhetorical ethics in addition to public affairs as he read about them in newspapers. In referring to Lincoln's second political career, Michael Burlingame writes, "No more would he [Lincoln] ridicule and belittle his opponents."[64] Yet between 1854 and 1860, as he fought against the demagoguery of Stephen A. Douglas, Lincoln would severely criticize his archrival's policies, rhetoric, and character. Sometimes that criticism included sharp personal attacks that Lincoln felt were appropriate in retaliation for Douglas's rhetorical abuses.

PART II

Emerging Republican Statesman

4

Introducing Arguments against Slavery and Douglas (1850–1856)

I object to slavery because it assumes that there CAN be MORAL RIGHT in the enslaving of one man by another.
—Lincoln, the Peoria speech, 1854

The epigraph states the principle that anchored Lincoln's second political career. After his first political career ended in 1849 with his only term in Congress, Lincoln tried but failed to become the commissioner of the General Land Office. His antislavery reputation may have disadvantaged him with the administration of President Zachary Taylor for that appointment.[1] Taylor's administration did offer Lincoln the governorship of the remote Oregon Territory, but he declined. Returning to Springfield and his law practice, Lincoln pursued limited political activity until his famous return to national politics in 1854. Before then Lincoln's fondness for reading about current events in newspapers would have given him information relating to slavery and Stephen A. Douglas.

In October 1854 Lincoln and Douglas engaged in a series of rhetorical exchanges that concluded at Springfield and Peoria. Lincoln's Peoria speech presented an array of arguments against slavery and Douglas that became the foundation of Lincoln's second political career.[2] Lincoln's compositions between 1850 and his 1854 entanglement with Douglas do not primarily address slavery, yet they offer clues to Lincoln's attitude toward it and Douglas that would be more fully expressed in his celebrated 1854 Peoria speech and beyond.

Speaking on Matters of National Significance in the Early 1850s

On July 25, 1850, Lincoln delivered a eulogy on Zachary Taylor, who died on July 9, 1850, sixteen months after his inauguration. As noted earlier, Lincoln actively campaigned for Taylor, speculating that he would resist efforts to extend slavery. When Taylor died, Lincoln was in Chicago on legal business and accepted city officials' invitation to deliver a eulogy, which Lincoln gave after finishing his legal business of the day. He devoted more than half of the eulogy to recounting Taylor's military successes in the Mexican War and leadership qualities, including "sober and steady judgment," tenacity, fair treatment of a fellow officer who had severely criticized him, and "uniform kindness" to the soldiers who served under him.[3] The qualities of "wisdom" and "patriotism" that Lincoln praised in Taylor were qualities for which Lincoln himself would be eulogized. Lincoln's Taylor eulogy makes a brief, ominous reference to slavery: "I fear the one *great* question of the day, is not now so likely to be partially acquiesced in by the different sections of the Union, as it would have been could Gen. Taylor have been spared to us."

In 1852 Lincoln delivered and published speeches that illustrate his ongoing fascination with politics. On January 8 in Springfield, he spoke at a meeting that citizens at the state and local levels had called to show support for Hungarian freedom from the Habsburg Empire, which in 1848 had retaken Hungary soon after it had revolted to gain independence. In 1851 the United States had offered asylum to the Hungarian freedom leader Louis Kossuth, who then came to the United States and for months gave well-received speeches in which he argued for liberty and US support against Russia's intervention in another Hungarian revolution.

According to the *Illinois Journal*, "Lincoln spoke to the meeting on the 8th in favor of sympathy but non-intervention," as participants in the meeting debated whether the United States should intervene if Russia attempted to suppress another Hungarian revolution.[4] Lincoln's noninterventionist position expressed in the Hungarian freedom resolutions reflects his thinking as a moderate in contrast to the zealous interventionists. There is no indication that Lincoln's position on the Hungarian freedom issue caused him any trouble, but many of the difficulties he would face in his forthcoming, second political career and presidency would force him to deal with extremists for and against slavery, including Republican radicals.

The most significant political speeches Lincoln delivered just before his 1854 return to politics were given in the summer of 1852: Eulogy on Henry Clay in July at the statehouse in Springfield and Speech to the Scott Club of Springfield a little more than a month later. The audience for the Clay eulogy most likely consisted of state politicians and leading local citizens. Many of them would have been formally educated, and Lincoln gave them an informative account of Clay's distinction as a national leader and eloquent speaker. In fact, this eulogy is partly a history lecture to a public audience. Clay was Lincoln's ideal statesman, and in this eulogy Lincoln reveals his own values by praising the ones he most admired in Clay. Lincoln describes Clay's devotion to the Union for its promise of freedom as a natural right and the resulting economic benefit. For its testimony to patriotic fervor grounded in implicit morality, the following passage in plain language qualifies as eloquent: "He loved his country . . . mostly because it was a free country; and he burned with a zeal for its advancement, prosperity and glory, because he saw in such, the advancement, prosperity and glory, of human liberty, human right and human nature. He desired the prosperity of his countrymen . . . chiefly to show the world that freemen could be prosperous."[5]

After giving a biographical sketch of Clay, Lincoln devotes much of the speech to an explanation of Clay's work to accomplish the Missouri Compromise of 1820 and the Compromise of 1850: vital measures for controlling slavery agitation and avoiding disunion. The importance of preserving the Union is a theme that would appear in many of Lincoln's future speeches, and it was the mission of his early presidency. Another primary concept seen in Clay that Lincoln would express in future speeches was opposition to "both extremes" on slavery. Extremists included those who rejected the constitutional protection of slavery where it existed at the founding (abolitionists) and those "increasing number of men, who, for the sake of perpetuating slavery [southern fire-eaters], are beginning to assail and to ridicule the white-man's charter of freedom—the declaration that 'all men are created free and equal.'"

In August Lincoln requested to speak to the Scott Club of Springfield, and his speech to this partisan, sympathetic Whig audience had a more explicit political purpose than the Clay eulogy. Lincoln spoke ostensibly in support of the Whig presidential candidate, General Winfield Scott, but more directly as a criticism of a speech Douglas had given on behalf of the Democratic presidential candidate, Franklin Pierce, in Richmond, Virginia, on July 9. With the Scott Club speech, Lincoln created an opportunity to entertain his audience at the expense of common political foes, and the speech required two dates (August 14 and 26).

Many Lincoln biographers and historians have ignored the Scott Club speech, and the scholars who do mention it are typically derisive, for example, calling it "a very poor effort," an "inelegant harangue," "a strained performance," and "Lincoln at his feeblest."[6] Michael Burlingame says this speech "reflected the immaturity of the pre-1854 Lincoln."[7] Biographer Fred Kaplan offers a more positive assessment: "With an election at stake, Lincoln hammered away at Douglas and Pierce with his usual combination of satiric wit, literary allusion, practical politics, and issues of principle, the speech a rallying of the faithful."[8]

The Scott Club speech is more revealing than Lincolnists have acknowledged: an innovative hybrid of stump speech with satire and political/history lecture. Douglas's outstanding political success as a leading US senator and Lincoln's frustrated ambition for political distinction probably motivated him to give this speech. It is reminiscent of Lincoln's 1848 Presidential Question speech, which showcased his stump-speech satire to amuse its bipartisan congressional audience. In the Scott Club speech, criticism of Douglas's rhetoric leads to criticism of his moral character. Lincoln constructs his lawyerly refutation of Douglas's Richmond speech with historical detail obtained through research.

Lincoln's introduction tries to get the audience to identify with him by remarking that he remembers when Douglas "was not so much greater than all the rest of us." Despite Douglas's elevation, Lincoln reminds the audience that he used to "*try* to answer many of his [Douglas's] speeches," and the one at Richmond, "though marked with the same species of 'shirks and quirks' as the old ones, was not marked with any greater ability."[9] Lincoln's criticism of Douglas's rhetoric frames the hyperbolic satire of the Democrats' overpraise of Pierce's military activity. The beginning of the Scott Club speech forecasts its structure based on the sequence of nearly a dozen topics that Lincoln identifies in Douglas's speech. Lincoln's introduction also describes a central theme of Douglas's speech: "In addition to these specific points, a constant repetition of something more than insinuations and yet something less than direct charges that Gen. Scott is wholly under the control of Seward of New York; and that abolitionism is controlling the whole Whig Party, forms a sort of key-note to the whole speech."[10]

The body of the 9,791-word Scott Club speech is a legalistic cross-examination of points in Douglas's speech. Lincoln explains and exploits Douglas's contradictions, distortions, and factual errors. Lincoln denies Douglas's accusation that the Whigs are trying to portray Pierce as a coward, averring that the Democrats' effort to paint Pierce as a "great general is simply ludicrous and laughable." Lincoln notes the contradiction in which Douglas first says "truth and honor" prevent him from "deprecating Scott's merits as a soldier" but then "implies ignorance and stupidity, and duplicity and knavery, against Gen. Scott in almost every paragraph." Douglas's claim, Lincoln argues, that the Whigs "stole" their slavery platform plank from the Democrats is unfounded. Lincoln maintains the Compromise of 1850 was a bipartisan effort, yet Whig leader Henry Clay "perhaps more than any other ten men was the originator of that system of measures." Douglas argues that Scott's nomination was forced by northern interests and would threaten the Union, but Lincoln insists that Scott would "adopt the platform or Union view of the slavery question." Lincoln denounces Douglas's speech for inaccurately claiming that Scott ambiguously phrased his nomination acceptance letter so that the North and South would interpret it to their respective advantage. Lincoln faults Douglas for claiming Scott accepted the nomination "*in spite of*" the Whig platform, whereas Scott said he accepted the nomination "*with*" the platform. This criticism shows Lincoln's careful attention to language, but he belabors the point with analogies and examples.

Lincoln closes the first day's speech by addressing Douglas's accusation that a new naturalization law proposed by Scott "to admit to the rights of citizenship, such foreigners as may serve one year in time of war, in the land or naval service of the United States" would be unconstitutional. Lincoln cites existing federal laws that contained different naturalization provisions for "adult aliens," their minor children, and foreigners who had been "proscribed by any State." Lincoln then asks whether Douglas has read the naturalization laws and comments sarcastically: "Even those adopted citizens, whose votes have given Judge Douglas all his consequence, came in under these very laws. Would not the Judge have considered the holding of those laws unconstitutional, and those particular votes illegal, as more deplorable, than even an army and navy, a million strong?" By pointing out Douglas's faulty logic, Lincoln undermines his credibility (ethical appeal).

Before Lincoln gave the second half of his Scott Club speech twelve days later, he must have been accused of attacking Douglas personally, for Lincoln opens his second-day speech by describing a "turning the tables" rhetorical strategy. He emphasizes that another critic of Douglas who had spoken to the Scott Club and he were not trying to attack Douglas personally but "only trying to meet his mode of conducting the assault which the whole party are making upon Gen. Scott." Lincoln rebukes Douglas for unsupported claims that Scott would dismiss Democratic office holders in favor of Whig abolitionists and that Scott would be an ineffective president because he has never held public office. Lincoln speculatively argues that Scott's proven military leadership well qualifies him for the presidency.

Lincoln's treatment of the question of whether generals make good presidents includes stinging satire of the Democrats' exaggerated portrayals of Pierce as a heroic general. Lincoln argues that their strategy is to build up the military image of Pierce in order to undermine Scott's political appeal. Lincoln rejects Douglas's views that historic developments disfavoring Whigs and favoring Democrats demonstrate Providence and that "proof of superiority of statesmanship" ought to be a prerequisite for nomination to public office. Lincoln explains that Pierce's congressional record shows no such proof.

Lincoln refutes various accusations that Douglas has made against the administration of Whig President Millard Fillmore. Lincoln flips Douglas's snide comment that Fillmore's accomplishment has been to do no harm to the country into a "turnabout is fair play" attack on the Democratic Party: "Take the present Democratic platform, and it does not propose to do a single thing. It is full of declarations as to what ought *not* to be done, but names not one to be done. If there is in it, even an inference in favor of any positive action by the Democracy, should they again get into power, it only extends to the collecting a sufficient revenue to pay their own salaries, including perhaps, constructive mileage to senators."[11] Lincoln's refutation of Douglas's criticism of the Fillmore administration bogs down in tedious recitation of detailed revenue expenditures comparing Democratic and Whig administrations, ending with a personal jab at Douglas: "Judge Douglas is only mistaken about twenty-five millions of dollars—a mere trifle for a giant!"

Lincoln concludes by addressing "the key-notes of the [Douglas's] Richmond speech—Seward—Abolition—free soil, &c. &c." According to Lincoln, the Democrats' "hatred to Seward" stems from their need to gain the Free Soilers' votes in New York that would ensure Pierce's election. Lincoln explains that the Democrats chose Pierce because of the appeal he would have to Free Soilers owing to his alleged opposition to the Fugitive Slave Law. Lincoln also implies duplicity in the Democrats by citing a letter from Pierce that Lincoln speculates "will deal in generalities and will be framed with a view of having it to pass at the South for a denial" of opposition to the Fugitive Slave Law. This speech ends with a racial slur referring to Pierce as a "mulatto." After Lincoln began his second political career in 1854, his speeches avoided such crudity. Lincoln's Scott Club speech does not make much of a case for Scott's qualifications to be president. Lincoln apparently did not feel a need to issue a direct call for his audience to vote for Scott, as he would do in 1856 for Frémont.

On September 17, 1852, Lincoln gave a campaign speech at Peoria as reported in the Peoria *Weekly Republican* in which he defended tariffs, speculating that Pierce as president would "veto such internal improvement bills as the one recently passed by Congress." Lincoln defended Scott's qualifications, citing his appointment as Andrew Jackson's secretary of war and assignment by Martin Van Buren to "adjust the difficulties on the Northern frontier."[12]

Lincoln's compositions of the early 1850s show that he applied his rhetorical know-how to various purposes, audiences, and genres to stay engaged in public life. Yet during that time he saw no issue substantial enough to draw him more deeply into politics. In 1854 Douglas would present him with just such an issue—the threat of slavery extension and more slavery agitation.

Composing the Foundational Peoria Speech

The Kansas-Nebraska Act (a.k.a. the Nebraska bill or just Nebraska), which Douglas maneuvered through Congress early in 1854 and President Pierce signed in May, repealed the Missouri Compromise of 1820 and replaced it with the principle of "popular sovereignty," which allowed voters in the newly created Kansas and Nebraska territories to determine the legal status of slavery. Douglas "predicted that popular sovereignty would result in the expansion of the area of freedom."[13] Lincoln was among the many who were outraged at the passage of this legislation because it opened the possibility for the extension of slavery into previously forbidden areas. The widespread, intense backlash to the passage of the Kansas-Nebraska Act caught Douglas by surprise.[14] He was then forced into self-defense. Lincoln described himself as "thunderstruck and stunned" by the passage, but he did not write or say anything about it until several weeks later, after carefully formulating his views. Besides conducting research in the state library, he was paying attention to local public affairs, witnessing at least one speech denouncing slavery.[15] Lincoln also had opportunities to discover Douglas's central arguments by studying newspaper reports of his speeches given in various Illinois communities.

While keeping up with his law practice, in August Lincoln began speaking and writing letters and at least one unsigned editorial attacking the Nebraska bill. Newspapers reported that Lincoln spoke against the Nebraska bill at Winchester (August 26) and Carrollton (August 28), and those speeches were the first to express his anti-Nebraska views. In early September Lincoln accepted the Whig Party's nomination for the Illinois state legislature. In a letter of September 7, Lincoln encouraged the anti-Nebraska Democrat John M. Palmer, praising him and asking him to deliver speeches that would explain the reasons for his opposition, if that activity would not cause him trouble. Two years later Lincoln's willingness to "fuse" with anti-Nebraska members of several political groups would help him form and develop the Illinois Republican Party.

On September 9 Lincoln debated local Democrat John Calhoun at the Sangamon County Courthouse with a speech in which Lincoln rejected the Know-Nothing Party. Then the September 11 edition of Springfield's *Illinois Journal* published an editorial attributed to Lincoln that "continued his debate with John Calhoun," featuring an apt antislavery analogy in which Lincoln described himself as a farmer with "a fine meadow, containing beautiful springs of water, and well fenced, which John Calhoun had agreed with Abraham . . . should be his, and the agreement had been consummated in the most solemn manner, regarded by both as sacred." Later Calhoun's cattle needed water during a drought, so "he then looks with a longing eye on Lincoln's meadow, and goes to it and throws down the fences, and exposes it to the ravages of his starving and famishing cattle." When Lincoln protests, Calhoun denies driving his cattle onto Lincoln's property, "leaving them perfectly free to form their own notions of the feed, and to direct their movements in their own way!" Lincoln is sure others will see Calhoun as a "knave and fool."[16]

In September Lincoln spoke twice at Bloomington, rehearsing research-based arguments that would later appear in the Peoria speech. Scholarship on the Peoria speech is vast, but discussion of Lincoln's political rhetoric just before and after it is limited.[17] In mid-September Douglas campaigned in Bloomington, and while Lincoln was there handling cases in the McLean County Circuit Court, his local political friend Jesse W. Fell proposed a joint debate between the adversaries, but Douglas refused, later in October admitting that Lincoln was "the most difficult and dangerous opponent that I have ever met."

The Bloomington speech Lincoln gave on September 12, reported in the Bloomington *Pantagraph* on September 20, opens with an expression of empathy for southerners because slavery there was authorized by the Constitution, and "if we were situated as they are, we should act and feel as they do; and if they were situated as we are, they should act and feel as we do." Lincoln then summarizes the post-Revolutionary history accounting for which new states were admitted as free and which with slavery. He explains the circumstances that brought about the Compromises of 1820 and 1850. Lincoln maintains that the Nebraska bill succeeded as a southern initiative to repeal the Compromise of 1820 and opened new territory to slavery, but the Nebraska bill passed "without the consent of the people, and against their wishes, for if the matter had been put to vote before the people directly, whether that should be made a slave territory, they would have indignantly voted it down." Lincoln closes by calling for citizens to elect a majority of anti-Nebraska members to the House of Representatives to repeal the Kansas-Nebraska Act, and he speculates that the Senate would comply: "If this state [Illinois] should instruct Douglas to vote for the repeal of the Nebraska bill, he must do it, for 'the doctrine of instructions' was part of his political creed. And he was not certain he would not be glad to vote its repeal anyhow, if it would help him out of the scrape [widespread denunciation for his role in passing the Nebraska bill]. It was so with other senators: they will be sure to improve the first opportunity to vote its repeal. The people could get it repealed, if they resolved to do it."[18] The Bloomington *Pantagraph* said the speech included a witty comment on the Fugitive Slave Law: "I own, if I were called upon by a marshal, to assist in catching a fugitive slave, I should suggest to him that others could run a great deal faster than I could."

In Bloomington on the afternoon of September 26, Lincoln was in the audience when Douglas spoke at a Democratic meeting, and Lincoln spoke in the evening at the McLean County Courthouse, with a report of that speech published by Peoria's *Weekly Republican* on October 6. Lincoln began by making light of the Know-Nothings and Douglas's familiarity with them. Douglas claimed that the Whigs and abolitionists have been "swallowed up" by the "Black Republican" Party. Turning Douglas's word choice against him, Lincoln notes the drop in Democratic majorities in New Hampshire, Maine, Connecticut, and Iowa since the 1852 election of President Pierce, adding that "the abolitionists had swallowed up a great many of the Judge's friends, more of them, if anything, than of Whigs."

Lincoln then gives a brief history of the federal legislation that included the Missouri Compromise of 1820 before criticizing Douglas for the hypocrisy of first supporting that measure then later working to repeal it. This criticism indicates that Lincoln was especially troubled by Douglas's demagogic rhetoric: "The Whigs voted against the extension of the Missouri Compromise to the

Pacific. Now could that pass as a reasonable argument in favor of the Judge's proposition that they were against the Compromise itself . . . ? Yet this was the same kind of sophistry used by Judge Douglas; and if you take away this foundation, all his arguments on this point fall to the ground. . . . Because no one interrupts him with a denial of his assertions, he takes them as admitted by the people, and builds upon them his monstrous and ridiculous propositions."[19] Lincoln was troubled by Douglas's demagogic methods throughout the 1850s.

Lincoln shifts to the question of new territories being open to slavery or freedom, contending that if slavery can be kept out of territories prior to statehood, "I will risk the chances of its ever being established there." Conceding that "men or states" have a moral and political right to self-government, subject to the Constitution, Lincoln says that the question of whether the federal government has authority over slavery ("a moral, social, and political evil") in the territories hinges on whether slaves are property or human: "If the Negro is not a man, it is consistent to apply the sacred right of popular sovereignty to the question as to whether the people of the territories shall or shall not have slavery, but if the Negro, upon soil where slavery is not legalized by law and sanctioned by custom, is a man, then there is not even the shadow of popular sovereignty in allowing the first settlers upon such soil to decide whether it shall be right in all future time to hold men in bondage there."[20] This speech closes by reminding the audience that Illinois citizens did not "instruct" Douglas to repeal the Missouri Compromise.

When Douglas planned to speak at the Illinois State Fair in west Springfield on October 3, the weather was threatening, so he spoke at the statehouse, where Lincoln responded with a speech the next day. Douglas spoke at the Peoria County Courthouse in the afternoon of October 16, and Lincoln followed that evening.[21] Similarities and differences between Lincoln's speeches at Springfield and Peoria afford insight into his rhetoric, including his writing and revising process, but comparing these speeches is challenging. First, no complete text of the speech at Springfield has been found. Second, the extant text of the Peoria speech is one Lincoln wrote specifically for newspaper publication, and it is known that he edited his text for the reading audience. The formal structure of Lincoln's speeches at Springfield and Peoria suggest that he may have had newspaper publication in mind early on. The most obvious difference between the speeches given at Springfield and Peoria is that the one at Peoria ends with a refutation of Douglas's response to Lincoln's Springfield speech of October 4.

On October 6 the Springfield *Daily Register* noted that Lincoln opened his speech there with "a number of jokes and witticisms," but they do not appear in the introduction of the speech at Peoria. Lincoln may have excluded such material at Peoria because he felt a need to get quickly to his message—perhaps a conscious effort to accommodate an interested but somewhat tired audience. Lincoln, however, did use a touch of humor when he appeared after Douglas's speech in Peoria to invite the audience to have dinner and then return in the early evening to hear him and Douglas's reply. In the voice of his characteristic, self-deprecating persona, Lincoln tells the audience that he had agreed to give "one of his [Douglas's] high reputation and known ability" the final word, "for I suspected if it were understood, that the Judge was entirely done, you Democrats would leave, and not hear me; but by giving him the close, I felt confident you would stay for the fun of hearing him skin me."[22]

Many Lincoln scholars have praised the Peoria speech for its fact-based, logical use of various kinds of arguments and unembellished style.[23] Yet Mark E. Neely Jr. says the Peoria speech could be interpreted as expressing a sectional view and is vague about when and how to end slavery.[24] The widely recognized significance of this speech has led to critical commentary on its every aspect, including its structure, but the assessment of the Peoria speech's structure has lacked depth. The *Illinois Journal* said the speech was "interlocking in all its parts."[25] Noah Brooks, a contemporary reporter, noted that witnesses of the speech called it "perfect in its construction, a marvel of logical force."[26] Historian John S. Wright extols, "It was well prepared and beautifully organized."[27] Among the qualities of the Peoria speech Lewis E. Lehrman admires is its structure: "The clarity and originality of the prose, the organization and the substance of the speech—rather more than its delivery—contributed to Peoria's intellectual and emotional power."[28] Fred Kaplan offers a limited analysis of the structure of the Peoria speech: "The audience heard a loosely structured presentation divided into four sections: (1) a statement of theme and purpose; (2) a history of slavery in relation to the territories; (3) an analysis of the ramifications of the Missouri Compromise and its revocation; and (4) a discussion of the relationship between slavery, self-government, and what it is to be human."[29] Graham A. Peck notes that Lincoln's speeches at Springfield and Peoria "are organized almost identically."[30] The Peoria speech is more carefully and significantly structured than Lincolnists have reported, and its elements of classical rhetoric reveal that structure.

With access to Douglas's speeches in newspapers, Lincoln could have created the Peoria speech with a structure based on a sequence of topics in those speeches. In a published speech Douglas gave November 9, 1854, in Chicago after the fall elections, he said it followed an outline for many of his earlier speeches that year.[31] Yet Lincoln decided not to base the Peoria speech on Douglas's topic-by-topic sequence, as Lincoln had done in the Scott Club speech.

In fact, the sections of the seminal 16,800-word Peoria speech present a textbook example of the structure of political (deliberative) discourse in classical rhetoric, as he had done in the 1839 Subtreasury speech. The structure of the Peoria speech is so important to understanding Lincoln's rhetorical strategy, and the speech is so long that indicating each section's percent of the whole is useful. The first section is the introduction, or exordium, (paragraphs 1–5 of 118 total paragraphs, or 4 percent of the speech). Beginning the body of the speech, the second section (paragraphs 6–19, 12 percent) is called a statement of facts. It provides a history of federal measures designed to end slavery agitation that culminated in the Compromise of 1850, and this section includes historical information and some of the anti-Nebraska Act arguments Lincoln gave in speeches at Bloomington, Illinois, on September 12 and 26. The third section (paragraphs 20–74, 47 percent), attacking the repeal of the Missouri Compromise and popular sovereignty, is refutation. A fourth section (paragraphs 75–91, 14 percent), arguing for the restoration of the Missouri Compromise, is called confirmation; and a fifth, two-paragraph section (paragraphs 92 and 93, 2 percent) is the conclusion, or peroration, of the speech Lincoln gave at Springfield on October 4. For clarity and force of argument, Lincoln logically places a refutation section before the confirmation section. As previously noted, the sixth section (paragraphs 94–118, 21 percent) cogently closes Lincoln's case with a refutation of Douglas's response to Lincoln's Springfield speech of October 4. The two refutation sections, exemplifying Lincoln's analytic, legalistic prowess, constitute 68 percent of the speech.

Except for his Subtreasury speech, Lincoln's previous speeches do not show such an explicit application of structure from classical rhetoric. Such a complex, derivative structure is evidence of consciously applied information rather than common sense/intuitively applied information. The use of classical structure suggests Lincoln was aspiring to create a major political document in a formal, elevated manner to appeal to the well-educated, influential members of a listening and reading audience.

An interesting and important question arises as to a derivative source of classical rhetoric that may have influenced the organization of the Peoria speech. As indicated in the introduction, scholars have disagreed over whether Lincoln had read Blair's *Lectures* as an individual work apart from material quoted in Murray's *English Reader*. *Lectures* contains two chapters on organizational strategy based on classical rhetoric, but that information does not correspond well to the organization of the Peoria speech, and Blair has nothing to say about refutation.[32] A more likely source is the rhetoric of Whig Senator Daniel Webster.

In the research Lincoln conducted as preparation for his 1854 Peoria speech, he most likely perused Webster's 1850 speech supporting Clay's compromise proposals to end slavery agitation. Often called the Seventh of March Address, it was published in the *National Intelligencer* and the *Congressional Globe*, and Lincoln said he read them.[33] Certain qualities of rhetoric seen in Webster's speech, including some elements in the classical tradition, have parallels in

Lincoln's Peoria speech and thus may have influenced it: for example, using a well-focused introduction, forecasting, providing a statement-of-facts section, offering conciliatory passages toward the South, using discrete passages of refutation and confirmation, appealing to reason by carefully sequencing paragraphs or sentences to build toward a main point, and calling for national unity.[34]

The introduction of Lincoln's Peoria speech states his subject and purpose in a series of five one-sentence paragraphs. The first sentence is direct, succinct: "The repeal of the Missouri Compromise, and the propriety of its restoration, constitute the subject of what I am about to say." The introduction asserts the importance of the Union, a recurring theme in this speech: "I also wish to be no less than national in all the positions I may take; and whenever I take ground which others have thought, or may think, narrow, sectional, and dangerous to the Union, I hope to give a reason . . . why I think differently." This introduction clarifies the scope of the speech, a technique in classical rhetoric, including what the speaker/writer will not do. Lincoln implies he will not base his presentation on a point-by-point response to a Douglas speech, preferring instead "to present my own connected view of this subject . . . ; yet, as I proceed, the main points he has presented will arise, and will receive such respectful attention as I may be able to give them."

In the tradition of classical rhetoric, Lincoln forecasts development from one section to another. Forecasting clarifies organization and strengthens coherence, especially important qualities in such a long composition as the Peoria speech. Lincoln starts section two with a statement of its subject and purpose: "In order to [get?] a clear understanding of what the Missouri Compromise is, a short history of the preceding kindred subjects will perhaps be proper." He similarly begins the third section: "I think, and shall try to show, that it is wrong; wrong in its direct effect, letting slavery into Kansas and Nebraska— and wrong in its prospective principle, allowing it to spread to every other part of the wide world, where men can be found inclined to take it." The Kansas-Nebraska Act thus threatens the Union, Lincoln maintains. Section four opens with a direct statement of its topic and central proposition of the speech: "The Missouri Compromise ought to be restored. For the sake of the Union, it ought to be restored." Lincoln begins section five, the peroration of his Springfield speech of October 4, by directly addressing his audience with one of his most famous passages, as quoted later.

In the Peoria speech Lincoln was careful to forecast organization and development not only from one section to another but also within sections. For example, in section three he identifies the arguments he will strive to refute: "First, that the Nebraska country needed a territorial government. Second, that in various ways, the public had repudiated it [Missouri Compromise], and demanded the repeal; and therefore should not complain of it. And lastly, that the repeal establishes a principle, which is intrinsically right. I will attempt an answer to each of them in its turn." In this third section he employs the principle in classical rhetoric of building toward the most significant point.[35] He often begins a paragraph with directional phrasing: for example, "But to return to history"; "Before proceeding, let me say"; "But it is next said"; "I now come to consider"; and "Let me here drop the main argument, to notice what I consider rather an inferior matter." Further, Lincoln throughout uses rhetorical questions, conjunctions, and such transitional adverbs as *again*, *thus*, and *further*.

At the beginning of the statement-of-facts section, Lincoln says a brief history shows "what the Missouri Compromise of 1820 is." Lincoln praises Thomas Jefferson's leadership for helping to establish the Northwest Ordinance of 1787 as a prohibition against slavery in the territory that became five states now with "five millions of free, enterprising people . . . [and] the rich fruits of this policy." Before he continues with history, Lincoln sneers at the violation of the principle of territorial freedom resulting from the Nebraska bill: the "'sacred right' of taking slaves to Nebraska. That perfect liberty they sign for—Jefferson never thought of." Lincoln cites Douglas's support for the Missouri Compromise of 1820 before he worked to repeal it, but Lincoln claims he does not seek to "involve Judge Douglas in an inconsistency. If he afterwards thought he had been wrong, it was right for him to change." Lincoln also cites Douglas's proposal to "extend the Missouri line" (its southern border, 36° 30' parallel) as the geographical demarcation between slavery and freedom in the territories of New Mexico and Utah gained by the treaty ending the Mexican War. Lincoln adds that in Congress he was among those voting against Douglas's proposal because they wanted all that territory to be free. In concluding the statement-of-facts section, Lincoln again points out that in developing the Compromise of 1850, Douglas favored retaining the provisions of the Missouri Compromise of 1820 before deciding against them, but again Lincoln does not accuse Douglas of hypocrisy, maintaining a tone of objectivity and civility.

Lincoln begins the third body section by condemning the repeal of the Missouri Compromise of 1820 for indifference to slavery that allows it to spread into Kansas and Nebraska. A cogent passage in this section melds rational, emotional, and ethical appeals, expressing and justifying outrage at slavery for its violation of natural-rights precepts that are foundational to the Union and internationally valued. The message develops with increasing momentum, beginning with declarative sentences and ending with a climactic, cumulative sentence. The tone is sincere, with language that is direct, plain, and emotive. This passage exemplifies Lincoln's eloquence:

This *declared* indifference, but as I must think, covert *real* zeal for the spread of slavery, I cannot but hate. I hate it because of the monstrous injustice of slavery itself. I hate it because it deprives our republican example of its just influence in the world—enables the enemies of free institutions, with plausibility, to taunt us as hypocrites—causes the real friends of freedom to doubt our sincerity, and especially because it forces so many really good men amongst ourselves into an open war with the very fundamental principles of civil liberty—criticizing the Declaration of Independence, and insisting that there is no right principle of action but *self-interest.*[36]

Lincoln follows this passage with the language he previously used on September 12 in a speech at Bloomington in which he refused to blame southerners for slavery, and he repeats his support for legislation requiring the return of fugitive slaves as long as its enforcement "should not, in its stringency, be more likely to carry a free man into slavery, than our ordinary criminal laws are to hang an innocent one." He adds that the same moral principle underpins both the law against the slave trade and a law that would forbid slaves from being taken into Nebraska.

The remainder of this section presents several historical arguments to refute the repeal of the Missouri Compromise of 1820. Lincoln argues that this legislation did not establish a principle that Missouri's southern border should be extended indefinitely as the line between slave and free areas. Lincoln again faults Douglas, this time with humor: "Senator Douglas sometimes says the Missouri line itself was, in principle, only an extension of the line of the ordinance of '87—that is to say, an extension of the Ohio River. I think this is weak enough on its face. I will remark, however that, as a glance at the map will show, the Missouri line is a long way farther South than the Ohio; and that if our senator, in proposing his extension, had stuck to the principle of jogging southward, perhaps it might not have been voted down so readily."[37]

Lincoln insists that the provision in the Compromise of 1850 authorizing popular sovereignty for the slavery question in Utah and New Mexico "had no more direct reference to Nebraska than it had to the territories of the moon." The North, he explains, agreed to that provision as payment for California as a free state and because "the area of slavery was somewhat narrowed in the settlement of the boundary of Texas" with New Mexico. Plus, the slave trade was abolished in the District of Columbia. Lincoln points out the inconsistency of Douglas at once saying the provision added to the Nebraska bill that repealed the Missouri Compromise of 1820 was not a "substantial alteration of the bill" but that he introduced it to solicit support for the entire bill, adding that "his own opinions, therefore, seem not to rest on a very firm basis even in his own mind—and I suppose the world believes, and will continue to believe, that precisely on the substance of that change this whole agitation has arisen."

Lincoln next rebuts arguments as "palliative," "lullaby" reasons that apologists for the Nebraska bill gave in claiming it would not establish slavery in the Nebraska territory. He rejects the argument that climate would prevent slavery north of the "Missouri compromise line," citing the slave population in five states and the District of Columbia—"all north of the Missouri compromise line"—as "being more than one-fourth of all the slaves in the nation." Also, a county in northwest Missouri has a higher proportion of black to white people than any other Missouri county. Lincoln also rejects the argument that taking slaves into territories without slavery law would ensure their freedom: "To get slaves into the country simultaneously with the whites, in the incipient stages of settlement, is the precise stake played for, and won in the Nebraska measure."

Lincoln alleges that other arguments for the Nebraska bill are flawed. He maintains that opening new territories to slavery contributes to the slave trade and "tends to the perpetuation of the institution." He also rejects the "equal justice" argument that southerners should be able to take their property with them when they move, just as northerners do: slaves are human beings, not property. Lincoln cites historical evidence to show that southerners understand "after all, there is humanity in the Negro."

Lincoln reserves discussing the "one great argument" to justify the repeal of the Missouri Compromise of 1820 for last: "the sacred right of self-government." Lincoln declares: "When the white man governs himself that is self-government; but when he governs himself, and also governs *another* man, that is *more* than self-government—that is despotism. If the Negro is a *man*, why then my ancient faith teaches me that 'all men are created equal;' and that there can be no moral right in connection with one man's making a slave of another."[38] Lincoln immediately follows this use of the Declaration of Independence with a qualification that he would need to repeat for years to come, owing to Douglas's mischaracterization of Lincoln's views: "Let it not be said I am contending for the establishment of political and social equality between the whites and blacks. I have already said the contrary. I am not now combating the argument of NECESSITY, arising from the fact that the blacks are already amongst us; but I am combating what is set up as MORAL argument for allowing them to be taken where they have never been—arguing against the EXTENSION of a bad thing, which where it already exists, we must of necessity manage as we best can."[39] Lincoln agrees with Douglas's use of the founders' insistence that "EACH STATE SHOULD BE ALLOWED TO REGULATE ITS DOMESTIC CONCERNS IN ITS OWN WAY" but denies that such a position applies to taking slaves into new territories, adding that the founders had passed the Northwest Ordinance of 1787 prohibiting slavery in that region. Lincoln argues at length that the federal government should have control of a territory, not its early settlers, but that he would agree to the extension of slavery if it would avoid dissolving the Union.

In winding down this refutation section, Lincoln, without naming Douglas, asks the rhetorical question of who is to blame for the renewed slavery agitation caused by the repeal of the Missouri Compromise of 1820: "It could not but be expected by its author, that it would be looked upon as a measure for the extension of slavery." In another eloquent passage, Lincoln strengthens his moral argument against slavery by using emotive language to argue that it violates the universal human need for freedom: "Slavery is founded in the selfishness of man's nature—opposition to it, is [(in?)] his love of justice. These principles are an eternal antagonism, and when brought into collision so fiercely, as slavery extension brings them, shocks, and throes, and convulsions must ceaselessly follow. Repeal the Missouri Compromise—repeal all compromises—repeal the Declaration of Independence—repeal all past history, you still cannot repeal human nature. It still will be the abundance of man's heart, that slavery extension is wrong; and out of the abundance of his heart, his mouth will continue to speak."[40] Despite this optimistic tone, Lincoln warns that slavery agitation threatens the Union. The failure of the Nebraska bill to define a process for determining slavery or freedom in the Nebraska Territory means settlers both for and against slavery are moving there: "Through all this, bowie-knives and six-shooters are seen plainly enough; but never a glimpse of the ballot-box," with inevitable "blows and bloodshed," and "will not the first drop of blood so shed, be the real knell of the Union?"

The next section calls for the restoration of the Missouri Compromise of 1820 as a patriotic solution to slavery agitation. The restoration can arrest the rising extremism in the North and South and will "restore the national faith, the national confidence, the national feeling of brotherhood. . . . The South ought to join in doing this. The peace of the nation is as dear to them as to us." Lincoln pleads with appeal to moral and foundational principles: "Stand with anybody that stands RIGHT. Stand with him while he is right and PART with him when he goes wrong. Stand WITH the abolitionist in restoring the Missouri Compromise; and stand AGAINST him when he attempts to repeal the fugitive slave law." Lincoln complains that the Nebraska bill introduces a "NEW position . . . that there CAN be MORAL RIGHT in the enslaving of one man by another." Restoring the Missouri Compromise of 1820 will mean returning to the founders' intention for "gradual emancipation."

In the conclusion of his October 4 speech at Springfield and repeated at Peoria as the next-to-last part, Lincoln says the world is watching how America handles slavery, as he exhorts with arguably the most famous and eloquent passage in the Peoria speech. He makes his case with rational and emotional appeals to patriotism, which he implies is similar to Christian faith. The soiled "republican robe" metaphor visually dramatizes the slavery problem with negative, emotional connotation, which is surpassed by the positive connotation of the robe's repurification through political and moral redemption. The repetition of phrasing at the beginning of several sentences (anaphora) enhances this passage. Lincoln opens with a patriotic appeal to resolve the national crisis at hand by adhering to the equality principle of the Declaration of Independence:

> Fellow countrymen—Americans south, as well as north, shall we make no effort to arrest this "spirit of Nebraska." . . . Our republican robe is soiled, and trailed in the dust. Let us repurify it. Let us turn and wash it white, in the spirit, if not the blood, of the Revolution. Let us turn slavery from its claims of "moral right," back upon its existing legal rights, and its arguments of "necessity." Let us return it to the position our fathers gave it; and there let it rest in peace. Let us re-adopt the Declaration of Independence, and with it, the practices, and policy, which harmonize with it.[41]

The steadfast commitment to this founding principle brings a call to action vital for sustaining the Union: "Let north and south—let all Americans—let all lovers of liberty everywhere—join the great and good work. If we do this, we shall not only have saved the Union; but we shall have so saved it, as to make, and to keep it, forever worthy of the saving. We shall have so saved it, that the succeeding millions of free happy people, the world over, shall rise up, and call us blessed, to the latest generations."[42] The bloodless return to the purity of founding principles to "harmonize" the nation shows Lincoln's hopefulness of avoiding disunion, but Douglas would repeatedly accuse him of calling for it, regardless.

During the dozen days between Lincoln's statehouse speech of October 4 and the version of it given at Peoria, he was busy with legal business in court at Pekin, but he found time to analyze Douglas's response to his statehouse speech and compose a rebuttal, which became the sixth and final section of the Peoria speech (paragraphs 94–118, 21 percent). Peck notes this final section "suggests the degree to which he chose to protect the cohesion" of his speech first given at Springfield.[43] Lincoln opens this section with a forecasting thesis: "At Springfield, twelve days ago, where I had spoken substantially as I have here, Judge Douglas replied to me—and as he is to reply to me here, I shall attempt to anticipate him [procatalepsis], by noticing some of the points he made there." Lincoln rejects Douglas's denial that the Kansas-Nebraska Act was conceived as an instrument of slavery extension.[44] Douglas's denial was not insincere, but much of this final section of Lincoln's Peoria speech corrects Douglas's errors and distortions of historical fact.[45]

Lincoln refutes Douglas's arguments that the Nebraska bill has precedence in the Compromise of 1850, in the Washington territorial law of 1853, or in the work of Daniel Webster and Henry Clay. Lincoln emphasizes that Congress has authority over the question of slavery in territories before they apply for statehood. Lincoln says he agrees with Douglas that "this government was made for the white people and not for the Negroes," but Lincoln reiterates his objection to the Nebraska bill that it fails to recognize that black people are humans and should not be treated as property. Lincoln again avers that "the great mass of mankind . . . consider slavery a great moral wrong; and their feelings against it, is [*sic*] not evanescent, but eternal. It lies at the very foundation of their sense of justice." The repetition of this moral criticism of slavery endows Lincoln's lengthy Peoria speech with a vital unity.

In closing, a frustrated Lincoln vents with moral criticism of Douglas owing to his disregard for the accurate use of historical facts and the principles of the Declaration of Independence: "If a man will stand up and assert, and repeat, and re-assert, that two and two do not make four, I know nothing in the power of argument that can stop him. I think I can answer the Judge so long as he sticks to the premises; but when he flies from them, I cannot work an argument into the consistency of a maternal [material?] gag, and actually close his mouth with it."[46] Lincoln says at the outset of the speech that he will refrain from personal criticism, but in the end he could not resist complaining about Douglas's demagoguery. This final section is somewhat redundant of material presented in the preceding body of the speech, but undoubtedly Lincoln felt his rejoinder served the purpose of gaining a chokehold on his feisty opponent.

In addition to structure, the style of Lincoln's Peoria speech accommodates his distinct message and diverse audience, which ranged from the illiterate in the listening audience to the minimally educated and the well educated in both his listening and reading audiences. Plain diction characterizes Lincoln's style, and this quality is evident in the preceding quotations. Some of Lincoln's language is witty and refined. He sharpens refutation with irony, a tactic traced to classical rhetoric.[47] In several instances he sarcastically refers to the Kansas-Nebraska Act as a "sacred right" of self-government. With hyperbole and prosopopoeia, he mocks: "Nebraska brings it [the 'sacred right'] forth, places it on the high road to extension and perpetuity; and, with a pat on the back, says to it, 'Go, and God speed you.'" He finds subterfuge in the argument that the Kansas-Nebraska Act does not necessarily mean slavery extension: "It is argued that slavery will not go to Kansas and Nebraska, *in any event*. This is *palliation*—a *lullaby*."[48] The style of the Peoria speech includes other techniques seen in classical rhetoric: for example, sentences with structural parallelism and contrasting ideas (antithesis).

The text of the speech Lincoln delivered at Springfield on October 4, 1854, has not survived, but he carefully edited the version he gave at Peoria, and this 16,800-word text was published in a series of seven issues of the Springfield *Illinois Journal* in the last week of October. The shrewd Lincoln appreciated the power of the press to reach a wide reading audience with his message, and the message of the Peoria speech was a new and vital one for him. Gabor S. Boritt gives perspective to the Peoria speech:

For the first period of his political life economics provided the central motif. Antislavery was also there but was pushed far in the background with its triumph placed at a very distant day. After 1854 antislavery became Lincoln's immediate goal, and the economic policies he continued to esteem highly and work for when possible were relegated to the background and to a future triumph. . . . His underlying assumptions, his moral underpinnings, remained unchanged. . . . The challenge of this moral ascent inspired him to enunciate more clearly and more beautifully than ever before the ideals he stood for.[49]

The tandem speeches Lincoln and Douglas gave at Peoria marked the last of the closely successive appearances of the rivals at the same place in the 1854 campaign, and they spoke separately at other places until election day in November.[50]

In a speech at Chicago on October 27, Lincoln's confidence in his rhetoric led him to quip that "he could not help feeling foolish in answering arguments which were no arguments at all."[51] After the November election through January 1855, Lincoln pursued his ambition for the US Senate. During the state legislature's deliberations in the first week of February, when he realized he could not get enough votes to win, he gave his support to the anti-Nebraska Democrat Lyman Trumbull, who later collaborated with Lincoln as a Republican senator.

Writing and Speaking to Form the Illinois Republican Party

Lincoln's unshakable political ambition moved him beyond the 1855 setback. By the 1856 presidential campaign, he had cautiously joined other anti-Nebraska advocates to form and build the Illinois Republican Party to oppose the extension of slavery into new territories.[52] Lincoln's communicative ability helped the party address its critics, attract members, and promote its first presidential candidate, John C. Frémont. In his speeches of 1856 Lincoln carefully assessed his audiences and showed resourceful adaptability in structuring and developing his arguments, although there is no evidence that he provided manuscripts for publication.

At the first Illinois Republican convention (Bloomington, May 1856), Lincoln delivered his controversial Lost speech. As with the Scott Club speech, Lincoln relished addressing a partisan, sympathetic audience, and scholars have speculated that the provocative assertions in this Bloomington speech led party associates to prevent its publication.[53] From summer until the November election, Lincoln took the lead in the Illinois Republican Party's promotional communication. He wrote personal letters, at least one form letter to solicit party support, and at least one editorial.[54] Additionally, he delivered campaign speeches throughout Illinois and in Kalamazoo, Michigan.[55] His political goal was to get old-line Whigs, anti-Nebraska Democrats, and Know-Nothings to "fuse" in support of Frémont. Lincoln's rhetorical goal was to convince these disparate groups that the Republican Party best represented the political and economic principles of the Founding Fathers and the Constitution. Specifically, Lincoln sought to persuade the supporters of the Know-Nothing presidential candidate, Millard Fillmore, that they could not carry Illinois and that if they wished to defeat the Democratic Party candidate, James Buchanan, they could do so only by casting their vote for Frémont. Democrats charged that Republicans were forming an abolitionist, sectional party that would fracture the Union.[56]

In 1856 Lincoln gave various stump speeches to campaign for Frémont, to answer the critics of the Republican Party, and to build its base. More text has survived from the speech he gave at Kalamazoo, Michigan, on August 27 than from any other he gave in that campaign.[57] The speech was given at a Republican rally open to the public. The message, structure, and development of the Kalamazoo speech are especially important to consider because, unlike the Subtreasury speech, the Scott Club speech, and the Peoria speech, Lincoln does not use speeches by Douglas as targets. Nor does Lincoln use as much of a formulaic and forecasted structure as he did in the more formal, longer Peoria speech. At Kalamazoo, Lincoln assumed his audience included not only Republicans but also members of the Know-Nothing and Democratic parties, and he courted them all. To establish his focus and get attention, Lincoln incisively proclaimed in the introduction that "slavery, at the present day, should be not only the greatest question, but very nearly the sole question." The 2,770-word text exhibits Lincoln's rhetorical ingenuity in arguing for the Republican cause.

The first body section of the speech combines explanation of principle (confirmation) and rejection of popular sovereignty (refutation). Lincoln's thesis is that slavery is a national problem that should concern all Americans and should be handled by the federal government. Lincoln rejects popular sovereignty and Douglas's argument that the Supreme Court should determine when and how such a policy would be implemented in Kansas. Further, Lincoln cautions that even the few slaveholders moving to Kansas could lead others eventually "to look upon slavery with complacency." Lincoln says Fillmore and Buchanan do not favor limiting slavery's extension, and he urges their antislavery supporters to turn to Frémont. In this speech Lincoln four times directly asks antislavery Fillmore and Buchanan supporters to vote for Frémont, whereas in the Scott Club and Peoria speeches, Lincoln does not explicitly ask the audience to vote for a particular candidate. He also argues against the complacent attitude that slavery extension is "none of our business" by citing the constitutional three-fifths clause advantage of the South. Extending slavery, he says, would increase that undesirable advantage.

Additionally, Lincoln maintains that the slavery question is a national problem because free labor, not slave labor, represents the founding principles that have made the nation great. Free labor deserves "an outlet, through which it may pass out to enrich our country." Lincoln attacks the southern shibboleth that "slaves are far better off than Northern freemen" by describing how freedom enables individuals to advance economically: "The man who labored for another last year, this year labors for himself, and next year he will hire others to labor for him. . . . When these reasons can be introduced, tell me not that we [all citizens] have no interest in keeping the territories free for the settlement of free laborers."[58]

Lincoln then shifts into refutation of the accusations that "our party is a sectional party" and that electing a Republican administration will dissolve the Union. First, he points out that the country has had both the president and vice president from the South "at the same time" without the Union being dissolved, and now both positions are occupied by northerners without disunion. Lincoln addresses the criticism that Frémont is an abolitionist and disunionist by stating that the accusers admit they have no proof. Somewhat abruptly, Lincoln predicts the nation will see either slavery's proponents or opponents eventually "triumph"—anticipating the thesis of the 1858 House Divided speech—and that voting for Buchanan endorses slavery while voting for Frémont opposes it.

Lincoln's rhetorical questions intensify his argumentation: "They [critics of Republicans] tell us that the Union is in danger. Who will divide it? Is it those who make the charge? Are they themselves the persons who wish to see this result?" Lincoln next argues with the critical question he would use in the 1861 secession crisis: "A majority will never dissolve the Union" and asks, "Can a minority do it?" Lincoln closes by saying the Democratic Party has always been "the friend of individual, universal freedom," and again urges Democrats to unite with the Republican cause "and not to Democrats alone do I make this appeal, but to all who love these great and true principles" of liberty and union. The flourish of the last sentence makes a strong emotional appeal to patriotism: "Come, and keep coming! Strike, and strike again! So sure as God lives, the victory shall be yours."

Newspaper reports of Lincoln's other 1856 campaign speeches are brief but insightful. He continued to use arguments from the Kalamazoo speech and strengthened them with the classical technique of citing or quoting testimony from authority (nonartistic proofs). In this case, Lincoln referenced first Clay and Webster, then Washington and Jefferson.[59] Lincoln engaged in humorous interaction with detractors, and he displayed rhetorical skill in customizing his message to his audience. For example, in his speech at Vandalia on September 23, as he faced an audience in which many had southern roots and were resistant to Frémont, Lincoln denied that Republicans were disunionists, quoting "from the disunion speeches of [southern politicians] Toombs, Slidell, Wise and Brooks."[60] On October 18 at Belleville, Lincoln spoke to an audience that included many Germans, including those who had come to America to escape oppression, and he played to their love of liberty by affirming the value of "free labor, 'that national capital,' in the language of Col. FRÉMONT, 'which constitutes the real wealth of this great country, and creates that intelligent power in the masses alone to be relied on as the bulwark of free institutions.'"[61]

Buchanan won the 1856 presidential election because the anti-Nebraska supporters split between Fillmore and Frémont, but Republican William Henry Bissell was elected governor of Illinois. On December 10 at a post-election Republican banquet in Chicago, Lincoln delivered a brief, 1,100-word congratulatory speech to members of the base he had helped to create, but he had more than a victory celebration and more than just Republicans in mind. The speech further exemplifies Lincoln's ability to synthesize various methods in his political rhetoric: it features the themes of liberty, union, and the immorality of slavery; folksy humor for satiric effect; problem analysis; numeric analysis of voting; refutation; solution development based on his political-social philosophy; and exhortation. The speech includes the stylistic techniques characteristic of Lincoln's skillful writing, including antithesis, metaphor, and anaphora. In this speech, Lincoln famously observes that public opinion shapes American government and that "whoever can change public opinion, can change the government."[62] He attacks Buchanan's accusation that Republicans are trying "to change the domestic institutions of existing states" and "doing everything in our power to deprive the Constitution and the laws of moral authority." Lincoln, rather, says the Democrats are the ones who are trying to shift from the American principle of "the practical equality of all men" to "the opposite idea that slavery is right." Lincoln denies that the majority of Americans believe slavery is right.

The conclusion of the Chicago banquet speech was the only part of it published in the Springfield *Illinois Journal*, appearing a week after the speech was given and provided "in manuscript" to the editors by Lincoln. The brief conclusion is a polished and moving call to action: its conciliatory tone, patriotic commitment to the Union, implied moral argument, and explicit religious appeal express a strong emotional plea in plain language, foreshadowing the eloquence of his inaugural addresses:

> In the late contest we were divided between Frémont and Fillmore. Can we not come together, for the future. Let everyone who really believes, and

is resolved, that free society is not, *and shall not be*, a failure, and who can conscientiously declare that in the past contest he has done only what he thought best—let every such one have charity to believe that every other one can say as much. Thus let bygones be bygones. Let past differences, as nothing be; and with steady eye on the real issue, let us reinaugurate the good old "central ideas" of the Republic. We *can* do it. The human heart *is* with us—God is with us. We shall again be able not to declare, that "all States as States, are equal," nor yet that "all citizens as citizens are equal," but to renew the broader, better declaration, including both these and much more, that "all *men* are created equal."[63]

Lincoln's immediate, primary audience at the banquet consisted of Republicans, but the conclusion also appeals to other partisans.

In this ceremonial speech Lincoln might have limited himself to entertaining his audience by using his well-known talent for telling stories and jokes. Instead, he spoke to inspire political unification. Burlingame writes that the Chicago banquet speech was "eloquent" and "helped clinch Lincoln's reputation as the leader of Illinois's Republicans."[64] The Chicago banquet speech capped the first phase of Lincoln's return to politics, and in just two years, he had found a compelling political/rhetorical purpose and was pursuing it through multiple roles and responsibilities that renewed his rivalry with Douglas.

Conclusion

From 1850 to 1856, as Lincoln continued to write and speak about subjects of national significance, he composed in diverse genres and addressed more partisan and public audiences than previously. The most notable of these compositions are the Eulogy on Henry Clay (a ceremonial speech), the Scott Club speech (a campaign speech), the Peoria speech (a debate speech intended for publication), the Kalamazoo speech (a campaign speech), and the Chicago banquet speech (a celebratory speech). All of these works use historical information with appeals to patriotism and are benchmarks in Lincoln's political/rhetorical development.

Of these compositions, Lincolnists agree that the Peoria speech is the most significant, for it launched Lincoln's second political career. Michael Burlingame writes that this speech "heralded the emergence of a new Lincoln. Like a butterfly hatching from a caterpillar's chrysalis, the partisan warrior of the 1830s and 1840s was transformed into a statesman. . . . He began to speak with authority as a principled, articulate, high-minded champion of the antislavery cause."[65] This metaphor suggests that the Peoria speech was quite unlike Lincoln's preceding compositions. True, in the Peoria speech for the first time Lincoln developed multiple kinds of antislavery arguments, emphasizing the immorality of slavery, and some of the language is Lincoln's most eloquent to date.

Yet the Peoria speech has antecedents in Lincoln's previous compositions, including the implicit moral appeals of his speeches in the Illinois legislature and Congress, the antislavery stances he expressed in the 1837 Protest in Illinois Legislature on Slavery and the 1852 Eulogy on Henry Clay, and the use of plain and figurative language. Another antecedent of the Peoria speech is its structure rooted in classical rhetoric that also especially characterizes Lincoln's 1839 Subtreasury speech. Lincoln's extensive use of historical argumentation in the Peoria speech has precedent in the most important speeches of his first political career. The Peoria speech shows that Douglas could provoke Lincoln into making personal attacks, but they are more judicious than many in his first political career. Perhaps during the interim of his two political careers Lincoln considered the political disadvantage he may have experienced owing to his personal attacks on President Polk in the Mexican War speech.

From 1854 to 1856 Lincoln became a leading strategist for the Illinois Republican Party, writing policy that would become essential to the success of his party at the state and later the national level. He was functioning as the director of communications for the new state party, writing editorials and corresponding to advance his party's development. He was writing his own speeches and addressing various kinds of audiences, becoming one of his party's chief spokesmen.

The attention Lincoln gained from 1854 to 1856 suggests he would have felt good about his political future, but a personal fragment dated December 1, 1856, reveals otherwise, as he describes his political misfortune compared to Douglas's political good fortune:

> Twenty-two years ago Judge Douglas and I first became acquainted. We were both young then: he a trifle younger than I. Even then, we were both ambitious; I, perhaps, quite as much so as he. With *me*, the race of ambition has been a failure—a flat failure; with *him* it has been one of splendid success. His name fills the nation; and is not unknown, even, in foreign lands. I affect no contempt for the high eminence he has reached. So reached, that the oppressed of my species, might have shared with me in the elevation. I would rather stand on that eminence, than wear the richest crown that ever pressed a monarch's brow.[66]

When Lincoln bemoaned his "flat failure," surely he was thinking only of his political career, for he was succeeding quite well in his legal career. History shows that Lincoln continued to pursue his determined political ambition, and the feelings expressed in this fragment may have spurred it.

Throughout the remainder of the 1850s, Lincoln would draw upon his rhetorical resourcefulness as he faced the challenges of working effectively at multiple levels: Republican operative, party leader, and emerging statesman. The greatest challenge would be how to handle Douglas's vigorous, demagogic rhetoric, including personal attacks, during the 1858 Illinois US Senate campaign that featured the Lincoln-Douglas debates—the most important American political debates of the nineteenth century.

5

Pursuing the Case against Slavery and Douglas for the US Senate (1857–1858)

> So I say in relation to the principle that all men are created equal, let it be as nearly reached as we can.
> —Lincoln, Speech at Chicago, July 10, 1858

The epigraph states Lincoln's belief in the moral ideal of perfectible social justice in a free society based on self-government. In 1857 Douglas and Lincoln renewed their political/rhetorical competition with speeches about the Supreme Court's controversial *Dred Scott* decision. Then in June 1858 the rivalry intensified when Lincoln gave his House Divided speech to accept the Illinois Republican Party's nomination for the US Senate, accusing Douglas of conspiring to nationalize slavery. Lincoln also accused Douglas of trying to usurp Republican leadership. That summer the combative Douglas often attacked Lincoln's House Divided speech. Lincoln vigorously defended his positions and rhetoric, refuted Douglas's positions and policy, and criticized his fiery rival's rhetorical methods as abusive. Lincoln insinuated that those methods derived from Douglas's moral deficiency. From early to late summer 1858, the rivals' speeches set the stage for the colorful drama of the Lincoln-Douglas debates, which began at Ottawa, August 21.

Criticizing the *Dred Scott* Decision and Douglas

On March 6, 1857, the US Supreme Court issued its *Dred Scott* decision (seven to two), which aggravated the debate over slavery extension. Dred Scott was a Missouri slave who had sued for his freedom: his master, a US Army doctor, had taken Scott with him during transfers to Illinois and the Wisconsin Territory (now Minnesota), where slavery was illegal. Slaves were often declared free after living in states that prohibited slavery. The Supreme Court's ruling in *Dred Scott v. Sandford* proclaimed that Scott's suit was invalid because no black person could be a citizen and thus no black person was qualified to sue in US courts. The ruling also declared the Missouri Compromise unconstitutional and determined that Congress had no authority to regulate slavery in US territories and no authority to prevent owners of slaves from taking them into those regions. This decision thus appeared to invalidate Douglas's popular sovereignty as the solution to slavery extension and aggravation. The court's decision provoked abolitionists and many Republicans, heightening North-South tension.

Douglas's speech in the Illinois statehouse on June 12, 1857, presented his views on the *Dred Scott* decision, prompting Lincoln's reply speech in Springfield on June 26. Douglas's speech explained that the present stability in Kansas and its future likelihood of entering the Union as a free state were due to the state elections there—an example of popular sovereignty.[1] He predicted that self-government in Kansas, with Democrats leading the way, would finally end slavery agitation, provided that "free state men" will participate in the elections and that Republicans will not "produce strife, anarchy, and bloodshed in Kansas, that their party may profit." Douglas acknowledged that *Dred Scott* repealed the Missouri Compromise of 1820 and enabled owners of slaves to take them into the Kansas-Nebraska Territory, but he contended that such a right "remains a barren and worthless right, unless sustained, protected and enforced, by appropriate police regulations and local legislation." Douglas thereby interpreted *Dred Scott* as a sanction for his "great principle of popular sovereignty," which he said Republicans opposed because they were abolitionists.[2]

Douglas gave his Dred Scott speech to a crowded audience, which included Lincoln, who later said he had also read it. Lincoln took two weeks before giving a rebuttal, also in the Springfield statehouse. In some ways Lincoln's speech reflects Republican positions; in other ways the speech attempts to shape them. Lincolnists have mainly praised this speech.[3] Lincoln's Dred Scott speech is noteworthy for its rational, direct criticism of Douglas's rhetorical methods and indirect criticism of his moral character.

Like his 1854 Peoria speech, Lincoln's 5,362-word Dred Scott speech does not merely follow the sequence of topics in Douglas's speech but addresses them in an original fashion that combines structural elements of classical rhetoric in a problem-solution pattern.[4] This speech illustrates Lincoln's characteristic strategy of using legalistic (forensic) methods to serve a political (deliberative) purpose. Lincoln develops this speech through a structure that expands from refutation of popular sovereignty and the *Dred Scott* decision as solutions to slavery agitation into an endorsement of the solution to the problems of slavery and race—colonization—that such other political leaders as Clay had long advocated but was not current Republican policy. Unlike the Peoria speech, Lincoln does not forecast the overall organization of his Dred Scott speech, but he does use transitions from one major topic to another.

The first body section moves directly into Douglas's positions on the problems of Mormons trying to gain statehood for Utah and of proslavery elements trying to gain statehood for Kansas. Lincoln appropriates the situations in Utah and Kansas to criticize Douglas's application of popular sovereignty: "That doctrine was a mere deceitful pretense for the benefit of slavery." The accusation of deceit is speculative, thus weakening the implied criticism of Douglas's moral character. Lincoln says that if the Mormons want to form a state constitution allowing polygamy, there is nothing in the US Constitution against it. He says that such a state constitution would demonstrate Douglas's "sacred right of self-government," but that neither Douglas nor the other Democrats will answer the question of whether they would accept such a state constitution.

Lincoln also faults Douglas's speech for conveniently excluding important information in his comments on politics in Kansas. Douglas expressed his hope that all Kansas citizens would participate in the vote on a proposed state constitution, but Lincoln says Douglas failed to acknowledge that "free state men place their refusal to vote on the ground that but few of them have been registered." With that election occurring between Douglas's and Lincoln's speeches, Lincoln observes that preliminary analysis of the voting shows only a fraction of registered voters went to the polls. He argues that with only about half of the eligible voters registered, the result is an election that appears to be "altogether the most exquisite farce ever enacted." Lincoln further expresses his opinion that in Kansas, free state Democrats are "mythical": "If there should prove to be one real living free state Democrat in Kansas, I suggest that it might be well to catch him, and stuff and preserve his skin, as an interesting specimen of that soon to be extinct variety of the genus, Democrat."

Lincoln delivers a double refutation, first of the *Dred Scott* decision and then of Douglas's position on it. Lincoln rejects Douglas's criticism that questioning *Dred Scott* is the same as resistance to it. Lincoln contends that *Dred Scott* "is erroneous," so he will work to have the court "over-rule" it. Without a unanimous court decision, Lincoln maintains that it is not "factious" or "disrespectful" to oppose it, as Douglas complained. Lincoln points to the inconsistency of Douglas praising President Jackson as a critic of the Supreme Court's sanction for a national bank while attacking Lincoln for questioning *Dred Scott*. Exposing inconsistency was a favorite technique Lincoln used to undermine Douglas's credibility.

Lincoln then disputes certain alleged historical facts underlying Chief Justice Roger B. Taney's majority opinion in *Dred Scott*. Taney wrote that the Declaration of Independence and the US Constitution did not pertain to black people, but Lincoln points out the Constitution authorizes individual states to determine qualifications for citizenship, and five of the original thirteen states had extended the vote to black people. Lincoln also disputes Taney's claim that for black people life has improved since the early years of the republic, explaining that voting rights for black people have been canceled in New Jersey and North Carolina, abridged in New York, and disallowed in new states. Further, the power of masters to emancipate their slaves has been severely reduced by various state legislatures. With loaded, metaphoric language Lincoln blames congressional inaction combined with *Dred Scott* and social conditions in general for confining black people to a "prison house" with "a lock of a hundred keys . . . in the hands of a hundred different men . . . scattered to a hundred different and distant places; and they stand musing as to what invention, in all the dominions of mind and matter, can be produced to make the impossibility of his escape more complete than it is."[5] This imagery may have been modeled on what Charles Sumner said in his famous Crime against Kansas speech in May 1856, in which he refers to "a hundred arms directed by a hundred eyes" bolstering slavery.[6]

Lincoln alleges an implicit moral abuse in Douglas's attempt to regain political strength by exploiting white people's "natural disgust" with racial amalgamation. Douglas, says Lincoln, uses Republicans' outcry over *Dred Scott* and their view that black people are included in the Declaration of Independence as his opportunity to render Republicans as promoters of social and political equality between the races. Lincoln exposes Douglas's fallacy of causal generalization, and Lincoln presents one of his best-known examples of antithesis: "Now I protest against that counterfeit logic which concludes that, because I do not want a black woman for a *slave* I must necessarily want her for a *wife*. I need not have her for either, I can just leave her alone. In some respects she certainly is not my equal; but in her natural right to eat the bread she earns with her own hands without asking leave of anyone else, she is my equal, and the equal of all others."[7] Lincoln rejects the argument, advanced by Taney and Douglas, that the Declaration of Independence did not include black people because its authors did not immediately establish black people's "equality with the whites." The founders, Lincoln points out, did not even establish equality among all white people.

In the following passage Lincoln gives his interpretation of the intended idealism of the Declaration of Independence. Beginning each sentence with the grammatical subject establishes directness, and after the main verb of the second sentence, the cumulative sentence structure unfolds his position with patriotic emotional appeal for the promise of the future:

> They [the founders] meant to set up a standard maxim for free society, which should be familiar to all, and revered by all; constantly looked to, constantly labored for, and even though never perfectly attained, constantly approximated, and thereby constantly spreading and deepening its influence, and augmenting the happiness and value of life to all people of all colors

everywhere. The assertion that "all men are created equal" was of no practical use in effecting our separation from Great Britain; and it was placed in the Declaration, nor [*sic*] for that, but for future use. Its authors meant it to be, thank God, it is now proving itself, a stumbling block to those who in after times might seek to turn a free people back into the hateful paths of despotism.[8]

This section of the speech ends with rejection of Douglas's view that the Declaration of Independence refers only to white people.

Lincoln argues that extending slavery would increase the problem of racial amalgamation. He uses one of his favorite legalistic gambits of first agreeing with adversaries before deflating them. Lincoln agrees "a thousand times" with Douglas in being "especially horrified at the thought" of amalgamation. He says the few "mulattoes" in free states were born in the South, and he uses the 1850 census to show that the South had 348,874 mulattoes, whereas the North had 56,649. He notes that "the North has a smaller proportion of free mulattoes to free blacks than the South." Lincoln concludes that supporters of the *Dred Scott* decision are endorsing the conditions that foster amalgamation.

The final section presents colonization (resettling US black people in foreign lands) as a solution to the problem of amalgamation. Lincoln acknowledges that this solution is not part of the Republican platform or the policy of any other party. Lincoln explains that colonization first requires finding a way to separate the races, and he maintains that Republican opposition to slavery extension because of the immorality of slavery is a step toward that separation. In a rhetorical sleight of hand, he conflates moral objection to slavery extension and slavery with moral justification for colonization. Cleverly, he supports this questionable assertion with an eloquent passage in which he emphasizes that his party's antislavery position derives from acknowledging black people's humanity, while Democrats reject it: "The Republicans inculcate, with whatever of ability they can, that the negro is a man; that his bondage is cruelly wrong, and that the field of his oppression ought not to be enlarged. The Democrats deny his manhood; deny, or dwarf to insignificance, the wrong of his bondage; so far as possible, crush all sympathy for him, and cultivate and excite hatred and disgust against him; compliment themselves as Union-savers for doing so; and call the indefinite outspreading of his bondage 'a sacred right of self-government.'"[9] Lincoln drives his argument home by ending the sentence with sarcasm.

Newspaper reports of Lincoln's Dred Scott speech brought it to the attention of readers throughout Illinois and to a lesser extent in the East. Ever mindful of the power of the press, Lincoln in July 1857 collaborated with other Republicans to provide financial backing for the St. Louis pro-Republican *Missouri Democrat* to gain more support in heavily Democratic southern Illinois.

After his Dred Scott speech, Lincoln closely monitored the ongoing rift within the national Democratic Party over the question of statehood for Kansas. Douglas's rejection of the proslavery Lecompton Constitution there conflicted with the Buchanan administration's support for it. Timing was always a primary consideration in Lincoln's decisions to voice a political stand, and in the second half of 1857 and the first half of 1858, he anxiously but patiently watched the Democratic drama, especially Douglas's role in it. Letters Lincoln wrote to Illinois Republican Senator Lyman Trumbull late in 1857 express concern that Douglas's anti–Lecompton Constitution position might attract Republicans to him.[10]

In December 1857 Lincoln composed 2,440 words of "fragments" (exploratory writing) in preparation for a speech, but he did not feel the time was right to express his views publicly until early summer 1858. In this fragment Lincoln notes that many church denominations were "wrangling, and cracking, and going to pieces" over slavery agitation. This fragment includes the biblical line that he would forgo using until he accepted the Illinois Republican Senate nomination: "*A house divided against itself cannot stand.*"[11] As previously noted, Lincoln used this statement of Jesus in 1843.

Boldly Launching the 1858 Illinois Republican Campaign for the US Senate

On the afternoon of June 16, 1858, the Illinois Republican Party, meeting in the Springfield statehouse, unanimously nominated Lincoln as its candidate for the US Senate, asserting unwillingness to be controlled by eastern party leaders. That evening also in the statehouse, Lincoln delivered a provocative acceptance speech: the famous House Divided speech. Anticipating his nomination and the political challenges he faced at the national level, Lincoln carefully prepared this 3,180-word speech (his shortest major speech before the Cooper Union address). Herndon said Lincoln worked hard on it, including "revising every line and every sentence."[12] This speech contains ideas Lincoln had previously considered but had waited for an appropriate time to present.[13] This speech is one of Lincoln's most controversial, and the controversy began even before he delivered it. He read it to Herndon in private, pausing after every sentence to gauge his reaction. Herndon said he questioned the practical wisdom of the house-divided message. When Lincoln showed the speech to other political allies, they advised him not to give it because of its incendiary potential.[14] Like the storied Lost speech and the widely panned Scott Club speech, the House Divided speech was intended for a partisan audience, including eastern Republican leaders who would read it. In disregarding his friends' advice, the self-assured Lincoln apparently made no attempt to soften his message, and subsequently never expressed regret for it.

The House Divided speech voices the fear that Lincoln shared with other Americans that slavery agitation would end in slavery becoming legal not only throughout territories but also in free states. Lincoln was, moreover, afraid of losing Republican Party leadership to Douglas. The speech carries implicit moral appeal: Republicans have the solution to slavery agitation, and they should not align with Douglas, for he is corrupt, as evidenced by his collaboration with Democratic Party leaders to nationalize slavery. (Scholars have debated the likelihood of slavery becoming nationalized.[15])

Lincoln's multiple purposes, then, in the House Divided speech were to increase his credibility with slavery opponents, especially with Republicans by defining his party's purpose, to explain why they should disassociate themselves from Douglas, and to inspire party unity. The speech features distinct sections logically interrelated in a problem-solution framework. The brevity of the speech and its tight structure perhaps explain why Lincoln saw no need to forecast the body sections in the introduction. It consists of ten one-sentence paragraphs, identifying the problem of what to do about slavery agitation: "If we could first know *where* we are, and *whither* we are tending, we could then better judge *what* to do, and *how* to do it." (This language echoes the opening of Daniel Webster's famous 1830 Second Reply to Senator Robert Y. Hayne.[16]) Lincoln predicts the nation "will become *all* one thing, or *all* the other."[17] That is, either the nation would eventually allow slavery throughout—including the free states—or the nation would eventually eliminate slavery. The well-known biblical quotation lends emotional appeal to his proposition: "A house divided against itself cannot stand." Further, Lincoln says a crisis would resolve the question of what to do about slavery agitation. He does not explicitly say the nation currently is in crisis, but he implies the imminence of such a crisis throughout the speech, beginning with the last sentence of the introduction, a rhetorical question: "Have we no *tendency* to the latter condition?" (nationalizing slavery).

Eminent Lincolnists have condoned the conspiracy accusation. Don E. Fehrenbacher writes that its hyperbolic language was justified: "It is not surprising that even reasonable men should have seen an ominous pattern in the sequence of events which had begun four years earlier with the Kansas-Nebraska Act. Nor was it hard for them to believe that behind such a pattern there must be some kind of concert. Lincoln, to be sure, was exercising the politician's privilege of overstating his case."[18] David Zarefsky explains the conspiracy accusation as "a carefully constructed argument that made plausible a charge for which there was scant external evidence," and the House Divided speech "brought the conspiracy argument into the political mainstream, gave Republicans of diverse persuasions a common enemy against which to rally, and brought to an end the talk about Douglas's becoming a Republican or furthering the Republicans' cause."[19] Lincoln believed his conspiracy argument was factual but could not prove it.

The three-part body of the House Divided speech incrementally builds a case against Douglas. The first is a statement-of-facts section consisting of thirty-one short paragraphs (many of one sentence). The second is a twenty-paragraph affirmative argument interpreting historical and current events to demonstrate the tendency toward nationalizing slavery and Douglas's role in it, and stating that the solution is to overcome the proslavery Democrats' control of the federal government. The third is an eleven-paragraph plan of action on how to accomplish that objective, and it includes Republicans rejecting alignment with Douglas. The five one-sentence paragraphs ending the speech issue a call to arms.

Each body section relies heavily on figurative language (metaphor or analogy) to support Lincoln's propositions, and he uses those techniques to make his conspiracy accusation seem feasible and elicit fear. Corbett and Connors point out that "analogy is always the most vulnerable of all modes of argument. . . . An analogy never proves anything; at best, it persuades someone on the grounds of probability. It is the *degree* of probability that will be susceptible to challenge."[20] Using his literary writing ability, Lincoln compares his alleged Democratic proslavery conspiracy to a machine and building construction. Those figures of speech are a rhetorical sleight of hand similar to the one cited previously in his 1857 Dred Scott speech, in this case to compensate for his inability to provide the facts that would verify his conspiracy allegation. Lincoln was fond of magic tricks and performed them in his youth.[21] Lincolnists have used the phrase *sleight of hand* to describe rhetorical/verbal manipulation in at least three of his other major compositions.[22] A rhetorical sleight of hand invites an accusation of demagoguery, yet paradoxically Lincoln's House Divided speech argumentation is driven by the moral underpinning of a statesman.

Lincoln begins the first body section by inviting anyone who doubts the tendency toward nationalizing slavery to consider the historic benchmarks pointing to that likelihood, comparing them to a "piece of *machinery* so to speak—compounded of the Nebraska doctrine and the *Dred Scott* decision. Let him consider not only *what work* the machinery is adapted to do, and *how well* adapted; but also let him study the *history* of its construction, and trace . . . the evidences of design, and concert of action, among its chief bosses, from the beginning." Historical "points gained" forming the parts of the machinery are 1. the 1854 Kansas-Nebraska Act that abolished the 1820 Missouri Compromise and opened new territories to slavery; 2. 1856 outgoing President Pierce's and incoming President Buchanan's apparent endorsement of popular sovereignty; 3. the 1857 *Dred Scott* decision's ruling that Congress could not prevent slavery in territories. This chronology insinuates a cause-effect relationship but lacks verification (causal fallacy). Lincoln remarks that Douglas defended the *Dred Scott* decision but "squabbled" with President Buchanan over the validity of the proslavery Lecompton Constitution. Lincoln does not compliment Douglas for fighting President Buchanan's support of the Lecompton Constitution, and Lincoln insists that Douglas "cares not whether slavery be voted down or voted up." Lincoln explains the only viable part of the Kansas-Nebraska Act to survive *Dred Scott* is "the right of a people to make their own decisions, upon which he and the Republicans have never differed." Lincoln infers that this history combined with the survival of popular sovereignty serves "to *educate* and *mould* public opinion, at least *Northern* public opinion, to not *care* whether slavery is voted *down* or voted *up.*"[23]

The second section includes two figures of speech appealing to fear in support of Lincoln's accusation of proslavery conspiracy among successive Democratic leaders. Lincoln's figurative language is original, but the conspiracy accusation is not.[24] First, "these things ["points gained"] *look* like the cautious *patting* and *petting* [of] a spirited horse, preparatory to mounting him, when it is dreaded that he may give the rider a fall." Second, Lincoln follows this metaphor with a construction analogy to insinuate conspiracy, and he begins by hedging and follows it with a detailed analogy to flesh out his case:

> We cannot absolutely *know* that all these exact adaptations are the result of preconcert. But when we see a lot of framed timbers, different portions of which we know have been gotten out at different times and places and by different workmen—Stephen [Douglas], Franklin [Pierce], Roger [Taney] and James [Buchanan], for instance—and when we see these timbers joined together, and see they exactly make the frame of a house or a mill, all the tenons and mortices exactly fitting, and all the lengths and proportions of the different pieces exactly adapted to their respective places, and not a piece too many or too few—not omitting even scaffolding—or, if a single piece be lacking, we can see the place in the frame exactly fitted and prepared to yet bring such a piece in—in *such* a case, we find it impossible to not *believe* that Stephen and Franklin and Roger and James all understood one another from the beginning, and all worked upon a common *plan* or *draft* drawn up before the first lick was struck.[25]

Lincoln's conspiracy accusation may have been a "turning the tables" strategy in response to the widespread rumor that Douglas was conspiring with Republicans.[26] Michael Burlingame notes, "Douglas later denied consorting with the Republicans, though abundant evidence suggests that he did."[27] By implicating Douglas in a Democratic conspiracy to nationalize slavery, Lincoln refutes the idea that Douglas and Republicans held common ground.

Lincoln contends that at any time the Supreme Court could issue a follow-up decision to *Dred Scott* to the effect that free states could not continue to prohibit slavery: "Such a decision is probably coming, and will soon be upon us, unless the power of the present political dynasty shall be met and overthrown."[28] With figurative language and antithesis, Lincoln's appeal to fear was not groundless, for as Burlingame points out the New York case of *Lemmon vs. the People* that prohibited slavery there was likely headed for the pro-southern US Supreme Court where it would likely be overturned[29]: "We shall *lie down* pleasantly dreaming that the people of *Missouri* are on the verge of making their State *free*; and we shall *awake* to the *reality*, instead, that the Supreme Court has made Illinois a slave State." Lincoln felt his message was timely, asserting that the nationalization of slavery was inevitable unless the Democratic national hold on power could be broken.

In the third body section, Lincoln urges Republicans not to embrace Douglas just because he rejects the proslavery Lecompton Constitution. Lincoln employs figurative language to render Douglas as a weakened leader: "Judge Douglas, if not a *dead* lion *for this work*, is at least a *caged* and *toothless* one." Lincoln argues that Douglas's indifference to slavery and its extension disqualifies him for Republican alignment: "But clearly, he is not now with us—he does not *pretend* to be—he does not *promise* to *ever* be. Our cause, then, must be intrusted to, and conducted by its own undoubted friends—those whose hands are free, whose hearts are in the work—who *do care* for the result."

The five one-sentence paragraphs ending the speech issue a call to action. Lincoln's language expresses rational and emotional appeals with justification based on righteousness, as he would often do more explicitly in subsequent speeches up through the Cooper Union address. Lincoln uses militaristic imagery to cite the Republican coalition "of *strange, discordant,* and even, *hostile* elements" that in the 1856 national elections "fought the battle through, under the constant hot fire of a disciplined, proud, and pampered enemy." Now, again adapting Webster's language, Lincoln exclaims: "When that same enemy is wavering, dissevered . . . , the result is not doubtful. We shall not fail—if we stand firm. We shall not fail!"[30]

Lincoln crafts the language of the House Divided speech to its pressing purpose, using methods that were both familiar and original to his rhetorical weaponry. As in previous compositions, he employs biblical quotations and other nonartistic proofs to support main points. In this speech, like his previous political rhetoric, he uses historical facts in logical argumentation with implicit moral appeal. Like other speeches, this one uses recursive, logical argumentation with incremental use of facts and inferences. As in previous speeches, Lincoln enhances points with figurative language for emphasis and emotional appeal. The short paragraphs and noncomplex sentence structure reflect Lincoln's urgency. His previous speeches have many long paragraphs, but the House Divided speech has none. In fact, it has seventy-seven para-graphs, averaging forty-one words per paragraph, with sentences averaging twenty-five words. Also, this speech has a higher proportion of one-sentence paragraphs than previous compositions. The brevity of the speech is appropri-ate for the celebratory occasion and political urgency.

Douglas was not present to hear the House Divided speech, but its news-paper publication allowed him to familiarize himself with it as he prepared his "homecoming" speech at Chicago on July 9. It launched his reelection campaign. Approximately the first third of Douglas's homecoming speech explains his criticism that the Lecompton Constitution violated popular sover-eignty. Much of the remainder of the speech rebuts the House Divided speech. Throughout the US Senate race Douglas did not miss an opportunity to use that speech to smear Lincoln as devious and his party and him as abolitionist and disunionist.

Before starting his attack, Douglas patronizes Lincoln "as a kind, amiable, and intelligent gentleman, a good citizen and an honorable opponent." Doug-las says he takes issue with Lincoln on principle "not involving personalities." Douglas, quoting the biblical house divided passage from Lincoln's speech, first complains that "Mr. Lincoln asserts, as a fundamental principle of this government, that there must be uniformity in the local laws and domestic institutions of each and all the States of the Union." Then Douglas stretches this claim to mean Lincoln advocates northern warfare upon all slave-holding states. Douglas also accuses Lincoln of going to war against the Supreme Court for *Dred Scott*. In fact, Douglas uses the fearmongering words *warfare* or *war* ten times. His next major criticism is that Lincoln advocates citizenship for black people throughout the nation. Douglas closes by denouncing coopera-tion between Republicans and Buchanan Democrats.

Douglas's 1858 campaign speeches typically repeated the arguments of the homecoming speech, occasionally supplemented with other accusations. While Lincoln's speeches attempted to refute the accusations, he often introduced additional subject matter to strengthen his arguments. Lincoln's speeches prior to the scheduled seven debates covered a wide range of subjects relating to slavery agitation, and those speeches well prepared him for the debates. Horace White, a reporter for the *Chicago Press and Tribune*, witnessed many of Lincoln's speeches during the 1858 Senate race and noted their variations. In September he commented to Lincoln about the contrast between the rivals' speeches, eliciting an insightful comment from Lincoln that "Douglas was not lacking in versatility, but that he had a theory that the popular sovereignty speech was the one to win on," whereas Lincoln said "that he could not repeat to-day what he had said yesterday. The subject kept enlarging and widening in his mind as he went on, and it was much easier to make a new speech than to repeat an old one."[31]

Lincoln witnessed Douglas's homecoming speech in Chicago on July 9 and spoke the next day on the same balcony of the hotel where Douglas had spoken, also with an audience of several thousand. Lincoln's 8,030-word speech was a prompt reply but not a perfunctory one: it was so well organized and so fully developed that he most likely composed most of it well before Douglas's speech. As in his Peoria speech, Lincoln observed in the introduction that his speech would not strictly follow the "point by point" sequence of Douglas's preceding speech.[32] Many Lincolnists have ignored this important speech or offered little critical commentary on it.[33]

In an effort to establish audience rapport, Lincoln takes a satirical swipe at Douglas's remark the previous day that he did not care whether his criticism hits Republicans or his Democratic detractors as Douglas compared himself to the Russians at Sebastopol (during the Crimean War) who did not care whether their fire hit the forces of one nationality or the other. Lincoln throws Douglas's phrasing back at him: "Well now, gentlemen, is not that very alarming? Just to think of it! Right at the outset of his canvass, I, a poor, kind, amiable, intelligent, gentleman [Douglas had used those adjectives to describe Lincoln], I am to be slain in this way. Why, my friend, the Judge, is not only, as it turns out, not a dead lion, nor even a living one—he is the rugged Russian Bear!" The humor elicited "roars of laughter and loud applause," and these kinds of responses occurred throughout the speech.

Prior to rebutting Douglas's criticism of the House Divided speech, Lincoln devotes separate sections to criticism of Republicans who favorably viewed the anti-Buchanan Democrats who objected to the president's support of the Lecompton Constitution, to a denial that Douglas's popular sovereignty remains viable, and to the assertions that Republicans were more important to the defeat of the Lecompton Constitution than anti-Buchanan Democrats and Douglas.

Lincoln argues that Douglas's criticism of the House Divided speech is based on the false inferences that Lincoln seeks to make "all states of this Union uniform in all their internal regulations" and that Lincoln aims to settle the slavery question through civil war. Lincoln urges the audience to read the passage in question to realize that he "made a prediction only—it may have been a foolish one perhaps. I did not even say that I desired that slavery should be put in course of ultimate extinction. I do say so now, however, so there need be no longer any difficulty about that." With his humble persona, Lincoln skirts the possibility that he could have been clearer in the House Divided speech and insists that Douglas has no justification for misinterpreting it: "I am not a master of language; I have not a fine education; I am not capable of entering into a disquisition upon dialectics, as I believe you call it; but I do not believe the language I employed bears any such construction as Judge Douglas put upon it. But I don't care about a quibble in regard to words. I know what I meant, and I will not leave this crowd in doubt, if I can explain it to them, what I really meant in the use of that paragraph."[34]

Lincoln explains his belief that the framers of the Constitution, who provided that after twenty years the slave trade could be abolished, implicitly expressed hope that slavery would face "ultimate extinction."[35] The impassioned Lincoln says Douglas has heard him say "as good as a hundred times" that he does not advocate "interfering with slavery where it exists" and has never implied "setting the sections [of the United States] at war with one another."

Lincoln utterly denies that he wants "a general consolidation of all the local institutions of the various states." Rather, he asserts his belief in "the principle of self-government." He does, however, qualify his belief: "Each community, as a state, has a right to do exactly as it pleases with all the concerns within that state that interfere with the rights of no other state, and that the general government, upon principle, has no right to interfere with anything other than that general class of things that does not concern the whole." He affirms that states have the right to legislate for their particular conditions: "I do not believe in the right of Illinois to interfere with the cranberry laws of Indiana, the oyster laws of Virginia, or the liquor laws of Maine." Lincoln voices frustration with Douglas's misleading rhetoric: "I have said these things over and over again." As this frustration continued during the Senate race, Lincoln sometimes grew angry.

Lincoln maintains his opposition to the *Dred Scott* decision but says that if he were in Congress and a bill prohibiting slavery in a new territory came up, he would vote for it but work "peaceably" to reverse *Dred Scott*. Douglas, insinuates Lincoln, is hypocritical for condemning his criticism of *Dred Scott*, because Douglas had approved President Jackson's rejection of the Supreme Court's ruling that a national bank was constitutional.

After first dealing with these matters of concern to members of both parties, Lincoln addresses Republicans about Douglas's appeal for their support based mainly on common opposition to the Lecompton Constitution, and Lincoln implies flaws in Douglas's character. Lincoln suggests that Douglas was untruthful in claiming that the "Illinois legislature instructed him to introduce the Nebraska bill" when in fact "there was nobody in that legislature who ever thought of such a thing." Lincoln notes Douglas's disregard for the immorality of slavery: "He cares not if slavery is voted up or down." If Republicans endorse Douglas, he will enslave them, Lincoln argues, for they will be "saddled, bridled and harnessed and waiting to be driven over to the slavery extension camp of the nation—just ready to be driven over tied together in a lot—to be driven over, every man with a rope around his neck, that halter being held by Judge Douglas." It would be a mistake, says Lincoln, for Republicans to abandon their opposition to slavery extension, their support for "the [territorial] settlement of free laborers, who want the land to bring up their families upon," and their belief in slavery's ultimate extinction. Lincoln agrees with Douglas that the government was "made for white men" but again faults Douglas for "the counterfeit logic" that if Lincoln does not want a black woman for a slave, he must want her for a wife. Lincoln closes this section by citing Douglas's argument that when races mix, "the inferior race bears the superior down" as a reason not to allow slavery to extend into the territories. Lincoln calls the need to disallow slavery in the territories "a self-evident truth."

Quoting the Declaration of Independence, Lincoln moves into the last, most important section, with reference to the recent July 4th celebrations. He gives a patriotic, historical, and moral basis for his and his party's opposition to slavery extension—and to Douglas—and this section has the most potent language of the speech. Here Lincoln eloquently celebrates the nation's progress as seen in its growing population composed of immigrants from various European nations. The Declaration of Independence bonds the new generations of immigrants to the founders' guiding principles. The biblical language suggests a religious/moral underpinning in the Declaration that is an essential component of the American heritage. The phrase "electric cord" implies a connection of moral principle from the founders' generation, when Franklin discovered electricity, to the present and into the future.

> When they [immigrants] look through that old Declaration of Independence they find that those old men say that "we hold these truths to be self-evident, that all men are created equal," and then they feel that that moral sentiment taught in that day evidences their relation to those men, that it is the father of all moral principle in them, and that they have a right to claim it as though they were blood of the blood, and flesh of the flesh of the men who wrote that Declaration, and so they are. That is the electric cord in that Declaration that links the hearts of patriotic and liberty-loving men together, that will link those patriotic hearts as long as the love of freedom exists in the minds of men throughout the world.[36]

Lincoln more famously used the electric cord metaphor in the First Inaugural Address.

Lincoln says Douglas's inaccurate interpretation of the Declaration of Independence presents a view that "Americans are equal to the people of England" and that such an interpretation excludes Germans. Transmitting that misinterpretation to succeeding generations will destroy the belief in liberty, which motivated many Germans to settle in America. A restrictive, condescending regard for "the inferior race" will lead to "the arguments that kings have made for enslaving the people in all ages of the world." Lincoln uses biblical allusion to impute evil to Douglas's position: "This argument of the Judge is the same old serpent that says you work and I eat, you toil and I will enjoy the fruits of it. . . . I hold if that course of argumentation that is made for the purpose of convincing the public mind that we should not care about this, should be granted, it does not stop with the Negro."

For emphasis Lincoln repeats this point in plain language charged with rational, moral, and emotional appeal. Here he suggests the logical possibility of a pernicious outcome from misinterpreting the Declaration of Independence, just as he did toward the end of the House Divided speech by suggesting that the extension of slavery into the territories would be followed by a Supreme Court decision that slavery could not be excluded from such a free state as Illinois: "I should like to know if taking this old Declaration of Independence, which declares that all men are equal upon principle and making exceptions to it, where will it stop? If one man says it does not mean a Negro, why not another say it does not mean some other man?"[37] Lincoln strengthens his argument by turning to the Constitution and Bible. He notes the founders' logic of compromising to establish the nation: the Constitution had to allow slavery in the original states where it existed. The founders' vision should be regarded as an aspirational, moral ideal analogous to Christ's exhortation: "As your Father in Heaven is perfect, be ye also perfect." Lincoln thus denigrates Douglas as an unwitting politician responsible for a policy that would nationalize slavery, refuting Douglas's argument for Republicans to align with him.

Lincoln eloquently asserts a rational/emotional appeal to national unity based on foundational commitment to social justice. Lincoln's plea gains emphasis through the repetition of "let us" (anaphora): "In relation to the principle that all men are created equal, let it be as nearly reached as we can. If we cannot give freedom to every creature, let us do nothing that will impose slavery upon any other creature. Let us then turn this government back into the channel in which the framers of the Constitution originally placed it. Let us stand firmly by each other. If we do so we are turning in the contrary direction, that our friend Judge Douglas proposes—not intentionally—as working in the traces tend to make this one universal slave nation."[38] Again Lincoln shrewdly gives Douglas an excuse.

Lincoln closes with an inspiring call to patriotic action: "My friends, I have detained you about as long as I desired to do, and I have only to say, let us discard all this quibbling about this man and the other man—this race and that race and the other race being inferior, and therefore they must be placed in an inferior position—discarding our standard that we have left us. Let us discard all these things, and unite as one people throughout this land, until we shall once more stand up declaring that all men are created equal." When he says he could not continue without introducing "some new topic," the audience cried, "Go on." He thanks them, saying he leaves them "hoping that the lamp of liberty will burn in your bosoms until there shall no longer be a doubt that all men are created free and equal."[39] Lincoln had used the phrase "free and equal" in reference to the equality language of the Declaration of Independence in his Eulogy on Henry Clay, and he would use that phrase again in a stump speech at Monticello later in July and in the fifth and seventh Lincoln-Douglas debates.

Lincoln's Chicago speech was published in the Democratic-leaning *Daily Democrat* and the Republican-leaning *Chicago Press and Tribune*. Those newspapers had reporters practicing shorthand techniques during the candidates' Chicago July speeches that would be used during the Lincoln-Douglas debates to try to capture every word. The newspapers' reports also cited audience comments, questions, and the speaker's response or lack of it.

From Chicago, the Douglas campaign traveled south by train to Springfield, with stops along the way for rallies and speeches. The well-dressed Douglas and his attractive wife enjoyed a private car, and a platform car featured a cannon named "Popular Sovereignty," whose blasts announced the train's approach to towns. The plainly dressed Lincoln was on the train so he could hear Douglas speak at stops that included Bloomington on July 16 and the next day at Atlanta and Lincoln—his first namesake town, established in 1853 before he became famous. Despite his supporters' call for Lincoln to speak after Douglas at the locations on the way to Springfield, he declined, except for unrecorded remarks at his first namesake town.[40] Lincoln delivered his next major campaign speech on the evening of July 17 in Springfield after Douglas's afternoon speech. Lincoln's speech that day included material from his earlier Chicago speech as well as new material, suggesting he must have been writing on the train to Springfield (he had his valise with him).

The speeches Douglas and Lincoln gave July 17 in Springfield, at the statehouse, highlighted the different positions on slavery between the candidates that would later be mixed with other arguments during the Lincoln-Douglas debates. According to Burlingame, Douglas's July 17 speech repeated his Chicago speech of the week before with a focus on attacking the House Divided speech. Douglas maintained that black people and such other minorities as "Indians" and "Chinese" should not be considered the social and political equals of white people and that Lincoln was trying to incite disunion. Douglas accused Lincoln of seeking full racial equality: "The Little Giant then went into graphic and extensive detail about the indignities of 'nigger equality' and race-mixing—hordes of blacks invading the state, holding office, becoming judges, and—horror of horrors, marrying with whites."[41] Burlingame notes that "Douglas regularly used the word 'nigger' for 'Negro,' though the *Congressional Globe* and his organ, the *Chicago Times*, sanitized his language."

Douglas said all matters concerning black people should be left to individual states, but he personally opposed racial equality, emphasizing that the federal government was created by and for white people only.

Speaking without the benefit of being able to study his opponent's speech in print, Lincoln nonetheless included references to Douglas's afternoon speech. Lincoln's speech appeared in the *Illinois State Journal*, and when he chose it over others to appear as a pamphlet, he reportedly said, it was "the most 'taking' speech I ever made."[42] It was also included in his 1860 published scrapbook of the Lincoln-Douglas debates. This 7,940-word speech receives little discussion in Lincoln literature.[43] Yet it comprehensively develops Lincoln's criticism of Douglas to date.

After a six-paragraph introduction, body sections of the speech attack Douglas on subjects in this order: popular sovereignty, the Lecompton Constitution, Douglas's criticism of the House Divided speech and of Lincoln's view of the *Dred Scott* decision, and Douglas aligning himself with old-line Whigs. This structure strategically positions Lincoln's defense of the House Divided speech between sections in which he takes the offense through strong refutations. The conclusion reiterates the striking theme of the House Divided speech: that recent history shows a growing movement toward the nationalization of slavery, contrary to the founders' intention. The informed arguments and cutting language of Lincoln's July 17 speech suggest increasing frustration with Douglas.

In this speech Lincoln weaves moralistic personal attacks on Douglas into criticism of his positions, policy, and rhetoric. Lincoln's growing frustration and anger over Douglas's demagoguery explain the aspersions. The introduction illustrates Lincoln's capacity for political analysis by providing a critique of the legislative conditions that put Illinois Republicans at a disadvantage for electing a US senator in 1858. First, the legislative apportionment in Illinois was antiquated, and since it favored Democrats, they would not reform it. Second, "There are one or two Democratic [state] senators who will be members of the next legislature, and will vote for the election of [US] senator, who are holding over in districts in which we could, on all reasonable calculation, elect men of our own, if we only had the chance of an election." Yet the fair-minded Lincoln says this circumstance is acceptable, while the apportionment problem is not. Third, Douglas has the advantage of "worldwide renown," and his incumbency and the expectation that he may rise to the presidency give him a particular appeal owing to the expected increase in patronage power he will have. A salient passage in this speech features a metaphorical, scornful description of Douglas's advantage of celebrity: Democrats "have been looking upon him as certainly, at no distant day, to be the president of the United States. They have seen in his round, jolly, fruitful face, post offices, land offices, marshalships, and cabinet appointments, chargeships and foreign missions, bursting and sprouting out in wonderful exuberance ready to be laid hold of by their greedy hands. . . . They rush about him, sustain him, and give him marches, triumphal entries, and receptions beyond what even in the days of his highest prosperity they could have brought about in his favor."[44]

Lincoln then humorously invokes his humble, self-deprecating persona: "On the contrary nobody has ever expected me to be president. In my poor, lean, lank, face, nobody has ever seen any cabbages were sprouting out." With the Democrats having these advantages, Lincoln says the Republicans will have "to fight this battle upon principle, and upon principle alone." Lincoln then forecasts the subjects he will address, and they are "the main points" he has observed in Douglas's campaign plan.

Lincoln next presents his most thorough critique of Douglas's use of popular sovereignty to date, beginning with figurative language to poke Douglas for assigning so much importance to it that he has it plastered on train cars and banners, and "it is to be dished up in as many varieties as a French cook can produce soups from potatoes." To Lincoln, Douglas's use of popular sovereignty reveals it to be "the most arrant Quixotism that was ever enacted before a community." Lincoln's examination of the concept first defines it concerning the question of extending slavery to new territories and raises the question of whether Douglas is "devoting his life" to using popular sovereignty to justify allowing slavery into those areas. If so, Douglas is acting contrary to the true meaning of popular sovereignty as local self-government and being inconsistent if not hypocritical for at once circumventing the *Dred Scott* decision while also criticizing Lincoln for resisting it.

As was his rhetorical strategy in court, Lincoln begins with lesser points he could concede to set up his main point. Lincoln acknowledges Douglas's belief in popular sovereignty as local self-government. Lincoln also acknowledges that those who criticize and oppose the Lecompton Constitution for approving slavery in Kansas without the participation of antislavery voters are agreed in principle, including Douglas and himself. Then, with hyperbole Lincoln tars Douglas as a fool: "This being so, what is Judge Douglas going to spend his life for? Is he going to spend his life in maintaining a principle that nobody on earth opposes? Does he expect to stand up in majestic dignity, and go through his apotheosis and become a god, in the maintaining of a principle which neither a man nor a mouse in all God's creation is opposing?" Lincoln next faults Douglas for trying to take disproportionate credit for defeating the endorsement of the Lecompton Constitution in Congress, citing Douglas's use of a rationale that Lincoln presented before Douglas used it without attribution.

Lincoln takes the high moral ground in defending his positions in the House Divided speech, and the language reveals disgust with his opponent's demagogic rhetoric. Again Lincoln testifies to the care he took in writing that speech, striving to avoid errors of fact and inference, "having made that speech with the most kindly feeling towards Judge Douglas" and giving assurances that he was entirely willing to correct any kind of mistake. Lincoln says that Douglas has thoroughly read and reread the House Divided speech without citing any errors. Nonetheless, Douglas "declares" he will make that speech a main issue in the campaign and misquotes it. Lincoln says he will presently quote from memory the passage from the House Divided speech in question and that if Douglas subsequently "repeats his misrepresentation, it shall be plain to all that he does so willfully." If Douglas persists in distorting Lincoln's views, Lincoln says he will have to change his campaign strategy according to "the real exigencies of the case." Here is a clear threat of "turnabout is fair play."

Lincoln is frustrated with Douglas's demagogic rhetoric, asserting that he intended to conduct his campaign "upon principle, and with fairness" and "as a gentleman," implicitly expecting the same from his opponent. Yet Douglas has misrepresented Lincoln's views by charging him with trying to incite "a war of sections." Douglas has used "language most able and ingenious for concealing what I really meant; and [saying] that while I had protested against entering into the slave states, I nevertheless did mean to go on the banks of the Ohio and throw missiles into Kentucky to disturb them in their domestic institutions."

Lincoln says his purpose is to return the institution of slavery to its status as intended by the framers of the Constitution, denying any other purpose or meaning in the controversial passage from the House Divided speech, which he then recites from memory. He next maintains he had no other intention than to make a prediction: "I simply expressed my *expectation*. Cannot the Judge perceive the distinction between a [political] *purpose* and an *expectation*. I have often expressed an expectation to die, but I have never expressed a wish to die."[45] He says he expected the "ultimate extinction" of slavery until the passage of the Nebraska bill marked the beginning of a conspiracy to make slavery "perpetual, national, and universal." Lincoln mocks Douglas's accusation that Lincoln seeks to abolish slavery entirely: "to annihilate the state legislatures—to force cotton to grow upon the tops of the Green Mountains—to freeze ice in Florida—to cut lumber on the broad Illinois prairies—that I am in favor of all these ridiculous and impossible things." Lincoln's hyperbole again expresses his frustration.

The next section is a 1,530-word refutation of Douglas's complaints about Lincoln's position on *Dred Scott*. Lincoln says Douglas is making his critique "one-half the onslaught, and one-third of the entire plan of the campaign." Lincoln repeats his previously announced position that the decision should be obeyed until it can be overturned and that he has pointed out an example of Douglas's refusal to acquiesce in a Supreme Court decision. Lincoln holds no hope of stopping Douglas from attacking him on this point and again uses cutting language: "I wish to show that I am sustained by authority, in addition to that heretofore presented. I do not expect to convince the Judge. It is part of the plan of his campaign, and he will cling to it with a desperate gripe [grip]. Even, turning it upon him—turn the sharp point against him, and gaff him through—he will still cling to it till he can invent some new dodge to take the place of it."

The nonartistic proof Lincoln cites for the first time to strengthen his view of the *Dred Scott* decision is an 1820 letter by Thomas Jefferson from his published correspondence (named by volume number and page number). Jefferson's letter says that "our judges are as honest as other men, and not more so. They have, with others, the same passions for party, for power, and the privilege of their corps." As a result, "to consider the judges as the ultimate arbiters of all constitutional questions [is] a very dangerous doctrine indeed and one which would place us under the despotism of an oligarchy." Jefferson points out that judges whose power derives from lifetime appointments are potentially dangerous. Applying the authority of Jefferson, Lincoln contends that Douglas's strict reliance on the Supreme Court as the final word "would reduce us to the despotism of an oligarchy."

Lincoln then notes that Douglas subscribes to the Democratic tradition of refusing to recognize the Supreme Court's decision that a national bank is constitutional. Lincoln is thus able to use one of his favorite methods of refutation: demonstrating an opponent's inconsistent views and undermining his credibility: "The plain truth is simply this: Judge Douglas is for Supreme Court decisions when he likes them and against them when he does not like them. He is for the *Dred Scott* decision because it tends to national- ize slavery—because it is part of the original combination for that object." Further, Lincoln finds irony in this conflict with his opponent, ending his complaint with the rational/emotional appeal of biblical-sounding language: "It so happens, singularly enough, that I never stood opposed to a decision of the Supreme Court till this. On the contrary, I have no recollection that he was ever particularly in favor of one till this. He never was in favor of any, nor opposed to any, till the present one, which helps to nationalize slavery. Free men of Sangamon—free men of Illinois—free men everywhere—judge ye between him and me, upon this issue."

Lincoln uses the authority of Whig icon Henry Clay to continue his attack on Douglas with more sarcasm. Clay pointed out that the British government allowed individuals to take slaves into the American colonies "in spite of the wishes of the people," and now, Lincoln maintains, the federal government is acting just like the British government in allowing slaves to be taken into the territories, asking pointed rhetorical questions of Douglas: "Will you not graciously allow us to do with the *Dred Scott* decision precisely what you did with the bank decision? You succeeded in breaking down the moral effect of that decision; did you find it necessary to amend the Constitution? or to set up a court of Negroes in order to do it?" Lincoln ridicules Douglas's account of visiting Clay on his deathbed to become his successor as a proponent of popular sovereignty: "By this part of the 'plan of the campaign,' the Judge has evidently promised himself that tears shall be drawn down the cheeks of all old Whigs, as large as half grown apples." Lincoln unsparingly continues his acerbic criticism of Douglas: "It would be amusing, if it were not disgusting, to see how quick these [Missouri] compromise-breakers administer on the political effects of their dead adversaries, trumping up claims never before heard of, and dividing the assets among themselves. If I should be found dead tomorrow morning, nothing but my insignificance could prevent a speech being made on my authority, before the end of next week."[46]

In the penultimate section Lincoln repeats his central idea: "I have said that I do not understand the Declaration to mean that all men were created equal in all respects. They are not our equal in color." Burlingame refers to the inequality in color as "bizarre," further saying "his meaning is obscure; what is a superior color? Perhaps he was being satirical." The inequality in color could be explained as an expression of limited racism that some writers have seen in Lincoln. Burlingame cites Lincoln's subsequent qualifying language as a "carefully hedged treatment of the racial inferiority argument [that] differed sharply from Douglas's unqualified racism": "Certainly the Negro is not our equal in color—perhaps not in many other respects; still, in the right to put into his mouth the bread that his own hands have earned, he is the equal of every other man, or black. In pointing out that more has been given you, you cannot be justified in taking away the little which has been given him. All I ask for the Negro is that if you do not like him, let him alone. If God gave him but little, that little let him enjoy."[47]

Lincoln closes the speech with three more points, emphasizing refutation and accusation without hyperbolic flourish. First, he reminds the audience that the framers of the Constitution recognized the expediency of allowing slavery where it was established but permitting the abolition of the slave trade twenty years into the future and prohibiting slavery in the new territories. Second, Lincoln confesses, "What I would most desire would be the separation of the white and black races." Third, Lincoln repeats his "belief in the existence of a conspiracy to perpetuate and nationalize slavery" although he cannot prove it. He repeats the accusation he made in the House Divided speech that people living in the territories were "deceived into carrying the last presidential election, by the impression" that they would be given the choice of prohibiting slavery although "it was known in advance by the conspirators that the Court was to decide that neither Congress nor the people could so exclude slavery." Lincoln says that despite Douglas's familiarity with the House Divided speech, he has not "contradicted those charges" in two speeches that Lincoln has recently witnessed. Thus, Lincoln says Douglas's silence is a "tacit admission," leading Lincoln again to charge Douglas with having a role in the conspiracy.

After these Springfield speeches, Lincoln corresponded with political allies and undertook the strategy, begun in 1854, of following Douglas on the campaign trail. Don E. Fehrenbacher noted the strategic importance of central Illinois in the state's 1850 politics because of the "even balance of opposing [political] forces": "The region that had previously been the heartland of Illinois Whiggery now became the battleground where each contest was decided. It was here, for instance, that Lincoln and Douglas concentrated most of their efforts in 1858, making only token expeditions into the north and south."[48]

No texts have been located for two other speeches Lincoln gave in July, but they were briefly reported in newspapers. At Clinton on July 27 Lincoln witnessed Douglas's afternoon speech, in which the Little Giant finally denied Lincoln's accusation of conspiring with Chief Justice Taney and Presidents Pierce and Buchanan to spread slavery. Douglas also denied he ever criticized the Supreme Court's ruling against the US Bank. That evening Lincoln mocked Douglas's bluster, denied the accusation that he failed to vote for troop supplies during the Mexican War, and denounced Douglas for failing to admit his frequent, public criticism of the Supreme Court's ruling on the federal bank.

Two days later, on July 29, Douglas spoke at Monticello in east central Illinois, and Lincoln followed there in the evening with an emphasis on refuting Douglas's accusation that Lincoln sought total equality between white people and black people. According to a newspaper report, Lincoln stressed the point he made in his earlier Chicago speech: that "*he only wanted that the words* of the Declaration of Independence should be applied, to wit: 'That all men are created free and equal.'"[49] The newspaper does not mention that Lincoln misquotes the Declaration of Independence by adding the word *free*.

Meanwhile, Lincoln's Republican advisors convinced him that greater advantages would result from joint debates rather than tandem speeches, so at the end of July Lincoln made the challenge. The renowned Douglas was reluctant to give the lesser-known Lincoln the prestige of sharing the stage, but Douglas was even more unwilling to look unmanly, so he accepted the debate challenge. Douglas limited the joint debates to one appearance in each of the seven congressional districts where Lincoln and he had not yet spoken. The first debate would be on August 21 at Ottawa.

Stumping in Former Whig Strongholds prior to the Debates

Lincoln agreed to the debate terms set by Douglas, and Lincoln said he would not subsequently be present at Douglas's stump speeches, in deference to his complaints that Lincoln was exploiting his audiences, which were large because of Douglas's celebrity. Unlike the 1854 campaign, when Douglas often spoke in the afternoon and Lincoln in the evening, on the 1858 campaign trail beginning in August, Lincoln often spoke the day after Douglas. With Lincoln absent from Douglas's audiences, Lincoln's friends told him what was said and done at Douglas's speeches. Thus Lincoln had several hours to make notes and form a mental outline of his points, although he preferred to have more time for writing before speaking. Burlingame says that many farmers who gathered to hear Douglas did not want to spend a second day away from work to hear Lincoln. The persistent Lincoln in early August followed Douglas up the Illinois River valley to Beardstown, Havana, Bath, Lewistown, and Peoria.

The newspapers reporting Lincoln's stump speeches quote them extensively. Those speeches demonstrate Lincoln's ability to adjust to context and audience. Douglas repeatedly charged Lincoln with making personal attacks, but at the same time Douglas called Lincoln such names as liar, coward, villain, sneak, pickpocket, and wretch.[50] Douglas also forcefully denied Lincoln's accusation of collaboration with Buchanan and Taney in a conspiracy to spread slavery. Sometimes Douglas's verbal abuses may have been fueled by alcohol: some newspaper reports said he was drinking heavily throughout the campaign.[51]

Lincoln's stump speeches prior to the debates show he anticipated the need to defend his accusation of the slavery-extension conspiracy against Douglas. At Beardstown on August 12, Lincoln criticized Douglas for temporizing in his response to the accusation of a Democratic proslavery conspiracy. Lincoln began with a summary of events supporting his accusation that Democratic national leaders for several years collaborated in "a symmetrical piece of workmanship," "an intelligent plan," to extend slavery throughout the nation. Lincoln said Douglas was given copies of the House Divided speech and had ample time to respond but failed to do so in his speeches at Chicago, Bloomington, and Springfield. Lincoln used a legalistic metaphor and legalistic, periodic sentence, with parallel introductory subordinate clauses leading to the main point at the end for emphasis, to indict Douglas for his lack of response: "Well, seeing that Douglas had had the process served on him, that he had taken notice of such service, that he had come into court and pleaded to a part of the complaint, but ignored the main issue, I took a default on him." Lincoln jabs: "Well, my friends, perhaps he so far lost his self-respect in Beardstown as to actually call it [conspiracy accusation] a falsehood."

Forest L. Whan quotes Douglas's autobiography to explain how he used silence as a rhetorical strategy: "Douglas came to believe early in life that it is well to 'admit nothing and require my adversary to prove everything material to the success of his case.' This philosophy lay behind his determination to keep his opponent always on the defensive."[52]

At Beardstown, to strengthen his conspiracy argument, Lincoln expanded the legalistic metaphor by adding new "charges" that he said he did not make in the House Divided speech. One new charge is that while the 1854 Nebraska bill was in progress, Douglas used his influence to reject language that would have given territorial residents "the right to exclude slavery if they chose." Douglas also said such a right was not in effect while the bill was pending. If Douglas denies these charges, Lincoln says he will prove him wrong "by such testimony as will confound him forever."

At Havana on August 14, Lincoln humorously attacked Douglas with insinuation about his drinking: "I am informed, that my distinguished friend yesterday became a little excited, nervous, perhaps, [laughter] and he said something about fighting, as though referring to a pugilistic encounter between him and myself. . . . I am informed, further, that somebody in his audience, rather more excited, or nervous, than himself, took off his coat, and offered to take the job off Judge Douglas' hands." Lincoln facetiously said he refuses to fight Douglas because he does not think his opponent really wants to and would no more fight Lincoln than his own wife. The question of muscularity is irrelevant to the campaign, says Lincoln, who also quips that he will not fight Douglas's "bottle-holder," either. Newspaper reports of Lincoln's other Senate campaign speeches reveal that he was restrained in his use of humor. In the debates Lincoln rarely told the kinds of humorous stories and jokes he had become famous for on the stump, allegedly saying, "The occasion is too serious; the issues are too grave."[53]

The Havana speech illustrates Lincoln's skill in adapting a stump speech to a local audience, as does his two-hour speech at Bath (August 16), a village on the banks of the Illinois River, between Beardstown and Havana. At Bath Lincoln identifies with the audience by acknowledging the several fellow veterans of the Black Hawk War from twenty-seven years ago who were with him on the stage in the town he had surveyed twenty-two years ago. Lincoln says many others in the audience are the sons of other friends of his youth, so he hopes they will listen with "respectful attention." The Bath speech criticizes Douglas for never saying slavery is wrong and for his attempts to claim he is a disciple of Henry Clay and rightful heir to his political legacy. To support this criticism, Lincoln read from Clay's speeches. Throughout the campaign Lincoln and Douglas competed for the Clay mantle.[54]

A few days before the first debate at Ottawa in northern Illinois, Lincoln ended his speeches in the Illinois River valley at Lewistown (August 17) and Peoria (August 19). The newspaper report of the two-and-a-half-hour Lewistown speech quotes Lincoln extensively. Roy P. Basler wrote that the Lewistown speech appeared in the *Chicago Press and Tribune* and was widely republished in other newspapers. The speech first attacks Douglas and then affirms the

Declaration of Independence as the founders' blueprint for developing the new nation.

At Lewistown Lincoln refutes Douglas's claim to be Clay's successor on political positions relating to slavery and faults Douglas for refusing to take a moral position on it. Lincoln says he is closer to Clay's positions on slavery than Douglas is, as evidenced in Clay's printed speeches. While speaking, Lincoln often read selected passages from important speeches of his own and of others. He knew that reading documents could bore an audience but felt that sometimes short passages should be read to clarify and emphasize main points. At Lewistown Lincoln said that his reading from Clay showed that Douglas was as opposite to Clay "as Beelzebub to an Angel of Light." Lincoln stresses that Clay's writing shows he sought gradual, "ultimate emancipation of the slave." Twice Lincoln says that Douglas is the only prominent public man "who had *never said to friend or enemy whether he believed human slavery in the abstract to be right or wrong.*" According to Lincoln, Douglas at Lewistown said he was open to slavery in Illinois. Lincoln berates Douglas for putting profit above morality: "If you can make more money by flogging niggers than by flogging oxen, there is no moral consideration which should interfere to prevent your doing so."[55]

The rest of the Lewistown speech presents one of Lincoln's most articulate encomiums on the equality principle of the Declaration of Independence. Lincoln claims the founders regarded slavery as evil and composed the Constitution to ensure that it would eventually end "by cutting off its source": the African slave trade. Blending rational, moral, and emotional appeals, Lincoln quotes the first sentence of the Declaration of Independence to foreground his assertion that the founders believed human rights were sanctioned by God: "their lofty, and wise, and noble understanding of the justice of the Creator to His creatures. Yes, gentlemen, to all His creatures, to the whole family of man. In their enlightened belief, nothing stamped with the Divine image and likeness was sent into the world to be trodden on, and degraded, and imbruted by its fellows."

Lincoln uses figurative language to endow the founders with profound wisdom: they constructed the Declaration of Independence as "a beacon to guide their children and their children's children, and the countless myriads who should inhabit the earth in other ages." Such a guiding principle was vital because the founders were prescient in anticipating "the tendency of prosperity to breed tyrants," and that tendency could lead some individual or group to establish a rationale for appropriating and twisting the language of the Declaration of Independence as a justification for bigotry and injustice: "That none but rich men, or none but men, were entitled to life, liberty and the pursuit of happiness." Lincoln believed that since the founders' generation, some leaders and other citizens had strayed from the original message of the Declaration, which he described in the Lewistown speech as the "chart[er] of liberty."

In the conclusion Lincoln, like a minister using biblical text as the basis for a born-again sermon on salvation, addresses those who tend to believe "that all men are *not* created equal in those inalienable rights enumerated by our chart[er] of liberty" to come back to foundational values. This conclusion makes rational, moral, and emotional appeals to patriotism, and the message is remarkable for its mix of directness, metaphoric language, and hyperbolic self-sacrifice. Perhaps Lincoln thought the use of language with evangelical overtones would be especially appropriate for a rural, largely uneducated audience accustomed to religious camp-meeting oratory; and such usage notwithstanding, the sentences are direct, brief, and eloquent:

> Return to the fountain whose waters spring close by the blood of the Revolution. Think nothing of me—take no thought for the political fate of any man whomsoever—but come back to the truths that are in the Declaration of Independence. You may do anything with me you choose, if you will but heed these sacred principles. You may not only defeat me for the Senate, but you may take me and put me to death. While pretending no indifference to earthy honors, I *do claim* to be actuated in this contest by something higher than an anxiety for office. I charge you to drop every paltry and insignificant thought for any man's success. It is nothing; I am nothing; Judge Douglas is nothing. But do not destroy that immortal emblem of Humanity—the Declaration of American Independence.[56]

Lincoln's biblical allusions and tone in the Lewistown speech and in previous quotations show, in Burlingame's words, that Lincoln "appealed to an audience of evangelical Christians even though he was not one himself." As Richard Carwardine elaborates, "Lincoln knew well enough the mainly Protestant sources of antislavery energy. Though cool toward the moral absolutism of the abolitionists, he still argued his case in terms which he knew would stir up the antislavery moderates of the mainstream churches. His fusion of Jeffersonian and scriptural precepts, set in the context of Whiggish self-improvement, was sweet music to the ears of those antislavery Christians whose church resolutions, circulating in the political as well as the religious press, likewise blended the Enlightenment idealism of the Founding Fathers with New Testament theology."[57] Carwardine emphasizes that Lincoln knew his audiences well.

Conclusion

In 1857 and 1858 Lincoln's rhetorical effectiveness advanced his antislavery political appeal to ordinary citizens and Republican Party leaders at the state and national levels. In 1857 Lincoln criticized the rhetoric of Douglas's Dred Scott speech with arguments against his political positions and with implied criticism of his moral character. Lincoln's Dred Scott speech supported black people based on the natural rights language of the Declaration of Independence.

In the House Divided speech Lincoln criticized Douglas's politics and policies, lack of empathy, and obtuseness to discredit him as a potential leader in the Republican Party and to paint him as unworthy of reelection to the US Senate. Lincoln attacked Douglas as corrupt for participating in a proslavery conspiracy whose purpose was to anesthetize public opinion into accepting slavery nationally. Like the Peoria speech, the House Divided speech is distinctive rhetoric for its diverse argumentation and principled appeal to fear. Lincoln's campaign speeches in Chicago, Springfield, and Lewistown feature passages that are evocative of the eloquent passages in the Peoria speech, including use of the Declaration of Independence and the Constitution, and showing the rhetorical readiness he took into the debates. Yet the demagogic rhetoric of Douglas's pre-debate speeches frustrated Lincoln, who responded often with sarcastic personal attacks but with lighter personal satire in the Havana speech.

Throughout the rest of the campaign, the rivals tried to destroy one another's credibility, and Lincoln had to face the question of how to handle his opponent's demagoguery, including personal attacks. In the first debate Douglas must have surprised Lincoln with the intensified charges of antislavery extremism and duplicity, including a counter conspiracy accusation, and those attacks put Lincoln's rhetorical savvy and patience to the ultimate test.

6

Sparring with Douglas over Credibility during Their First Four Debates (1858)

I don't want to be unjustly accused of dealing illiberally or unfairly with an adversary, either in court, or in a political canvas, or anywhere else. I would despise myself if I supposed myself ready to deal less liberally with an adversary than I was willing to be treated myself.
—Lincoln, the Fourth Debate, 1858

The epigraph resonates with the importance Lincoln placed on earning the respect of others in political activity that he expressed in his first announcement to run for public office and on keeping his self-respect, as seen in his efforts to secure a congressional nomination. The Lincoln-Douglas debates were the highlight of the 1858 Illinois race for the US Senate and advanced Lincoln's rise to national politics that began with his 1854 Peoria speech. Scholarship on the debates is extensive but typically with more emphasis on political positions and policy than on rhetorical methods.[1] Rhetorical/textual analyses, however, do not capture the pageantry and excitement of the debates and related stump speeches.[2]

The rivals disputed only slavery, slavery agitation, and race. Douglas's work in the Senate gave him far more formal debating experience than Lincoln, and Douglas was a world-renowned orator. In the tangled rhetorical vine of the campaign—twenty-one debate speeches and numerous stump speeches—the rivals' moral character was a central concern as they fought for credibility. Each candidate used conspiracy theories to portray the other as a corrupt extremist: Douglas said Lincoln collaborated with abolitionists; Lincoln said Douglas conspired with other Democrats to nationalize slavery. The rivals also charged one another with other rhetorical abuses. Previously, dating to the 1830s, Lincoln had been frustrated with Douglas's provocative rhetoric; now, as never before, Lincoln would face his rival's full-bore criticism.

The debates forced Lincoln to respond to Douglas's abolitionist conspiracy accusation, other inaccuracies, dodges, and personal attacks; and Lincoln had to decide whether, when, or how to use "turnabout is fair play" responses. The joint debate format was disadvantageous to Lincoln's occasional need to make quick decisions about "turnabout is fair play." As Allen C. Guelzo observes, "Lincoln never advertised himself as an off-the-cuff speaker, and in his cautious, lawyerly way, he was more inclined to wait until he had thought through the questions and the answers he wanted to give."[3]

In the first four debates, the rivals complained about personal attacks and repeated other criticisms. Both rivals employed the demagogic technique of appealing to the biases of local audiences. Lincoln has been criticized for repeating his rejection of social/political equality for black people when he spoke to a strongly negrophobic audience in the fourth debate, echoing points he had made in the first debate. In the first four debates, however, Lincoln introduced more new arguments than Douglas did, relying more on rational appeal than demagogic emotional appeal. Lincoln forced Douglas to defend his role in guiding the Kansas-Nebraska Act through Congress and to admit he did not support congressional protection of slavery in territories.

Debate Schedule and Context

In previous encounters, including their 1854 close exchanges, the rivals never had to follow one another immediately in such a formal, timed competition. In making the challenge of joint debates to the famous incumbent, the lesser-known Lincoln had to accept Douglas's conditions, including the requirement of holding one debate in each of the seven congressional districts where the contestants had not campaigned. Because of the backgrounds of residents in different parts of the state, northern audiences tended to be more antislavery than audiences in southern Illinois, where many families had come from such slave states as Virginia, Tennessee, and Kentucky. Central Illinois presented a mixture of political affiliations and would prove crucial to the contest.

Douglas stipulated that he would begin and close the first, third, fifth, and seventh debates. Opening speeches would be one hour; the rival's following speech would be one and a half hours; and the closing speech would be a half hour. Douglas would thus deliver eleven debate speeches; Lincoln, ten. Stump speaking during and after the debates gave the candidates opportunities to test, adapt, and hone argumentation to targeted audiences. The rivals committed to the following sites and dates: 1. Ottawa (August 21), 2. Freeport (August 27), 3. Jonesboro (September 15), 4. Charleston (September 18), 5. Galesburg (October 7), 6. Quincy (October 13), and 7. Alton (October 15). The time the candidates had to prepare between debates varied from almost three weeks to just two days. Despite reporters' efforts to capture every word, Democratic editors demagogically misreported Lincoln's speeches, whereas Republican editors' tampering may have been limited to tweaking his language.

The four debates opened and closed by Douglas gave him the advantage of the final word. The debates eliminated or reduced opponents' opportunities to study speeches in print before responding and deciding the timing of response, although between debates they consulted with political allies. Neither candidate delivered a debate speech by reading a manuscript of it, but they did read from material supporting their claims. In the first debates the rivals introduced the accusations, counteraccusations, and insinuations that would be repeated throughout the campaign, in the long, taxing struggle to election day, November 2. Lincoln would not emphasize his antislavery moral argumentation until the last three debates. From that standpoint the first four debates were the rising action in the debate drama.

Faulting Douglas's Rhetorical Ethics in the First Debate (Ottawa)

Ottawa, site of the first debate, is eighty miles southwest of Chicago. Ottawa in 1858 had a population of 7,000, and it was heavily Democratic. In the opening speech, with an audience of 10,000, Douglas accused Lincoln of political intrigues and extremes, intending to destroy his credibility as a politician who would accurately represent the values and beliefs of the Illinois citizens on the crucial questions of slavery and race. The series of accusations began with the charge that Lincoln was a leader in an abolitionist conspiracy and ended with the assertion that Lincoln favored the complete social and political equality of white people and black people.[4] Douglas predicted that such a policy would dissolve the Union. His accusations suggested a deliberate attempt to establish a case against Lincoln that would appeal to both negrophobes and patriots. Many Illinoisans, including old-line Whigs whose votes Lincoln needed and Democrats whose votes Lincoln sought, hated both slavery and abolition.

In his opening speech Douglas claims that after the passage of the 1854 Nebraska bill, which had bipartisan support, Lincoln and Illinois Senator Lyman Trumbull began a clandestine conspiracy to "abolitionize" old-line Whigs and Democrats. Trumbull had been a Democratic senator who left that party to help form the Illinois Republican Party. Lincoln and Trumbull, says Douglas, slanted their political methods to appeal to their respective audiences: "Mr. Lincoln went to work industriously to abolitionize the old Whig party all over the state, pretending that he was as good a Whig as he ever was." Meanwhile, Trumbull engaged in "preaching abolitionism in a milder and a lighter form, and of not quite as dark a color" to Democrats. Douglas uses figurative language in alleging Trumbull's demagogic effort to "bring the old Democrats handcuffed, bound hand and foot into the abolition camp."

Douglas's accusation of abolitionist conspiracy is a "turning the tables" response to an opponent who had accused him of a proslavery conspiracy in the recent House Divided speech. Douglas's characterizations are demagogic because they present a misleading use of the facts: neither Lincoln nor Trumbull ever aligned with the abolitionist mission of advocating immediate, complete freedom of all slaves and granting them social and political equality with white people.

Douglas at Ottawa confronts his opponent with several indirect rhetorical questions. First, Douglas wants to know whether Lincoln "will stand by each article" of an 1854 abolitionist platform that Douglas alleged Lincoln had helped to write for a Springfield Republican meeting.[5] Other questions imply that Lincoln favored repealing the Fugitive Slave Law, that Lincoln sought to disallow new slave states regardless of residents of a new state or territory having decided to permit slavery (one possible outcome of Douglas's doctrine of popular sovereignty), that Lincoln sought to ban slavery in the District of Columbia, that Lincoln wanted to prohibit interstate slave trading, and that Lincoln opposed annexing territory without first banning slavery there.

After making his accusations, Douglas describes how Lincoln's life and his had intersected in their young adulthood, and Douglas says that now he "means nothing personally disrespectful or unkind to that gentleman." Douglas praises Lincoln before he became a politician, then belittles him as a financially irresponsible Illinois state legislator and unpatriotic congressman for opposing the Mexican War. Douglas then devotes the majority of his opening speech to complaints about the House Divided speech.

Douglas contends that Lincoln advocates a uniform, national antislavery policy, suggesting that Lincoln was willing to sacrifice the Union for that purpose. Douglas also asserts that Lincoln declares war on the Supreme Court for its *Dred Scott* decision. Douglas inaccurately maintains that Lincoln advocates social and political equality between white people and black people, emphasizing that such a policy would result in sectional strife and civil war. Douglas's opening speech defining Lincoln as an abolitionist appeals to the biases of an audience in a decidedly negrophobic northern state.

Lincoln divides his single speech at Ottawa about equally between refuting most of Douglas's accusations and taking the offense with counter accusations. Throughout this speech Lincoln directly or indirectly critiques the ethics of Douglas's rhetoric. Lincoln rejects Douglas's charge that he was connected to an 1854 Illinois Republican abolitionist platform. Initially Lincoln makes light of Douglas's criticism: "When a man hears himself misrepresented just a little, why, it rather provokes him, at least so I find it with me, but when he finds the misrepresentations very gross, why it sometimes amuses him."

Lincoln denies that Trumbull and he have worked together to serve in the Senate simultaneously: "Judge Douglas cannot prove that because it is not true, nor nothing like it. I have no doubt he is conscientious in saying so." Lincoln's use of the word *conscientious* is sarcastic, for Douglas in his earlier Springfield speech had referred to Lincoln as *conscientious*—sincere but wrong; Lincoln was now saying Douglas was both insincere and wrong.

Lincoln accuses Douglas of fabrications: "Anything that argues me into his idea of perfect social and political equality with the Negro, is but a specious and fantastic arrangement of words, by which a man can prove a horse chestnut to be a chestnut horse." For emphasis Lincoln then asserts that he does not seek "to introduce political and social equality between the white and black races," as he said at other times beginning with the Peoria speech. He advocates only "natural rights" for black people according to the Declaration of Independence. Next Lincoln denies Douglas's long-repeated accusation that he withheld support for US soldiers during the Mexican War, explaining that he supported the soldiers as much as Douglas did and that the historical record verifies it. Then, in a short, humorous passage, Lincoln dismisses Douglas's accusation that he had been a saloon keeper.

Defending his House Divided speech, Lincoln acknowledges that local institutions "spring" from geographical variations and that such diversity helps to strengthen the nation, but slavery has been and is divisive, so he is justified in arguing that such division ultimately threatens the nation. In his lawyerly mode he first agrees with Douglas that slavery has existed in some states and not in others because the founders intended to prevent slavery in new territories as a measure toward its "ultimate extinction." Lately, however, Douglas and others have abandoned the founders' intention in favor of "*the perpetuity and nationalization of slavery.*"[6] Thus, Lincoln holds firm to the proposition that slavery will either be restored to the status established by the founders or be nationalized. Lincoln briefly argues that because of *Dred Scott*, popular sovereignty allows territorial residents to have slaves. Lincoln repeats his position in the House Divided speech that "there was a tendency, if not a conspiracy" to nationalize slavery, although the existence of such "pre-concert" cannot be known for sure.

At this point the speech shifts from defense to offense, and the target is Douglas's integrity. At first continuing the light approach, Lincoln says Douglas's description of him as a "kind, amiable, and intelligent gentleman" in Douglas's Chicago speech (of July 9) led Lincoln to be distracted by the flattery and to believe his opponent's accusations derived from an honest misinterpretation of the House Divided speech. "As the Judge so flattered me, I could not make up my mind that he meant to deal unfairly with me, so I went to work to show him that he misunderstood the whole scope of my speech, and that I really never intended to set the people at war with one another."

Lincoln says that in a subsequent speech at Springfield, he denied an intention to interfere with slavery in the South, but Douglas claimed Lincoln would dissolve the Union if he could not end slavery in all the states. Labeling this deliberate distortion "the horse-chestnut style of argument" (calling a horse chestnut a chestnut-colored horse), Lincoln sarcastically says, "Now I don't think that was exactly the way to treat a kind, amiable, intelligent gentleman."

Lincoln casts Douglas as a political pawn and protests his personal attacks, insisting that in the alleged Democratic proslavery conspiracy, Douglas "was used by conspirators, and was not a leader of them." Lincoln repeats the qualification he made in the House Divided speech that he cannot prove conspiracy but believes it took place and challenges Douglas to point out errors of fact and reasoning: "If I have brought forward anything not a fact, if he will point it out, it will not even ruffle me to take it back. But if he will not point out anything erroneous in the evidence, is it not rather for him to show, by a comparison of the evidence that I have reasoned falsely, than to call the 'kind, amiable, intelligent gentleman,' a liar?"

Lincoln charges Douglas with hypocrisy for claiming popular sovereignty was neutral on slavery extension while he maneuvered in the Senate to ensure that the 1854 Nebraska bill was proslavery. Douglas and other proponents of the Nebraska bill had rejected an amendment to it that would have prohibited slavery from being introduced into that territory. Lincoln maintains that the rejection was a deliberate "niche" to prepare for *Dred Scott* and its sanction of slavery extension. Lincoln bristles, "And now, I say again, if this was not the reason, it will avail the Judge much more calmly and good-humoredly to point out to these people what that other reason was for voting the amendment down, than, swelling himself up, to vociferate that he may be provoked to call somebody a liar."[7] Lincoln says Douglas's role in this matter verifies his culpability in the Democratic proslavery conspiracy.

Another fact of the Nebraska bill that Lincoln says Douglas put there with ulterior motive was stipulating that the bill's purpose applied to both territories and states. Lincoln says he was at first puzzled why legislation designed to apply to territories would be written also to apply to states but that he finally realized Douglas wanted to prepare the way for a second *Dred Scott* decision that states could not prohibit slavery. If there is some other reason, says Lincoln, Douglas should reveal it rather than call him a liar. Clearly offended by Douglas's insinuation of Lincoln's character failure and delay in responding to the conspiracy charge, Lincoln criticizes Douglas's excuse for not responding sooner to that charge.

Lincoln accelerates his criticism that Douglas's political activity lacks moral underpinning. First, Lincoln attempts to turn the tables on Douglas by demonstrating that Douglas is the one with "the deep corruption of the heart he has thought fit to ascribe to me." Lincoln argues that Douglas is hypocritical for criticizing Lincoln's accusation of a conspiracy to nationalize slavery while Douglas has criticized the Washington *Union* and the authors of the Lecompton Constitution for the same thing. Second, Lincoln contends that Douglas is conducting a campaign to nationalize slavery by preparing the public mind to accept that eventuality. Lincoln reasons from the premise that "he who molds public sentiment, goes deeper than he who enacts statutes or pronounces decisions. He makes statutes and decisions possible or impossible to be executed."[8] Douglas's influence in his party is so strong, says Lincoln, that many would acquiesce in whatever position Douglas takes, including the unquestioned acceptance of *Dred Scott* as if it were a divine decree ("Thus saith the Lord"). In Lincoln's view, Douglas will accept the next *Dred Scott* decision (allowing slavery into free states), despite its contradiction of Jeffersonian principles.

Lincoln continues to hammer Douglas for hypocrisy. Douglas had complained that Lincoln does not accept *Dred Scott*. In retaliation, Lincoln explains that years ago in Illinois, Douglas had collaborated in "adding five new Judges to break down four old ones" on that state's Supreme Court because Douglas disagreed with one of its decisions. Douglas became one of the five new judges. Lincoln ends this section with hyperbolic figurative language that expresses contempt for Douglas's adherence to *Dred Scott* (the denial of disrespect seems disingenuous):

> Like some obstinate animal (I mean no disrespect,) that will hang on when he has once got his teeth fixed, you may cut off a leg, or you may tear away an arm, still he will not relax his hold. And so I may point out to the Judge, and say that he is bespattered all over, from the beginning of his political life to the present time, with attacks upon judicial decisions—I may cut off limb after limb of his public record, and strive to wrench him from a single dictum of the Court—yet I cannot divert him from it. He hangs to the last, to the *Dred Scott* decision.[9]

The single-paragraph conclusion predicts the harm Douglas's moral indifference toward slavery will have by undercutting the freedom and equality principle of the founders as expressed in the Declaration of Independence. Lincoln cites Henry Clay's observation of the possibility that "a class of men" might attempt such a political deviation, and Lincoln says he considers Douglas to be such a person. This passage is eloquent owing to its moral argumentation developed with rational and emotional appeals, reprising Clay's figurative language: "Judge Douglas is going back to the era of our Revolution, and to the extent of his ability, muzzling the cannon which thunders its annual joyous return. When he invites any people willing to have slavery, to establish it, he is blowing out the moral lights around us. When he says he 'cares not whether slavery is voted down or voted up,'—that it is a sacred right of self-government—he is in my judgment penetrating the human soul and eradicating the light of reason and the love of liberty in this American people."[10]

Douglas's rejoinder at Ottawa cites Lincoln's failure to discuss the accusation that he collaborated in writing the 1854 abolitionist platform at Springfield. Michael Burlingame explains that Lincoln "did not recognize Douglas's mistake in attributing to the Springfield Republicans of 1854 the radicalism of the Aurora Republicans [in northern Illinois], [so] he failed to call attention to it."[11] Rodney O. Davis points out that within two days following the debate, Douglas's error was detected and that throughout the remainder of the race, the Republican press repeatedly harped on "Douglas's unfairness and misrepresentation of Lincoln and Republicans at the least, and his complicity in the use of forged documents at the most."[12] Douglas rightly points out that Lincoln did not respond to some of the questions asked in the opening speech, and Douglas questions whether Lincoln's positions truly reflected the Illinois Republican platform and whether his party should trust him. Douglas's rejoinder upset Lincoln so much that he had to be physically restrained. Douglas says he will not charge Lincoln with "moral turpitude" and will not waste time trying to refute his Democratic conspiracy accusation because Lincoln admits "he does not know [it] to be true."[13]

Questioning Douglas in the Second Debate (Freeport)

Lincoln traveled by train on the morning of August 27 to arrive at Freeport for the second debate. Freeport, located 140 miles west of Chicago and near Wisconsin, had a population of 5,000 and was a Republican stronghold. The audience for the second debate was estimated at 15,000. Lincoln opened and closed the second debate. His advisors had urged him to be more aggressive at Freeport. Despite Lincoln's full speaking schedule in the week between debates, his opening speech at Freeport was so well designed that it suggests he wrote substantial portions of it and memorized them, beginning with answers to Douglas's Ottawa questions, then asking "turnabout is fair play" questions of Douglas and criticizing him for inadequate refutation of Lincoln's Democratic conspiracy accusation.

Lincoln asserts that he is bound by his party's platform, will take responsibility for anything he says beyond that policy, then turns to the questions Douglas posed in the first debate. Lincoln had been cautious in not giving impromptu answers at Ottawa, preferring instead to have time to compose thoughtful responses. To each question Lincoln gives a one-sentence answer. He is not pledged to repealing the Fugitive Slave Law, nor to opposing the admission of more slave states, nor to the admission of a new state with a constitution written by its citizens, nor to abolishing slavery in the District of Columbia, nor to opposing the "prohibition of the slave trade between the different states," nor to opposing the "honest acquisition of territory." Rather, he is pledged to "the right and duty of Congress to prohibit slavery in all the United States territories."

Lincoln says Douglas has not asked for any explanations but that he will offer some, implying a commitment to rhetorical integrity. Accordingly, Lincoln says the Fugitive Slave Law could have been better written to prevent certain objections to it, but he would not propose revision now, to avoid further agitation. He admits he would be "sorry" to have to vote on whether to admit a new slave state. In such a case he hopes slavery would have been prohibited before a state constitution would be written. He would support abolishing slavery in the District of Columbia if that process would be gradual, would reflect the will of most residents there, and would compensate the "unwilling owners" of slaves. He admits he has not given much thought to abolishing the slave trade between states, but if Congress would so act, he hopes such legislation would include provisions like those he has stipulated for abolishing slavery in the District of Columbia. He emphasizes that he has formerly explained his opposition to allowing slavery into the territories and can now add nothing. He ends this section by asserting that he holds firm positions that would not change from one place to another.

Taking the offensive, Lincoln next asks four one-sentence questions of his opponent. Would Douglas vote to admit Kansas as a state prior to having the required 93,000 population, as required in the English bill? Can residents of a territory legally "exclude slavery from its limits prior to the formation of a state constitution?" Would Douglas accept a Supreme Court ruling that prevents states from excluding slavery? Would Douglas "favor" adding territory regardless of the slavery question? Douglas had answered the second question prior to the debates, but Lincoln wanted that answer repeated and published so a wider audience could see it. Douglas's affirmative answer would alienate many southern Democrats.

Lincoln asserts that Douglas was in error in attributing the 1854 Illinois abolitionist resolutions to Trumbull and him. Lincoln says that at Ottawa he did not know that those resolutions originated in some place other than Springfield. He says regardless of the site of origin, he has no more responsibility for them than if they had been "a set of resolutions passed in the moon." Lincoln contrasts his conspiracy accusation against Douglas's abolitionist accusation. Lincoln allows that his accusation of Douglas's conspiracy with other Democrats to extend slavery was not based on fact but on belief—in contrast to Douglas's claim that Lincoln's participation in abolitionist politics was a fact: "Judge Douglas did not make his statement upon that occasion as matters that he believed to be true, but he stated them roundly as *being true*, in such form as to pledge his veracity for their truth."

Then Lincoln pounces on Douglas's demagogic rhetoric, delivering a blistering attack on his lack of integrity:

> When the whole matter turns out as it does, and when we consider who Judge Douglas is—that he is a distinguished senator of the United States— that he has served nearly twelve years as such—that his character is not at all limited as an ordinary senator of the United States, but that his name has become of world-wide renown—it is *most extraordinary* that he should go so far [as to] forget all the suggestions of justice to an adversary, or of prudence to himself, as to venture upon the assertion of that which the slightest investigation would have shown him to be wholly false.[14]

Lincoln twists the blade by observing the irony that Douglas has always "charged falsehood upon his adversaries."

Lincoln continues to assault Douglas's moral character. Lincoln first notes that when Douglas falsely accuses Lincoln of something, Douglas cleverly says Lincoln is "conscientious" in holding such an allegedly wrong position. Lincoln accuses Douglas of chicanery in shaping the Kansas-Nebraska Act. Lincoln repeats the criticism he gave at Ottawa that Douglas and others were hypocrites for claiming to want a bill that would allow territorial residents to decide for or against slavery in establishing a state constitution but rejecting the Chase amendment that would have given the territorial legislature the authority to prohibit slavery if it so chose. Lincoln asserts that the rejection created a "niche" for a second proslavery *Dred Scott* decision. In getting into the weeds of the Senate's legislative process concerning the Chase amendment, Lincoln attempts to bolster his conspiracy charge against Douglas and weaken his credibility.[15] Lincoln finishes his opening speech by claiming he presents the accusation of Democratic proslavery conspiracy ethically: "I have only arrayed the evidence tending to prove [Democratic proslavery conspiracy], and presented it to the understanding of others, saying what I think it proves, but giving you the means of judging whether it proves it or not."

When Douglas rose to speak, a melon hit him on the shoulder, but he was undeterred in his efforts to control the narrative, complimenting himself on getting Lincoln to answer questions avoided at Ottawa. Douglas says he will first give direct answers to the questions Lincoln has just asked before "reviewing" the answers Lincoln has given to Douglas's questions. Lincoln had left his written questions on the podium at Freeport, and Douglas read each one aloud before answering it. History shows that Douglas's answer to the second question as to whether residents have any lawful means of excluding slavery before creating a state constitution was the most significant and became known as the Freeport Doctrine.

Douglas was annoyed at the second question because he knew Lincoln was forcing him to repeat a previously given answer, which would be widely read in print and prove divisive to the Democratic Party. Douglas complains that Lincoln is overreaching by making him repeat the position that Lincoln heard him give "all over the state in 1854, 1855, and 1856, and Lincoln has no excuse for pretending to be in doubt as to my position on that question." Douglas's answer (again, the Freeport Doctrine) is that people can exclude or include slavery through local laws and local enforcement, and he implies that credit is due him for making this measure of self-government possible through congressional legislation that he shaped: "Hence, no matter what the decision of the Supreme Court may be on that abstract question, still the right of the people to make a slave territory or a free territory is perfect and complete under the Nebraska bill."[16]

Douglas concludes his answers with demagogic techniques. First, he denigrates Lincoln's intellect: "He racked his brain so much in devising these four questions that he exhausted himself, and had not strength enough to invent the others." For Lincoln to "invent" additional questions, says Douglas, he would have to consult with his abolitionist advisors, including Frederick Douglass. Douglas says the last time he was in Freeport he saw "Fred" Douglass riding in a carriage next to a white woman while the carriage owner, a white man, was driving it. Douglas race-baits: "If you Black Republicans think that the Negro ought to be on a social equality with your wives and daughters and ride in a carriage with your wife, whilst you drive the team, you have a perfect right to do so." Douglas's race-baiting in this speech includes his use of the term *Black Republicans* twenty-nine times. Often someone in the audience responds, "White, white, white."

Douglas disputes Lincoln's denial that he had anything to do with the 1854 Illinois Republican platform as published in the Springfield *Illinois State Register*. Douglas says Lincoln's "ecstasies over the mistake I made in stating the place where it was done" have distracted him from the significance of that platform. Douglas insists that the "spot" where the 1854 Republican resolutions were written is immaterial because they reflected the unwavering abolitionist "creed" of the Illinois Republican Party from its inception. Douglas insinuates that Lincoln is as misguided to quarrel over the "spot" where the 1854 published resolutions originated as he was over the "spot" where hostilities began in the Mexican War. (Douglas often took a Mexican War "spot" swipe at Lincoln during the campaign.) Douglas says when he gets to Springfield he will further investigate the place of origination of the 1854 published resolutions.

At this point Douglas repeats criticism of the House Divided speech, calling Lincoln's conspiracy accusation "an infamous lie." Using a stretched "turnabout is fair play" gambit, Douglas accuses Lincoln of "trying to protect himself in this charge, because I made a charge against the Washington *Union.*" Douglas says he condemned that paper because it "advocated a revolutionary doctrine, by declaring that the free states had not the right to prohibit slavery within their own limits." Douglas explains that the owner of the Washington *Union,* Cornelius Wendell, who had lost his job as the printer of "the Black Republican House of Representatives," bought that paper as a Democratic organ but now uses it to support Lincoln's candidacy. These circumstances lead Douglas to argue that "Mr. Lincoln therefore considers any attack upon Wendell and his corrupt gang as a personal attack upon him. This only proves what I have charged that there is an alliance between Lincoln and his supporters and the federal officeholders of this state, and presidential aspirants out of it, to break me down at home." Douglas concludes by claiming his dispute with President Buchanan, a fellow Democrat, has "passed away." Douglas is confident that the president and he share the position that "hereafter all state constitutions ought to be submitted to the people before the admission of the state into the Union." Douglas claims that Lincoln seeks to defeat him by dividing the Democratic Party.

Lincoln's Freeport rejoinder is mostly refutation but ends with accusation. In the refutation section Lincoln makes it clear that he believes accuracy and honesty are important in political discourse. He acknowledges that as Republican groups formed in different parts of Illinois, their resolutions varied; but since the 1856 state-wide party was formed, Republicans have "agreed on a common platform." Lincoln assures the audience that he is not committed to any "secret purposes or pledges." Douglas, says Lincoln, most fears Republican unity. Lincoln commits also to rhetorical integrity: "And if I should never be elected to any office, I trust I may go down with no stain of falsehood upon my reputation—notwithstanding the hard opinions Judge Douglas chooses to entertain of me." Lincoln complains that he has so repeatedly had to correct Douglas's distortions of the House Divided speech that "I almost turn with disgust from the discussion—from the repetition of an answer to it." Lincoln contends that Douglas's debate rhetoric reflects his effort to regain status within his Democratic Party. Lincoln suspected that Douglas was playing a "double game" of criticizing the Buchanan administration for supporting the proslavery Lecompton Constitution while at other times maintaining that his rift with the Buchanan administration was healed.[17]

Stumping prior to the Third Debate

During the three weeks before the third debate (Jonesboro), Douglas and Lincoln stumped central Illinois with particular interest in soliciting votes from the tens of thousands of former Whigs who in the presidential election of 1856 had voted for former President Millard Fillmore, the American Party candidate. Zigzagging his way through central Illinois and southward toward Jonesboro in far southern Illinois, Lincoln spoke, successively, at El Paso, Peoria, Tremont, Carlinville, Clinton, Bloomington, Monticello, Mattoon, Paris, Hillsboro, Alton, Edwardsville, Highland, and Greenville. Newspaper reports on these speeches vary in length and amount of text attributed to Lincoln.

In these stump speeches Lincoln repeated his main positions, including refutation of Douglas's critique of the House Divided speech, and Lincoln expanded his criticism of popular sovereignty and denial that he favored social and political equality between white people and black people. At Carlinville Lincoln gave an economic argument against extending slavery: "Sustain these men [Buchanan and others who would allow slavery extension] and Negro equality will be abundant, as every white laborer will have occasion to regret when he is elbowed from his plow or his anvil by slave niggers. . . . Is it not rather our duty to make labor more respectable by preventing all black competition, especially in the territories?"[18] Lincoln avers that an advantage of preventing slavery extension is that it also prevents mixing races.

At Clinton, where Douglas preceded him, Lincoln denied Douglas's accusation that Republicans favor interracial marriage and all other social and political equality. Lincoln said Douglas knows he "misrepresents" Republicans and does so only to gain votes. Lincoln cited figures from the 1850 US census that reveal the South had 348,000 "mulattoes," "all of home production," compared to fewer than 60,000 in all the free states, with many of them "imported from the South."[19] At Clinton Lincoln cited the popular sovereignty provision in the 1854 Kansas-Nebraska Act as the central cause of increased slavery agitation. At Bloomington Lincoln rejected Douglas's claim of inventing popular sovereignty, explaining that self-government was a central idea in the Declaration of Independence. Lincoln protested that Douglas's definition of popular sovereignty was that territorial residents should have "the right to have slaves if they want them, but not the right *not* to have them if they don't want them." At Paris Lincoln said Douglas perverted the concept of self-government that US Senator Lewis Cass had earlier presented.[20]

Lincoln delivered his Edwardsville speech just four days before the third debate, and its 1,850-word text, published by the Alton *Weekly Courier*, is the longest account of a stump speech by Lincoln in this series. At Edwardsville Lincoln gave a lengthy criticism of Douglas's interpretation of popular sovereignty. Accordingly, Lincoln quoted the language in the Declaration of Independence asserting that governments are formed to ensure a people's natural rights, with such governments *"deriving their just powers from the consent of the governed."* Lincoln again contrasted this principle with Douglas's notion that self-government means white people can beat slaves. Lincoln explains that Republicans consider slavery "a moral, social, and political wrong," while

Democrats do not. He says he will not go so far as to assert that Democrats consider slavery "*right*" in these areas, but his opinion is that the last five years suggest such a "maxim." Douglas, he says, has been responsible for "this notion of utter indifference whether slavery or freedom shall outrun in the race of empire across the Pacific—every measure, I say, up to the *Dred Scott* decision, where, it seems to me, the idea is boldly suggested that slavery is *better* than freedom."

Republicans regard slavery as "an unqualified evil to the Negro, to the white man, to the soil, and to the state" but will adhere to its protection as guaranteed by the Constitution. Otherwise, Republicans will use "every constitutional method to prevent the evil from becoming larger and involving more Negroes, more white men, more soil, and more states in its deplorable consequences." Republicans seek to place slavery in "the public mind" and "rest in the belief that it is in the course of ultimate peaceable extinction, in God's own good time."[21] Lincoln had often used the phrase "ultimate extinction" but may have added "peaceable" because of Douglas's accusation that Lincoln preferred disunion and civil war rather than allow the extension of slavery. Citing Henry Clay, Lincoln warned that "among the white races of the world anyone might properly be enslaved by any other which had made greater advances in civilization. And, if this rule applies to nations there is no reason why it should not apply to individuals; and it might easily be proved that the wisest man in the world could rightfully reduce all other men and women to bondage."[22]

Lincoln claimed that Douglas's rhetoric would lead to acceptance of another *Dred Scott* decision declaring it illegal to exclude slavery from free states, and that condition would jeopardize liberty for all Americans. Lincoln says the "bulwark" of American freedom is not its military, which tyranny can use to overcome liberty. The true source of liberty is spiritual: "Our reliance is in the *love of liberty* which God has planted in our bosoms." The way to protect liberty is to sustain this spirit through vigilant action. The implicit moral message is clear—political action is needed to prevent the next *Dred Scott* decision that would nationalize slavery, and voting for the Republican Party will sustain liberty for all into the future:

> Our defense is in the preservation of the spirit which prizes liberty as the heritage of all men, in all lands, everywhere. Destroy this spirit, and you have planted the seeds of despotism around your own doors. Familiarize yourselves with the chains of bondage, and you are preparing your own limbs to wear them. Accustomed to trample on the rights of those around you, you have lost the genius of your own independence, and become the fit subjects of the first cunning tyrant who rises. And let me tell you, all these things are prepared for you with the logic of history, if the elections

shall promise that the next *Dred Scott* decision and all future decisions will be quietly acquiesced in by the people.[23]

Pressing Douglas and Proclaiming Southern Roots in the Third Debate (Jonesboro)

Jonesboro is in far southern Illinois, known as Little Egypt or just Egypt, and only thirty-six miles north of Cairo, Illinois, which is immediately north of the confluence of the Ohio and Mississippi rivers and Kentucky. Many families in southern Illinois had come from the slave states of Virginia, Tennessee, and Kentucky. Jonesboro is about ten miles east of Missouri, also a slave state. Many southern Illinoisans were pro-Buchanan Democrats. Southern Illinois has been far less prosperous, then and now, than central and northern Illinois. In 1858 Jonesboro was a backward village of eight hundred, and the railroad had only recently reached this area. The Jonesboro debate audience at approximately 1,400 was the smallest of the series and mostly indifferent.

Douglas opened the debate with a speech that shows he was carefully targeting a pro-southern audience, for he stressed the Republican Party was a sectional organization advocating an abolitionist agenda "in hostility to the Southern states, Southern people, and Southern institutions." In this speech Douglas interprets history to support this thesis. He argues that the Compromise of 1850 assured "every state and every community the right to form and regulate their domestic institutions to suit themselves." After the passage of the 1854 Nebraska bill, Douglas claims that Lincoln and Trumbull abolitionized their respective parties: "In fact, every article in their creed related to this slavery question, and pointed to a Northern geographical party in hostility to the Southern states of this Union."

Douglas then attacks the House Divided speech as he did relentlessly throughout the campaign. He says Lincoln advocates sectional warfare as the only way to resolve the slavery question. Douglas also accuses Lincoln of making "war on the decision of the Supreme Court in the case known as the *Dred Scott* case." Douglas uses his typical race-baiting in denying that the equality language of the Declaration of Independence applied "to the Negro, the savage Indians, the Fejee, the Malay, or any other inferior or degraded race." Douglas argues that the founders also intended for the nation to allow slavery and freedom to coexist and saw no reason that arrangement could not continue indefinitely. Douglas explains that the reason he opposed the Lecompton Constitution was that it violated the principle of popular sovereignty.

Douglas closes by using self-government as a strategy to maintain unity in the Democratic Party: "President Buchanan declared in his annual message that hereafter the rule adopted in the Minnesota case, requiring a constitution to be submitted to the people, should be followed in all future cases. And if he stands by the recommendation, there will be no division in the Democratic Party on that principle in the future." With rational and emotional appeals to patriotism, Douglas argues that such a Democratic policy will preserve the Union as the founders intended.[24]

Lincoln began his single speech at Jonesboro calmly, with good humor, but ended it with outrage and a harsh personal attack. Lincoln's Jonesboro speech is a more aggressive critique of Douglas's policies, rhetorical methods, and moral character than in previous debates. Throughout this speech Lincoln expresses frustration with Douglas's distortions.

Beginning with a favorite legalistic technique of first conceding a point Douglas made and then disagreeing with something else, Lincoln says he aligns with Douglas's expressed desire for states to "govern their domestic relations, including that of slavery." Lincoln then faults Douglas for helping to change the founders' intention that slavery should end eventually to a policy that slavery "is to become national and perpetual." Lincoln voices frustration at being unable to deter Douglas from repeating the false claim that Trumbull and he conspired to abolitionize their political parties, with figurative language he had used in the 1854 Peoria address: "I don't know how to meet this kind of argument. I don't want to have a fight with Judge Douglas, and I have no way of making an argument up into the consistency of a corn-cob and stopping his mouth with it." A central question Lincoln keeps repeating without gaining a satisfactory answer is why Douglas insisted on repealing the Missouri Compromise when it had mitigated slavery agitation. Lincoln defends his House Divided prediction that the nation cannot continue indefinitely split between freedom and slavery because history shows increasing slavery agitation.

Lincoln accuses Douglas of using a double standard. Lincoln asks Douglas whether he disagrees that "it is not a good rule for either of us" to be held responsible for the opinions of their respective friends, and Douglas blurts, "I do not." Lincoln then asks why Douglas insists that Lincoln subscribes to others' platforms that he denies are his. With a "turning the tables" rationale, Lincoln prosecutes his lawyer rival: "At Freeport Judge Douglas occupied a large part of his time in producing resolutions and documents of various sorts, as I understood to make me somehow responsible for them; and I propose now doing a little of the same sort of thing for him." Lincoln reads spoken and written statements at length from Democratic politicians who were also friends of Douglas, and these statements made in 1850 clearly show these friends belonged to the antislavery contingent of the Democratic Party. Lincoln adds that he does not think Douglas "is responsible for this article; but he is quite as responsible for it, as I would be if one of my friends had said it. I think that is fair enough."

The last section refutes the answers Douglas gave to the four questions Lincoln had asked at Freeport. Lincoln disputes Douglas's Freeport Doctrine at length. Lincoln points to the contradiction that in 1856 Douglas said a Supreme Court decision should answer the question of slavery in new territories, but now Douglas says *Dred Scott* does not prevent local legislation and police action from excluding slavery. Additionally, Lincoln maintains that Douglas's argument for "police regulations is historically false," citing Dred Scott's being held as a slave in Minnesota "even against unfriendly legislation." Lincoln also argues that as a senator, Douglas would be sworn to uphold the Constitution and that Douglas cannot logically interpret the Constitution as both allowing and disallowing slavery in territories.[25] To emphasize his allegiance to the Constitution, Lincoln explains that "many of us" who reject slavery on principle are willing to yield to the Constitution's provision for the Fugitive Slave Law.

Lincoln presents a new, fifth question for Douglas, which relates to the Freeport Doctrine: "If the slaveholding citizens of a United States Territory should need and demand congressional legislation for the protection of their slave property in such territory, would you, as a member of Congress, vote for or against such legislation?" Lincoln considered it important enough to reserve it for near the end of his Jonesboro speech for impact, although Lincoln said his opponent could "answer at his leisure." Douglas could not answer the question yes or no without compromising his often-stated position of being indifferent to whether slavery in the territories is voted down or up. Burlingame explains the significance of the question: "Lyman Trumbull had advised him [Lincoln] to ask Douglas that question, anticipating that the Little Giant would 'answer promptly that Congress possessed no such power, or that he was opposed to its exercise if it did.' Prophetically, Trumbull argued that such a response 'would effectually use him up with the South and set the whole proslavery Democracy against him.'"[26]

Lincoln anticipates Douglas's attempt to dodge the question (procatalepsis) by citing his past ambivalence: Douglas "has spoken as if he did not know or think that the Supreme Court had decided that a territorial legislature cannot exclude slavery," and Lincoln does not know "whether he would say definitely that he does not understand they have so decided, or whether he would say he does understand that the Court have so decided." Douglas, says Lincoln, at Springfield and Freeport claimed the Supreme Court had not decided whether slavery could be excluded from a territory. Lincoln says that Douglas is "not mistaken" if he means that the Court has determined that it has "jurisdiction" on the status of slavery in the territories. Lincoln reasons that the *Dred Scott* decision prevents congressional and territorial legislation against slavery.[27]

Lincoln's conclusion at Jonesboro is an angry personal attack on his rival. Lincoln contrasts his integrity and manhood with Douglas's to a rural audience that valued the manliness associated with farm labor and hunting. Lincoln reads a newspaper report of a speech Douglas made at Joliet after the Freeport debate in which speech Douglas claimed that Lincoln had to be carried from the Ottawa debate because of a nervous breakdown, which then put him to bed for a week. Douglas alleged that Lincoln had to consult with "political physician" abolitionists to prescribe his strategy at Freeport. Lincoln says the only reason Douglas would say things that could be denied by several thousand people who attended the Ottawa debate is that "the Judge is crazy." Lincoln's remarks had prompted an immediate retort from Douglas, "Didn't they carry you off?" Lincoln insists that he was not carried off because he was "broken down" by Douglas's speech. In fact, some of Lincoln's jubilant supporters paraded him on their shoulders.

Twice Lincoln insinuates that alcohol fuels Douglas's demagogic rhetoric. Douglas's false statement that Lincoln "was laid up seven days" could be attributed to drinking, for "if Douglas had been in his sober senses he would not have risked that barefacedness in the presence of thousands of his own friends" who knew Lincoln was on the stump in several counties during that period. Lincoln also suggests that Douglas was "wholly out of his sober senses" for saying he forced Lincoln to appear at Jonesboro. Lincoln taunts Douglas by saying, "Let the Judge go on, and after he is done with his half hour, I want you all, if I can't go home myself, to let me stay and rot here; and if anything happens to the Judge, if I cannot carry him to the hotel and put him to bed, let me stay here and rot."

Lincoln's final remarks stress his manliness, his opponent's dishonesty, and his affiliation with southern Illinoisans. In denying Douglas's boast that he forced Lincoln down to "Egypt," Lincoln says, "Did the Judge talk of trotting me down to Egypt to scare me to death? I know this people better than he does. I was raised just a little east of here. I am a part of this people. But the Judge was raised further north, and perhaps has some horrid idea of what this people might be induced to do."[28] Jonesboro was closer to southwest Indiana, where Lincoln spent fourteen formative years, than to Springfield. It galls Lincoln that Douglas tries to portray him as "a poor, helpless, decrepit mouse, and that I can do nothing at all." Lincoln closes by calling Douglas a liar, as he did in his 1854 Peoria address, and vowing to "reserve all my fighting powers for necessary occasions."

Much of the criticism Lincoln has received for the Jonesboro speech relates to the conclusion. Lincoln must have felt that a "turnabout is fair play" display of raw criticism of a devious opponent was appropriate for an audience that was less educated, closer to the frontier cultural heritage of prizing masculinity, and thus likely to be more impressed by harsh verbal assaults than northern Illinois audiences.

Douglas opens his Jonesboro rejoinder by observing that his remarks about Lincoln's being carried off at Ottawa were "playful," adding that indeed if ever he allowed his friends to carry him on their shoulders when he was able to walk, "I am willing to be deemed crazy." Douglas dismisses the significance of Lincoln's claim that he is one of the people of the Jonesboro region by saying he does not know that a person's place of origin "has much to do with his political principles," explaining that the "worst abolitionists" he has known in Illinois are men who were born in the South and who profited from selling their slaves. Douglas implies deficiency in Lincoln's moral character by claiming he "slanders the graves of his father and mother, and breathes curses upon the institutions under which he was born, and his father and mother bred." In fact, one reason Lincoln's parents left Kentucky for Indiana was to get away from slavery.

Douglas continues to argue that Republicans' platforms throughout time and place in Illinois are abolitionist despite their attempts to conceal the truth by shaping their messages differently in northern, central, and southern Illinois. Douglas continues to insist that Lincoln refuses to answer his questions, including the question of whether Lincoln would "vote to admit Kansas whenever the people applied with a constitution of their own making," despite Lincoln's statement that he would accept a new slave state if confronted with such a vote. Douglas quibbles with Lincoln's position that if he had to, he would vote to add a slave state, asking, "Why not give the vote admitting them cheerfully?" Douglas responds to Lincoln's new, fifth question about congressional protection for slavery in Kansas: "The Democratic Party have always stood by that great principle of non-interference and non-intervention by Congress with slavery in the states and territories alike, and I stand on that platform now."[29] Douglas concludes the rejoinder by repeating and defending his support for both *Dred Scott* and his Freeport Doctrine.

Only three days separated the third and fourth debates, and on the way to the fourth debate (Charleston), both Douglas and Lincoln stopped at Centralia, where the state fair was being held. Douglas spoke but not Lincoln. Douglas was less inhibited on the stump than on the debate platform. Burlingame reports that Douglas at Centralia was "evidently drunk," citing a newspaper account describing his speech there as a "'harangue' that . . . 'asked if his audience wished to eat with, ride with, go to church with, travel with, and in other ways bring Congo odor into their nostrils and to their senses.'"[30]

Reiterating Views on Racial Equality in the Fourth Debate (Charleston)

Charleston, the seat of Coles County, is ninety-five miles east and a little south of Springfield, and Lincoln practiced law there on the circuit. His father and stepmother had established their home in rural Coles County after leaving Indiana. Rodney O. Davis explains the political significance of this location: "Charleston was the first debate site to be located in the central region of the state where, after the collapse of the Whig Party, partisan divisions were least distinct, and where it was felt that the outcome of the senatorial campaign would be determined. . . . The county was also highly negrophobic: 94.9 percent of its citizens had voted in 1848 to ban African Americans from living in the state."[31] As Allen C. Guelzo explains, by the time of the fourth debate, these circumstances seemed auspicious for Douglas: "If anything, Douglas was moving appeals to the white racial fear further and further to the front of the campaign. Elect Lincoln to the Senate, Douglas warned, and he will move heaven and earth to abolish slavery in the South. When that happened, 'he would then give' the freed slaves 'citizenship, the right to vote, to hold office, to become legislators, jurors and judges and finally to marry white women.'"[32]

Lincoln's advisors encouraged him to respond directly to Douglas's race-baiting, but surely Lincoln thought that if he accepted this advice, he could do no more than repeat the disclaimer he had made for years that he rejected social/political equality between white people and black people. Lincoln's advisors also encouraged him to respond to Douglas's accusation that Lincoln was responsible for Senator Lyman Trumbull's criticism that Douglas in 1856 had killed a bill proposed by Senator Robert Toombs that would have enabled Kansas residents to vote on a proposed state constitution. Republicans argued that Douglas's action against the Toombs bill exposed Douglas's insincerity as a proponent of popular sovereignty, and Republicans advised Lincoln to argue this point at Charleston because citizens there were especially interested in this matter. In accepting his advisors' suggestion, Lincoln at Charleston demonstrated his ability to accommodate a particular audience.

The first part of Lincoln's opening speech at Charleston is a 612-word repetition of the denial that he favors civil rights for free black people. He had made that denial in his Peoria speech and in the Ottawa debate. (James Oakes explains that Lincoln's expressed rejection of black citizenship was for political expediency of the moment, but at other times he implicitly supported it.[33]) In negrophobic Charleston, Lincoln also repeated his position of favoring natural rights for black people: "I say upon this occasion I do not perceive that because the white man is to have the superior position the Negro should be denied everything. I do not understand that because I do not want a Negro woman for a slave I must necessarily want her for a wife." Lincoln further remarked that he had never known "a man, woman or child who was in favor of" complete racial equality.

At Charleston Lincoln tries more than in previous speeches to shade the controversial subject of race with humor. He says the only person he has ever known to be "entirely satisfied" with the "correctness" of total equality is Colonel Richard M. Johnson, an old friend of Douglas, who had been Martin Van Buren's vice president and who had sired "mulattos."[34] Lincoln denies "apprehension" that any of his friends or he would "marry Negroes" if lawful.

As a mocking reference to Douglas's questions at Ottawa asking whether Lincoln was "pledged" to one thing or another, Lincoln says he offers "the most solemn pledge that I will to the very last stand by the law of this state, which forbids the marrying of white people with Negroes." Noting that such laws are the province of state legislatures, not Congress, Lincoln quips that since Douglas suffers such "constant horror" of impending total racial equality, he should be "kept at home" and in the state legislature to protect the Illinois black code.

The remainder of Lincoln's opening speech refutes Douglas's attack on Senator Lyman Trumbull for charging Douglas with obstructing the passage of Senator Robert Toombs's 1856 proposed bill that would have given Kansans the vote on a state constitution and thus on the question of slavery. Douglas had said he held Lincoln "responsible for the slanders" that Trumbull had allegedly made against him. The crux of that dispute was Douglas's accusation that Trumbull had maligned him with forged evidence but was vague about exactly what had been forged. Lincoln observes that the legislative process relating to the Toombs bill was public record. Lincoln's defense of Trumbull's critique of Douglas's role in the Toombs bill's fate appealed to local interest, and Lincoln may have thought it helped to offset local disapproval of his support for black people's natural rights that he expressed at the beginning of his opening Charleston speech.

Lincoln ends his discussion of Douglas's accusation that Trumbull had used forged evidence against him by emphasizing commitment to an honest, rational approach in determining the truth, asserting an honorable persona: "I repeat again, if he will point out which one is a forgery, I will carefully examine it, and if it proves that any one of them is really a forgery it will not be me who will hold it any longer. I have always wanted to deal with everyone I meet candidly and honestly. If I have made any assertion not warranted by facts, and it is pointed out to me, I will withdraw it cheerfully. But I do not choose to see Judge Trumbull calumniated."[35] Lincoln's Charleston opening speech is so well planned that he presented all his points in the allotted time, ending with a summary paragraph replete with rhetorical questions.

Douglas's Charleston speech addresses three subjects: first, Lincoln's discussion of Douglas and the Toombs bill; second, Lincoln's accusation of a Democratic conspiracy to spread slavery; and third, Trumbull's and Lincoln's alleged efforts to abolitionize their respective former parties. Douglas opens by denying that Lincoln's preceding speech has anything to do with the understood purpose of a debate speech concerning "questions of public policy relating to the welfare of this state or the Union." The only relevant matter in Lincoln's speech, Douglas says, was the denial of favoring social and political equality of white people and black people. Douglas claims he has been trying to get Lincoln to clarify this matter since the beginning of the campaign.

(In the first debate, at Ottawa, and as early as the Peoria speech, Lincoln had expressed his opposition to social and political equality between white people and black people.)

Douglas intersperses his discussion of various aspects of Lincoln's comments on Douglas's relationship to the Toombs bill with the complaint that Trumbull and Lincoln have slandered him, and he does not want to "waste much of my time with these personal matters . . . these petty, malicious assaults." Yet Douglas devotes almost half of his speech to this subject, and his extensive discussion includes so many quotations from sources that it hardly seems possible his preparation could have been limited exclusively to listening to Lincoln's opening speech. According to Guelzo, "what was curious was how unusually well-prepared Douglas was to produce just the right clippings at just the right debate. Something like this had happened at Jonesboro, when Douglas had easily produced exact recollections of what certain Illinois Democrats had said at certain times about abolition, all of which raises the tantalizing question of whether there was a Douglas mole in the Republican state committee."[36]

Douglas says his only dispute with the Senate committee dealing with the Toombs bill was over the population needed for Kansas to be admitted to the Union and that the Toombs bill needed no language specifically calling for a vote by Kansas residents because of the long-standing tradition that such a vote was implicit in the bill. Douglas complains that Trumbull has accused him of removing language from the bill authorizing Kansas elections, whereas in fact Douglas was responsible for the bill's language authorizing them. Douglas thus argues that if Lincoln will examine the public records, he will be able to verify Douglas's accusation that Trumbull's account of them is a fabrication. Douglas says that from the beginning of the debates he held a high regard for Lincoln's character, but now Lincoln has become "the endorser for these and other slanders against me."

Douglas argues that he has disproved Lincoln's House Divided conspiracy accusation but that Lincoln fails to correct its inaccuracy. Douglas says that at the time the Nebraska bill was passed, there had been no *Dred Scott* decision, "hence that it was impossible there could have been any such conspiracy between the Judges of the Supreme Court and the other parties involved." Further, Douglas says Lincoln's conspiracy accusation is false because Lincoln claimed Dred Scott's owners were Democrats, whereas Douglas had proved they were abolitionists. Another error Douglas says he has pointed out is that President Buchanan was not in Washington in the winter of 1854 when the Nebraska bill was being considered because he was then a US official serving in Great Britain. Lincoln, Douglas insists, "keeps repeating this charge of conspiracy" contrary to the public records. In an emotional appeal for sympathy, Douglas says he is willing for his entire public and private life to be examined and that he has experienced "perhaps more abuse than any man living of my age, or whoever did live, and having survived it all and still commanded your confidence." He says he trusts the public and will not defend himself further "against these assaults."

Douglas devotes the second half of his speech to repeating his accusation that Trumbull and Lincoln are collaborating to lead the Illinois Republican Party as an abolitionist organization, and Douglas accuses Trumbull of over-reaching ambition. Douglas repeats the argument he made in the first debate that in 1854 Trumbull and Lincoln reached an agreement in which Lincoln would try to succeed James Shields in the US Senate and Trumbull would enter the Senate when Douglas "would be accommodating enough either to die or resign for his benefit." But, says Douglas, Trumbull's ambition was so strong that he "compelled" Lincoln's "friends" to abandon him in favor of Trumbull.

Douglas's loaded language alleging Trumbull's villainy suggests that Lincoln's supporters would have good reason to be bitter: "The mean, low-lived, sneaking Trumbull succeeded by pleading all that was required by any party, in thrusting Lincoln aside and foisting himself, an excrescence from the rotten bowels of the Democracy into the United States Senate: and thus it has ever been, that an *honest* man makes a bad bargain when he conspires or contracts with rogues."[37] Douglas says the Republicans have unanimously nominated Lincoln for the Senate "in order to keep Lincoln's friends quiet about the bargain in which Trumbull cheated them four years ago." Thus, argues Douglas, Trumbull and Lincoln now conspire to "break down" Douglas by attacking his "public character." Douglas further contends that the Republicans change their name and message to appeal to audiences in three geographical sections of the state: "Their principles in the North are jet black, in the centre they are in color a decent mulatto, and in lower Egypt they are almost white." In a "turnabout is fair play" twist, Douglas wonders how the Illinois "abolition party" can expect to stand as a "house divided against itself."

Douglas concludes the speech with two of his favorite arguments appealing to negrophobia. First, he reminds the audience that *Dred Scott* ruled that the Constitution prohibited black citizenship. Thus, Lincoln's opposition to *Dred Scott* means he favors citizenship for "a race incapable of self-government, and for that reason ought not to be on an equality with white men." Douglas says he lacks time to develop this argument, because he has been forced to devote the earlier part of his speech to defend himself against "those gross slanders and falsehoods that Trumbull has invented against me and put in circulation." By keeping Trumbull's alleged abuse in focus, Douglas is clearly trying to appeal to former and current Democrats. Second, Douglas emphasizes his belief that the nation was founded "on the white basis. It was made by white men, for the benefit of white men." Lincoln's "house divided" argument is fallacious in Douglas's view: The founders established the US government as half free and half slave, and it can continue to prosper under that principle.

Two-thirds of Lincoln's Charleston rejoinder is a loosely organized refutation of various criticisms Douglas has made about Lincoln over the years, while the last third continues to attack Douglas for his vagueness about his role in the Toombs bill. Lincoln repeats his denial of supporting racial equality and "Negro citizenship" and that he changes his message from one part of the state to another. He challenges any "fair-minded" people who read his speeches to find any such differences. Next Lincoln responds to Douglas's position that the nation could endure half slave and half free. Lincoln's concise statement-of-facts section uses a series of rhetorical questions to point out that from 1850 to the present, every legislative action taken by the federal government designed to end slavery agitation has failed. The nation now faces the question of whether to prevent slavery from the territories, consistent with the founders' wishes, or "to surrender and let Judge Douglas and his friends have their way and plant slavery over all the states." Lincoln again rejects the accusation that Trumbull and he have abolitionized their respective former parties, and Lincoln says the only basis Douglas has cited for that accusation is an 1856 speech by a Democrat that Lincoln calls a "cock-and-bull" story.

As Lincoln proceeds, he accuses Douglas of unethical rhetoric. Lincoln denies that Trumbull broke a bargain with him, and Lincoln repeats his confidence in Trumbull's "veracity." Lincoln defends his criticism of Douglas: "I don't want to be unjustly accused of dealing illiberally or unfairly with an adversary, either in court, or in a political canvas, or anywhere else. I would despise myself if I supposed myself ready to deal less liberally with an adversary than I was willing to be treated myself."[38] Perhaps Lincoln was trying to compensate for the bitter personal attack on Douglas at the end of the third debate. Lincoln insinuates that Douglas deviates from principled rhetoric. For example, Douglas complains that Trumbull and Lincoln criticize him for his involvement in the Toombs bill two years ago, whereas Douglas continues inaccurately to criticize Lincoln for his alleged failure to support US forces in the Mexican War ten years ago: "the more respectable papers of his own party throughout the state have been compelled to take it back and acknowledge that it was a lie."

At this point Lincoln's temper flared, and he grabbed former Democratic Congressman Orlando B. Ficklin from his seat and forced him to come forward to verify that Lincoln never failed to vote in favor of supplies for the Army during the Mexican War, giving "all the votes that Ficklin or Douglas did, and perhaps more." So pressed, all Ficklin says is to admit that Lincoln had asserted that the Mexican War was needlessly and unconstitutionally started by the US president. Lincoln notes that Douglas had included the false accusation in the first debate.

Lincoln moves into the conclusion of his rejoinder, recounting how Douglas insinuated him into the dispute over Douglas's role in the Toombs bill. Lincoln asks the audience whether Douglas has effectively rebutted the evidence Lincoln has cited in support of Trumbull's criticism. In a series of rhetorical questions, Lincoln asks whether Douglas has proved that specific documents or passages from them are forgeries. Lincoln sarcastically asks whether the quotations from Douglas's own speech are forgeries. He asks how it is possible for an entire story to be considered false when each piece of it is true. Lincoln metaphorically characterizes Douglas's willful vagueness: "I take it these people [audience] have some sense: they see plainly that Judge Douglas is playing cuttlefish, a small species of fish that has no mode of defending itself when pursued except by throwing out a black fluid, which makes the water so dark the enemy cannot see it and thus escapes."

Finally, Lincoln examines particulars reported in the legislative process of the Toombs bill that point to fallacies in Douglas's argumentation. According to Lincoln, Douglas dodges Trumbull's accusation by calling him a liar instead of fully explaining his role in the Toombs bill episode. Lincoln uses examples to emphasize the red herring nature of Douglas's ad hominem complaint: "I assert that you (pointing to an individual), are here to-day, and you undertake to prove me a liar by showing that you were in Mattoon yesterday. I say you took your hat off your head, and you prove me a liar by putting it on your head. That is the whole force of Douglas's argument." Lincoln maintains that by withholding comment on the committee developing the Toombs bill as reported by others, Douglas makes himself look suspicious: "He [Douglas] stands in the attitude of an accused thief who has stolen goods in his possession, and when called to account, refuses to tell where he got them." Without Douglas's adequate testimony, Lincoln says he has "a right to infer that Judge Douglas understood it was the purpose of his party, in engineering that bill through, to make a [proslavery] Constitution and have Kansas come into the Union with that Constitution, without its being submitted to a vote of the people." Further, unless Douglas can refute the evidence against him, Lincoln argues that "it will not avail him at all that he swells himself up, takes on dignity, and calls people liars."

Lincoln ends by saying that Euclid's proposition of all angles in a triangle being equal to two right angles cannot be disproved by calling him a liar. Scholars have voiced the criticism of the debates that they sometimes were unclearly related to the question of what makes a good US senator, but despite its tedium, Lincoln's defense of Trumbull suggests that integrity and credibility were pertinent.

Conclusion

As the debates began, both rivals used the rational appeal of historical and legalistic arguments in advocating their solutions to slavery agitation: Douglas for popular sovereignty, Lincoln for the need to stop slavery extension and slavery itself by restoring the Missouri Compromise and adhering to the Constitution's implied intention of eventually ending slavery. Throughout the debates the rivals aimed to destroy one another's credibility. Both used arguments based on "turnabout is fair play" strategy that included personal attacks to diminish one another's ethical appeal. In the first debate Douglas argued that Lincoln and Trumbull were abolitionist conspirators. Douglas's accusation seemed to be retaliation for Lincoln's House Divided speech that charged Douglas with conspiracy to nationalize slavery. Just as Lincoln struggled to defend the House Divided speech, Douglas struggled to defend popular sovereignty, especially the Freeport Doctrine. Lincoln was forced to refute Douglas's wrongful argument that Lincoln's interpretation of the Declaration of Independence meant he advocated social/political equality between white people and black people, and that Lincoln was willing to risk disunion for that purpose.

Lincoln's responses to Douglas's provocative methods were versatile. Sometimes Lincoln used humor, and he always used logical, fact-based refutation before resorting to a personal attack out of exasperation. Lincoln was skillful in asking rhetorical and leading questions to get at the facts. Confident in his arguments, he frequently advised audiences to read his published speeches to verify his truthfulness.

In the first four debates, Lincoln introduced the moral argumentation that he first presented in the Peoria speech but did not emphasize it. Perhaps he was then too distracted by Douglas's demagogic methods to pursue that argumentation, or perhaps he was deliberately reserving it for impact in the later debates. In the sixth debate, at Quincy, Lincoln would say he regarded the debates as acts in a drama, and his fondness for the theater would have taught him the heightened importance of the last act. Also in his presentations at court, Lincoln often reserved his main points for the conclusion. The last three debates would give Lincoln the opportunity to assert his antislavery moral argumentation against an opponent who professed moral indifference to slavery.

Lincoln's rhetoric of the first four debates paradoxically includes the eloquence of a statesman and the personal criticism of a rhetorical wrestler. Of particular interest in the closing action of the debate drama would be how Lincoln would continue to respond to Douglas's demagoguery. Lincoln was capable of losing his temper in frustration with his crafty rival, as seen in the physical restraint Lincoln received at the end of the first debate, his scathing attack on Douglas at the end of the third debate, and the Ficklin episode of the fourth debate. Yet rationality and rhetorical ethics mattered to Lincoln and would be important as he finished the contest for credibility and votes.

Concluding the Senate Race and Gaining National Distinction (1858)

> I was aware, when it was first agreed that Judge
> Douglas and I were to have these seven joint
> discussions, that they were the successive acts of
> a drama . . . to be enacted not merely in the face of
> audiences like this, but in the face of the nation, and
> to some extent . . . in the face of the world; and I am
> anxious that they should be conducted with dignity
> and in the good temper which would be befitting
> the vast audience before which it was conducted.
> —Lincoln, the Sixth Debate, 1858

The epigraph reiterates Lincoln's ongoing desire for ethical political discourse. Nearly seven weeks passed from the first to the fifth debate, but the last three debates occurred in only nine days. The short time of the last debates added stress for Lincoln because he preferred to plan his speeches carefully, with practice writing whenever possible. The interim and post-debate stump speeches enabled the candidates to focus on the crucial Whig belt, in communities from the eastern Illinois border with the free state of Indiana to the western border with the slave state of Missouri. The last three debates moved from west-central to southwestern Illinois.

Those debates brought the rivals' respective solutions to slavery agitation and rhetorical methods into focus as never before. In the final debates, at Galesburg, Quincy, and Alton, the rivals disputed founding principles related to slavery, moral perspectives on slavery and related policies, and rhetorical methods. The next section suggests that Lincoln continued to use exploratory writing for private brainstorming as the campaign advanced.

Private Brainstorming between the Fourth and Fifth Debates

Between the fourth and fifth debates, both candidates continued with a rigorous schedule of stump speeches, mostly in west-central Illinois. None of Lincoln's texts for those speeches are extant. While the dates attributed to Lincoln's fragments are not entirely reliable, his fragments associated with this period offer clues to what he might have said on the stump or planned to say in the remaining debates. These fragments suggest he was anticipating arguments he might face and practicing their refutation (procatalepsis). A common subject of these fragments concerns religious perspective on the morality of slavery.[1]

Religious justification for slavery was widespread: "Proslavery theology, as part of a larger proslavery, political ideology, exerted a deep influence over sizable parts of the population, and not just in the South. Proslavery theology connected with a public steeped in religion by arguing that its beliefs were rooted in the Bible and the Judeo-Christian tradition. Lincoln did not underestimate the power of this theology."[2] In one fragment Lincoln asserts that Douglas and the proslavery southern press are unified in hoping to "subvert" the equality principle of the Declaration of Independence with religious/moral justification, that is, "to deny the equality of men, and to assert the natural, moral, and religious right of one class to enslave another."[3]

In another fragment Lincoln judges slavery to be un-Christian: "Suppose it is true that the Negro is inferior to the white, in the gifts of nature; is it not the exact reverse justice that the white should, for that reason, take from the Negro, any part of the little which has been given him? '*Give* to him that is needy' is the Christian rule of charity; but 'Take from him that is needy' is the rule of slavery." In other passages Lincoln sarcastically describes a religious rationalization for slavery, and it outrages him:

> The sum of proslavery theology seems to be this: "Slavery is not universally *right*, nor yet universally *wrong*; it is better for *some* people to be slaves; and, in such cases, it is the Will of God that they be such. . . . " But slavery is good for some people!!! As a *good* thing, slavery is strikingly peculiar, in this, that it is the only good thing which no man ever seeks the good of, *for himself*. Nonsense! Wolves devouring lambs, not because it is good for their own greedy maws, but because it [is] good for the lambs!!![4]

Lincoln tended to modulate the intensity of his antislavery feelings in public speeches.

Sites and Audiences of the
Final Three Debates

The fifth debate (October 7) was at Knox College in Galesburg, thirty-two miles east of the Mississippi River, and an abolitionist stronghold. Galesburg was also home to Lombard University (1853–1930), which was founded by the Universalist Church and originally named the Illinois Liberal Institute. Galesburg, population nearly 5,000 in 1858, was a crossroads of two railroads and a hub of the Underground Railroad. Small industry was beginning to augment Galesburg's agricultural economy. The town was more Republican than the surrounding area. At this debate the rivals faced the largest campaign audience, estimated at between 15,000 to 20,000, with many traveling there by rail.

Quincy, site of the sixth debate (October 13) and the seat of Adams County, is on the Mississippi River directly across from the then-slave state of Missouri and approximately 140 miles north of St. Louis. Both a river and railroad hub, Quincy, population 13,000, was the largest community of the debate sites, a Democratic stronghold, and a major depot of the Underground Railroad. The surrounding area held a large population of moderate voters. The Quincy audience was large but not quite so large as the one at Galesburg.

The final debate (October 15), at Alton, followed the Quincy debate by just two days. Alton is in Madison County on the Mississippi River across from Missouri, 115 miles downstream from Quincy and fifteen miles above St. Louis. Complacency held the audience to about 5,000, and only the Jonesboro debate had a smaller audience. The Madison County electorate was diverse, including old-line Whigs and German immigrants as well as both southern sympathizers and anti-Nebraska advocates. Twenty years earlier Alton was the site of the murder of Elijah Lovejoy, an abolitionist newspaper editor/publisher, and in 1858 anti-abolitionist feelings continued.

Disputing Founding Principles
Related to Slavery

Conflicting interpretations of the Declaration of Independence were a main reason for the candidates' differences on the moral aspect of slavery. In his opening speech at the fifth debate, at Galesburg, Douglas expounds on his position that the founders did not view white people and black people as equals and that the founders saw self-government as the principle that would answer the question of freedom or slavery in a particular location. He cites Thomas Jefferson as both author of the Declaration and slave owner, then asserts:

Every man who signed that instrument represented a slaveholding constituency. Recollect, also, that no one of them emancipated his slaves, much less put them on an equality with himself, after he signed the Declaration. . . . Now, do you believe . . . that every man who signed the Declaration of Independence declared the Negro his equal, and then was hypocrite enough to continue to hold him as a slave, in violation of what he believed to be the divine law? And yet when you say that the Declaration of Independence includes the Negro, you charge the signers of it with hypocrisy. I say to you, frankly, that in my opinion this government was made by our Fathers on the white basis.[5]

Douglas held firm to several related positions: that the answer to questions of whether black people should be slaves or freemen and citizens should be left to individual states, that the Compromise of 1850 applied the states' rights principle to the territories, and that the *Dred Scott* decision determined that slaves as property can be taken into territories, where local legislation and law enforcement will either sanction or disallow slavery.

Also in opening the fifth debate, Douglas rejects Lincoln's house-divided argument that the nation could not continue indefinitely half free and half slave, citing the conditions under which the nation was founded. Douglas says at the time of the constitutional convention, there were twelve slave states represented and one free state, arguing that if Lincoln had been there to proclaim that a nation half free and half slave could not endure, "would not the twelve slaveholding states have out-voted the one free state and, under his doctrine, have fastened slavery by an irrevocable constitutional provision upon every inch of the American Republic?" Douglas asks the rhetorical question of whether the North now as the "majority" section should "exercise power" that it would not have "submitted to" when it was in the minority. He thus concludes: "I say to you that there is but one path of peace in this republic, and that is to administer this government as our Fathers made it, divided into free and slave states, allowing each state to decide for itself whether it wants slavery or not."[6]

In his fifth debate speech, Lincoln denies that the "framers" of the Declaration of Independence did not intend its equality language to apply to black people. He argues that no US president or major member of Congress or other "living man" had ever made such a claim "until the necessities of the present policy of the Democratic Party, in regard to slavery, had to invent that affirmation." He says that Jefferson "trembled for his country, when he remembered that God was just."

Lincoln's closing speech of the sixth debate refutes Douglas's statement that the founders "made" the nation half free and half slave as an ideal condition. Lincoln says Douglas "assumes what is historically a falsehood." The founders, rather, had no choice because slavery was already well established and had to be accommodated. Lincoln cites the founders' goal of abolishing the slave trade as evidence of their intention to place slavery "in the course of ultimate extinction." He also cites the testimony of Congressman Preston Brooks of South Carolina that "no one expected the institution of slavery to last until this day and that the men who formed this government were wiser and better men than the men of these days."[7] Douglas, says Lincoln, does not approach slavery as the founders did but as an expediency to meet the increased demand for cotton resulting from the invention of the cotton gin. Lincoln dismisses the validity of Douglas's rhetoric: "Then what becomes of all his eloquence in behalf of the rights of states, which are assailed by no living man?"[8] Lincoln directly and metaphorically asserts his keystone principle of natural rights: "I agree with Judge Douglas that he [the Negro] is not my equal in many respects, certainly not in color—perhaps not in intellectual and moral endowments; but in the right to eat the bread without leave of anybody else which his own hand earns, he is my equal and the equal of Judge Douglas, and the equal of every other man."

In his opening speech of the last debate, Douglas contends that he has successfully "controverted" Lincoln's proposition that "the Declaration of Independence included and meant the Negroes as well as the white men, when it declared all men to be created equal." In that speech Douglas also expresses an attitude that seems to coincide with Lincoln's view that black people deserve sympathetic treatment but ends with qualifying language that appeals to negrophobia:

> But it does not follow, by any means, that merely because the Negro is not a citizen, and merely because he is not our equal, that therefore he should be a slave. On the contrary, it does follow that we ought to extend to the Negro race, and to all other dependent races, all the rights, all the privileges, and *all the immunities which they can exercise consistently with the safety of society* [emphasis mine]. Humanity requires that we should give them all these privileges. Christianity commands that we should extend those privileges to them.[9]

This attitude appears similar to Lincoln's except for the hedging of "consistently with the safety of society," which Douglas also expressed in the fifth debate. Douglas equivocated on natural rights by acknowledging black people's humanity but insinuating they are dangerous and stating that their rights and privileges should be limited for "the safety of society." Douglas poses the question of what the rights and privileges of black people should be and finds the answer in local self-government, using Illinois as an example: "We [Illinoisans] tried slavery, kept it up for twelve years, and finding that it was not profitable, we abolished it for that reason and became a free state. We adopted in its stead the policy that a Negro in this state shall not be a slave and shall not be a citizen. We have a right to adopt that policy." For clarity Douglas repeats that if each state would "mind its own business," peace will prevail throughout the nation. He concludes by asserting that the Republican Party represents the North, and it has become more politically powerful than the South. Now, he adds, "a few ambitious men may ride into power on a sectional hobby" to control the nation.

Also in his opening speech of the last debate, Douglas insists that the nation can endure half free and half slave by allowing "each locality" to decide for or against slavery, as he alleges the "framers of the Constitution" intended. Douglas repeats his argument that if Lincoln had presented the founders with the house-divided argument, they would have enshrined slavery in the Constitution and "on every foot of the American republic forever . . . in all the states whether they wanted it or not." Douglas says that at the founding, slavery prevailed in twelve of the thirteen states. Yet according to Rodney O. Davis, by the time of the federal Constitutional Convention in 1787, "slavery had been abolished outright in Vermont, Massachusetts, and New Hampshire, and provisions had been made for its gradual extinction in Pennsylvania, Rhode Island, and Connecticut."[10] Douglas's reference to the prevalence of slavery at the founding was not the full truth.

Lincoln in the seventh debate venerates the Declaration of Independence as "the charter of our liberties," as he had twice referred to it with this metaphor earlier in the campaign. He reads from his 1857 Dred Scott speech, without naming it, in which he states his view that the authors of the Declaration did not mean all men were entirely equal, but the founders were establishing "a standard maxim for free society which should be familiar to all: constantly looked to, constantly labored for, and even though never perfectly attained, constantly approximated and thereby constantly spreading and deepening its influence and augmenting the happiness and value of life to all people, of all colors, everywhere."[11] Lincoln reminds his audience that he has repeatedly voiced these beliefs and positions, and had them published so that people could better understand them.

Lincoln next observes that only in the last few years have some people argued that the equality language of the Declaration of Independence was not meant to include black people as "men" (human), and in demonstrating this proposition, he aligns himself with Henry Clay. Lincoln explains that the argument against black people as "men" originated only recently: "The first man who ever said it [black people are not human] was Chief Justice Taney in the *Dred Scott* case, and the next to him was our friend Stephen A. Douglas. And now it has become the catch-word of the entire [Democratic] Party. I would like to call upon his friends everywhere to consider how they have come in so short a time to view this matter in a way so entirely different from their former belief? To ask whether they are not being borne along by an irresistible current—whither, they know not?"[12]

Lincoln refutes a letter published in the *Chicago Times* after the fifth debate in which the writer, signing himself as "an Old Line Whig," claims that Henry Clay had not accepted black people as human. Acknowledging the likelihood of many old-line Whigs in the audience, Lincoln flatters them by saying that "they always had some sense" and reads two paragraphs from a Clay speech to show that Clay saw the equality language of the Declaration of Independence as stating "an abstract principle that all men are created equal, but that we cannot practically apply it in all cases." Lincoln explains that Clay was stating a guiding principle for organizing an original society. Lincoln reads a short passage from the same Clay speech that explicitly condemns slavery "as a great evil" and expresses Clay's argument of applying the equality principle: "If a state of nature existed and we were about to lay the foundations of society, no man would be more strongly opposed than I should be, to incorporating the institution of slavery among its elements."

Lincoln complains that when he applies Clay's interpretation of the Declaration of Independence to "new territories and societies," he is "vilified." In the following passage Lincoln insists that denying the Declaration's equality principle is a moral abuse leading to slavery nationally. Sentences in this passage repeat the simple grammatical subject and verb for emphasis (anaphora): "And when this new principle—this new proposition that no human being ever thought of three years ago,—is brought forward, *I combat* it as having an evil tendency, if not an evil design; I combat it as having a tendency to dehumanize the Negro—to take away from him the right of ever striving to be a man. I combat it as being one of the thousand things constantly done in these days to prepare the public mind to make property, and nothing but property of the *Negro in all the States of this Union.*"[13] Lincoln condemns the accusation that he seeks to "abolish slavery" where it exists as "a miserable perversion of what I have said." In his last speech of the debates, Douglas did not further comment on the Declaration of Independence.

Lincoln's final debate speech attacks Douglas's Nebraska bill as an incitement to ongoing slavery agitation, rather than a solution to it, as Douglas had claimed it would be. Douglas's Nebraska bill, Lincoln insists, failed to achieve its purpose in Kansas and was "a living, creeping lie from the time of its introduction." At this point Lincoln asserts his purpose of "arresting" slavery by preventing its spread to new territories, thereby placing it "where the public mind shall rest in the belief that it is in the course of ultimate extinction" as the founders had intended.

Lincoln contends that the Constitution's provision to stop the African slave trade twenty years into the future indicates the founders' intention of eliminating slavery gradually, and he points out that the Constitution's several oblique references to slaves as "persons held to service or labor" was deliberate so that after the passing of slavery "there should be nothing on the face of the great charter of liberty suggesting that such a thing as Negro slavery had ever existed among us."[14] Lincoln denounces as false Douglas's argument that the founders had intended to introduce "slavery as a rightful thing within itself." The founders' policy, Lincoln insists, is "the only wise policy—the only policy that we can ever safely continue upon—that will ever give us peace unless this dangerous element masters us all and becomes a national institution."

In a series of rhetorical questions, Lincoln asks why Douglas had to change the founders' policy. Their policy had not led to civil war, and neither will a return to that policy. Lincoln again rejects Douglas's insinuation that the house-divided metaphor means that Lincoln seeks to deny individual states the right to enact laws peculiar to their economic conditions, but slavery is a national, transcending matter. Individual states do not dispute one another's particular laws pertaining to their economies, but slavery provokes agitation among all states.

In his last speech of the debates, Douglas rejects Lincoln's claims that he is politically aligned with Clay and that slavery is the only issue that has threatened the stability of the Union. Douglas reminds the audience that Lincoln supported Taylor over Clay in the 1848 presidential contest. In fact, Douglas cites Lincoln's speech that a leading Whig claimed had "the effect of cutting Clay's throat." With additional hyperbole Douglas describes Lincoln as "the bitter and deadly enemy of Clay." Douglas blames the Wilmot Proviso and Lincoln's support of it for renewing slavery agitation at the end of the 1840s (the Wilmot Proviso proposed to prohibit slavery in the territories acquired from Mexico). Douglas says he has heard Lincoln "boast that he voted forty-two times for the Wilmot Proviso, and that he would have voted as many times more if he could." Douglas says the Democratic Party "rallied under Clay, then as you Whigs in nullification time [1832–33] rallied under the banner of old Jackson, forgetting party when the country was in danger, in order that we might have a country first and parties afterward." Douglas also cites the nullification crisis as a threat to the Union in order to refute Lincoln's claim that only slavery agitation has ever carried such a threat.

Douglas rejects Lincoln's argument that the founders had planned for the gradual, complete elimination of slavery from the Union. Douglas acknowledges that the founders did not establish slavery in all states, but he emphasizes that the founders intended "to guarantee forever to each state the right to do as it pleased on the slavery question" and that the nation can indefinitely "exist" with both "free and slave states." In referring to Lincoln's quote from Representative Preston Brooks of South Carolina that "our fathers then thought that probably slavery would be abolished by each state acting for itself before this time," Douglas contends that such an expectation does not really matter: "Suppose they did. Suppose they did not foresee what has occurred. Does that change the principles of our government? They did not probably foresee the telegraph that transmits intelligence by lightning, nor did they foresee the railroads that now form the bonds of union between the different states, or the thousand mechanical inventions that have elevated mankind." Douglas perhaps alludes to the invention of the cotton gin, which Lincoln sometimes cited as the reason for increased slavery in the South. Douglas insists that the founders established the states' rights of self-government, compatible with the Constitution, to "allow the people of each to apply to every new change of circumstances such remedy as they may see fit to improve their condition." This right, Douglas asserts, continues forever.[15]

Disputing Moral Perspectives on Slavery and Related Policies

In his only speech in the fifth debate, Lincoln addresses the failure of Douglas and his supporters to acknowledge the moral aspect of slavery, and he delineates his reasoning in plain language:

> Judge Douglas declares that if any community want slavery they have a right to have it. He can say that logically, if he says there is no wrong in slavery; but if you admit that there is a wrong in it, he cannot logically say that anybody has a right to a wrong. He insists that, upon the score of equality, the owners of slaves and owners of property—of horses and every other sort of property—should be alike and hold them alike in a new territory. That is perfectly logical, if the two species of property are alike and are equally founded in right. But if you admit that one of them is wrong, you cannot institute any equality between right and wrong.[16]

For emphasis and clarity, Lincoln restates his principles and applies them to political policy: Republicans seek to "arrest of the enlargement of that wrong," whereas Douglas and other Democrats take the opposite view.[17]

Near the end of his speech in the fifth debate, Lincoln faults Douglas for disregarding the moral aspect of slavery in the *Dred Scott* decision and its implications. Douglas, says Lincoln, maintains an absolute adherence to *Dred Scott* without considering "whether this opinion is right or wrong" and that such a position is conditioning the public to accept the next *Dred Scott* decision that will nationalize slavery. Lincoln cleverly attacks Douglas by suggesting that he is a proslavery dupe: "I do not charge that he means it so; but I call upon your minds to inquire, if you were going to get the best instrument you could, and then set it to work in the most ingenious way, to prepare the public mind for this movement, operating in the free states, where there is now an abhorrence of the institution of slavery, could you find an instrument so capable of doing it as Judge Douglas? Or one employed in so apt a way to do it?"[18] (A major section of Lincoln's 1859 Cincinnati speech satirically elaborates on Douglas as a proslavery asset.) Lincoln repeats Henry Clay's eloquent warning that those who would "repress all tendencies to liberty and ultimate emancipation" must first "blot out the moral lights around us—they must penetrate the human soul, and eradicate the light of reason and the love of liberty."

In his opening speech of the sixth debate, Lincoln explains that Republicans view slavery as a "disturbing" and "dangerous" element and as "a moral, a social, and a political wrong." Lincoln notes that Republican opposition to slavery is constrained by the Constitution. Thus Republicans will not "disturb" slavery where it exists, favoring gradual, compensated emancipation but will fight its spread. Lincoln affirms that Republicans will not act "as a mob" in opposing *Dred Scott* but will resist it "because we think it lays the foundation not merely for enlarging and spreading out what we consider an evil, but it lays the foundation for spreading that evil into the [free] states themselves."[19] Lincoln admonishes that any person in the Republican Party who is "impatient" with these principles is "misplaced, and ought to leave us."

Lincoln points out that Douglas, the leader of the Democratic Party, "has the high distinction, so far as I know, of never having said slavery is right or wrong. Almost everybody else says one or the other, but the Judge never does." Lincoln addresses Democrats dissatisfied with slavery and anticipates their reluctance to take action against it: "You say it must not be opposed in the free states, because slavery is not here; it must not be opposed in the slave states, because it is there; it must not be opposed in politics, because that will make a fuss; it must not be opposed in the pulpit, because it is not religion. Then where is the place to oppose it?"

Lincoln admits Douglas can logically be indifferent to slavery on the basis of equating slaves with "horse and hog property," and on that basis slaves could be taken into new territories, "but if you admit that it [slavery] is wrong, he cannot logically say that anybody has a right to do wrong . . . [;] but if the one is property, held rightfully, and the other is wrong, then there is no equality between the right and wrong; so that, turn it in any way you can, in all the arguments sustaining the Democratic policy, and in that policy itself, there is a careful, studied exclusion of the idea that there is anything wrong in slavery."[20] In a nonpartisan call to arms, Lincoln asks for all who find slavery wrong "to stand and act with us in treating it as a wrong."

In his only speech of the sixth debate, Douglas explains the reasons he does not discuss the moral aspect of slavery: "I tell you why I will not do it. I hold that under the Constitution of the United States, each state of this Union has a right to do as it pleases on the subject of slavery." He cites Illinois and Missouri as "sovereign states" that have effectively done so. Douglas further explains his position on the relationship of morality to the politics of slavery, as he pitches for southern support: "I hold that the people of the slaveholding states are civilized men as well as ourselves; that they have consciences as well as we, and they are accountable to God and their posterity and not to us. It is for them to decide therefore the moral and religious right of the slavery question for themselves within their own limits."[21] Citing the constitutional guarantee of slavery where it exists, he simply calls on each state to "mind its own business and let its neighbors alone, and there will be no trouble on this question." That advice does not address questions relating to slavery in the process of the territories gaining statehood.

Douglas says the stability resulting from his policy will ensure national growth. He phrases this prediction in language with chauvinistic appeal—a promise to fulfill the dream of divinely inspired manifest destiny. In the following passage Douglas is eloquent for the implicit moral argumentation of gaining a greater good expressed through an emotional/rational appeal to patriotism and religion. The sentences are well crafted, including the repetition of *great* and *principle*, and the use of a cumulative sentence for rhetorical impact to conclude the passage:

> Stand by that great principle [self-government] and we can go on as we have done, increasing in wealth, in population, in power, and in all the elements of greatness, until we shall be the admiration and terror of the world. . . . Under that principle, the United States can perform that great mission, that destiny which Providence has marked out for us. Under that principle, we can receive with entire safety that stream of intelligence which is constantly flowing from the Old World to the New, filling up our prairies, clearing our wildernesses, and building cities, towns, railroads and other internal improvements, and thus make this the asylum of the oppressed of the whole earth.[22]

Douglas reiterates his belief that morality in politics derives from the conscience of individuals: "It does not become Mr. Lincoln, or anybody else, to tell the people of Kentucky that they have no consciences, that they are living in a state of iniquity, and they are cherishing an institution to their bosoms in violation of the law of God. Better for him to adopt the doctrine of 'judge not lest ye be judged.'"[23] The biblical quotation mocks Lincoln because he often used that technique.

In his last debate speech, Lincoln repudiates the insinuation made by Douglas and others that "office seekers and ambitious Northern politicians" are to blame for slavery agitation. Lincoln cites the divisions throughout American society and culture in "politics, in religion, in literature, in morals, in all the manifold relations of life" as evidence that politicians alone are not responsible for turmoil relating to slavery. With a clear rationale and plain but emotive language, Lincoln denounces Douglas's position that slavery is an inappropriate subject for political activity and policy.

> Where is the philosophy or statesmanship which assumes that you can quiet that disturbing element in our society which has disturbed us for more than half a century, which has been the only serious danger that has threatened our institutions—I say, where is the philosophy or the statesmanship based on the assumption that we are to quit talking about it, and that the public mind is all at once to pass being agitated about it? Yet this is the policy here in the North that Douglas is advocating—that we are to care nothing about it! I ask you if it is not a false philosophy? Is it not a false statesmanship that undertakes to build up a system of policy upon the basis of caring nothing about *the very thing that everybody does care the most about?*—a thing which all experience has shown we care a very great deal about?[24]

By characterizing Douglas's indifference to the national slavery problem as unstatesmanlike, Lincoln brands his opponent as unsuited for such a high office as the US Senate.

Lincoln denounces as fallacious the charge that he seeks to interfere with states' rights and strengthens his antislavery moral position with an argument for economic opportunity: "He is fighting a man of straw [the straw man fallacy is a recognized rhetorical technique] when he assumes that I am contending against the right of states to do as they please about it" (slavery). Lincoln reiterates his argument that the federal government needs to have control of the territories, so that white people have opportunities to settle in areas where slavery is prohibited and "where they can better their condition." He directs his argument to members of the opposing party: "I will ask you [Democrats], if the policy you are now advocating had prevailed when this country was in a territorial condition, where would you have gone to get rid of it? Where would you have found your free state or territory to go to? And when hereafter, for any cause, the people in this place shall desire to find new homes, if they wish to be rid of the institution, where will they find the place to go?"[25] This argument indicates Lincoln is aware of Americans' restlessness, their ever-increasing numbers, and their veneration of freedom.

Lincoln's moral objection to slavery is the subject of the lengthiest portion of his last debate speech. He denounces Douglas's "false issues" that he seeks to eliminate slavery in the South and to develop social and political equality between the races. Lincoln contends that the moral question divides not just political factions but all of society: "The real issue in this controversy—the one pressing upon every mind—is the sentiment on the part of one class that looks upon the institution of slavery as a wrong, and of another class that does not look upon it as a wrong." Republicans know the solution to slavery agitation is complicated, for it must be accomplished within the constitutional framework, and Republicans want to avoid further agitation: "They desire a policy in regard to it that looks to its not creating any more danger. They insist that it should as far as may be, be treated as a wrong, and one of the methods of treating it as a wrong is to make provision that it shall grow no larger." Lincoln amplifies his point through emotive figurative language:

> You may have a wen or a cancer upon your person and not be able to cut it out lest you bleed to death; but surely it is no way to cure it, to engraft it and spread it over your whole body. That is no proper way of treating what you regard a wrong. You see this peaceful way of dealing with it as a wrong—restricting the spread of it, and not allowing it to go into new countries where it has not already existed. That is the peaceful way, the old-fashioned way, the way in which the Fathers themselves set us the example.[26]

Lincoln might have added that just as cancer is life threatening, slavery threatens the national welfare, but in using that comparison he could have invited more of the grievous repercussion he received from the ominous house-divided metaphor. Lincoln acknowledges that some Democrats are "as much opposed to slavery as anybody," and he urges them not to be dissuaded by the failed efforts of such Democrats as Frank Blair and Benjamin Gratz Brown of Missouri to promote gradual emancipation.

Lincoln repeats his dissection of Douglas's refusal to regard the immorality of slavery as an appropriate political problem. The poignant figurative language that defines slavery as a universal, timeless problem is one of the most eloquent statements of the debates and the entire Lincoln canon and was prefigured in the Chicago speech of July 10, 1858:

> That is the real issue. That is the issue that will continue in this country when these poor tongues of Judge Douglas and myself shall be silent. It is the eternal struggle between these two principles—right and wrong—throughout the world. They are the two principles that have stood face to face from the beginning of time; and will ever continue to struggle. The one is the common right of humanity and the other the divine right of kings. It is the same principle in whatever shape it develops itself. It is the same spirit that says, "You work and toil and earn bread, and I'll eat it." No matter in what shape it comes, whether from the mouth of a king who seeks to bestride the people of his own nation and live by the fruit of their labor, or from one race of men as an apology for enslaving another race, it is the same tyrannical principle.[27]

Using a metaphor insinuating obfuscation in Douglas's rhetoric, Lincoln points to the need to "get rid of the fog which obscures the real question" and to convince the Douglasites of the evil of slavery. Then, slavery "will be placed again where the wisest and best men of the world placed it."

In the last speech of the debates, Douglas uses overwrought language to belittle Lincoln's moral/religious argument against slavery:

> [Lincoln] is going to extinguish slavery by surrounding the slave states, hemming in the slaves, and starving them out of existence as you smoke a fox out of his hole. And he intends to do that in the name of humanity and Christianity, in order that we may get rid of the terrible crime and sin entailed upon our fathers of holding slaves. Mr. Lincoln marks out that line of policy, and appeals to the moral sense and justice and to the Christian feeling of the community to sustain him. He says that any man who holds to the contrary doctrine is in the position of the king who claimed to govern by divine right.[28]

In "turnabout is fair play" language, Douglas then attacks Lincoln's divine-right argument with a hyperbolic comparison between Lincoln's policies and British King George the Third's: "We went to war on the principle that the home government should not control and govern distant colonies without giving them a representation. Now, Mr. Lincoln proposes to govern the territories without giving the people a representation, and calls on Congress to pass laws controlling their property and domestic concerns without their consent against their will. Thus, he asserts for his party the identical principles asserted by George III and the Tories of the revolution."[29] Douglas emphasizes that Republicans are abolitionists and that the Democratic Party stands in sharp contrast by advocating for the right of self-government as the only way to gain a peaceful solution to the slavery problem.

In the final debates Lincoln and Douglas especially argued over slavery relating to popular sovereignty, sectional vs. national political policy, and implications of the *Dred Scott* decision. In the first speech of the fifth debate, Douglas summarizes his political/legalistic case for popular sovereignty as the solution to slavery agitation. Beginning with a statement-of-facts justification for his political history, Douglas reminds his audience that in 1854 he "vindicated" himself as a proponent of "the great fundamental principle that the people of each state and each territory of this Union have the right, and ought to be permitted to exercise the right, of regulating their own domestic concerns in their own way, subject to no other limitations or restriction than that which the Constitution of the United States imposes upon them."[30] He insists that the Kansas-Nebraska Act embodied that principle and was not intended to legislate slavery in or out of the territory but to leave the decision to locals.

Douglas defends popular sovereignty as a national policy: "And I can appeal to all men, friends and foes, Democrats and Republicans, Northern men, Southern men, that during the whole of that fight I carried the banner of popular sovereignty aloft, and never allowed it to trail in the dust, or lowered my flag until victory perched upon our arms." Douglas ultimately supports the "rule" that a territory should not become a state until it reaches the required population to qualify for statehood, and he reemphasizes the importance of self-government as the basis for allowing Kansas residents to decide the question of being a free or slave state.

Douglas says that unlike the Whig and Democratic Parties, the Republican Party serves only the interests of the North. With antithesis he emphasizes that the Republican Party promotes itself exclusively through emotional appeals: it is "a party which appeals to Northern passion, Northern pride, Northern ambition, and Northern prejudices, against Southern people, the Southern states, and Southern institutions." Framing his position with implicit fearmongering, he asserts that Republicans intend to gain and exercise power over the South, adding that no "political creed is sound which cannot be proclaimed fearlessly in every state of this Union where the federal Constitution is the supreme law of the land."

In his speech at the fifth debate, Lincoln rejects Douglas's accusation that the Republican Party is sectional. Lincoln tries to demonstrate the fallacy of Douglas's position that the test of validity for political doctrine is whether it would be universally accepted. For example, Douglas, says Lincoln, could not propound democracy in Russia. Lincoln alleges southern intolerance for Republican positions: "In some places we may not be able to proclaim a doctrine as clearly true as the truth of democracy, because there is a section so directly opposed to it that they will not tolerate us in doing so." Lincoln wonders whether Douglas would regard the open resistance to his Chicago speech in July as a "test of its unsoundness."

With "turning the tables" sarcasm, Lincoln cites southern criticism of Douglas for his Freeport Doctrine: "His pill of sectionalism, which he had been thrusting down the throats of Republicans for years past, will be crowded down his throat." Lincoln denies that the Compromise of 1850 established a national precedent for popular sovereignty in Kansas and Nebraska. He maintains that the New Mexico and Utah bills that organized those territories and allowed them to decide in favor of slavery or freedom were individual parts of that legislation and not intended to be "models" or a "pattern" for answering the slavery question in other territories. Lincoln maintains that Douglas's positions inadequately address the question of slavery extension and that Douglas has not in fact answered Lincoln's question of whether Douglas would "acquiesce" in a Supreme Court decision that free states cannot exclude slavery. Douglas, claims Lincoln, has only "sneered" at the question and at Lincoln for asking it.

In the fifth debate Lincoln introduces his discussion of the *Dred Scott* decision and Douglas's interpretation of it by showing an understanding of the relationship between logic and rhetoric, observing that the validity of conclusions depends on "the truth of the premises." Lincoln's main premise is that "the right of property in a slave is not distinctly and expressly affirmed in the Constitution, and Judge Douglas thinks it is." Lincoln allows he is stating his own view of the significance of the *Dred Scott* decision: "My own opinion is that the new *Dred Scott* decision, deciding against the right of the people of the states to exclude slavery, will never be made if that party is not sustained by the elections." Lincoln tempers his criticism of Douglas: "I have said, upon a former occasion, and I repeat it now, that the course of argument that Judge Douglas makes use of upon this subject, (I charge not his motives in this), is preparing the public mind for that new *Dred Scott* decision."[31]

The lack of specific policy and procedure for acquiring new territory, Lincoln warns, could be exploited by proslavery factions, increasing slavery agitation, which Lincoln describes as the only problem "that has ever threatened or menaced a dissolution of the Union—that has ever disturbed us in such a way as to make us fear for the perpetuity of our liberty." Thus, Lincoln insists, the voting public needs to pay close attention to Douglas's views on the "important and practical question" of slavery or freedom in new territories.

In his fifth debate closing speech, Douglas rejects Lincoln's prediction of a second *Dred Scott* decision that would nationalize slavery, saying Lincoln charged him with favoring such an outcome despite knowing of Douglas's public disavowals of it. Lincoln, says Douglas, predicts a second *Dred Scott* decision while knowing that current Supreme Court justices do not favor nationalization of slavery. Douglas charges Lincoln with conducting a grassroots campaign to undermine and destroy "public confidence in the Court," thus perverting "the government of the laws into that of a mob." Douglas ends by accusing Republicans with the hypocrisy of claiming the right to repudiate Supreme Court decisions but holding Democrats to them.

In his speech of the sixth debate, Douglas argues that the policies advocated by Lincoln and his party favor the North and are unworkable in the South. Douglas again accuses Lincoln and the Republican Party of pitting the North against the South, contending that Republican rhetoric emphasizes not logical argumentation but emotional appeal. Fearmongering, Douglas portrays Lincoln as a religious zealot: "Mr. Lincoln thinks that it is his duty to preach a crusade in the free states against slavery because it is a crime, as he believes, and ought to be extinguished and because the people of the slave states will never abolish it."

In the sixth debate Douglas begins his attack on Lincoln's treatment of *Dred Scott* by asserting that a US senator should not dispute the judiciary. Douglas asks whether Lincoln intends to overthrow *Dred Scott* by "strife and rebellion," despite Lincoln's repeated rejection of "mob" action. Douglas says he always accepted a court's unfavorable decision, whereas Lincoln would "get mad at the judge and talk about appealing." Douglas boasts, "I never dreamed of going out of the courthouse and making a stump speech to the people against the judge, merely because I had found out that I did not know the law as well as he did." Douglas maintains that when he appealed cases, he accepted the higher court's rulings. With a personal attack, Douglas curtly dismisses Lincoln's prediction of a second *Dred Scott* ruling that would deny a state the right to exclude slavery: "There was not a man possessing any brains in America, lawyer or not, who ever dreamed such a thing." Douglas portrays Lincoln as an extremist in his own party for "preaching the doctrine" of urging rebellion against the Supreme Court, and Douglas predicts that Lincoln "will find some honest Republicans, some law abiding men in that party, who will repudiate such a monstrous doctrine." All Democrats, Douglas insists, abide by the law.

Lincoln's closing speech of the sixth debate criticizes Douglas's position on *Dred Scott* and popular sovereignty. First, Lincoln notes that Douglas continues to ignore the question of what he would do in Congress should the Supreme Court determine that no state could exclude slavery. Douglas has also failed to respond to Lincoln's challenge of pinpointing language in *Dred Scott* that verifies Douglas's claim that members of the Supreme Court have said they would make no such ruling. In response to Douglas's question of how Lincoln's party would "reverse" *Dred Scott*, Lincoln repeats his position that it would be done in the same lawful ways Douglas and his party have reversed judicial decisions, including the legislation that flipped the Court's position that the National Bank was constitutional and the maneuvering years ago in Illinois that placed Douglas on that state's supreme court.

Lincoln's criticism of popular sovereignty is so logical and polished that he must have developed it earlier with the intention of saving it for this closing speech. He begins by acknowledging that the two parties interpret *Dred Scott* differently, quoting Jackson as saying that "each man was bound to support the Constitution 'as he understood it.'" Using rhetorical questions, however, Lincoln belittles (reductio ad absurdum) Douglas's Freeport Doctrine for contradicting the *Dred Scott* ruling that taking slaves into a territory is guaranteed by the Constitution: "Does the Judge mean to say that the territorial legislature in legislating may, by withholding necessary laws, or by passing unfriendly laws, nullify that constitutional right? Does he mean to say that? Does he mean to ignore the proposition so long known and well established in the law, that what you cannot do directly, you cannot do indirectly? Does he mean that?" Lincoln further mocks this contradiction, proclaiming that *Dred Scott* "has *squatted* Douglas's 'squatter sovereignty' out" but that Douglas will persist in this "humbuggery" of "*do nothing sovereignty*."[32] Lincoln uses metaphoric language to disparage his rival's defense of popular sovereignty: "Has it not got down as thin as the homeopathic soup that was made by boiling the shadow of a pigeon that had starved to death? . . . It is precisely no other than the putting of that most unphilosophical proposition, that two bodies may occupy the same space at the same time."

In his opening speech of the final debate, Douglas observes that local self-government accounts for the sectional shift in power away from the South to the North, giving the North the power to control both houses of Congress and to elect a president. With fearmongering language Douglas then poses a rhetorical question of whether that power should be used to "wage a war against the Southern states and their institutions until you force them to abolish slavery everywhere." Douglas insists that during the debates Lincoln had time and again refused to answer the question of whether he would vote to allow a territory to become a slave state "if Congress had not prohibited slavery in it during its territorial existence, as Congress never pretended to do under Clay's compromise measures of 1850."[33] Douglas repeats his position that in Illinois "it is none of our business" what people in other states and territories want to do about slavery.

Douglas asserts that the slavery question requires "sectional men" to put aside their differences and unite as they have in the past under the leadership of the Democratic Party. He claims Democrats "welcomed Henry Clay" for his work on the Compromise of 1850, with Whigs and Democrats, North and South, combining to defeat abolitionism and "restoring tranquility and good feeling." Douglas maintains that such collaboration stemmed from adherence to the common belief in self-government. He cites the 1854 Kansas-Nebraska Act as a further embodiment of that principle, claiming that he has consistently advocated that principle from 1850 through the present.

Douglas cites Democratic leaders who support the basic principle of the Freeport Doctrine and quotes from a recent speech by Democratic Senator Jefferson Davis of Mississippi: "If the inhabitants of any territory should refuse to enact such laws and police regulations as would give security to their property or to his, it would be rendered more or less valueless in proportion to the difficulty of holding it without such protection. In the case of property in the labour of man or what is usually called slave property, the insecurity would be so great that the owner could not ordinarily retain it." Douglas is inaccurate and misleading when he contends "the whole South are rallying" in support of local self-government as the answer to the slavery question. Douglas renews his pledge to adhere to this principle, arguing that he has consistently fought for it "when assailed by Northern mobs, or threatened by Southern hostility." He will stick to it "wherever its logical conclusions lead me."

Lincoln's last debate speech sharply attacks both *Dred Scott* and the Freeport Doctrine: "I do not believe it is a constitutional right to hold slaves in a territory of the United States. I believe the decision was improperly made and I go for reversing it. Judge Douglas is furious against those who go for reversing a decision. But he is for legislating it out of all force while the law itself stands. I repeat that there has never been so monstrous a doctrine uttered from the mouth of a respectable man."[34] Then Lincoln turns his reasoning for acquiescing in the Fugitive Slave Law into a fresh legalistic argument against Douglas's proposition that local "unfriendly legislation" with law enforcement can keep slavery out of a new territory:

> I defy anybody to go before a body of men whose minds are educated to estimating evidence and reasoning, and show that there is an iota of difference between the constitutional right to reclaim a fugitive, and the constitutional right to hold a slave, in a territory, provided this *Dred Scott* decision is correct. I defy any man to make an argument that will justify unfriendly legislation to deprive a slaveholder of his right to hold his slave in a territory, that will not equally, in all its length, breadth and thickness furnish an argument for nullifying the Fugitive Slave Law.[35]

Extrapolating from the preceding logic, Lincoln closes with a punch line satirizing Douglas for his effort, beginning with the first debate, to tar Lincoln as an abolitionist: "Why, there is not such an abolitionist in the nation as Douglas, after all." Lincoln thus asserts a tu quoque refutation—but with the good humor that he said early on in his first debate speech was the key to coping with his devious opponent. Burlingame praises Lincoln's Alton speech as "his finest rhetorical hour."[36]

The quick-witted Douglas begins the last speech of the debates with a retort to Lincoln's allegation that Douglas is an abolitionist: "If he could make the abolitionists of Illinois believe that, he would not have much show for the Senate. Let him make the abolitionists believe the truth of that statement and his political back is broken."[37] Douglas remarks that all of his speeches in Illinois testify to his fight against the Lecompton Constitution because it violated the principle of self-government, and he again denounces those Democrats who supported Lecompton "not because it was right" but because it was "expedient" for party unity: "There is no safety or success for our party unless we always do right and trust the consequences to God and the people."

Disputing Rhetorical Methods

The rivals charged one another with using such demagogic methods as making unverified conspiracy accusations, being deviously inconsistent, and making personal attacks. In other words, the rivals criticized one another's moral character to denigrate their credibility and prove unworthiness to serve in the US Senate. Douglas charged Lincoln with ignoring the facts that disproved his Democratic proslavery conspiracy accusation made in the House Divided speech. Lincoln charged Douglas with ignoring the facts that disproved his accusation that Lincoln was an abolitionist.

In the fifth debate Lincoln rejects Douglas's claim that Republican resolutions passed at Springfield in 1854 exposed Lincoln and Trumbull as abolitionists. Previously journalists pointed out that abolitionist resolutions in the 1854 Springfield Republican platform as published in the Democratic *Illinois State Register* were actually the work of northern Illinois abolitionists, and Lincoln avers he had nothing to do with that Springfield platform. In 1854 Douglas claimed he had been misled by the *Register*'s editor, Charles Lanphier. Several weeks before the fifth debate Douglas said he would investigate when he got to Springfield. At Galesburg Lincoln points out that a month after promising that investigation Douglas had not reported on it, and Lincoln argues this silence implied guilt for misrepresenting the facts of the platform's origin. Lincoln maintains that the inclusion of abolitionist resolutions in the platform could not have been "by mistake."

Lincoln insists on finding out whether Lanphier or Douglas can be "exonerated." Lincoln deduces that Lanphier has "but little room for escape." Douglas and fellow Democrat Thomas L. Harris, Lincoln claims, have repeatedly tried to use the forgery to their advantage. Lincoln makes his allegation with metaphoric language: "As the fisherman's wife, whose drowned husband was brought home with his body full of eels, said when she was asked, 'What was to be done with him?' '*Take the eels out and set him again,*' so Harris and Douglas have shown a disposition to take the eels out of that stale fraud by which they gained Harris's election [to Congress], and set the fraud again more than once."[38] Lincoln says that Douglas's mere claim of a Republican platform with abolitionist resolutions does not validate the charge, adding that "Douglas requires an endorsement of his truth and honor by a reelection to the United States Senate."

In his closing speech of the fifth debate, Douglas first cites historical facts to disprove proslavery collusion among Presidents Pierce and Buchanan, Chief Justice Taney, and himself, as Lincoln alleged, and then Douglas complains that Lincoln is so underhanded as to use the question of the 1854 Illinois Republican platform as an instrument of personal attack that Douglas participates in a "conspiracy . . . to perpetuate a forgery." Douglas reviews his previous admission of mistakenly believing an 1854 newspaper report that falsely presented northern Illinois abolitionist resolutions as the Illinois state Republican platform, and then he expresses outrage at the remarks Lincoln has made in his Galesburg speech: "I will now say that I do not believe that there is an honest man on the face of the globe who will not regard with abhorrence and disgust Mr. Lincoln's insinuations of my complicity in that forgery, if it was a forgery." Douglas bitterly alleges that Lincoln abuses him:

"I commenced this contest by treating him courteously and kindly. . . . In return he has sought, and is now seeking, to divert public attention from the enormity of his revolutionary principles by impeaching men's sincerity and integrity, and inviting personal quarrels. . . . I spurn the insinuation of complicity and fraud made upon the simple circumstance of an editor of a newspaper having made a mistake as to the place where a thing was done, but not as to the thing itself."[39] Douglas insists that from the beginning he sought to debate like a "gentleman," and he alleges that Lincoln attacks his character by wrongly charging him with collaborating in the erroneous newspaper report of the Republican resolutions.

Also in the fifth debate, Douglas charges Lincoln with arguing inconsistently in different parts of the state. Douglas first reads from Lincoln's Chicago speech asserting that the equality language of the Declaration of Independence applies to black people. Douglas later calls this position Lincoln's "Chicago Doctrine," a derogatory counterpoint to the term *Freeport Doctrine*. Then Douglas quotes from Lincoln's Charleston speech and charges him with duplicity: "He gave the people to understand that there was no moral question involved, because the inferiority being established, it was only a question of degree and not a question of right. Here today, instead of making it a question of degree, he makes it a moral question, says that it is a great crime to hold the Negro in that inferior condition."[40] Douglas declares, "I would despise myself if I thought that I was procuring your votes by concealing my opinions, and by avowing one set of principles in one part of the state and a different set in another part."

Douglas says that Lincoln will not commit to the "doctrine" of opposing the addition of other slave states that prevails in northern Illinois, but Republicans in the rest of the state "repudiate" that doctrine. With "turnabout is fair play" language, Douglas "wonders whether Mr. Lincoln and his party do not present the case which he cited from the scriptures, of a house divided against itself cannot stand!" In contrast to this alleged division, Douglas maintains that his party and he are united on the principle of self-government to answer the slavery question in new territories.

Lincoln's fifth debate speech denies the accusation of presenting inconsistent messages in various parts of Illinois. Douglas, notes Lincoln, attempts to support that accusation by quoting him out of context. Lincoln succinctly repeats his central position of accepting slavery where it exists and opposing its extension: "And these declarations I have constantly made in reference to the abstract moral question, to contemplate and consider when we are legislating about any new country, which is not already cursed with the actual presence of the evil—slavery."

In the fifth debate Lincoln mentions more than once that his printed speeches present his views so that the only misunderstanding possible would come from "men interested to misunderstand" him. As he often observed, he valued his reading audience: "I take it that I have to address *an intelligent and reading community* [emphasis mine], who will peruse what I say, weight it, and then judge whether I advance improper or unsound views, or whether I advance hypocritical, and deceptive, and contrary views in different portions of the country. I believe myself to be guilty of no such things as the latter."[41] Since Lincoln was speaking in a community with two colleges (Galesburg), it made sense for him to remind an audience with educated citizens of the availability of his positions in print.

In his opening speech of the sixth debate, Lincoln delivers a source-based refutation of Douglas's ongoing complaint that Lincoln plays "a double part" by making "speeches of a certain sort in the South which I would not make in the North." Lincoln first quotes the portion of his Charleston speech denying that he favors social and political equality between white people and black people and then explains that he had stated this position at the Ottawa debate, when he had read from a speech "made nearly four years ago" (1854, the Peoria speech) expressing the same views. Lincoln reads a lengthy passage from his Ottawa speech that he delivered after reading from the Peoria speech, and it explains the similarities and differences between Douglas and him on race and slavery. Somewhat apologetic for reading "perhaps too much so for good taste," Lincoln emphasizes that he had stated his full views on slavery and race in the northern, abolitionist section of Illinois despite Douglas's repeated contrary assertions. Lincoln also notes that his views were the same as those of "our old Whig leader, Henry Clay."

Continuing, in the sixth debate, Lincoln explains that during the campaign Douglas has attempted to stigmatize him with abolitionist resolutions that he had nothing to do with. Lincoln says Douglas wants to hold him responsible for all of his friends' political beliefs, and Lincoln recalls that at Jonesboro he did likewise to Douglas. Lincoln expresses exasperation with Douglas's persistent complaints that Lincoln engages in personal attacks. Lincoln cites the outrage that Douglas voiced at Galesburg over Lincoln's use of the word *forgery* to characterize the erroneous attribution of the 1854 northern Illinois abolitionist resolutions as representing the statewide Republican platform then and now. In a temper flare Lincoln turns directly toward Douglas on the stage and exclaims, "Yes, Judge, I dared to say forgery. But in this political canvas, the Judge ought to remember that I was not the first who dared to say forgery." Lincoln says Douglas had condemned the evidence as a forgery that Trumbull had cited in criticizing Douglas but that Douglas had offered no proof that any of the evidence had been falsified. Lincoln says he is justified in daring Douglas to vindicate himself from connection to the proven fraud of the 1854 abolitionist resolutions. Douglas's complaint that he would never have believed Lincoln would make personal insinuations leads Lincoln to comment on the ethics of the debate rhetoric:

I was aware, when it was first agreed that Judge Douglas and I were to have these seven joint discussions, that they were the successive acts of a drama— perhaps I should say, to be enacted not merely in the face of audiences like this, but in the face of the nation, and to some extent, by my relation to him, not from anything in myself, in the face of the world; and I am anxious that they should be conducted with dignity and in the good temper which would be befitting the vast audience before which it was conducted.[42]

Lincoln's commitment to debate with "dignity" and "good temper," thus maintaining his credibility and honor, reaffirms the desire he expressed at the beginning of his political career to earn public esteem.

In the sixth debate Lincoln argues that Douglas has, from his July Chicago speech through the Galesburg debate, repeatedly accused him of unethical rhetoric. Lincoln maintains that Douglas has claimed Lincoln used language "ingeniously to conceal [his] intentions," that Lincoln and Trumbull made a corrupt bargain in which each tried to abolitionize their respective parties, and that Lincoln has presented different messages in different sections of the state "to cheat the public, and get votes." Lincoln protests that Douglas "impeaches my honor, my veracity and my candor, and because he does this, I do not understand that I am bound, if I see a truthful ground for it, to keep my hands off of him." Just as Lincoln had stood up for himself in 1846 by insisting he had a right to run for Congress based on a "gentleman's agreement," he again responds to political challenge on the basis that "turnabout is fair play." Douglas, says Lincoln, started the personal attacks, and "when he quits, I *probably* will" (emphasis mine).

In the sixth debate several more of Lincoln's remarks indicate that after losing his temper in the fourth debate, he was trying not to let that happen again, for example, controlling his anger with self-deprecating humor: "He [Douglas] did not make a mistake, in one of his early speeches, when he called me an 'amiable' man, though perhaps he did when he called me an 'intelligent' man." Notwithstanding his brutal personal assault on Douglas in the third debate, Lincoln claims the ethical high ground in debate rhetoric: "It really hurts me very much to suppose that I have wronged anybody on earth. I again tell him, no! I very much prefer, when this canvas shall be over, however it may result, that we at least part without any bitter recollections of personal difficulties." Lincoln recalls that at Galesburg Douglas accused him of making personal attacks as a way to avoid debating the principles, and now Lincoln challenges Douglas "to confine himself to a war upon these principles."[43]

In his single speech of the sixth debate, Douglas expounds on one of his favorite complaints that Lincoln slants messages to suit the biases of audiences in different parts of the state. Douglas acknowledges that Lincoln said he was not "pledged" against adding new slave states but complains that

Lincoln dodges the question of whether he would vote for a new slave state if Congress did not prohibit slavery there in its territorial phase. Douglas argues that Lincoln refuses to answer this question in order to appease his abolitionist constituency. Douglas attempts to demonstrate Lincoln's "double dealing" by first reading passages from his Chicago speech that Lincoln used to show black people's entitlement to the natural rights of the Declaration of Independence and then passages from Lincoln's Charleston speech that, Douglas maintains, contradict Lincoln's Chicago speech. Douglas insinuates Lincoln is hypocritical and thus unworthy of election to the Senate.

In his closing speech of the sixth debate, Lincoln again repudiates the ongoing criticism that he delivers conflicting messages to audiences in different parts of the state, and he emphasizes that his position on the natural rights of black people derives from the Declaration of Independence. He quotes from an 1842 speech by Henry Clay stating his belief that natural rights are a "fundamental principle" in "*the original construction of society.*" Lincoln also uses fresh language to repeat his denial of wanting "a nigger wife": Douglas "never can be brought to understand that there is a middle ground on this subject. I have lived until my fiftieth year and have never had a Negro woman either for a slave or a wife, and I think I can live fifty centuries, for that matter, without having had one for either." Lincoln appeals to his audience to read and compare the passages that Douglas has quoted from Lincoln's speeches, denying that those passages "show rascality or double dealing."

Then Lincoln becomes angry over Douglas's criticism that Lincoln disrespects Supreme Court decisions, delivering a harsh personal attack expressed in some of the sharpest language of the debates: "If there is villainy in using disrespect or making opposition to Supreme Court decisions, I commend it to Judge Douglas's earnest consideration. I know of no man in the State of Illinois who ought to know so well about how much villainy it takes to oppose a decision of the Supreme Court as our honorable friend, Stephen A. Douglas."

Lincoln, observing that Douglas insists on making personal attacks, retaliates. Lincoln reminds the audience that Douglas had promised to investigate the source of the 1854 forged abolitionist resolutions that Douglas had been associating Lincoln with: "I demand of him to tell why he did not investigate it, if he did not. And if he did, *why he won't tell the result.*" Moreover, Lincoln says that Douglas's claim that he "magnanimously" admitted his error in the place where the controversial resolutions originated came only after Republican newspapers had announced it. Lincoln attacks Douglas's rhetoric with "turnabout is fair play" argumentation: "He has taken credit for great magnanimity in coming forward and acknowledging what is proved on him beyond even the capacity of Judge Douglas to deny, and he has more capacity in that way than any other living man. Then he wants to know why I won't withdraw the charge in regard to a conspiracy to make slavery national, as he has withdrawn the one he made." That is, Lincoln will withdraw the House Divided conspiracy accusation when it is proved to be as false as Douglas's accusation of Lincoln's association with the 1854 abolitionist resolutions has been proved false. Lincoln adds, "I will withdraw it whenever a reasonable man shall be brought to believe that the charge is not true."

As noted previously, Douglas's reluctance to own up to a mistake was a rhetorical strategy that as a young attorney in the 1830s he had first learned to use as a legal strategy.[44] Thus in his closing speech of the sixth debate, Douglas seems disingenuous when he asserts that as an honest man, he admits mistakes and corrects them; but when Lincoln "makes a false charge, he sticks to it, and never corrects it."[45]

In Lincoln's final debate speech, he says Douglas is inaccurate to claim that he objects to the *Dred Scott* decision because it denies the possibility of black people becoming citizens. Lincoln complains this charge reveals "a pre-determination on his part to misrepresent me." Lincoln reviews several facts about *Dred Scott* that he had cited in his House Divided speech as part of the evidence he says demonstrates a tendency toward nationalizing slavery. Then Lincoln criticizes Douglas for an unfounded, accusatory generalization: "Out of this, Judge Douglas builds his beautiful fabrication—of my purposes to introduce a perfect, social, and political equality between the white and black races. His assertion that I made an 'especial objection' (that is his exact language) to the decision on this account, is untrue in point of fact."

Lincoln notes the importance of clarifying his "connection" with Henry Clay (understood to be a moderate) because Douglas is attempting to brand Lincoln as an abolitionist (radical) before an audience of many with "sympathies southward." Lincoln explains that Douglas has selectively quoted from Lincoln's speeches in order to mislead. Lincoln says this practice, familiar today as cherry-picking or quote mining, "is called garbling—taking portions of a speech which, when taken by themselves, do not present the entire sense of the speaker as expressed at the time. . . . (taking an extract before and after) will give a different idea [from] the true idea I intended to convey." Specifically, Douglas has attempted to show that Lincoln aims "to interfere with the institution of slavery and establish a perfect social and political equality between Negroes and white people." Lincoln reads the passage from his Chicago speech that demonstrates his understanding that the founders composed a Constitution that both allowed slavery where it existed and did "not destroy the principle that is the charter of our liberties" (the Declaration of Independence).

Both candidates resumed stump speaking immediately after their last debate, not appearing in the same place at about the same time. As an example of Lincoln's stamina and tenacity, after the last debate he traveled north 115 miles by rail to appear the next day to deliver a two-hour stump speech at a "monster" political rally in Lincoln, Illinois—his first namesake town—thirty miles north of Springfield.[46] After this central Illinois speech, most of Lincoln's speeches were in western Illinois. No text of those speeches is known, but newspaper reports tell about audience size and behavior. One of Lincoln's most common arguments of these post-debate speeches in the Whig belt was claiming alignment with Henry Clay's views on slavery. During stump speeches Lincoln had to deal with hecklers, and Burlingame observes that "he usually got the better of them," although Lincoln later commented disingenuously that he "made no attempt at a retort." Lincoln gave his last campaign speech to a friendly audience in Springfield on October 30, reflecting on the campaign, summarizing his purposes, and again denying the accusations of his opponent. He admitted to ambition but said if the Missouri Compromise could be restored, he would "gladly agree, that Judge Douglas should never be *out*, and I never *in*, so long as we both or either, live."[47]

Conclusion

In the last three debates the rivals propounded their conflicting solutions to slavery agitation—Lincoln claiming the founders meant for slavery to end gradually, thus his opposition to slavery extension into new territories and free states; Douglas contending that the founders intended for the nation to exist forever half free and half slave, thus his arguments for popular sovereignty. Both candidates were brilliant debaters, each practicing his particular version of intrepid rhetoric.

The rivals' speeches featured "turnabout is fair play" argumentation. In responding to the accusation that the Republican Party was sectional, Lincoln argued that the Democratic Party failed to acknowledge the national significance of the immorality of slavery. Lincoln also pointed out the irony that Douglas had to contend with southern rejection of his Freeport Doctrine, which Lincoln described as "his pill of sectionalism, which he had been thrusting down the throats of Republicans for years past, will be crowded down his throat." Douglas accused Lincoln of saying he advocated natural rights for black people in some parts of Illinois but not others, dubbing this practice Lincoln's Chicago Doctrine, a sarcastic counterpoint to the term *Freeport Doctrine*. Douglas maintained that Republicans' inconsistent messaging from one part of the state to another betrayed them as a "house divided," a play on Lincoln's reference to the nation's split over slavery expressed in the House Divided speech.

In the final debates Lincoln's antislavery moral argumentation prompted a qualified, corresponding position from Douglas, who maintained that slavery was a matter for the conscience of individuals and was thus a concern for local jurisdiction as provided for in his version of popular sovereignty. Given Lincoln's repetition of his antislavery moral argumentation, it is surprising that Douglas did not do likewise with his counterargument valorizing individual conscience. Lincoln insisted that the humanity of black people meant they should have natural rights, but he denied black people's social/political equality with white people, and this chapter cites two examples of Lincoln's eloquence based on natural rights equality. Douglas's only language cited in this book as eloquent concerns his celebration of the national aspiration of westward expansion, not popular sovereignty. Douglas thought popular sovereignty could be used to define black people's rights and privileges, and he was willing to sacrifice their natural rights and privileges to eliminate the national problem of slavery agitation. In the final debates Lincoln missed no opportunity to criticize Douglas's moral character, for example, charging him with chicanery for his legislative role in maneuvering the 1854 Nebraska bill through Congress.

The rivals' dispute over rhetorical methods intensified as they tried to close their cases for credibility, and in these disputes the rivals faulted one another's moral character. Both rivals claimed the high ground in rhetorical ethics, and they argued more over personal attacks than any other rhetorical method. In the fourth debate Lincoln claimed commitment to ethical debating, notwithstanding his brutal personal attack on Douglas in the third debate. In the fifth debate the rivals accused one another of unethical rhetoric as they disputed the newspaper publication of the 1854 Republican platform at Springfield.

In the sixth debate Lincoln declared he was "anxious" for the debates to "be conducted with dignity and in good temper." Also in that debate Lincoln noted that in the campaign Douglas had repeatedly accused him of unethical rhetoric, beginning with Douglas's July Chicago speech. Lincoln contended that Douglas's attacks justified "turnabout is fair play" responses but urged Douglas "to confine himself to a war upon the principles." Lincoln said he would "probably" stop casting aspersions when Douglas did, but Lincoln could not resist ending his last debate speech with a jab at Douglas.

Ironically, while Douglas claimed the high ground in debate rhetoric, he dodged, lied, and used racial fearmongering, falsely claiming that Lincoln advocated social/political equality between white people and black people, and that Lincoln was willing to risk civil war in order to end slavery. Lincoln was frustrated in repeatedly having to refute Douglas's demagoguery, but he held his temper somewhat better in the last three debates than he did in the first four.

Lincoln was confident that people who read his speeches would come to know he was truthful, so that in every debate he either read from or referred to his printed speeches or advised listeners to read them, as his remark in the third debate signifies: "Douglas places me wrong in spite of all I can tell him.

. . . I have made a great many speeches, some of which have been printed, and it will be utterly impossible for him to find anything that I have ever put in print contrary to what I now say."[48] In the seventh debate Lincoln said, "[Here] again are the sentiments I have expressed in regard to the Declaration of Independence upon a former occasion—sentiments which have been put in print and read wherever anybody cared to know what so humble an individual as myself chose to say in regard to it."[49] Douglas was not known to give similar advice to his audiences.

In January 1859 the Illinois legislature, with a Democratic majority, again chose Douglas to serve in the US Senate, but Lincoln had won the popular vote—suggesting that his humanistic, forceful rhetoric was effective. Newspaper reports of the Lincoln-Douglas debates elevated Lincoln to the national political stage, and the publication of those debates in 1860 brought attention to Lincoln as a prospective presidential candidate. More than three dozen editions of the Lincoln-Douglas debates have been published, with most of them based on Lincoln's scrapbook collection of texts published in the pro-Republican *Chicago Press and Tribune* and Douglas's texts published in the pro-Democratic *Chicago Times*.[50]

The rivals expanded their arguments in 1859. Lincoln's speeches continued to respond to Douglas and address other concerns as they spoke beyond Illinois. The rivals would not speak at the same place at the same time, so Lincoln usually had more time to consider how to handle Douglas's politics and rhetoric, including whether to criticize his moral character and, if so, how.

Expanding Arguments against Slavery and Douglas (1859–1860)

Stick to the proposition, that the men of the revolution
understood this subject [slavery] better than we do
now, *and with that better understanding they acted
better than you* [Douglas] *are trying to act now.*
—Lincoln, the Columbus, Ohio, speech, 1859

The epigraph, an ironic twist to Douglas's thesis in his 1859 *Harper's Magazine* essay, applies a "turning the tables" argument against Douglas's solution to slavery agitation. Lincoln would also adapt the founders' "better understanding" proposition as the thesis of the celebrated Cooper Union address. Newspaper reports of the 1858 Lincoln-Douglas debates established Lincoln as a national political figure, and interest in his presidential prospects improved with the publication of those debates early in 1860. In most of 1859 Lincoln publicly dismissed the idea of a presidential run, but circumstances must have stimulated his consideration of it: "Lincoln took encouragement from the ever-widening rift in the Democratic Party over such issues as a federal slave code for the territories and the reopening of the African slave trade."[1] As a Republican Party leader, Lincoln contended with the challenges of Douglas's ongoing push for popular sovereignty, the attraction Douglas continued to hold for some Republicans, and abolitionism. In 1859 Lincoln wrote letters and gave speeches to unify the Republican Party at the state and national levels. Those compositions, the Cooper Union address, and subsequent speeches in the East strengthened his reputation as a party leader with potential to become its 1860 presidential candidate.

Until the fall of 1859, Lincoln mostly relied on correspondence to clarify and promote his political views and work for party unity, turning down invitations to travel and speak as he pursued his law practice. Then in the fall he spoke in Ohio, Wisconsin, and Kansas at the invitation of Republican leaders in those places, and he corresponded with party leaders in eastern states. These activities suggest he was beginning to maneuver for a presidential run. Fighting Douglas's initiatives continued to be a priority. In January and February Lincoln wrote to Senator Lyman Trumbull at Washington, DC, asking to be kept informed about Douglas's "movements" and assuring Trumbull of commitment to party unity and of no intention to rival him. Trumbull was not considered to be a potential presidential candidate, so he would have understood Lincoln meant he would not run against him for the US Senate. With presidential aspirations, Lincoln would have to consider such potential rivals in his own party as William H. Seward of New York and Salmon P. Chase of Ohio.

Corresponding to Strengthen Republican Unity at the State and National Levels

In 1859 Lincoln sent tactful letters declining to speak in Philadelphia, Boston, and Osawatomie, Kansas. Those letters included brief statements of his political views, and in several letters he responded to inquiries about his views, or he initiated correspondence to shape Republican policy. On May 17 Lincoln responded by letter to a "note" from Dr. Theodore Canisius of Springfield in which Lincoln urged such disparate groups as foreign-born citizens and southerners to "fuse" for the Republican cause. Canisius owned and published a German-American newspaper, the *Illinois Staats-Anzeiger*. Lincoln did not ask that his response be kept private. Canisius published this letter, which many other newspapers then also published. In May Lincoln purchased a printing press and gave it to Canisius with the understanding he would use it in Springfield to publish pro-Republican material in German prior to the 1860 election.

In June Lincoln wrote two letters to Salmon P. Chase, Republican governor of Ohio, on party policy. Lincoln had written Chase in April to thank him for publicly supporting the Illinois Republican cause in the 1858 Senate race, noting that if Illinois Republicans had then embraced Douglas, they would have destroyed the party there.[2] Previously, as an attorney, Chase had defended fugitive slaves, and he advocated for the repeal of the Fugitive Slave Law. On June 9 Lincoln wrote to let Chase know that the Ohio Republican Party platform's plank calling for the repeal of the Fugitive Slave Law was "already damaging us here." Lincoln maintains that advancing such a repeal would make Republicanism in Illinois "hopeless," and "I have no doubt that if that plank be even introduced into the next Republican National Convention, it will explode it."[3] Lincoln closes by asking whether Chase can do something to reduce this concern. Chase replied to say he believed the repeal of the Fugitive Slave Law was essential and that Illinois Republicans would accept that repeal.

The letter Lincoln sent Chase on June 20 notes that the Constitution requires fugitive slaves to be returned to their owners but without giving the procedure for it, and Lincoln says that Congress has that responsibility. Lincoln uses historical argument to make his point, reminding Chase that the founders included the Fugitive Slave provision in the Constitution as necessary to form a central government that "could execute its own behests," contrary to the Articles of Confederation's emphasis on laws created by individual states.

The Fugitive Slave Law was a central question for the forthcoming 1860 Republican platform, and another concern was reopening the slave trade. In a letter of June 23 to Nathan Sargent, a former Whig living in Washington, DC, Lincoln advised that a Republican platform emphasizing opposition to the reopening of the slave trade rather than opposition to slavery extension would lose those members who came into the Republican Party from the Democratic Party, and the Republican Party would "dissolve into thin air."[4]

On July 3 the private letter Lincoln sent to the editor of the *Central Transcript*, which was published at Clinton, the county seat of DeWitt County, Illinois, demonstrates just how determined Lincoln was to maintain party unity. Lincoln's letter objected to the newspaper's claim that the middle and southern parts of the state should determine gubernatorial candidates. Lincoln tactfully advises the editor: "Surely, on reflection, you will agree that the matter must be controlled, in due proportions, by all parts of the state." Lincoln also objects to the newspaper's statement blaming the "ultra men" (abolitionists) of northern Illinois for Lincoln's Senate race loss the previous year. He points out that northern Illinois did not advance extremist candidates in the 1856 and 1858 state elections. Insisting that his letter remain private, Lincoln says he would have preferred to discuss these matters in person.[5] As a small-town newspaper, the *Central Transcript* did not have a wide circulation, but Lincoln did not want to overlook an opportunity to curtail threats to party unity that he felt might result from further publication of ideas that he found inaccurate and misleading.

Lincoln's most comprehensive explanation for his concern about the 1860 Republican platform and its effect on the presidential election that year appears in a letter he sent to Indiana Congressman Schuyler Colfax on July 6. Lincoln stipulates that his letter be for Colfax's "eye only," but clearly Lincoln was trying to influence a Republican leader at the national level. Lincoln's message was that local Republican "convocations" should avoid adopting a position that would be a "firebrand" to Republicans in other locations. Colfax's reply expressed agreement and awareness of the great challenge of assimilating disparate antislavery elements.

On July 28 Lincoln wrote to Samuel Galloway, a lawyer and former US congressman and an Ohio leader of the Opposition Party (a short-lived antislavery group), in response to Galloway's request for correspondence. Besides regret for Ohio Republicans' support for the repeal of the Fugitive Slave Law, Lincoln is troubled by Ohio Republicans "leaning" toward support for popular sovereignty. Lincoln denounces Douglas as "the most dangerous enemy of liberty" and "the most insidious one," adding that in the future Douglas would not find support in either the North or South. Most notable about this letter is that Lincoln is no longer hesitant to take a stand against reviving the slave trade, which he links to popular sovereignty: "Taking slaves into new territories, and buying slaves in Africa, are identical things—identical *rights* or identical *wrongs*—and the argument which establishes one will establish the other. Try a thousand years for a sound reason why Congress shall not hinder the people of Kansas from having slaves, and when you have found it, it will be an equally good one why Congress should not hinder the people of Georgia from importing slaves from Africa."[6] Lincoln compliments Chase but says he does not consider him "the most suitable as a candidate for the presidency." Lincoln adds that he does not think himself "fit" for that office, but he does not ask for this letter to remain private. On September 21 Lincoln wrote to Chase to urge him "not to let your approaching election in Ohio so result as to give encouragement to Douglasism. That ism is all which now stands in the way of an early and complete success of Republicanism."[7]

Diminishing Douglas and Strengthening Illinois Republican Unity

In February 1859 Lincoln delivered his Second Lecture on Discoveries and Inventions in Jacksonville, Decatur, and Springfield, Illinois. It was a revision of a lecture he had first delivered in April 1858 at Bloomington. This lecture was implicitly political. Lincolnists discuss this composition for its treatment of a reform movement often referred to as Young America, which Robert W. Johannsen describes as a "movement of ardent, evangelical nationalism" that applied to a "group within the Democratic Party that was determined to restore the party to its former Jacksonian vigor."[8] Douglas was especially associated with this movement for his advocation of national expansion. David S. Reynolds, however, maintains that the "Second Lecture on Discoveries and Inventions" shows that Lincoln aligned Young America with the Republican Party: it not only fought "for the liberation of enslaved nations and colonies" but "like the Whigs before them, were the party of technological and social improvement. . . . " Reynolds points out antislavery elements in this composition.[9]

Michael Burlingame cites this composition's 450-word opening paragraph as a satire of Douglas.[10] Lincoln, writes Burlingame, uses Douglas's reputation as the "chief spokesman" for Young America to poke fun at him.[11] Lincoln's satire of Douglas as an expansionist is personal but mild: "If there be any thing old which he can endure, it is only old whiskey and old tobacco." Burlingame's commentary stops at that point, but there is more to the political and personal satire, including self-deprecating humor. Lincoln continues, "If the said Young America really is, as he claims to be, the owner of all present, it must be admitted that he has considerable advantage of Old Fogy."[12] The audience would have readily interpreted "Old Fogy" as a reference to Lincoln because he often described himself as "an old line Whig," and by the 1850s Lincoln was widely known as "Old Abe" but not called that to his face.[13] Thus, the Old Fogy/Lincoln connection would have served a tactical purpose of trying to get and hold audience interest. From that point, Lincoln creates a version of the biblical figure of Adam, "the first of all fogies," as an instrument of double-edged satire. Adam is a Lincoln self-parody: "very ignorant, and simple in his habits." Mixed with the self-parody is implicit criticism of Young America/Douglas:

> It is very plain, he [Adam/Lincoln] was no equal of Young America; the most that can be said is, that *according to his chance* he may have been quite as much of a man as his very self-complaisant descendant. Little as was what he knew, let the Youngster discard all he has learned from others, and then show, if he can, any advantage on his side. In the way of *land* and *livestock*, Adam was quite in the ascendant. He had dominion over all the earth, and all the living things upon, and round about it. The land has been sadly divided out since; but never fret, Young America will *re-annex* it. The great difference between Young America and Old Fogy, is the result of *Discoveries*, *Inventions*, and *Improvements*. These, in turn, are the result of *observation*, *reflection* and *experiment*.[14]

Lincoln illustrates this process: the invention of "steam-power" and its inventor succeeded because he had learned "no doubt, from those who, to him, were old fogies." Lincoln may have chosen steam power because, beginning in the early 1850s, Douglas was an influential proponent of railroad construction first in Illinois and then across North America. Before Adam's descendants could develop the "unexplored mine" of nature, they had to develop not just the ability to observe but the habit of observing. Adam may be slow, but he does develop that habit; Lincoln, too, was somewhat plodding but keenly observant of the political world, Douglas's activity in particular.

Lincoln's lecture then takes on a more serious tone as he narrates a brief history of communication, from speech to writing to printing. In this account Lincoln makes only one more allusion to Young America/Douglas, and it relates to writing, with a "turning the tables" twist: "With all conception of it, [if writing] were this day lost to the world, how long, think you, would it be, before even Young America could get up with the letter A with any adequate notion of using it to advantage?" Lincoln notes the first inventors of writing "were very old fogies." Thus, if Young America/Douglas had to reinvent writing and could do so, he would also be an old fogy.

On March 1 Lincoln delivered a 2,535-word speech to a Republican rally in Chicago, and it was his first explicitly political speech since his 1858 Senate race. His purposes were to strengthen his party affiliation and to extend his case against Douglas. Lincoln begins by thanking Chicago and Cook County for the support they gave him in a common cause—"brothers in the work." Lincoln admonishes his party, "suggesting that we consider whether it would not be better and wiser, so long as we all agree that this matter of slavery is a moral, political, and social wrong, and ought to be treated as a wrong, not to let anything minor or subsidiary to that main principle and purpose make us fail to cooperate."[15]

Lincoln then cautiously begins his discussion of Douglas by mentioning that some Illinois Republicans considered voting for him in the 1858 Senate race, denying that he said any "unkind words" about them. Lincoln believes Douglas's Republican friends were "sincerely the friends of our cause as I claim to be myself; yet I thought they were mistaken, and I speak of this now for the purpose of justifying the course that I took and the course of those who supported me," adding that he means "no unkindness toward Judge Douglas." Lincoln asserts that if Republicans had made Douglas their 1858 Senate candidate, their party would no longer exist. They would not have "absorbed him"; he would have "absorbed them": his "doctrines" would have become theirs, and they would have ceded the moral argument against slavery and opened the way for slavery to spread not only to the territories but also to the free states. Lincoln reminds his audience that slavery extension is a proxy for slavery itself: "Never forget that we have before us this whole matter of the right or wrong of slavery in this Union, though the immediate question is as to its spreading out into new Territories and States." Adhering to this moral argument against slavery means that "the future of the Republican cause is safe and victory assured."[16]

In closing the speech, Lincoln uses imperative, anaphoric sentences with emotive, militaristic imagery to enhance the rational appeal of a call for unity: "All you have to do is to keep the faith, to remain steadfast to the right, to stand by your banner. Nothing should lead you to leave your guns. Stand together, ready, with match in hand. Allow nothing to turn you to the right or to the left. Remember how long you have been in setting out on the true course; how long you have been in getting your neighborhood to understand and believe as you now do. Stand by your principles; stand by your guns; and victory complete and permanent is sure at the last."[17] Lincoln would use the theme of keeping the faith in party principle in the perorations of future speeches, most famously in the Cooper Union address.

Spreading His Message and Reputation
Eastward and Southward: The Ohio Speeches

The Ohio Republicans had capable stump speakers, but the divergent views and intense intraparty rivals, including Salmon P. Chase, "indicated to the Republican high command that the man to send against Douglas must be brought in from outside the state. The result was that Abraham Lincoln received two invitations to speak in the Buckeye hustings of 1859 almost simultaneously."[18] Illinois Republican Senator Lyman Trumbull, more outwardly liberal than Lincoln, was invited to speak in northern Ohio, which like northern Illinois was the most antislavery part of the state: "Lincoln [was] a progressive conservative in 1859—progressive enough for central Ohio and conservative enough for southern Ohio."[19]

Lincoln eagerly accepted the Ohio speaking invitations.[20] His main speeches were at Columbus and Cincinnati. Lincoln sometimes suggested that Douglas may have been a dupe of proslavery proponents but not in these speeches. Both insinuate that Douglas's rhetoric is too revealing to be the work of a mere pawn. By stressing the willfulness of Douglas's wrongful indifference to slavery, Lincoln convicts him of moral turpitude. Lincoln spoke at Columbus on September 16, 1859, following a speech Douglas had made there on September 7. Columbus, the capital of Ohio, had a population of 18,554 in 1860. Like the Illinois capital of Springfield, Columbus was located at the center of the state, with a mix of northern and southern sympathizers. Douglas's Columbus speech continued his battle against the Buchanan Democrats and "sounded the opening gun of the senator's expanding presidential campaign for 1860."[21] Lincoln was able to study newspaper reports of Douglas's Columbus speech, which drew heavily on his essay published in the September 1859 issue of *Harper's Magazine* titled "The Dividing Line between Federal and Local Authority: Popular Sovereignty in the Territories," which presented Douglas's research-based justification for his solution to slavery agitation. Lincoln's Columbus speech rebuts Douglas's *Harper's* essay.

In composing his essay, Douglas withdrew books from the Library of Congress, including histories of early American colonies, and solicited help from historian George Bancroft, perhaps hoping to gain from the kind of research-based argumentation that Douglas saw Lincoln often used to his advantage. Douglas's *Harper's* essay extended the Lincoln-Douglas debates and attempted to refute criticism of the Freeport Doctrine, with the claim of constitutional justification for it.

Robert W. Johannsen explains that Douglas believed the political process in the American colonies served as a precedent for local control of slavery in the western territories.[22] Douglas's omission of a Supreme Court decision and historic federal enactments weakened his argumentation. Burlingame suggests some of this omission may have been unintentional: "Unaware of the crucial Supreme Court decision in *Barron vs. Baltimore* (1833), Douglas mistakenly argued that the Bill of Rights in the Constitution limited the power of the states as well as the federal government."[23] Johannsen writes that some of Douglas's omissions were deliberate: "For judicial support, Douglas quoted the *Dred Scott* decision at length. He made free use of ellipses, however, citing only those portions which seemed to substantiate his position most fully, and at one point he transposed sentences in order to heighten the effect."[24]

Lincoln's Columbus speech was one of his most important between the Lincoln-Douglas debates and his presidential nomination. Speaking to a small audience from a terrace outside the statehouse, Lincoln repeated many of the points made during his Senate race. While Lincoln and his views were known to some Ohio Republican leaders, rank-and-file party members and other citizens lacked familiarity with him or his positions. This speech also had currency because it addressed the fresh arguments of Douglas's two-columned, nineteen-page *Harper's* essay. The *Illinois State Journal* published Lincoln's Columbus speech on September 24, 1859. At 11,959 words, the speech is long, and its sentences are lengthy, with an average of thirty words. As in some other speeches Lincoln gave as refutations to a Douglas speech, the body of the Columbus speech develops with an original structure rather than a point-by-point sequence reflecting the structure of the targeted Douglas speech. In the Columbus speech Lincoln links the allegedly wrongheaded political views in Douglas's *Harper's* essay to rhetorical abuses—inaccuracies, obfuscation, equivocation, contradictions, and omissions—that insinuate corrupt intention.

Opening the Columbus speech, Lincoln compliments Ohio Republicans Thomas Corwin, Salmon P. Chase, and Benjamin Wade; and he expresses the hope that his audience will view his speech with "moderate expectations" in comparison to the oratory of these native-state speakers. In the introduction Lincoln humorously repeats the denial he has frequently made that his friends or he would marry black people if no law prohibited it but that Douglas and his friends "seem to be in great apprehension that they might." Lincoln's introduction ends with a stab at Douglas: that the editor of the *Statesman* (Columbus newspaper) should be thankful Lincoln has given him the timely chance "to correct the misrepresentation" before "malicious people can call him a liar." Lincoln says Douglas's speech was about black people, so his speech will be, too.

The body of Lincoln's wide-ranging Columbus speech has six parts. The first is a statement of facts covering the relevant history of slavery agitation from the 1854 Kansas-Nebraska Act to the present. The second body section defines popular sovereignty as the problem preventing an end to the long history of

American slavery agitation. The third discusses the implied assumption in Douglas's *Harper's* essay that constitutional law mandates equal status for states and territories. The fourth discusses contradiction in Douglas's policy of popular sovereignty. The fifth refutes what Lincoln identifies as the two purposes of Douglas's *Harper's* essay, and the sixth discusses the problems of the nationalization of slavery and the return of the African slave trade. The single concluding paragraph is an implicit call to action.

In the statement-of-facts section, Lincoln asserts that the probable continuation of legislative and judicial response to slavery agitation will be to nationalize slavery, and thus the goal of the Republican Party is "eminently conservative": restoring slavery to its status at the nation's founding. The immediate danger of nationalizing slavery is not "the African slave trade or the passage of a congressional slave code or the declaring of a second *Dred Scott* decision" but "that insidious Douglas popular sovereignty." This is "the miner and sapper" because it prepares the public mind for the other measures that would bring about slavery nationally.

The appeal of Douglas and his conception of popular sovereignty thus threatens the Republican Party and the nation, says Lincoln, and this proposition leads into the second part of the speech's body, which begins by clarifying the distinction between what Lincoln considers "genuine" popular sovereignty and Douglas's version. In Lincoln's view, genuine popular sovereignty means "that each man shall do precisely as he pleases with himself, and with all those things which exclusively concern him," and that is the foundational principle of the federal government. Douglas's version means "if one man chooses to make a slave of another man, neither that other man nor anybody else has a right to object." Douglas's version as applied to settlement of a new territory means that the first "few people" to enter there, whether for or against slavery, set the precedent for "the infinitely greater number of persons who are afterward to inhabit that territory." Douglas's equivocation entangles him: "He has a good deal of trouble with his popular sovereignty. His explanations explanatory of explanations explained are interminable," the most recent being his *Harper's* essay, which Lincoln belittles as "great."

Lincoln says much of his speech that day will concern Douglas's *Harper's* essay. Lincoln quotes a passage from the House Divided speech that he claims Douglas has misquoted, then asks "right-minded men" whether the fifteen months since the House Divided speech have not verified the truth of the passage in question: that with Douglas's introduction of popular sovereignty, slavery agitation has "constantly augmented." Lincoln maintains that since the House Divided speech, slavery agitation has brought more and more people into the Republican ranks, including such former Democrats as Congressman John Hickman of Pennsylvania. In a rare request for audience response, Lincoln calls for three cheers for Hickman, and the audience complies.

The next aspect of Douglas's *Harper's* essay Lincoln addresses is the Constitution's implied authorization for the federal government to treat territories the same as states and that states have the right to do as they please with "all those things that pertain exclusively to themselves—that are local in their nature. That have no connection with the general government." Lincoln insists that Douglas errs in viewing slavery as a local, "trivial" matter—"no moral question about it"—like livestock, crops, and the "Canada thistle, or some other of those pests of the soil, which when first planted cannot be dug out by the millions of men who will come thereafter." Douglas is wrong to equate the national concern over slavery agitation "as only on a par with onions and potatoes."

Using more figurative language with negative connotation, Lincoln emphasizes the irony that Douglas believes territorial political appointments are significant enough to require federal control, but slavery is not: "Planting slavery upon a soil—a thing which once planted cannot be eradicated by the succeeding millions who have as much right there as the first comers or if eradicated, not without infinite difficulty and a long struggle—he considers the power to prohibit it, as one of these little, local, trivial things that the nation ought not so say a word about; that it affects nobody save the few men who are there."[25] Lincoln explains that slavery appears "small" to Douglas: "He is so put up by nature that a lash upon his back would hurt him, but a lash upon anybody else's back does not hurt him. That is the build of the man, and consequently he looks upon the matter of slavery in this unimportant light."

Lincoln then quotes Jefferson's warning that "I tremble for my country when I remember that God is Just!" and asserts that Douglas's version of popular sovereignty risks invoking "the avenging justice of God." Lincoln valorizes this point with the language of a biblical command: "Choose ye between Jefferson and Douglas as to what is the true view of this element among us." Lincoln suggests that under Douglas's policy a geographical area could be organized as a state without the need for a territorial phase, repeating with sarcastic emphasis that Douglas would allow territories "from the jump" to determine "this little Negro question."

Lincoln quips that near the end of Douglas's "copyright essay" he "comes very near kicking his own fat into the fire." Lincoln reads a passage from Douglas's essay that says territorial legislatures have the right to determine "all case[s] of taxation and internal polity." Lincoln says Douglas is equivocating by using the euphemistic phrase "internal polity" for slavery. Lincoln points out that Douglas's language betrays faulty logic: that in Douglas's version of popular sovereignty, Congress has no authority to legislate on the question of slavery in a territory; but when Congress determines a minimum population for a territory to qualify for statehood, it can address that question. Lincoln's blade cuts both the faulty logic and the verbosity in the *Harper's* essay that attempts to conceal it: "After fighting through more than three hours, if you undertake to read it, he at last places the whole matter under the control of that power which he had been contending against, and arrives at a result directly contrary to what he had been laboring to do. He at last leaves the whole matter to the control of Congress."

The next section addresses "the two main objects" of the *Harper's* essay: that Douglas tries to prove the founders supported his version of popular sovereignty and that *Dred Scott* "had not entirely squelched out this popular sovereignty." Lincoln declines to examine Douglas's use of history in detail but believes it to be inaccurate and incomplete. Examining individual statements, Lincoln says, would be like "crawling through a crack" in a fence and unnecessary because he can jump the fence in "a single bound." Lincoln finds Douglas's argument of the founders' support for popular sovereignty unconvincing because of its factual errors of omitting consideration of the Ordinance of 1787 and the Missouri Compromise of 1820. Lincoln says the federal government's adherence to the principles of those documents has been thorough and ongoing.

Lincoln argues that Douglas's exclusion of these foundational documents is deliberate and shameless from "a man who has occupied a position upon the floor of the Senate of the United States, who is now in his third term, and who looks to see the government of this whole country fall into his own hands, pretending to give a truthful and accurate history of the slavery question in this country, should so entirely ignore the whole of that portion of our history—the most important of all." In Douglas's rhetorical abuse, he "is as impudent and absurd as if a prosecuting attorney should stand up before a jury, and ask them to convict A as the murderer of B, while B was walking alive before them." Lincoln argues that Douglas fails to "demonstrate upon reason . . . as Euclid demonstrated propositions" that the founders endorsed his concept of popular sovereignty.

Lincoln also maintains that Douglas does not succeed in using the founders' testimony to verify that claim, turning a quotation from Douglas's recent Columbus speech back upon him. Douglas had said, "Our Fathers, when they formed this government under which we live, understood this question just as well as and even better than we do now." Lincoln emphatically agrees with this statement and then challenges Douglas with pointed irony, exhorting him to "stick to the proposition, that the men of the revolution understood this subject better than we do now, *and with that better understanding they acted better than you are trying to act now.*"[26] The Cooper Union address would more famously turn Douglas's claim against him that the founders understood slavery "even better than we do now."

Refuting Douglas's treatment of the *Dred Scott* decision, Lincoln reminds the audience of the contradiction inherent in Douglas's Freeport Doctrine that local legal action could exclude slavery despite the Supreme Court's determination that Congress had no authority to prevent owners of slaves from taking them into territories. According to Lincoln, after the "verbiage" is removed from Douglas's position, what remains is "a bare absurdity—*no less than a thing may be lawfully driven away from where it has a lawful right to be.*" Further, since Douglas gave his position at Freeport, he has never once repeated the language he used but has altered his diction to mislead people into thinking that popular sovereignty will prevent slavery extension: "He does not say the people can drive it [slavery] out, but they can control it as other property." Lincoln creates an earthy analogy to underscore his point:

> Driving a horse out of this lot, is too plain a proposition to be mistaken about; it is putting him on the other side of the fence. Or it might be a sort of exclusion of him from the lot if you were to kill him and let the worms devour him; but neither of these things is the same as "controlling him as other property." That would be to feed him, to pamper him, to ride him, to use and abuse him, to make the most money out of him "as other property"; but, please you, what do the men who are in favor of slavery want more than this? What do they really want, other than that slavery being in the territories, shall be controlled as other property?[27]

For emphasis and clarity, Lincoln restates the meaning of the *Dred Scott* decision and repeats his prediction that the Supreme Court would rule against any antislavery legislation in the territories.

Lincoln reminds his audience that because of Douglas's "insidious" popular sovereignty, he is not the friend of either the Republican Party or the nation, repeating that Douglas's brand of popular sovereignty "now threatens the purpose of the Republican Party, to prevent slavery from being nationalized in the United States." Lincoln asserts that there is no difference between allowing slaves in territories and allowing the reopening of the African slave trade, despite Douglas's equivocating contention of their difference. Lincoln denies Douglas's claim that the abolition of the slave trade came about as "a compromise of the Constitution," arguing that nothing in history or the Constitution supports Douglas's position. Both the abolition of the slave trade and the restriction of slavery extension were "the public expectation at the time," in Lincoln's view.

Lincoln stresses the "gradual and steady debauching of public opinion" caused by disregarding the immorality of slavery and trusting in popular sovereignty to end slavery agitation. Democrats who hope to maintain party loyalty but who "nevertheless hate slavery" are especially vulnerable to the false appeal of popular sovereignty that will lead to reopening the slave trade and spreading slavery to the territories and free states. As proof that the public mind is already moving in this fateful direction, Lincoln argues that five years ago nobody held the position presently advocated by Douglas and others that black people are excluded from the equality language of the Declaration of Independence. Lincoln repeatedly challenges anyone to prove otherwise. Excluding black people from the Declaration has enabled Douglas and others to reduce black people "from the rank of man to that of a brute. They are taking him down, and placing him, when spoken of, among reptiles and crocodiles, as Judge Douglas expresses it." Lincoln quotes Henry Clay to affirm the hope that preventing slavery extension would eventually end slavery itself.[28] Lincoln asks both Ohio Republicans and Democrats to give "serious consideration of this fact, that there is now going on among you a steady process of debauching public opinion on this subject." The speech thus ends not with hyperbolic exhortation but with direct admonition.

Afterward Lincoln spoke more briefly to the Young Men's Republican Club, and on the way to Cincinnati the next day, he spoke for two hours in Dayton, where he argued for free labor, as he did in his next major speech at Cincinnati. On September 17, the day after his Columbus speech, Lincoln spoke for two hours at Cincinnati, whose population in 1860 was 161,044, and it was the largest city west of the Appalachians and the largest city where Lincoln had spoken to date. The Cincinnati speech extends the Columbus speech's criticism of Douglas's political views, rhetoric, and moral character. With distinctive originality, the Cincinnati speech adapts some of Lincoln's familiar arguments to this particular setting, just across the river from Kentucky. At 11,112 words, the Cincinnati speech is only a few hundred words shorter than the Columbus speech.

In the brief introduction Lincoln presents himself with humility, saying that his appearance "in so great a city as this" gives him "some degree of embarrassment." Lincoln used the same technique at Columbus. At Columbus and Cincinnati Lincoln devoted the first body section to refutation of Douglas's criticism of the House Divided speech, just as Lincoln felt necessary in so many other speeches. In more than half of his Cincinnati speech, Lincoln directly addresses Kentuckians, sensibly assuming some are in the audience, and indirectly addresses other Kentuckians and the southerners they represent (prosopoeia/synecdoche). Lincoln then directly addresses Ohioans.

Feigning spontaneity, Lincoln begins by saying it has occurred to him just "tonight" that the location immediately across from Kentucky gives him the opportunity to "shoot over the line at the people on the other side of the line into a slave state" and still "keep his skin safe." Lincoln candidly admits to the Kentuckians/southerners that he would not mind if slavery "should gradually terminate in the whole Union." He says he knows southerners believe the opposite, and he admits it would be futile to try "proselyting [*sic*] you." When someone in the Cincinnati crowd told him to address Ohio men, not

Kentuckians, the self-assured Lincoln retorted, "I beg permission to speak as I please," and that reply prompted laughter.

The section addressing Kentuckians is a sweeping satire of Douglas as a clever politician whose rhetorical prowess makes him the last, best hope to sustain the South. Lincoln urges Kentuckians/southerners to nominate Douglas for the presidency because he "is as sincerely for you, and more wisely for you, than you are for yourselves." Lincoln repeats this language to be sure he is correctly understood, adding he will "demonstrate the proposition" that the only way for the South to "succeed" is to keep northern support. Without it, "you are in the minority, and you are beaten at once." Douglas, claims Lincoln, is the only man who can deliver northern support for the South.

This admonition is timely because some southern leaders were then questioning whether Douglasism would truly work to their advantage.[29] Lincoln's satire in this section is the most extended creative writing and use of irony in the entire Lincoln canon. The irony is that Douglas's rhetoric had alienated many proslavery Democrats, North and South, but this section maintains that Douglas's rhetoric in fact will benefit southerners by aligning proslavery northern Democrats with them. This satire is a fresh approach to Lincoln's ongoing effort to define Douglas as proslavery. As seen above, Lincoln's political letters after the debates predicted that the future would see continued split in the Democratic Party, and Lincoln's portrayal of Douglas as a willful apologist for slavery could promote division between free-soil Democrats and proslavery Democrats. Such a depiction would also work to destroy any residual appeal Douglas might have with Republicans, increasing Lincoln's political capital.

This section of the Cincinnati speech discusses several subjects of concern to the South that Lincoln says Douglas can relate to the North for southern benefit: southerners' proslavery theology, the African slave trade, and the legal status of slavery in territories. Lincoln's discussion of these subjects renders Douglas as a schemer who "moulds the public opinion of the North" in favor of the southern view of slavery. Lincoln explains that Douglas sometimes appears otherwise by things he says or does not say, but if he does not behave in those ways, he would "lose his capacity to serve" the South. Several times Lincoln repeats Douglas's refusal to say whether slavery is wrong or right. Lincoln allows that Douglas "takes all the chances that he has for inveigling the sentiment of the North, opposed to slavery, into your support, by never saying it is right." Further, Douglas has stated in the Senate and repeated at many other places that he is indifferent whether slavery is voted down or up, and this position is another way he shows that he believes the South's "favorite institution which you would have spread out, and made perpetual, is no wrong." In further demonstrating how Douglas shapes public opinion in favor of the South, Lincoln cites a "proposition" Douglas made in a post-debate speech in Memphis that the Almighty had drawn a line across North America to decree slavery perpetual on one side. Lincoln evokes laughter when he says Douglas "did not pretend to know exactly where that line was."

Lincoln continues to elaborate on Douglas's effort to influence northern political belief, attributing a religious/moral ethos to Douglas's strategy, as seen in the carefully written passage below. It begins with a periodic sentence that builds to his main point at the end for emphasis; then he uses a cumulative sentence first to repeat his main point and then augment it with explanatory phrases. These artistically formed sentences suggest that Lincoln composed his speech well in advance:

> Whenever you can get these Northern audiences to adopt the opinion that slavery is right on the other side of the Ohio; whenever you can get them, in pursuance of Douglas' views, to adopt that sentiment, they will very readily make the other argument, which is perfectly logical, that that which is right on that side of the Ohio, under the seal and stamp of the Almighty, when by any means it escapes over here, it is wrong to have constitutional laws, "to devil" you about it. So Douglas is moulding the public opinion of the North, first to say that the thing is right in your state over the Ohio River, and hence to say that that which if right there is not wrong here and that all laws and constitutions here, recognizing it as being wrong, are themselves wrong, and ought to be repealed and abrogated.[30]

Lincoln cites several examples of Douglas's attempt to demean black people in advancing the southern cause for slavery. Again, Lincoln says Douglas is even more successful than the South in this regard. According to Lincoln, the strongest example of Douglas's success in shaping public opinion in favor of the South is promoting the misinterpretation of the Declaration of Independence that black people are excluded from its equality language. Lincoln says this misconception was unheard of five years ago before Douglas introduced it.

The next example of how Douglas advocates for slavery concerns southerners' use of the Bible in defense of slavery. Lincoln says Douglas knows this argument fails to convince northerners because they interpret slaves in the Bible to be white, so Douglas argues for black slavery as "right": "He thereby brings to your support Northern voters who could not for a moment be brought by your own argument of the Bible-right of slavery. Will you not give him credit for that?" In making this point, Lincoln hyperbolically and inaccurately claims that Douglas's rhetoric is successful "with his entire party." Lincoln says Douglas is responsible for the implication that "if you do not enslave the Negro you are wronging the white man in some way or other and that whoever is opposed to the Negro being enslaved is in some way or other against the white man." Lincoln says he does not agree with this fallacy but tells the Kentuckians/southerners they should thank Douglas because that implication benefits them.

Lincoln argues that Douglas's version of popular sovereignty "if carried to its logical conclusion" also justifies the revival of the African slave trade. Lincoln challenges anyone to disprove the argument that allowing someone to take slaves to Kansas also allows "the people of Georgia . . . to buy them in Africa." Lincoln denies Douglas's claim that the founders were compromising when they agreed to abolish the slave trade twenty years after the passage of the Constitution. He maintains the founders expected both the abolition of the slave trade and the prohibition of slavery from new territories.

Citing the relationship between the authors of the Northwest Ordinance of 1787 and the Constitution, Lincoln explains, "that generation of men, though not to the full extent members of the convention that framed the Constitution, were to some extent members of that convention, holding seats, at the same time in one body and the other, so that if there was any compromise on either of these subjects, the strong evidence is that that compromise was in favor of the restriction of slavery from the new territories." Lincoln's position that the founders believed in the "ultimate extinction of slavery" is a central argument of his Cooper Union address the following February.

Lincoln discusses two Douglas positions that Lincoln says should not be regarded as objectionable by Kentuckians. In the first, Lincoln senses Kentuckians are "offended" by Douglas's opposition to repealing antislavery measures, but Lincoln assures them that unless Douglas takes this position, "he would lose the power of 'lugging' the Northern states to your support." Further, if Kentuckians will just be patient, they will be rewarded by Douglas abandoning his objection to repealing abolition of the slave trade, for Douglas has a history of changing positions. For example, Douglas in 1849 fully supported the Missouri Compromise of 1820, but the Douglas-backed 1854 Kansas-Nebraska Act canceled the Missouri Compromise. Accordingly, Lincoln predicts: "It will only be four years more until he is ready to take back his profession about the sacredness of the [constitutional] compromise abolishing the slave trade." The gibe drew applause and laughter: "Precisely as soon as you are ready to have his services in that direction, by fair calculation you may be sure of having them." As he did in the Columbus speech, Lincoln cites Douglas's discontinuation of his "unfriendly legislation" argument to ensure slavery in the territories because of the "naked absurdity" of that position. In fact, when a territorial legislature attempts to enact and enforce "unfriendly legislation" and the Supreme Court strikes it down as unconstitutional, Douglas will support that decision. Lincoln thus assures Kentuckians: "In this again he serves you faithfully, and as I say, more wisely than you serve yourselves."

Lincoln cites two more examples of Douglas's talent for serviceable rhetoric. The first example explains that Douglas attacks only northerners' prediction that slavery threatens the future of the Union, not some southerners' prediction to that effect, including the position of the Richmond *Enquirer*, which, according to Lincoln, originated the prediction in 1856. The second example explains that during the 1858 Senate race, Douglas amazingly managed to gain the endorsement of both proslavery and antislavery proponents. Again, Lincoln maintains that Kentuckians should take advantage of Douglas's skill in rhetorical maneuvering: "If he was [successful in 1858], then it is for you to consider whether that power to perform wonders, is one for you lightly to throw away."

Lincoln makes two points in the climax of his advice to Kentuckians/southerners. The first is a bold prophecy that if the South does not "take" Douglas, it will surely be defeated—and may be defeated regardless. The language is direct and plain, and the repetition speaks determination: "We, the Republicans and others forming the opposition of the country, intend to 'stand by our guns,' to be patient and firm, and in the long run to beat you. . . . We don't intend to be very impatient about it. We mean to be as deliberate and calm about it as it is possible to be, but as firm and resolved, as it is possible for men to be." In a surprising conciliatory twist, he then tells "what we will do with you," repeating what he has said on other occasions:

> We mean to treat you as near as we possibly can, like Washington, Jefferson and Madison treated you. We mean to leave you alone, and in no way to interfere with your institution; to abide by all and every compromise of the Constitution, and, in a word, coming back to the original proposition, to treat you . . . according to the examples of those noble fathers—Washington, Jefferson, and Madison. . . . We mean to recognize and bear in mind always that you have as good hearts in your bosoms as other people, or as we claim to have, and treat you accordingly.[31]

(The Cooper Union address would reiterate Republican commitment to non-interference with slavery in the South.) The first point ends with humor: "We mean to marry your girls when we have a chance—the white ones I mean—and I have the honor to inform you that I once did have a chance in that way."

The second point of the advice develops with a series of rhetorical questions and predictions emphasizing the disadvantages of southern secession and the improbability of a southern victory in a civil war. Lincoln mocks the idea of secession by asking whether the South will try to wall itself off from the North, and he faults the notion of economic advantage in secession by asking, "Do you think you can better yourselves . . . by leaving us here under no obligation whatever to return those specimens of your moveable property [runaway slaves] that come hither?" In the event of civil war, he compliments the South for being "as gallant and as brave men as live," but it will lose simply for "being inferior in numbers." In fact, that advantage proved essential to northern victory in the Civil War.

Lincoln turns from "the Kentuckians" to address "our friends," and he states that his purpose is to discuss the "best means" of defeating the southern opposition. He attacks Douglas's insistence that popular sovereignty was the key to forming free states in the upper Midwest, discussing Ohio, Indiana, and Illinois, with particular attention to the latter. Lincoln says that differences in soil and climate cannot explain why some states became free and others chose slavery, as Douglas argues, because some areas of these free states are similar in soil and climate to adjacent slave states. Rather, the Northwest Ordinance of 1787 set the expectation and legal precedent for those three states becoming free. Lincoln disputes Douglas's inaccurate assertion that Illinois had come into the Union as a slave state by citing the state's constitutional history that documented its rejection of slavery and eventually indentured servitude in the southern part of the state. Here was an example of a political process that would accomplish Lincoln's often-stated desire for "ultimate extinction" of slavery, but of course this process could also be cited as an example of Douglas's argument for popular sovereignty. This ambiguity may explain why Lincoln did not more often cite Illinois history in making his case for ultimate extinction. At this point Lincoln repeats his criticism that Douglas's version of popular sovereignty is misguided because it grants absolute authority to the local level of government to answer the question of slavery or freedom—a question that has national significance and thus should be answered at that level.

Next Lincoln offers his familiar argument that free labor gives "industrious, and sober, and honest men" the opportunity to acquire enough capital to hire others, but he estimates those who gain enough capital to do so amount only to "one-eighth of the labor of this country." Free labor affords the hope for advancement that motivates, and Lincoln observes that even the "slave-master" understands the advantage of reward over punishment.

The conclusion is a recommendation developed by policy and procedure exposition rather than the emotional, hyperbolic exhortation characteristic of much nineteenth-century oratory, including some of Lincoln's previous compositions. The conclusion opens with a call for "a national policy" opposed to slavery. Preventing its extension and perpetuation is necessary for the nation's "general welfare." Lincoln asserts that slavery is the only problem "that has ever threatened the perpetuity of the Union itself." The call for action includes preventing both the revival of the African slave trade and a congressional black code that would protect slavery in the territories. He recommends unity of appropriate political action through conventions, platforms, and candidates, with special admonition not to choose a candidate who claims to be "tired of hearing anything about it" (slavery). A candidate using that argument, says Lincoln, will surely fail to have the support of both proslavery and antislavery voters.

Lincoln makes the surprising assertion that there are "plenty of men in the slave states that are altogether good enough for me to be either president or vice president, provided they will profess their sympathy with our purpose." These good men, he further notes, have the right character, intelligence, talent, and integrity. Lincoln says he would be for one of these men to have a place on the next Republican "or opposition ticket." Clearly Lincoln is trying to defuse the criticism that the Republican Party is sectional. Lincoln says he "should be glad to have some of the many good, and able, and noble men of the South to place themselves where we can confer upon them the high honor of an election upon one or the other end of our ticket."

The Cincinnati speech illustrates Lincoln's masterful ability to advance his political goals by creatively adjusting his message to a particular place and addressing multiple audiences, sometimes individually, sometimes collectively. Gary Ecelbarger comments on the significance of the speech: "It not only received widespread national attention for Lincoln (North, South, East, and West), it immediately elevated him in the eyes of those outside Illinois from a two-time Senate loser to a viable candidate for president. It is likely the only one of the thirty addresses delivered within nine months of Lincoln's nomination that appears to have influenced non-Illinois delegates to vote for him. These reasons support the argument that the Cincinnati address was not only Abraham Lincoln's most underrated speech, it ranks as one of the most important addresses of his pre-presidential career."[32] Yet the 1858 debates were far more important in advancing Lincoln's national reputation. On his trip back to Illinois, Lincoln gave a speech at Indianapolis, and a newspaper report of it indicates he repeated the arguments of his Ohio speeches. The October elections in Ohio brought major victories to Republicans, and Burlingame notes "the Ohio result damaged Douglas."[33]

Spreading His Message and Reputation Northward: The Wisconsin Speeches

After the Ohio speeches, a telling speech Lincoln gave prior to the Cooper Union address was his "Address before the Wisconsin State Agricultural Society," delivered on September 30, 1859, at the Wisconsin State Fair in Milwaukee. Like the Cooper Union address, this Milwaukee speech was an invited lecture. It discussed Lincoln's views on labor, human nature, and society that supported his Republican positions. While in Springfield practicing law and developing his Ohio speeches, Lincoln must have thought about his remarks at Milwaukee, and after speaking in Ohio he had less than two weeks before giving the Milwaukee address, for which he earned $100.[34] He delivered his Milwaukee lecture from a manuscript to a small audience of 200 to 300.[35]

Like his overtly political speeches, the Milwaukee address informs and avers through facts obtained from research.

The 4,700-word Milwaukee speech opens with an introduction of eight short paragraphs followed by sections on farm productivity, including thoughts on steam-powered machinery, free labor vs. slave labor, and the importance of education. The three-paragraph conclusion aims to motivate farmers. Daniel Kilham Dodge suggested that Lincoln's reading gave him familiarity with agricultural information, and his reading included such newspapers as Horace Greeley's weekly *Tribune* and "the writings, speeches, and conversation of his friend Jonathan B. Turner, of Jacksonville, Illinois, the real father of the Morrill Act" (legislation that Lincoln signed as president in 1862 establishing land-grant colleges).[36] The logical relationships among the sections of this speech establish coherence.

The introduction shows Lincoln's thoughtful attention to the occasion, audience, and his communicative purpose. The first half of the introduction attributes considerable significance to agricultural fairs and to the American farmer. While politics is not emphasized, that subject is in the background from the beginning: fairs "make more pleasant, and more strong, and more durable, the bond of social and political union among us," and Lincoln quotes Alexander Pope's aphoristic line that "happiness is our being's end and aim." Lincoln says that agricultural fairs are "a present pleasure, making the future more pleasant," and he explains that these fairs allow sharing new information and inventions for prizes and "pride and honor of success," which in turn stimulate emulation. He acknowledges the custom of fairs to "feature . . . a regular address" and expresses gratitude for the honor of this speech invitation.

The second half of the introduction attempts to establish rapport with the audience. Lincoln candidly says that he assumes he is not there to flatter them but humorously suggests that their large numbers do establish them as a favorite audience to court for their votes. He further jokes, using a characteristic double negative for understatement: "I am not quite sure that there is not cause of suspicion against you, in selecting me, in some sort a politician, and in no sort a farmer, to address you." With humility he says, "Any one of your own number, or class, would be more able to furnish" "specific information on agriculture" than he can, and he will try only "to make some general suggestions, on practical matters." Yet, his address excels at synthesizing theory, factual details, and rational/emotional appeals.

The first body section develops like a modern-day problem/solution report. The problem is that agricultural production in the upper Midwest and throughout America lags far behind its potential. Lincoln gives statistics of wheat and corn harvest per acre as evidence, citing a Patent Office Report as the source, also indicating that he has spoken to farmers about yields. Lincoln's solution is more "thorough cultivation," that is, "to push the soil up to something near its full potential," and this goal is accomplished by concentrating on limited acreage rather than expanded acreage. Accordingly, he recommends such innovative techniques as "deeper plowing, analysis of soils, experiments with manures, and varieties of seeds." He asserts that the advantage of more intensive cultivation is a "self-evident proposition": "It is certain that thorough cultivation would spare half or more than half the cost of land, simply because the same product would be got from half, or from less than half the quantity of land."[37]

Lincoln explains the importance of farm tools and machines for improving productivity, and the relationship between productivity and work satisfaction. Lincoln says machinery is superior to horse-drawn equipment for improving productivity because "horse power" involves inefficient use of energy. "The effect of thorough cultivation upon the farmer's own mind, and, in reaction through his mind, back upon his business, is perhaps quite equal to any other of its effects. Every man is proud of what he does well; and no man is proud of what he does not do well. With the former, his heart is in his work; and he will do twice as much of it with less fatigue." Lincoln says he has seen "even men of energy" fail who had invested heavily in acreage: "Mammoth farms are like tools or weapons, which are too heavy to be handled. Ere long they are thrown aside, at a great loss."[38]

The next section opens with the proposition that the application of steam power to farm work, especially "a steam plow," is desirable, "a *desideratum*" (one of the few words in the speech that farmers might not understand but perhaps reflects the speaker's desire to impress them). Lincoln is aware of the speculative/experimental nature of this technology, admitting that he has never seen such machinery and that a steam plow would have to beat horsepower in cost and speed. Such technology appeals to Lincoln's interest in inventions.[39] He says he has given considerable thought to it "in an abstract way" and identifies some of the specific performance and operational challenges in developing a steam plow, including those of fuel supply and water, but he expresses the belief that "ingenious men" can meet those challenges. He has identified the problems, not to discourage invention but to spur it, and he says even "the unsuccessful" will be useful in the process.

In discussing the work of farm laborers and farming technology, Lincoln lays the foundation for his shift into explaining his views on labor, capital, and education. Some of Lincoln's contemporary proponents of the "mud-sill theory" (that society requires an underclass to perform manual labor) found uselessness and even danger in education.[40] In contrast, Lincoln believes that "the Author of man" endowed him with head and hands so that they "should co-operate as friends; and that that particular head, should direct and control that particular pair of hands." The mind should be "cultivated" to facilitate improved labor: "Free labor insists on universal education."[41] He observes that many independent workers, including some in his audience, earn enough to buy tools and land, and to hire others. Lincoln observes it had been widely accepted "that *educated* people did not perform manual labor," for they relied on the uneducated to produce necessities. Lincoln maintains that "this was not an insupportable evil to the working bees, so long as the class of drones remained very small." Presently, however, especially in the free states, education is nearly universal, so that educated people must now work because a nation cannot be sustained by excessive "idleness."

Lincoln asserts that agriculture is the most suitable occupation for "the profitable and agreeable combination of labor and cultivated thought." The expansive field of agriculture invites discovery, and the expectation of useful discovery "lightens and sweetens toil." Lincoln uses details in plain language to endorse the potential value of education in agriculture:

> And how vast, and how varied a field is agriculture for such discovery. The mind, already trained to thought, in the country school, or higher school, cannot fail to find there an exhaustless source of profitable enjoyment. Every blade of grass is a study; and to produce two, where there was but one, is both a profit and a pleasure. And not grass alone; but soils, seeds, and seasons—hedges, ditches, and fences, draining, droughts, and irrigation—plowing, hoeing, and harrowing—reaping, mowing, and threshing—saving crops, pests of crops, diseases of crops, and what will prevent or cure them—implements, utensils, and machines, their relative merits, and how to improve them—hogs, horses, and cattle—sheep, goats, and poultry—trees, shrubs, fruits, plants, and flowers—the thousand things of which these are specimens—each a world of study within itself.[42]

Some readers have found this passage suggestive of Walt Whitman's celebration of nature in free-verse style as seen in *Leaves of Grass* (1855).[43] Lincoln cites the availability of scientific and technical writing that can inform farmers about available methods and machinery. "Thorough work" in any field requires education, described as "cultivated thought." For emphasis and clarity, he repeats that "thorough work" makes "the smallest quantity of ground" adequate, and this condition accommodates the contemporary world trending more to peace than to war. Lincoln's emphasis on education for small farmers follows Jeffersonian principles. Lincoln contends that intensive cultivation will facilitate subsistence and prevent oppression as population increases, concluding that "such community will be alike independent of crowned-kings, money-kings, and land-kings."

Olivier Fraysse explains Lincoln's political message in his rejection of large-scale farming and his advocacy of small-scale, intensive farming based on scientific methods achieved through education:

Lincoln compared it [intensive] agriculture to extensive agriculture solely because of his desire to contrast free labor and slavery. . . . Modern agriculture requires education, slave society requires ignorance; modern agriculture needs a free society. . . . Mechanized, scientific agriculture presupposes an educated labor force. The antagonism between the progress of civilization and the maintenance of slavery is sharply defined. This antagonism is not abstract, but rather is embodied in the competition between the slave plantation and individual agriculture. . . . The degradation that accompanied extensive agriculture opened the way to another, more serious degradation. That is why Lincoln stressed the sentiment of the dignity of work and the ambition for education that characterized his audience to win them to his firm opposition to the extension of slavery.[44]

Reflecting the Victorian faith in progress, Lincoln's conclusion encourages hopefulness. He urges those who do not win awards this year not to be discouraged but to continue to strive, and the concluding eloquent sentence encompasses a broad optimism and moral concern for all aspects of civilization, including the political realm: "Let us hope . . . that by the best cultivation of the physical world, beneath and around us; and the intellectual and moral world within us, we shall secure an individual, social, and political prosperity and happiness, whose course shall be onward and upward, and which, while the earth endures, shall not pass away."[45]

In an afternoon reception following this lecture, Lincoln participated in a political question-and-answer session and that evening delivered a political speech at a hotel. In 1902 a Lincoln admirer who said he had witnessed the Milwaukee lecture claimed: "I can only say that we had here in Milwaukee substantially the Cooper Institute speech some months later in New York."[46] (Lincoln had not seen the telegram invitation that led to the Cooper Union address until two weeks after his Milwaukee speeches.[47])

The day after the Milwaukee speeches, Lincoln spoke in two other Wisconsin communities before returning to Springfield: first at Beloit in the afternoon, then at Janesville in the evening. The newspaper reports of those speeches did not include their texts, indicating only that Lincoln repeated familiar arguments, including the charge that popular sovereignty will spread slavery throughout the nation and the complaint that the southern leaders "sedulously strive, by misrepresentation and falsehood, to produce the impression that the Republicans desire to meddle with their existing institutions."[48]

Persevering on the Home Front:
The Illinois Speeches

Lincoln gave his next political speeches in central Illinois during celebratory occasions for recent Republican victories in other states: at Clinton on October 14 while he was practicing law on the circuit and the next day at Springfield in the Capitol rotunda. At Clinton Lincoln accommodated his Republican audience by including a history of the party's formation, noting that the influential American Party of 1856 had faded as its members had since been "absorbed into both the other great parties," so that with recent victories in other states Republicans can now "rejoice." The only part of the Clinton speech that the pro-Republican Clinton *Weekly Central Transcript* quoted was part of the conclusion: "Our position . . . is right—our principles are good and just, but I would desire to impress on every Republican present to have patience and steadiness under all circumstances—whether defeated or successful. But I do hope that as there is a just and righteous God in Heaven, our principles will and shall prevail sooner or later."[49] The language voicing confidence in the righteousness of the Republican cause foreshadows the more famous expression of that idea in the conclusion of the Cooper Union address, as quoted below in the discussion of that speech. The Clinton paper said the audience responded with "loud, prolonged and stentorian cheering . . . that made the rafters of the court-house ring again."

The next day at Springfield, Lincoln was called upon to speak when a crowd gathered at his home after a parade, and he agreed to accompany citizens to the statehouse, where he spoke. The one-paragraph report of that speech in the pro-Republican *Illinois State Journal* said that in this "unpremeditated" speech, Lincoln "again and again brought down the crowd." Lincoln preferred to make careful preparation for speeches, and he sometimes declined invitations to speak impromptu, but at other times he must have enjoyed short-notice invitations to speak when he could deliver well-rehearsed arguments to sympathetic audiences under informal circumstances. The day after this Springfield speech, the radical abolitionist John Brown raided the federal arsenal at Harper's Ferry, Virginia. This violence shocked the nation, terrorized the South, and made Republicans fearful of serious damage to their cause. This fear must have encouraged and perhaps benefited Lincoln as a moderate in public discourse.

Spreading His Message and Reputation
Westward: The Kansas Speeches

In the first week of December, just days before Kansas elections, Lincoln traveled there in response to Kansas Republican leaders' speaking invitations. As in Ohio, Lincoln was not well known to ordinary citizens. He appeared at Elwood, Troy, Doniphan, Atchison, and Leavenworth, where he spoke three times: briefly upon his arrival and twice more extensively. These locations were strongly Democratic, and Kansas Republicans favored Seward as a leader of the national party. No full texts of the Kansas speeches have been located.[50] Newspaper reports exist for his speeches at Elwood and Leavenworth.

The Kansas speeches further demonstrate Lincoln's ability to consider local and national concerns and events in adapting his message to a particular audience. In his first Kansas speech, at Elwood, Lincoln explained the reason the citizens of that territory should be concerned about not only local "internal improvements" but also slavery as a national problem. He explained that after Kansas becomes a free state, its citizens will have the responsibility of being concerned with how other territories should handle the slavery question as they prepare for statehood. Regarding the violence of slavery agitation in recent Kansas history, Lincoln avoided placing blame on either party and refrained from explicitly blaming Douglas and popular sovereignty. Perhaps he was trying to test Democratic response. In subsequent Kansas speeches he was less restrained. Lincoln rejected the radical abolitionist John Brown's violence and advocated "the ballot box" as the way to handle the slavery question.[51]

According to the Leavenworth Democratic *Daily Times*, the large audiences Lincoln addressed there twice on December 3 included many Democrats, and Lincoln spoke from notes.[52] Lincoln describes the shift away from the founders' regard for slavery as wrong to a new, failed policy that did not. Under the new policy in effect for almost five years in Kansas, federally appointed governors failed to prevent "almost continual struggles, fire and bloodshed . . . and after having framed several state constitutions, you have, at last, secured a free state constitution, under which you will probably be admitted into the Union." Lincoln asks the indirect rhetorical question of whether the states coming into the Union under "the old way—the way adopted by Washington and his compeers—was not the better way."

Lincoln maintains that popular sovereignty had the potential in Kansas for the first settlers to "plant five thousand slaves on your soil." In that case, adopting a free constitution would have been impossible, and "you would not know what to do with the slaves after you had made them free." He says slave states would not want them, and Kansans would not want them as "underlings" or as social and political equals. He remarks, "You could have disposed of, not merely five, but five hundred governors easier." Taking slaves into the Kansas Territory was legal, but extensive slave holding did not develop.[53] Lincoln faults Kansas Democrats who profess opposition to popular sovereignty but who find excuses not to take action against proponents of slavery who would "go for" not only legalizing slavery in free states but also "surrendering fugitive slaves in Canada."

Lincoln repeats the centrist Republican position of leaving slavery alone where it exists, advising Kansas Republicans, especially the radical ones, to "leave Missouri neighbors alone. Have nothing whatever to do with their slaves. Have nothing to do with the white people, save in a friendly way. Drop past differences, and so conduct yourselves that if you cannot be at peace with them, the fault shall be wholly theirs."[54] Lincoln dismisses the accusation that Republicans have been responsible for increased slavery agitation, claiming that just the opposite is true and that Democrats support the troublesome new policy (popular sovereignty).

Denying that Republicans want disunion, Lincoln contends that proslavery southern Democrats will want to leave the Union if a Republican president is elected in 1860. As he questions whether Democrats can justify secession, he emphasizes that Republican policy is the same as "the men who made the Union." Lincoln says Republicans reject the rebellion of abolitionist John Brown. In blunt, prophetic language Lincoln asserts that Republicans would ensure the same fate for other traitors:

> Old John Brown has just been executed for treason against a state. We cannot object, even though he agreed with us in thinking slavery wrong. That cannot excuse violence, bloodshed, and treason. It could avail him nothing that he might think himself right. So, if constitutionally we elect a president, and therefore you undertake to destroy the Union, it will be our duty to deal with you as old John Brown has been dealt with. We shall try to do our duty. We hope and believe that in no section will a majority so act as to render such extreme measures necessary.[55]

Lincoln's remarks about Brown to clarify the Republican cause and to warn proslavery southern Democrats show the confidence he had developed in his antislavery arguments and willingness to express them to an unsympathetic audience.

The day after Lincoln's first full-length speech at Leavenworth was a Sunday, on which he refrained from political activity, resuming it the next day with a second full-length Leavenworth speech in front of a large audience. The newspaper report of that speech is much briefer than the report on the first Leavenworth speech, presenting hardly any alleged text. The report suggests Lincoln's fondness for enhancing familiar arguments, but the cryptic nature of the report only teases the reader about this aspect of the speech. Early in the speech, as Lincoln cites the Democrats' indifference to the immorality of slavery and the consequential implication of its eventual extension into free states, he offers a strained twist to the house-divided metaphor: "If a house was on fire there could be but two parties. One in favor of putting out the fire. Another in favor of the house burning. But these popular sovereignty fellows would stand aloof and argue against interfering."[56]

Lincoln reiterates repudiation of Brown's lawless actions and blames slavery, citing earlier slave insurrections and predicting more. Lincoln denies the Democrats' accusation that Republicans favor black suffrage and racial amalgamation, and he closes the speech by explaining how Republican principles aligned with the founders. Lincoln asserts that Republican "predominance was essential to the proper development of our country—its progress and its glory—to the salvation of the Union and the perpetuity of free Institutions."[57] The second Leavenworth speech was Lincoln's last overtly political speech before the Cooper Union address. Democrats gained in the Kansas elections despite Lincoln's speeches there. His Kansas trip took him to sparsely populated areas during harsh winter conditions (he was somewhat ill). The trip, made at his own expense, demonstrated his devotion to the Republican cause.

Strengthening Ties on the Home Front before Leaving for Cooper Union

Upon returning to Illinois, Lincoln resumed his busy law practice, and his main political activity was dealing with an Illinois Republican Party feud between two powerful party leaders that jeopardized that state party's unity and success in the 1860 election.[58] In late December Lincoln also complied with Illinois Republican ally Jesse W. Fell's suggestion to provide an autobiographical sketch requested by a journalist in Pennsylvania. The four-paragraph, 600-word composition Lincoln offered plays down his self-education, which he says he "picked up from time to time under the pressure of necessity." He repeated his previous, often-quoted comment that he "was losing interest in politics when the repeal of the Missouri Compromise aroused me again." He observed that his loss in his first run at the Illinois legislature (1832) was "the only time I ever have been beaten by the people." Such a statement was thus an accurate cover for not mentioning his two failed attempts to gain the US Senate. The brevity of this autobiography reflects the modest political persona Lincoln often presented. Even so, when he sent the autobiography to Fell, he said he would not object to material being added from his speeches, but he stipulated that the autobiography "must not appear to have been written by myself."[59] Clearly, he did not want to appear overly ambitious.

On February 9 Lincoln wrote a one-paragraph letter to Norman B. Judd, a leading Chicago Republican involved in the intraparty feud, soliciting his help and specifying privacy. Lincoln must have known that Judd would support him for their party's presidential nomination, rather than vice presidential nomination, as some other Illinois Republicans favored. The directness and figurative language of Lincoln's letter convey his urgency in gaining strategic positioning:

I am not in a position where it would hurt much for me to not be nominated on the national ticket; but I am where it would hurt some for me to not get the Illinois delegates. What I expected when I wrote the letter to Messrs. Dole and others is now happening. Your discomfited assailants are most bitter against me; and they will, for revenge upon me, lay to the [Edward] Bates egg in the South, and to the [William H.] Seward egg in the North, and go far towards squeezing me out in the middle with nothing. Can you not help me a little in this matter, in your end of the vineyard?[60]

In the week following this letter to Judd, the *Chicago Press and Tribune* endorsed Lincoln for president with high praise. Historians credit Judd's influence with that paper for securing the endorsement.

Lincoln's last significant political composition before traveling to New York to deliver the Cooper Union address was a letter of February 14 addressed to three Sangamon County farmers, who sought clarification of the House Divided speech. This letter shows that speech continued to be problematic for Lincoln well beyond his many refutations of Douglas's criticism of it before, during, and after the debates. Lincoln defensively responds, "It puzzles me to make my meaning plainer." He notes that Douglas has accused him of trying to incite civil war, but again Lincoln denies it. He closes by telling his readers he will offer answers to other questions they may have.[61] In writing to these farmers, Lincoln shows a scrupulous commitment to personal communication with ordinary citizens to make his political views clear. With this letter, like the Milwaukee address, Lincoln was reaching out to members of the large, rural population in an effort to fight Douglas and popular sovereignty.

Defining and Defending Republicanism in the Cooper Union Address

On February 27, 1860, Lincoln delivered the Cooper Union address to an elite New York audience of 1,500, and this composition is sometimes referred to as the speech that made him president.[62] In mid-October 1859 Lincoln was pleased to receive a mailed invitation to speak in Henry Ward Beecher's church at Brooklyn, New York. Lincoln then spent weeks researching in the Illinois State Library and writing the speech that he would deliver on the appointed date but at the changed location of New York's Cooper Union Institute. He received $200 for this speech.[63] (In 2023 that amount equals about $7,416.60.[64]) At 7,600 words the Cooper Union address falls between the length of the Peoria speech at 16,800 words (his longest political speech) and the House Divided speech at 3,180 words (one of his shortest formal speeches). Each of his two major 1859 speeches in Ohio is over 11,000 words.

The Cooper Union address is one of Lincoln's most extensively discussed and praised compositions.[65] Yet a couple of critical commentaries on this speech suggest that additional analysis could yield more insight. Harold Holzer remarks, "Stylistically, it [Cooper Union address] is so completely unlike anything that Lincoln produced either before or after his New York appearance. . . . It is infinitely more restrained, intricate, and statesmanlike than the stem-winding oratory with which Lincoln earned his reputation as a public speaker in the West. . . . It represents an altogether unique rhetorical watershed, the transforming moment separating the prairie stump speaker and the presidential orator."[66] True, in Lincoln's previous frequent use of historical research, he never presented such an extensive, inductive analysis of archival data as that seen in the first section of the Cooper Union address, but otherwise Holzer's characterization of this speech warrants qualification. A common understanding is that in matters of communication, *style* refers to language usage, not a range of rhetorical or literary qualities, and Lincoln's language in the Cooper Union address features the same direct, plain, and figurative language with occasional eloquent passages as seen in his previous major speeches.

Although characterizing the Cooper Union address as unlike any of Lincoln's speeches before and after it, Holzer briefly acknowledges that Lincoln "had offered many of [this speech's] arguments before, rehearsing and refining them across the West." The Cooper Union address's rhetorical antecedents could have been more usefully and specifically identified beginning with the Peoria speech. As the foundational speech of Lincoln's second political career, the Peoria speech blends historical, legal, and moral antislavery argumentation and use of satire to criticize Douglas. All of these elements appear in the Cooper Union address. The Peoria speech and the Cooper Union address are the rhetorical bookends of Lincoln's rise to the presidential nomination. Between those speeches are other milestone speeches, for example: the Chicago speech of July 10, 1858, the final speech of the Lincoln-Douglas debates, and the Ohio speeches. Burlingame maintains that "there is little new in this speech" (Cooper Union address).[67] Yet he does not elaborate, owing to the biographer's need to prioritize historical context, summarize, and report effects of the speech.

The sponsors of the Cooper Union address invited a political lecture, and the audience surely was curious about what the rising westerner would say. Lincoln delivered a hybrid cross between a political lecture and a campaign speech that deferred emphatically emotional appeals to near the end of the speech, as he often did in previous speeches. This book has noted political implications in Lincoln's other lectures, and lecture qualities in his political speeches, especially beginning with the 1854 Peoria speech.

The Cooper Union address refutes multiple claims against the Republican Party and defines its cause with broad appeal. In this speech Lincoln often refutes those claims with ironic reversal, giving a biting, satirical edge to those refutations, whose cleverness surely amused the sophisticated New York listening audience and wider eastern reading audience. This speech consists of three main sections: the first, 45 percent of the speech, implicitly addresses Douglas and his supporters. It exploits Douglas's thesis that the nation's fathers "understood this question [of slavery] just as well, and even better, than we do now." The second section, 41 percent of the speech, ostensibly addresses southerners (prosopoeia) but northerners as well. It attacks southerners' accusation that the Republican Party is sectional. The third section, 14 percent of the speech, rallies Republicans to adhere to their moral stance against slavery.

In the first body section Lincoln extended the "turning the tables" refutation of Douglas's argument from the preceding fall that "Our Fathers, when they framed the government under which we live, understood this question just as well, and even better, than we do now." Douglas had broadly conceived of the fathers as consisting of the generation of Americans at the establishment of the republic, but his rhetoric excluded foundational documents. In contrast, Lincoln defined the founders as the thirty-nine signers of the Constitution and first twelve amendments. Lincoln maintained that the thirty-nine fathers' voting records before, during, and after signing the Constitution show that they believed there was nothing in the Constitution prohibiting Congress from controlling slavery in the territories.

Graham A. Peck writes that Lincoln's adaptation of the founders' voting records is "carefully researched" and "straightforward" but finds Lincoln's inductive leap manipulative that the founders' voting records are evidence that they favored the eventual abolition of slavery: "In a masterful sleight of hand Lincoln inferred from it [the founders' voting records] that the Founders intended to put slavery in the course of ultimate extinction, a conclusion that did not follow from the premises. After all, as Lincoln conceded in a different context [passage] in the speech, the power to prohibit slavery did not imply the expediency of doing so. This was no small discrepancy considering that Lincoln's idea of an antislavery nation rested upon his historical argument."[68] John Channing Briggs scrupulously identifies limitations in Lincoln's selection of the founders and in their voting records he cites.[69] Regardless, Lincoln's antislavery argumentation in various previous compositions, beginning with the Peoria speech, repeatedly cited provisions in the Constitution as evidence of the founders' intention for the eventual end of slavery, and his ongoing case against slavery depended heavily on moral suasion.

A close reading of the Cooper Union address reveals another, less important example of Lincoln's rhetorical sleight of hand that reflects his attention to detail: the use of the word *probably* to hedge a point. For example, Lincoln writes: "The sum of the whole is, that of our thirty-nine fathers who framed the Constitution, twenty-one—a clear majority of the whole—certainly understood that no proper division of local from federal authority, nor any part of the Constitution, forbade the Federal Government to control slavery in the federal territories; while all the rest *probably* [emphasis mine] had the same understanding."[70] Lincoln uses *probably* six times in this speech, more times than in any of his other compositions. Yet the prevailing high regard for this speech confirms that the limitations of his selection of founders, use of their voting records, and minor verbal hedging do not overshadow the overall merits of the speech.

With sarcastic criticism of Douglas, Lincoln argues that anyone who questions congressional authorization to control slavery in territories is entitled to do so but "should, at the same time, brave the responsibility of declaring that, in his opinion, he understands their [the founders'] principles better than they did themselves; and especially should he not shirk that responsibility by asserting that they 'understood the question just as well, and even better, than we do now.'"[71] Lincoln closes the first section by aligning Republican policy with his interpretation of the founders' regard for slavery: "As those Fathers marked it, so let it be again marked as evil not to be extended, but to be tolerated and protected only because of and so far as its actual presence among us makes that toleration and protection a necessity."[72] Lincoln had observed the constitutional necessity of protection for existing slavery in previous speeches, beginning with the Peoria speech.

The second section of the Cooper Union address broadens Lincoln's refutational targets, which paint Republicans as extremists, beginning with the accusation that southerners refuse even to listen to northerners on slavery. In addressing the southern accusation that the Republican Party is sectional, Lincoln challenges southerners to prove that Republican "principle or practice" harms them. Reversing the southerners' accusation of northern sectionalism, Lincoln cites their refusal to agree with the prohibition of slavery in western territories established by the Northwest Ordinance and thus their rejection of a foundational, national policy endorsed by Washington. Lincoln also reverses the southerners' claim to conservatism by pointing out that the North accepts and the South rejects the "old policy" on slavery established by "our Fathers who framed the government under which we live,' [as] you with one accord reject, and scout, and spit upon that old policy, and insist on substituting something new."[73] Lincoln cites this fact to reverse the southern charge that the North has made the "slavery question more prominent than it formerly was." Holzer notes that Lincoln used the phrase "our Fathers who framed this government" "no fewer than fifteen times, and one can only imagine how he delights his audience each time he renews the refrain." In refuting the accusation that Republicans are radical and promote slave insurrections, Lincoln at length criticizes John Brown's attack on the federal arsenal at Harper's Ferry, to distance the Republican cause from radical abolitionism.

Lincoln also repeats his 1857 criticism of *Dred Scott*, arguing that in due time and due process the Supreme Court will correct its mistaken, proslavery ruling. Lincoln recalls that signers of the Constitution resolved their differences over slavery "without division among themselves . . . without basing it upon any mistaken statement of facts." With that historical precedent and Republicans' commitment to upholding the Constitution, Lincoln caps his refutation by asking whether the South will "break up this government" unless its views on slavery prevail as national policy. In this speech emphasizing rational appeals, Lincoln cannot refrain from also voicing his feeling about the South's refusal to accept a Republican president, expressing his outrage with ironic figurative language: "In that supposed event, you say, you will destroy the Union; and then, you say, the great crime of having destroyed it will be upon us! This is cool [insolent]. A highwayman holds a pistol to my ear, and mutters through his teeth, 'Stand and deliver, or I shall kill you, and then you will be a murderer!'"[74] Lincoln compares extortion of money with extortion of votes—a striking conclusion to the second section, with emphasis on rational and emotional appeals.

The last section addresses Republicans, presenting the dilemma and challenge Lincoln sees for their party. First, Lincoln advises that Republicans must do their part to accomplish national peace and harmony, and in the face of southern provocation they must "do nothing through passion and ill temper," echoing an emphasis on rationality to solve a political problem as seen in his 1838 Lyceum address. Repeating the theme of the House Divided speech but with less emotion-charged language, Lincoln predicts that southern provocation will increase: "Holding, as they [southerners] do, that slavery is morally right, and socially elevating, they cannot cease to demand full national recognition of it, as a legal right, and a social blessing."[75] With a call to reject Douglas and popular sovereignty, Lincoln urges Republicans to use their votes to reject "some middle ground between the right and the wrong, vain as the search for a man who would be neither a living man nor a dead man—such as the policy of 'don't care' on a question about which all men do care—such as Union appeals beseeching true Union men to yield to disunionists." In language with religious and patriotic appeal, Lincoln admonishes that yielding to southern intransigence, slander, and "false accusations" would be "reversing divine rule, and calling, not the sinners, but the righteous to repentance—such as invocations to Washington, imploring men to unsay what Washington said, and undo what Washington did." Lincoln invokes Washington's name eight times in this speech and Jefferson's twice.

The preceding irony-laden quotation leads to one of the most famous examples of Lincoln's eloquence in his rise to the presidency—the call to moral action that concludes the Cooper Union address: "LET US HAVE FAITH THAT RIGHT MAKES MIGHT, AND IN THAT FAITH, LET US, TO

THE END, DARE TO DO OUR DUTY AS WE UNDERSTAND IT."
(Typographers often used all-capitals to highlight passages that Lincoln under-lined for emphasis.) The day after Lincoln gave this speech, at least 170,000 copies appeared in various newspapers, with widespread positive reaction.[76]

The Cooper Union address extended Lincoln's aspirational approach to fight slavery. Holzer maintains that the second section of that speech "has misled some historians for generations, leading them to judge the Cooper Union address as conservative." Holzer explains that Lincoln's conservatism differs from southern calls to reinstate the slave trade and from Douglas's popular sovereignty. Holzer points out that Lincoln's conservatism rests in his belief that the founders intended to "curtail the spread of slavery," characterizing the second section of the Cooper Union address as "conservative in tone, but liberal in message."[77] In the last section Lincoln's plea that Republicans stand by their condemnation of slavery as wrong is arguably an even stronger suggestion of liberal inclination, and throughout Lincoln's second political career he often cited the immorality of slavery. Burlingame has written that "Abraham Lincoln disguised the wolf of radical antislavery nationalism with conservative sheep's clothing."[78]

Conclusion

From the Peoria speech through the Cooper Union address, the masterful compositions of Lincoln's second political career show that he was emerging as a Republican statesman. His 1859 and early 1860 compositions exemplify the inventiveness and rhetorical growth that accounted for that emergence, as he strengthened his antislavery messages and delivered them to a broader geographical and social/cultural range of audiences than before. The genre of those compositions is diverse: letters sent to Republican leaders beyond Illinois, lectures in Illinois and New York, a ceremonial address and political speeches in Wisconsin, and campaign speeches in Ohio and Kansas. Lincoln's use of genre was versatile. For example, his ceremonial Wisconsin address is a motivational lecture championing free labor and promoting education as the key to improving the small farmer's production and satisfaction. The lecture at Cooper Union includes a campaign-style, inspirational message. Lincoln adapted his December 1859 Kansas messages and the Cooper Union address to denounce John Brown's raid at Harper's Ferry, asserting Republicans' rejection of radicalism.

Several of Lincoln's compositions of this period continued to defend his House Divided speech thesis that US history and Douglasism indicated a trend toward the nationalization of slavery. In his Second Lecture on Discoveries and Inventions, Lincoln employed satire to deflate Douglas through criticism not only of popular sovereignty but also of his ambitious support for westward expansion, limited intellectual ability, and indulgence in liquor and cigars. Lincoln's Columbus and Cincinnati speeches argue that Douglas's popular sovereignty was a proslavery policy that he advocated through devious rhetorical methods betraying moral deficiency. The result of that rhetoric, Lincoln maintained, is to corrupt public opinion to be indifferent to slavery and accept its spread to free states. Lincoln's moral indictment of Douglas in the Ohio speeches is more elaborate than in previous compositions.

The Columbus speech is a comprehensive refutation of popular sovereignty achieved through incisive rhetorical analysis of Douglas's *Harper's* essay. Lincoln's Columbus speech prefigures the political/rhetorical thesis of the Cooper Union address: that the founders had understood slavery better than his contemporaries. Lincoln's use of that proposition is a "turning the tables" refutation of Douglas's use of it in his *Harper's* essay. Douglas may have conceived his proposition as a reversal of Lincoln's "turnabout is fair play" response in the sixth Lincoln-Douglas debate to the southern Representative Preston Brooks's claim that "the men who formed this government were wiser and better men than the men of these days."

The moral deficiency Lincoln imputes to Douglas in the Columbus speech makes Lincoln vulnerable to a charge of demagogic aspersion, but this personal criticism derives from astute assessment of the *Harper's* essay. The part of Lincoln's Cincinnati speech addressing Kentuckians (and other southerners) to show them how Douglas is a proslavery northern asset is sugar-coated with humor and irony. This part of the Cincinnati speech carried a mirrored message to antislavery northern Democrats that Douglas did not serve their interests. Lincoln's use of extended irony for political satire in that speech is unparalleled in his rhetoric, exemplifying adaptation of a literary mode as a political/rhetorical strategy.

The satire in the Cincinnati speech risked alienating southerners who might have thought that Lincoln was mocking them for being gullible enough to believe Douglas was their benefactor. Lincoln is blunt in predicting the failure of secession, but he says he is open to a southerner as president or vice president. Lincoln's post-Ohio speeches show his determination to take his pro-Republican messages to more and more places and audiences, including unfriendly, proslavery Democrats in Kansas, who heard Lincoln warn them against the use of violence, and friendly audiences in the East, including countless readers. Lincoln is also blunt toward the South in the Cooper Union address, chastising it for considering disunion unless its proslavery cause prevails.

The Cooper Union address and subsequent speeches in the East closed Lincoln's prepresidential case against slavery and Douglas, defined Republicanism with broad appeal, and opened the door wider to a presidential nomination. By early 1860 Douglas's chances that Republicans would adopt him as a leader had greatly lessened, and Douglasism had heavily contributed to the fragmentation of the Democratic Party. Yet even after the Cooper Union address Lincoln "remained concerned that Douglas continued to spread what he termed the 'infernal stereotypical lye'—perhaps a mere misspelling, perhaps a homonym to suggest Douglas's corrosive falsification of Lincoln's position on 'Negro equality.'"[79]

Conclusions

Lincoln's prepresidential compositions tell a decades-long, complicated story of how he applied foundational rhetorical principles in his struggle to rise in the Whig and Republican parties. Lincoln learned how to leverage his values, beliefs, and relationships to formulate messages with implicit or explicit moral appeal appropriate for various purposes and audiences. His compositions enabled him to gain political capital incrementally, culminating in the presidential nomination. Through his evolving rhetorical ability, he achieved eloquence and statesmanship, and he left a distinguished rhetorical record and legacy even before his presidential election. Lincoln entered the presidency remarkably well prepared for the communicative challenges of that office.

Lincoln's two prepresidential political careers show determined ambition in that field, and his political/rhetorical activities benefited from intellectual curiosity and growth guided by a moral compass. His combined expertise as a political/rhetorical critic, writer, and promoter of his writing helped him to surmount ongoing political challenges and major setbacks. In the six years of his second political career (1854–1860), Lincoln twice failed to achieve his goal of becoming a US senator, yet his rhetorical power gave him political resilience. His prepresidential political achievements demonstrate the principle that rhetorical skill is essential for success in a profession. Knowledge of foundational genre and rhetorical elements, traced to classical antiquity, helps us understand Lincoln's rhetorical consistency, versatility, and growth.

Lincoln's rhetoric aimed to advance the greater good according to his values and beliefs, and he blended historical, legalistic, and moral argumentation with rational, emotional, and ethical appeals to reach for credibility, political advancement, and esteem. Paradoxically, Lincoln's argumentation for just causes and purposes included methods that could be considered demagogic. Those purposes included criticism of political opponents and their policies that Lincoln believed did not serve economic and social justice. Lincoln's most controversial rhetorical methods were rhetorical sleight of hand, loaded language, and personal attacks. Lincoln used rhetorical sleight of hand in three major prepresidential speeches: the Dred Scott speech, the House Divided speech, and the Cooper Union address. Lincoln's most conspicuous use of sleight of hand was in the House Divided speech, with extended analogies to allege Democratic proslavery conspiracy. Lincoln always used language with emotional appeal, often in other kinds of figures of speech, and such usage is vulnerable to criticism as demagogic. A striking example of his use of figurative language was the extended irony in the Cincinnati speech to satirize Douglas as a savior for the South. Lincoln knew well that personal attacks were controversial, and in the Lincoln-Douglas debates, he defended his use of them. Significantly, his last major criticism of Douglas, in the Cincinnati speech, humorously attacked his policies and rhetorical methods.

The term *ethical political rhetoric* seems like an oxymoron, but Lincoln developed one. From the beginning, his compositions indirectly or directly appealed to the moral consciousness that he well understood was embedded in a predominantly Christian society. His rhetoric grew especially commendable in his second political career, owing to his multifaceted antislavery argumentation with patriotic and altruistic appeals. Those qualities offset his use of less-noble but expedient rhetorical elements. Lincoln's qualified use of demagogic methods did not make him a demagogue, and sometimes his writing rose to eloquence and statesmanship.

Lincoln's first announcement to run for public office expressed a worthy ambition that accounted for the ethical rhetoric he developed in his two prepresidential political careers and rewarded him with the presidential nomination: pursuing political goals while wanting to be respected: "I can say for one that I have no other [ambition] so great as that of being truly esteemed of [by] my fellow men, by rendering myself worthy of their esteem." Lincoln saw public service as the path to gain that advantage, but he did not seek political advancement at the cost of losing self-respect. Lincoln's greatest challenge in fulfilling his political ambition was how to respond to the often demagogic rhetoric of his chief rival, Stephen A. Douglas. To do so, Lincoln learned how to become an astute critic of Douglas's policies, rhetoric, and moral qualities.

Except for stump speeches, Lincoln's immediate audience in his first political career was not the public, but he reached it because his speeches and other writings were published in government documents, newspapers, or pamphlets. Early on, Lincoln began revising some of his compositions for publication and taking personal action to get his work in print. The compositions of his first political career show a surprisingly high level of skill for a young adult who had grown up in rural areas and was mainly self-educated, and those compositions—not his meager legislative accomplishments—advanced him from a rustic political novice to a state party leader. In his second political career, the public was often Lincoln's immediate audience, and his published speeches reached a wider readership than before. Those compositions show an increasing resourcefulness to adapt his rhetoric to greater and greater political challenges, enabling his elevation to national leadership. An example of this resourcefulness is that often his compositions are genre hybrids: his application of historical information, including nonartistic proofs, gives lecture quality to his eulogies and political compositions, and his lectures convey indirect or direct political messages.

Consistency and Versatility

In his prepresidential life, Lincoln composed in various genres: legal documents, campaign announcements, stump speeches for his own campaigns and for presidential campaigns (Whigs in 1836, 1840, 1844, 1848, and 1852; Republicans in 1856), debate speeches, addresses in the Illinois legislature and Congress, legislative resolutions and remarks, handbills, lectures, eulogies for President Zachary Taylor and Senator Henry Clay, private and public letters, and even poetry. He adapted his political messages to fellow members of the Whig and Republican parties, oppositional parties, political rivals, the Illinois state legislature, the US House of Representatives, and the public (sometimes with northerners, southerners, or Christians especially in mind). His compositions show a tendency to view public affairs with a businesslike, problem-solution perspective, combining arguments for his party's positions and policies with refutation/criticism of the opposition. Often his rhetoric not only reflected Whig or Republican positions and policies but also attempted to shape them. Lincoln thus established partisan leadership, built the Republican base, and gained increasing political advantage.

Lincoln's moral argumentation reflected his sense of social justice, and his political compositions advocated for qualified economic, social, and political progress. His moral argumentation was mostly implicit in his first political career as he promoted internal improvements and sought to obtain their economic and social benefits. Lincoln and Dan Stone's 1837 Protest in the Illinois Legislature on Slavery was overtly legalistic, with an antislavery moral message as the subtext. Lincoln never wavered from this antislavery position. Lincoln's 1838 Lyceum address calling for "a reverence for the Constitution and laws" to sustain the Union was an implicit moral plea for righteousness in society and government. His 1848 Mexican War speech accused President Polk of beginning an unconstitutional war, but the harsh personal satire overshadowed the moral message of criticizing Polk for excessive ambition. In his 1852 Eulogy on Henry Clay, during the interim of Lincoln's two political careers, he praised Clay for his antislavery stance, aligning himself with it.

Beginning his second political career with the 1854 Peoria speech, Lincoln often used explicit, antislavery moral argumentation as the most potent weapon in his rhetorical arsenal, besides formidable refutation of his critics, especially Douglas. Lincoln qualified his antislavery moral argumentation with the admission that he did not favor social and political equality between white people and black people. (His Last speech indicated a willingness to change that position, endorsing voting rights for black Civil War veterans.)

The introductions of Lincoln's major political speeches identify a problem, often including the need for refutation because he wanted to present a timely, direct rejoinder to something a Democrat said or wrote. The body sections of Lincoln's speeches creatively blend argument for his policy positions with refutation sections or passages and vice versa. His refutations fault the contradictions, distortions, and factual errors in an opponent's rhetoric. Lincoln typically uses the legalistic and dramatic strategy of reserving his most important points for near the end of a composition, including his most cutting satire and calls for certain ways of thinking, making decisions, or taking action.

Lincoln's sequencing of sections in the body of his compositions shows he understood fundamentals derived from classical rhetoric. Two of his political speeches are textbook examples of using structural design according to classical rhetoric: the 1839 Subtreasury speech (the last major speech of his time in the Illinois legislature) and the 1854 Peoria speech (the first major speech of his second political career). Lincoln's other compositions employ structural elements with flexibility according to his purposes and audiences. All his compositions show rhetorical inventiveness, including his responses to demagoguery and qualified use of it.

Thirteen key speeches illustrate Lincoln's rhetorical consistency and versatility, and they serve as benchmarks in his political/rhetorical evolution: five from his first political career, one from between his political careers, and seven from his second.[1] Lincoln's rhetoric benefited immensely from the lawyerly, robust refutations for which he had a distinct talent, and they defined his political positions and policy—what he faulted revealed what he believed and advocated. Lincoln often strengthened his arguments with such nonartistic proofs as the Northwest Ordinance of 1787, the Declaration of Independence, and the Constitution, and their use adds an emotional appeal of patriotism. Besides using foundational documents, Lincoln invoked the name of George Washington and sometimes such other founders as John Adams, Thomas Jefferson, and James Madison. Lincoln enriched his compositions with biblical quotations and allusions, which appealed to the many Christians in his audiences. Lincoln's use of such words as *ethical, justice, moral,* and *truth* expressed his appeal to righteousness—the essential element in this book's working definition of eloquence as the use of cogent moral argumentation and emotive language to inspire belief in a cause for social justice or action to achieve it.

Lincoln developed political/moral messages strengthened by strong refutation without being self-righteous, using appeals traced to classical rhetoric.

The Declaration of Independence contains the central proposition of natural human rights that anchored Lincoln's antislavery moral argumentation, and he metaphorically referred to this document three times as "the charter of our liberties." All three references were in speeches during the 1858 Senate campaign (Chicago, July 10; Lewistown, August 17; and Alton, October 15). Before he became president, Lincoln had emerged as one of the nation's preeminent voices on the relationship between the Constitution and slavery. Then in Fragment on the Constitution and the Union, January 1861 (perhaps earlier), Lincoln wrote that the "liberty to all" principle of the Declaration of Independence was America's "apple of gold," and "the *Union*, and the *Constitution*, are the *picture of silver*, subsequently framed around it. The picture was made, not to *conceal*, or *destroy* the apple; but to *adorn*, and *preserve* it. The *picture* was made *for* the apple—*not* the apple for the picture."[2]

One of the most significant findings of this study's rhetorical/textual analyses of the thirteen key speeches concerns the comparative number of references to the Declaration of Independence and Constitution. In those speeches Lincoln referred to the Declaration fifty-four times and to the Constitution 284 times, with a ratio of 1 to 5.3. In his first political career, Lincoln cited the Declaration very little: once in the Lyceum address and once in the Subtreasury speech. During that time he cited the Constitution most often in the 1839 Subtreasury speech (twenty times), 1848 Internal Improvements speech (twenty-one times), and 1848 Presidential Question speech (sixteen times). In the Subtreasury speech Lincoln reminded the audience that the Whigs had refuted the opposition's claim that a national bank is unconstitutional by claiming that Washington and Jackson, as well as many signers of the Declaration of Independence, "framers of the Constitution," and the Supreme Court sanctioned such a federal enterprise. In the Internal Improvements speech, Lincoln discussed how prominent politicians and jurists have debated whether congressional expenditure for those kinds of improvements may or may not be constitutional, concluding that expediency justifies that expenditure. In the Presidential Question speech, Lincoln quoted Taylor's correspondence testifying to the general's belief that policy and legislation need to conform to constitutional constraint, and Lincoln referred to Taylor as a dutiful military leader in the Mexican War despite its unconstitutionality.

Lincoln's most extensive use of the Declaration of Independence and Constitution came in his second political career, in the 1850s. During that period Lincoln used the Constitution much more frequently than the Declaration, citing the Declaration fifty times and the Constitution 218 times, with a ratio of 1 to 4.4. The most frequent citations of the Declaration in his second political career were in the Dred Scott speech (seventeen times) and his final speech of the Lincoln-Douglas debates (eighteen times). Lincoln cited the Constitution frequently in seven main speeches of this period: twenty-three times in the Peoria speech, twenty-two times in the Dred Scott speech, fifteen times in the House Divided speech, twenty-nine times in his final speech of the Lincoln-Douglas debates, forty-one times in the Columbus speech, twenty-six times in the Cincinnati speech, and sixty-two times in the Cooper Union address. At Cooper Union Lincoln made no direct reference to the Declaration of Independence.

Beginning with his Peoria speech, the frequent use of the Constitution that Lincoln made in his major speeches contributed significantly to the synthesis of rational, emotional, and ethical appeals of his antislavery argumentation. In that speech Lincoln acknowledged the protections of slavery under the Constitution and maintained that its signers intended for slavery to end eventually. He cited the constitutional provision that fugitive slaves must be returned, that after twenty years the source of the slave trade should be "cut off," and that free states suffered the injustice of southerners having the advantage of additional members in the House of Representatives by counting three-fifths of the slave population. Lincoln did not call for amendments to the Constitution to eliminate any of its provisions sanctioning slavery, saying that he stood for the Constitution "fairly, fully, and firmly." He also pointed out that the founders who signed the Constitution also enacted the Ordinance of 1787, which prohibited slavery in the northwestern territories. Lincoln declared that this historical consistency denied credibility to Douglas's interpretation of history in support of popular sovereignty. Lincoln maintained that the foundational documents proved that slavery concerned the entire nation, not just a local entity, and that the question of slavery in new territories was thus subject to congressional authority.

In the Peoria speech Lincoln called for the restoration of the Missouri Compromise to return slavery to "that spirit which first gave us the Constitution, and which has thrice saved the Union." Otherwise, he predicted, the South and North will be divided, and government under the Constitution will be threatened: "Already a few in the North, defy all constitutional restraints, resist the execution of the Fugitive Slave Law, and even menace the institution of slavery in the states where it exists." Further, Lincoln cited the constitutional provision to mitigate the slave trade and said the founders were limited in what they could do about slavery out of the necessity to get the Constitution approved.

Drawing on the Constitution in the Dred Scott speech, Lincoln denied that he advocated defying the *Dred Scott* decision, as Douglas charged, but regarded it as "erroneous" and subject to correction. Lincoln noted that the Constitution allows for individual interpretation of judicial decisions at the highest level, and he maintained that because *Dred Scott* was not a unanimous decision, it was not settled law. Lincoln observed that the Supreme Court had reversed itself on other questions.

The House Divided speech argued that the proponents of slavery extension had deliberately included reference to the Constitution in the 1854 Kansas-Nebraska Act in preparation of advancing their cause in the 1857 *Dred Scott* decision: "What the *Constitution* had to do with it [the Kansas-Nebraska Act], outsiders could not *then* see. Plainly enough *now*, it was an exactly fitted *niche*, for the *Dred Scott* decision to afterwards come in, and declare the *perfect freedom* of the people, to be just no freedom at all." That is, the majority of the Supreme Court in that decision, Lincoln noted, "declared that the Constitution of the United States neither permits Congress nor a territorial legislature to exclude slavery from any United States territory[;] they all *omit* to declare whether or not the same Constitution permits a state, or the people of a *state*, to exclude it." Lincoln argued that deliberately leaving unanswered the question of when a state's power to legislate about slavery is "restrained" by the Constitution forms "another nice little niche" that in due time may be "filled with another Supreme Court decision, declaring that the Constitution of the United States does not permit a *state* to exclude slavery from its limits."

In the last Lincoln-Douglas debate, at Alton, Lincoln cited the Constitution to refute Douglas's "beautiful fabrication" that he sought "a perfect, social, and political equality between the white and black races." Lincoln did so by repeating his previous emphasis on the treatment of slavery in the Constitution to indicate his alignment with the founders' intention that eventually "the institution of slavery [should] come to an end." In his final debate speech, Lincoln placed most of his references to the Constitution in the last two paragraphs, for emphasis. He pointed out the inconsistency between the *Dred Scott* decision's declaration that introducing slavery into territories is constitutional and Douglas's insistence that local legislation and police enforcement can prevent that introduction. Lincoln rejected Douglas's policy with insinuated aspersion: "I repeat that there has never been so monstrous a doctrine uttered from the mouth of a respectable man."

Lincoln concluded his final Lincoln-Douglas debate speech with blade-twisting criticism of Douglas based on the conflict between *Dred Scott* and Douglas's definition of popular sovereignty: "The man who argues that by unfriendly legislation, in spite of that constitutional right [to take slaves into a territory], slavery may be driven from the territories, cannot avoid furnishing an argument by which abolitionists may deny the obligation to return fugitives. . . . " Lincoln denied that there is an "iota of difference between the constitutional right to reclaim a fugitive, and the constitutional right to hold a slave, in a territory, provided this *Dred Scott* decision is correct." In turning Douglas's popular sovereignty position against him, Lincoln shrewdly ended his final debate speech with the irony of reversing the charge Douglas made against Lincoln in the first debate that he was an abolitionist. This reversal is one of the best examples of Lincoln's intellectual capacity to create a "turning the tables" argument.

In the 1859 speech at Columbus, Ohio, Lincoln reasserted his position that the Kansas-Nebraska Act and *Dred Scott* removed the constitutional power of Congress to prohibit slavery in new territories and could as well do that in free states. Lincoln explains: "From the adoption of the Constitution down to 1820 is the precise period of our history when we had comparative peace upon this question—the precise period of time when we came nearer to having peace about it than any other time of that entire one hundred and sixty years, in which he [Douglas] says it began, or of the eighty years of our own constitution." In critiquing Douglas's *Harper's Magazine* essay, Lincoln said that Douglas is wrong to consider the question of slavery in territories to be one of those "little, unimportant, trivial matters" that are exclusively of local significance and thus of no concern to the federal government.

The compositions of Lincoln's political careers demonstrate consistent use of figurative language to enhance his argumentation: the positive or negative connotations of his figurative language strengthen his rational and emotional appeals. Lincoln used figurative language in his pre-1854 rhetoric to belittle individuals, for example, referring to Usher Linder as a snobbish hunter in the 1837 State Bank speech, to President Polk as a deranged animal in the 1848 Mexican War speech, and to Lewis Cass as a glutton in the 1848 Presidential Question speech. In the speeches of his second political career, Lincoln consistently supported his views with figures of speech (some examples quoted in the preceding chapters are cited again below for emphasis). In the Peoria speech and in his final speech of the Lincoln-Douglas debates, Lincoln compared slavery to a disease: "Thus, the thing [slavery] is hid away, in the Constitution, just as an afflicted man hides away a wen or a cancer, which he dares not cut out at once, lest he bleed to death; with the promise, nevertheless, that the cutting may begin at the end of a given time." Without the restoration of the Missouri Compromise, Lincoln argued (with mixed metaphors) that slavery "is to be transformed into a 'sacred right.' Nebraska [Kansas-Nebraska Act] brings it forth, places it on the high road to extension and perpetuity; and, with a pat on its back, says to it, 'Go, and God speed you.' Henceforth it is to be the chief jewel of the nation—the very figure-head of the ship of state. Little by little, but steadily as man's march to the grave, we have been giving up the OLD for the NEW faith."

In the second half of the Dred Scott speech, Lincoln used figurative language with negative connotation to express how in present times Congress and the Supreme Court were ignoring the equality language of the Declaration of Independence "to aid in making the bondage of the Negro universal and eternal." The current power structure holds the Negro "in a prison house."

He is "bolted in with a lock of a hundred keys, which can never be unlocked without the concurrence of every key; the keys in the hands of a hundred different men, and they scattered to a hundred different and distant places; and they stand musing as to what invention, in all the dominions of mind and matter, can be produced to make the impossibility of his escape more complete than it is."

Figurative language—specifically, metaphor and analogy—permeates the House Divided speech and drives its purposes. The house-divided metaphor expressed the fear of an imminent existential crisis for the nation. It was also a critical time for Lincoln to secure his leadership in the Republican Party because some of its eastern members were considering Douglas for such a role. Lincoln's analogies comparing the roles of the Kansas-Nebraska Act, Douglas, Presidents Pierce and Buchanan, and *Dred Scott* with machinery and building construction expressed his alleged Democratic collaboration to advance slavery into the territories and free states. Lincoln mocked popular sovereignty as "squatter sovereignty," comparing its folly owing to the *Dred Scott* decision to "temporary scaffolding—like the mould at the foundry [that] served through one blast and fell back to loose sand—and helped to carry an election, and then was kicked to the winds." Lincoln used metaphor to say that he as a "living dog" is preferable to Douglas as "a caged and toothless" lion: "How can he oppose the advances of slavery? He don't [*sic*] care anything about it. His avowed mission is impressing the 'public heart' to *care* nothing about it." Lincoln's comparison of himself to a "living dog" is hardly flattering, but his comparison of Douglas to a "caged and toothless lion" is truly denigrating.

Lincoln's final speech of the Lincoln-Douglas debates featured loaded metaphoric language to support his views. Referring to Douglas's sharp, repeated criticisms of the House Divided speech, Lincoln said, "He has warred upon them as Satan does upon the Bible." Lincoln contended that the Kansas-Nebraska Act, which gave territorial residents the power (popular sovereignty) to decide the slavery question, "clothed the people of the territories with a superior degree of self-government beyond what they had ever had before." Lincoln reiterated that the problems arising from efforts to spread slavery yielded experience that "speaks in thunder tones, telling us that the policy which has given peace to the country heretofore, being returned to, gives the greatest promise of peace again." He repeated his comparison of slavery to "a wen or a cancer." He referred to Douglas's rhetoric that obscures the immorality and injustice of slavery as a "fog" to be "rid of."

Lincoln used a considerable amount of metaphoric language in the 1859 Columbus speech to mock Douglas's view of slavery as strictly a local concern without moral significance. Lincoln compared introducing slavery into new territories to introducing an invasive species: the first occupants of a new territory "may plant there a thing which, like the Canada thistle, or some other of those pests of the soil, cannot be dug out by the millions of men who will come thereafter." Lincoln asserted that it is "a very well-known fact, that we have never had a serious menace to our political existence, except it sprang from this thing which he [Douglas] chooses to regard as only upon a par with onions and potatoes." Lincoln sarcastically charged that in Douglas's view the federal government has the right to appoint such local officials as governors and judges because the good or evil they may leave behind is of "a vast national magnitude," but the "planting of slavery upon a soil—a thing which once planted cannot be eradicated by the succeeding millions . . . without infinite difficulty and a long struggle—he considers . . . as one of these little, local, trivial things that the nation ought not to say a word about." Lincoln referred to the confusing contradiction between the *Dred Scott* decision allowing slavery into territories and Douglas's popular sovereignty disallowing it as "trash," "collateral matter," and "chaff." Once this "verbiage" is "cleared away," the "bare absurdity" emerges: "that a thing may be lawfully driven from the place where it has a lawful right to stay."

Lincoln explained that because Douglas began to see this contradiction, he began using devious, figurative language to convince northerners that he intended for "the territories to remain free." Lincoln claimed that Douglas dissimulated with the use of new, deceptive language to describe the relationship between the territories and slavery: "It is now the *Dred Scott* decision, or rather the Constitution under that decision, does not carry slavery into the territories beyond the power of the people of the territories *to control it as other property.*" Lincoln used an analogy to demonstrate that this language was an attempt to obscure Douglas's unchanged position. "Driving a horse out of his lot, is too plain a proposition to be mistaken about; it is putting him on the other side of the fence. Or it might be a sort of exclusion of him from the lot if you were to kill him and let the worms devour him; but neither of these things is the same as 'controlling him as other property.' That would be to feed him, to pamper him, to ride him, to use and abuse him, to make the most money out of him 'as other property.'" This latter meaning, Lincoln maintained, reflects the southern interpretation of controlling other property by taking slaves into territories.

Metaphoric language enhances the conclusion of the Columbus speech. There Lincoln twice used Douglas's metaphor of comparing black people to "reptiles and crocodiles" to describe what Lincoln claimed is the recent change in attitude toward black people "from the rank of man to that of a brute." Douglas's dehumanization of black people was "a new turn of the screw." Lincoln twice referred to Henry Clay's language that "repressing all tendencies to liberty and ultimate emancipation" is "blowing out the moral lights around us." This strategy, Lincoln insisted, was "a steady process of debauching public opinion on this subject."

Beginning early in the Cincinnati speech, Lincoln directly addressed "my brother Kentuckians," and all southerners by implication (prosopopoeia/synecdoche) and said his purpose was to "demonstrate the proposition" that Douglas is "for you, and more wisely for you, than you are for yourselves." Even before taking that direction, Lincoln assured his audience that he accepted the constitutional protection of slavery "or any other of the institutions of our sister states, be they free or slave states." Lincoln included his reasons for maintaining that the Constitution's framers intended for slavery to end eventually as he cleverly interprets Douglas's positions to show he was working to benefit southern proslavery positions.

The section addressing Kentuckians/southerners is Lincoln's most sustained use of figurative language (irony) to claim that Douglas is a proslavery proponent, using extended satire to mock his positions and policies and to fault his character. The proposition that Douglas was more for Kentuckians/southerners than they were for themselves anticipates Lincoln's claim in the Cooper Union address that the founders understood slavery better than his contemporaries.

The Cooper Union address omits direct reference to the Declaration of Independence but invokes the Constitution more than in any other composition as he criticizes Douglas and the intransigent southern defense of slavery, defending and defining Republicanism. That speech features selective, poignant use of metaphors to bolster Lincoln's case, including the comparison of the founders with fathers and the accusation that southerners compare Republicans with reptiles or outlaws, and treat pirates or murderers better. Lincoln also denigrates popular sovereignty by comparing it with "the search for a man who should be neither a living man nor a dead man."

The Evolution of Lincoln's Prepresidential Political Rhetoric

From young adulthood Lincoln was an ambitious but principled politician. He succeeded in politics by shaping and promoting public policy through compelling rhetoric, including extraordinary refutations. Most of that refutation was direct and serious, but some of it was humorous. When Lincoln began his public life in the 1830s, he entered a political culture that often featured sarcastic personal attacks and such other demagogic methods as conspiracy theories and emotional appeals to prejudice and bigotry. Even before he reached maturity, Lincoln became popular for telling stories in which he mimicked people's behavior and speech, and he applied that satirical talent when he began to debate, speak on the stump, and publish pseudonymous and anonymous letters in the *Sangamo Journal* beginning in the mid-1830s.

Lincoln wrestled rhetorically not only with political opponents but also sometimes with himself over rhetorical methods, especially when he contended with Douglas. As an aspiring politician and quick wit, Lincoln could not resist using demagogic methods, but he faced the dilemma of whether and how to apply them because their controversial use could endanger his goals of gaining public esteem and preserving self-esteem. Lincoln knew he could not succeed in politics by always taking the high road, and some of the compositions in his first political career included such demagogic methods as exaggeration, withholding negative information, race-baiting, and personal attacks.

Lincoln's speeches aimed at partisan, sympathetic audiences are his most controversial owing to their caustic elements. He delivered his 1848 Mexican War speech in the House of Representatives with an apparent purpose of try-ing to impress fellow Whigs by denouncing President Polk's war policy and personally ridiculing him as an incompetent, morally deficient leader. In the 1852 Scott Club speech, Lincoln at length entertained local Whigs with satire of the case the Democratic Party made for its presidential nominee, Lewis Cass, and of Cass personally. No text has been found for the 1856 Lost speech that Lincoln gave at a Republican convention. It may have featured demagogic elements, radical antislavery views, or both as suggested by contemporaneous accounts that say it was so controversial that it was not recorded. The 1858 House Divided speech is arguably his most controversial, owing to its pre-diction of national crisis over slavery and the complex conspiracy accusation against Democratic leaders, including Douglas.

From his early political life, Lincoln's greatest political/rhetorical challenge was responding effectively to Douglas's policies and rhetoric. Lincoln's first observations of Douglas, in the 1830s, revealed an unscrupulous political operative. In the 1838 Lyceum address, Lincoln fearfully described a future, autocratic "towering genius" who would jeopardize self-government, and Douglas was the likely target. From then on, Lincoln often refuted Doug-las's positions and policies with multiple modes of argumentation, including satire. Lincoln's Douglas satire is a manifestation of the moral theme that runs throughout Lincoln's political rhetoric, for satire implies the need for improvement in the human condition. In his 1839 Subtreasury speech, Lincoln criticized Douglas for his endorsement in the Illinois legislature of a national subtreasury and for lying about expenditures made by the Democratic Van Buren administration. That speech focused more on Douglas's politics and rhetoric than on his personal qualities. After the 1830s Lincoln and Douglas did not become embroiled again until the 1854 Kansas-Nebraska Act repealed the Missouri Compromise and motivated Lincoln to reenter national politics. Apparently Lincoln and Douglas did not quarrel when they shared time in Congress from 1847 to 1849, when Lincoln was in the House of Representa-tives; Douglas, in the Senate.

In the 1840s Lincoln gained considerable experience with personal attacks in political rhetoric. In 1842 his second Rebecca letter ridiculed James Shields, the vain state auditor, who was so outraged that Lincoln almost fought a duel with him. That fiasco humiliated Lincoln, and afterward he wrote no more anonymous letters devoted to personal attacks. Yet when politicians attacked Lincoln, he sometimes responded with disparagement of individuals in addition to criticism of oppositional policy and rhetoric. Lincoln in the early 1840s developed a rationale for fighting back at his detractors as he maneuvered to gain his Whig Party's congressional nomination. In 1845 Lincoln felt that fellow Whig John J. Hardin was violating honorable protocol by seeking another congressional nomination out of turn. Lincoln successfully countered that move with a "turnabout is fair play" argument developed not with personal attacks but with serious, rational argumentation expressed in a candid, respectful tone.

After using "turnabout is fair play" argumentation to dispose of Hardin, Lincoln felt that the implicit moral sense of that strategy justified its future use. In his 1852 Eulogy on Henry Clay, Lincoln turned the tables on Douglas (without naming him) by alleging that Douglas's mourning of Clay was gratuitous, emphasizing that in political "sentiment" those two were "as far apart as party could make them." Lincoln's use of foundational documents was a "turnabout is fair play" strategy to refute Douglas's racist interpretation of the Declaration of Independence. Lincoln's Democratic conspiracy accusation in the House Divided speech could be understood as a "turnabout is fair play" response to the collaboration of Douglas and some of his supporters with eastern Republicans. In the 1858 Senate race, Lincoln's criticism of Douglas for demagoguery included retaliation (with professed reluctance) for personal attacks. Lincoln's 1859 Columbus speech used a "turnabout is fair play" appropriation of the claim Douglas made in his *Harper's* essay that the founders understood slavery "just as well and even better than we do now," and that proposition anchored the Cooper Union address.

The compositions of Lincoln's second political career typically meld controversial elements and moral suasion. Lincoln's fearmongering over slavery and Douglas in this period would appear to be demagogic. Yet, as noted in the introduction, rhetoricians point out that whether emotional appeals are demagogic depends on their ethical quality. Beginning with his 1854 Peoria speech, Lincoln invoked the fear that the indifference to the immorality of slavery promoted by Douglas would lead to its extension into new territories. In the 1858 House Divided speech, the Democratic conspiracy accusation, developed with figurative language, insinuated a fearful tendency toward nationalizing slavery. In those speeches and throughout the 1850s, a paradoxical, principled fearmongering was a vital component of the moral suasion of Lincoln's bold, antislavery rhetoric, in contrast to Douglas's racial fearmongering.

Another emotional appeal with potential demagogic application seen in Lincoln's rhetoric was patriotism, but he did not invoke it to argue merely for power to the state for its own sake but for national stability. For example, at the end of the 1838 Lyceum address, the call to patriotism was straightforward, urging a rational approach to social unrest and linking "morality" to "a reverence for the Constitution and laws" and to the memory of George Washington. Sometimes Lincoln's use of the patriotic theme involved righteous personal criticism. The conclusion of the 1848 Mexican War speech praised the US military but sarcastically rendered President Polk as "a deranged animal," "bewildered, confounded, and miserably perplexed." In his 1848 Presidential Question speech, Lincoln praised the Whig presidential candidate Zachary Taylor as a citizen military commander for serving his country in the Mexican War without questioning its purpose, while belittling the Democratic presidential candidate, Lewis Cass, as a pompous fool. Toward the end of the 1852 Eulogy on Henry Clay, Lincoln expressed the patriotic aspiration that if the nation will become free from "the dangerous presence of slavery," it will be "a glorious consummation" of "the efforts of Mr. Clay." In his 1852 Scott Club speech, Lincoln denounced Douglas for claiming that the 1852 Whig presidential nominee, General Winfield Scott, would threaten "the safety of the Union."

Lincoln's Peoria speech braced antislavery argumentation with an emotional, eloquent appeal to patriotism: "Our republican robe is soiled, and trailed in the dust. Let us repurify it. . . . Let us turn slavery from its claims of 'moral right,' back upon its existing legal rights, and its arguments of 'necessity.' Let us re-adopt the Declaration of Independence, and with it, the practices, and policy, which harmonize with it." Throughout the 1850s Lincoln often cited the Declaration of Independence and the Constitution in his argumentation, implicitly drawing on patriotic-rational/emotional appeals in response to Douglas.

In responding to his archrival's provocative rhetoric, Lincoln used historical, legalistic, and moral argumentation to expose Douglas's contradictions, distortions, and factual errors. Lincoln was especially challenged in dealing with Douglas's personal attacks. In the Peoria speech Lincoln said he would not use personal attacks—"not assail the motives of any man, or class of men; but rather to strictly confine myself to the naked merits of the question." The conclusion of the Peoria speech vented Lincoln's frustration with Douglas for his demagogic response to the earlier version of Lincoln's speech at Springfield: "If a man will stand up and assert, and repeat, and re-assert, that two and two do not make four, I know nothing in the power of argument, that can stop him. I think I can answer the Judge so long as he sticks to the premises, but when he flies from them, I cannot work an argument into the consistency of a maternal [material?] gag, and actually close his mouth with it."

In the Dred Scott speech Lincoln rejected Douglas's view that the equality language of the Declaration of Independence excluded black people, and

Lincoln condemned Douglas's popular sovereignty as "a mere deceitful pretense for the benefit of slavery." That implied criticism of Douglas's character could be considered demagogic because it was based on speculation. Lincoln points out that the US Constitution has nothing to prevent Mormons in Utah from exercising "the sacred right of self-government" to legalize polygamy but that Douglas refuses to address that particular issue. Lincoln thus insinuates that Douglas is inconsistent for his silence on it while maintaining that self-government can decide the slavery question in territories. Lincoln also criticized Douglas's fallacious generalization that because Lincoln does not want a black woman for a slave he "must necessarily want her for a wife."

In the 1858 Illinois Senate race, Lincoln and Douglas often deviated from explaining and defending their respective solutions to slavery agitation (rational appeal) by using conspiracy accusations to appeal to the public's fear (ad populum fallacy) as they attempted to undermine one another's credibility (ethical appeal). Both candidates were powerful, articulate speakers, and this campaign is thus a case study in the relationship of those various kinds of appeals to demagoguery, satire, moral argumentation, and eloquence in a debate format and related stump speeches. In this campaign, "turnabout is fair play" was one of Lincoln's strategies used to criticize Douglas's politics, rhetoric, and moral character.

Douglas often repeated his various, demagogic criticism of Lincoln: the race-baiting of inaccurately accusing him of favoring political and social equality between white people and black people, including their intermarriage; falsely accusing him of being a radical abolitionist; deliberately misrepresenting his brand of Republicanism; inaccurately accusing him of failing to support troops during the Mexican War when he was a member of Congress; and wrongly accusing him of fostering disunion and civil war. Douglas complained of personal attacks but expressed little desire to eschew them. Lincoln repeatedly protested that Douglas was using personal attacks, exaggerating, and lying. Lincoln criticized Douglas's rhetoric for cherry-picking evidence and for using "language most able and ingenious for concealing what I really meant." Lincoln's personal criticism of Douglas included frequent jabs whose brevity suggested that Lincoln was mostly in control of his frustration and anger. Douglas's repeated offenses especially troubled Lincoln, for they were implicit criticisms of his integrity and sense of honor. In the fifth Lincoln-Douglas debate, Lincoln said he would "probably" stop personal attacks when Douglas did. Regardless, "turnabout is fair play" must have always been on his mind.

Ultimately, Lincoln's 1858 antislavery moral argumentation associated freedom with universal good, slavery with universal evil. Voicing those associations, Lincoln achieved eloquence and statesmanship: "That is the real issue. That is the issue that will continue in this country when these poor tongues of Judge Douglas and myself shall be silent. It is the eternal struggle between these two principles—right and wrong—throughout the world. They are the two principles that have stood face to face from the beginning of time; and will ever continue to struggle." Lincoln deployed figurative language to emphasize his point: "The one is the common right of humanity and the other the divine right of kings. It is the same spirit that says, 'You work and toil and earn bread, and I'll eat it.' No matter in what shape it comes, whether from the mouth of a king who seeks to bestride the people of his own nation and live by the fruit of their labor, or from one race of men as an apology for enslaving another race, it is the same tyrannical principle." Lincoln's language expressed an appeal to credibility based on implacable support for a humanistic, universal truth and humility (his role is transitory). In the thirteen speeches cited in these conclusions, he expressed humility in the 1839 Subtreasury speech, the 1848 Internal Improvements speech, and in certain 1859 speeches.

After the 1858 Senate race, Lincoln tempered his tone as he continued to criticize Douglas, sometimes with satire of his positions, rhetoric, and personal traits. In his 1859 Second Lecture on Discoveries and Inventions, Lincoln caricatured Douglas as Young America, the zealous proponent of territorial expansion, who was also fond of whiskey and cigars. The 1859 speaking invitations Lincoln received from outside Illinois enabled him to take his messages, including criticism of Douglas, to more and more audiences. With those opportunities perhaps Lincoln felt he was finally winning the war with his decades-long rival, but he was not gloating. In beginning his speech at Columbus, Ohio, Lincoln adopted a humble tone, advising his audience to listen with "very moderate expectations." In that speech Lincoln poked fun at Douglas and his Democratic friends' racism by claiming they were fearful they might marry black women. Lincoln also referred to his complaint that if the Constitution allows slavery in the territories, it would allow it in the free states, saying that only his "excessive modesty" stopped him from reading that printed argument aloud. This language, expressing self-deprecation, was an appeal to his credibility.

When Lincoln spoke at Cincinnati the day after he spoke at Columbus, he continued to frame his arguments with appeal to his credibility. He began this speech with an expression of humility by saying he was self-conscious in "appearing before an audience in so great a city as this." Also early in this speech he humorously confessed he is a "Black Republican." At Cincinnati Lincoln cleverly mocked Douglas's popular sovereignty through the extended irony that he would be southerners' best hope for promoting their support of slavery, and that argument also potentially alienated Douglas from antislavery proponents in his own northern Democratic Party. The modesty with which Lincoln opened the Cooper Union address surely helped put the audience in a receptive mood: "The facts with which I shall deal this evening are mainly old and familiar; nor is there anything new in the general use I shall make of them."

Passages of Lincoln's antislavery moral argumentation, for example, in the Peoria speech, the last three Lincoln-Douglas debates, and the Cooper Union address, qualify as eloquent, but the traditional practice of labeling entire, acclaimed compositions in the Lincoln canon as eloquent should be viewed with caution, for many of them include harsh personal attacks. Lincoln's prepresidential rhetoric demonstrates Reinhard H. Luthin's observation, worth repeating, that "there exists a bit of demagoguery in the most lofty of statesmen." Some people may interpret Douglas's most articulate passages supporting popular sovereignty as eloquent for their implicit moral appeal of potentially preventing slavery extension through local control. Not until hard pressed by Lincoln does Douglas offer an explicit, qualified moral defense of popular sovereignty. Douglas's rhetoric is heavily demagogic, and he mainly denies that slavery is a subject of moral concern. As noted in chapter 7, Douglas's only language cited in this book as eloquent concerns his celebration of the national aspiration of westward expansion.

The invitation to speak at the prestigious Cooper Union followed many years in which Lincoln learned how to compose messages geared to both listening and reading audiences. During that long political/rhetorical rise, Lincoln learned how to apply fundamentals originating in classical antiquity, with rhetorical strategies, including satire, that focused on his opponents' positions, rhetorical methods, and personal qualities. He learned how to infuse his major discourse with historical, legalistic, and moral argumentation to advance his positions without a self-righteous tone. He consistently argued from principles inferred from compositions of the founders and contemporaneous political leaders. He structured his compositions with versatility and for impact. He clothed his messages in plain language, often with figures of speech using familiar imagery to clarify and enhance his meaning.

In effect, Lincoln had developed a multifaceted, ethical rhetoric that subsumed demagogic elements into poignant pleas for political/social justice. His prepresidential eloquence and statesmanship reveal that he had attained the potential for literary distinction, and later circumstances would give him the opportunity to create it—to compose messages resonating with universal truth and hope for the human condition—specifically, the United States as the "last best hope on earth" for self-government. Lincoln's main prepresidential compositions are an original contribution to American political discourse and deserve to be further read, studied, and taught.

At Cooper Union Lincoln stepped onto a national stage leading to the presidency and literary statesmanship achieved in such works as the Inaugural addresses, the Gettysburg address, and the Last speech. Those imperishable compositions contribute immeasurably to the classical heritage of American and world literature.

Notes

Preface

1. For William H. Herndon's description of Lincoln delivering political speeches, see William H. Herndon and Jesse W. Weik, *Herndon's Lincoln,* ed. Douglas L. Wilson and Rodney O. Davis (Galesburg, IL: Lincoln Studies Center, Knox College; Champaign: University of Illinois Press, 2006), 248–49. This work was originally published in 1889.

2. For scholarship on how a great number of Lincoln's speeches and other writings have been treated, in chronological order, see Thomas L. Krannawitter, *Vindicating Lincoln: Defending the Politics of our Greatest President* (New York: Rowan and Littlefield Publishers, 2008); John McKee Barr, *Loathing Lincoln: An American Tradition from the Civil War to the Present* (Baton Rouge: Louisiana State University Press, 2014); D. Leigh Henson, *Inventing Lincoln: Approaches to His Rhetoric* (CreateSpace/Amazon, 2017).

3. For selected biographers' approaches to Lincoln's rhetoric, in chronological order, see Herndon and Weik, *Herndon's Lincoln*, 127; Horace White, *The Lincoln and Douglas Debates: An Address Before the Chicago Historical Society, February 17, 1914* (Chicago: University of Chicago Press, 1914), 28. White paraphrases what Lincoln told him about his opponent's stump speeches: "Douglas was not lacking in versatility, but that he [Douglas] had formed a theory that the speech which he was delivering at his small meetings was the best adapted to secure votes and since the voters at one meeting would not be likely to hear him at any other, they would never know that he was repeating himself, or, if they did know, they would probably think that it was the proper thing to do." Albert J. Beveridge, *Abraham Lincoln, 1809–1858*, vol. 1 (New York: Harcourt, Brace and Co., 1928), 301–2; Benjamin P. Thomas, *Abraham Lincoln: A Biography* (New York: Alfred A. Knopf, 1952), 135. Thomas notes that Lincoln's early legal experience taught him "political astuteness . . . the thought-processes of the people and how they might be guided, when to speak and when to maintain silence, what to say and how to say it," 94; and his second law partner, Stephen T. Logan, "showed him the value of exactitude and

thorough preparation as opposed to mere cleverness and high flown rhetoric," 96. Michael Burlingame, *Abraham Lincoln: A Life,* 2 vols. (Baltimore: Johns Hopkins University Press, 2008), 1:376; Douglas L. Wilson, "Lincoln's Rhetoric," *Journal of the Abraham Lincoln Association* 34, no. 1 (Winter 2013): 2.

4. For studies of Lincoln's literary stylistic techniques, in chronological order, see Daniel Kilham Dodge, *Abraham Lincoln: The Evolution of His Literary Style* (reprint, 2000; Champaign: University of Illinois Press, 1900); Luther Emerson Robinson, *Abraham Lincoln as a Man of Letters* (Chicago: Reilly and Britton, 1918); Roy P. Basler, "Abraham Lincoln's Rhetoric," *American Literature* 11, no. 2 (May 1939): 167–82; Herbert J. Edwards and John E. Hankins, *Lincoln the Writer: The Development of His Literary Style,* University of Maine Studies, Second Series, No. 76 (Orono: University of Maine Press, 1962); James Hurt, "All the Living and the Dead: Lincoln's Imagery," *American Literature* 52, no. 3 (November 1980): 351–80; Alan G. Gross, "Lincoln's Use of Constitutive Metaphors," *Rhetoric & Public Affairs* 7, no. 2 (2004): 173–90; Marshall Myers, "'Rugged Grandeur': A Study of the Influences on the Writing Style of Abraham Lincoln and a Brief Study of His Writing Habits," *Rhetoric Review* 23, no. 4 (2004): 350–67; John Channing Briggs, *Lincoln's Speeches Reconsidered* (Baltimore: Johns Hopkins University Press, 2005); Fred Kaplan, *Lincoln: The Biography of a Writer* (New York: Harper, 2008); Douglas L. Wilson, "Lincoln's Rhetoric," *Journal of the Abraham Lincoln Association* 34, no. 1 (Winter 2013): 1–17; David S. Reynolds, *Abe: Abraham Lincoln in His Times* (New York: Penguin Books, 2020), 145–46.

5. William Lee Miller, *Lincoln's Virtues: An Ethical Biography* (New York: Vintage Books, 2003), 103.

6. Reinhard H. Luthin, *American Demagogues* (Boston: Beacon Press, 1954), 355, quoted in Gustainis, "Demagoguery and Political Rhetoric: A Review of the Literature," *Rhetoric Society Quarterly* 20, no. 2 (Spring 1990): 155.

7. Gustainis, "Demagoguery and Political Rhetoric," 155.

8. For critiques of Bradford's and Bennett's accusations of demagoguery against Lincoln, see Henson, *Inventing Lincoln,* 187–209, 223–40.

9. Graham A. Peck, *Making an Antislavery Nation: Lincoln, Douglas, and the Battle over Freedom* (Urbana: University of Illinois Press, 2017), 176–78.

10. Edward P.J. Corbett and Robert J. Connors, *Classical Rhetoric for the Modern Student* (New York: Oxford University Press, 1999), 23–24. This book, published in multiple editions, is an excellent primer on rhetoric and the history of its development in western civilization.

11. Benjamin P. Thomas, *Lincoln's New Salem: Its History, Its Influence on Lincoln, Its Lincoln Legends and the Story of Its Restoration* (Chicago and Lincoln's New Salem: Lincoln's New Salem Enterprises, 1973), 6.

12. For an extended bibliographical essay on Lincoln's rhetoric, including technical discussions, see D. Leigh Henson, *Inventing Lincoln: Approaches to His Rhetoric* (CreateSpace/Amazon, 2017).

13. Don E. Fehrenbacher, *Lincoln in Text and Context: Collected Essays* (Stanford, CA: Stanford University Press, 1987), 270.

14. Don E. Fehrenbacher, ed., Introduction to *Abraham Lincoln: A Documentary Portrait through His Speeches and Writings* (Stanford, CA: Stanford University Press, 1964), xxix.

Introduction

1. Andrew King and Jim A. Kuypers, Introduction to "Our Roots Run Deep," *Twentieth-Century Roots of Rhetorical Studies* (Westport, CT: Praeger Publishers, 2001), ix.

2. Edward P.J. Corbett and Robert J. Connors, *Classical Rhetoric for the Modern Student*, 4th ed. (New York: Oxford University Press, 1999), 1.

3. Theresa Enos, ed., *Encyclopedia of Rhetoric and Composition: Communication from Ancient Times to the Information Age*, s.v. "Contextuality." (London: Routledge, 2013), 143. See also Corbett and Connors, *Classical Rhetoric for the Modern Student*, 17–23. Once communicative purpose and audience are well defined and the medium selected, content (including argumentation), structure/organization, and style (language features) can be developed and adapted accordingly.

4. Corbett and Connors, *Classical Rhetoric for the Modern Student*, 518.

5. Corbett and Connors explain Aristotle's artistic and nonartistic proofs. Artistic proofs consist of deductive and inductive reasoning: "The deductive mode of arguing is commonly referred to by the term that Aristotle used, the *syllogism*. In rhetoric, the equivalent of the syllogism is the *enthymeme*. The rhetorical equivalent of *full induction* in logic is the *example*" (18). Corbett and Connors also assert that a knowledge of the fallacies in reasoning is useful in refutation and in avoiding deception. Nonartistic proofs do not originate with a speaker/writer but derive from such sources as laws and testimonials. *Classical Rhetoric for the Modern Student*, 62.

6. A basic source for the structural elements of classical rhetoric is *Rhetorica ad Herennium*. This anonymous work from the 80s BC has been called the oldest Roman book on rhetoric, and it continues to be an influential source. Corbett and Connors, *Classical Rhetoric for the Modern Student*, 29, 256–92.

7. For an overview of the history and development of the theory, practice, and teaching of rhetoric in Lincoln's time, including the use of textbooks, see Nan Johnson, Introduction to "A Profile of Nineteenth-Century Rhetoric," *Nineteenth-Century Rhetoric in North America* (Carbondale: Southern Illinois University Press, 1991), 3–17.

8. For information about books that Lincoln read or might have read in Indiana, including discussion of Lindley Murray's use of Blair's *Lectures*, see Robert Bray, *Reading with Lincoln* (Carbondale: Southern Illinois University Press, 2010), 1–40. Bray's work is a painstaking effort, which includes rating each book on the likelihood that Lincoln read it. For a discussion of the rhetorical theory of Hugh Blair, including the influence of classical rhetoric on it, see Linda Ferreira-Buckley and S. Michael Halloran, eds., editors' Introduction to Hugh Blair, *Lectures on Rhetoric and Belles Lettres* (Carbondale: Southern Illinois University Press, 2005), XV–LIV.

9. Bray, *Reading with Lincoln*, 5.

10. William H. Herndon and Jesse W. Weik, *Herndon's Lincoln*, ed. Douglas L. Wilson and Rodney O. Davis (Galesburg, IL: Lincoln Studies Center, Knox College; Champaign: University of Illinois Press, 2006), 36.

11. William Lee Miller, *Lincoln's Virtues: An Ethical Biography* (New York: Vintage Books, 2002), 81.

12. Bray, *Reading with Lincoln*, 8.

13. Corbett and Connors, *Classical Rhetoric for the Modern Student*, 411–13.

14. James T. Hickey, "Three R's in Lincoln's Education: Rogers, Riggin and Rankin," in *The Collected Writings of James T. Hickey* (Springfield: The Illinois State Historical Society, 1990), 5–13.

15. Robert Bray, "What Abraham Lincoln Read—An Evaluative and Annotated List," *Journal of the Abraham Lincoln Association* 28, no. 2 (Summer 2007): 39.

16. Douglas L. Wilson, *Lincoln's Sword* (New York: Alfred A. Knopf, 2006), 147.

17. Ronald C. White Jr., *The Eloquent President: A Portrait of Lincoln through His Words* (New York: Random House, 2005), xxi.

18. Roy P. Basler, "Abraham Lincoln's Rhetoric," *American Literature* 11, no. 2 (May 1939): 171.

19. David Zarefsky, "Rhetoric in Lincoln's Time," *Lincoln Lore* (Fall 2008): 26.

20. Zarefsky, "Rhetoric in Lincoln's Time," 26.

21. Hugh Blair, *Lectures on Rhetoric and Belles Lettres*, ed. Linda Ferreira-Buckley and S. Michael Halloran (Carbondale: Southern Illinois Press, 2005), 344–67.

22. For an account of the primary sources of classical rhetoric included in Webster's formal education and his adaptation of classical rhetoric in his speeches, see Glen E. Mills, "Daniel Webster's Principles of Rhetoric," *Speech Monographs* 9, no. 1 (1942): 124–140; Craig R. Smith, Introduction to *Defender of the Union: The Oratory of Daniel Webster* (New York: Greenwood Press, 1989), 1–9.

23. Texts of selected 1830s speeches by Daniel Webster, https://www.loc.gov/rr/program/bib/webster/index.html.

24. Roy P. Basler et al., eds., *The Collected Works of Abraham Lincoln*, 9 vols. (New Brunswick, NJ: Rutgers University Press, 1953–55), 2:154, 4–66. Hereafter cited as *CW*. Quotations from *CW* retain italics denoting emphasis.

25. Melvyn Dubofsky, "Daniel Webster and the Whig Theory of Economic Growth, 1828–1848," *The New England Quarterly* 42, no. 4 (Dec. 1969): 563.

26. Michael Burlingame, *Abraham Lincoln: A Life*, 2 vols. (Baltimore: Johns Hopkins University Press, 2008), 1:141.

27. Burlingame, *Lincoln: A Life*, 1:418.

28. Burlingame, *Lincoln: A Life*, 1:458. The 1830 passage in Webster that Lincoln paraphrases in his 1858 House Divided speech is ornate in contrast to Lincoln's plain style. Webster had developed a somewhat plainer style by the time he wrote his 1850 speeches in support of Clay's compromise proposals. Both the ornate, or grand, style and the plain style have roots in classical rhetoric. Corbett and Connors, *Classical Rhetoric for the Modern Student*, 461–63.

29. Abraham Lincoln, Eulogy on Henry Clay, July 6, 1852, *CW* 2:126. The question of how much rhetorical terminology Lincoln knew is intriguing but ultimately unknowable.

30. For a discussion of Lincoln's motivation in studying Euclid and its possible influences on his thinking and professional work, see Glenn W. LaFantasie, "Lincoln, Euclid, and the Satisfaction of Success," *Journal of the Abraham Lincoln Association* 41, no. 1 (Winter 2020): 24–46. LaFantasie cites additional publications that discuss how Lincoln's compositions allegedly show the influence of his study of Euclid (44).

31. Wilson, *Lincoln's Sword*, 4–7.

32. Corbett and Connors, *Classical Rhetoric for the Modern Student*, 72.

33. J. Justin Gustainis, "Demagoguery and Political Rhetoric: A Review of the Literature," *Rhetoric Society Quarterly* 20, no. 2 (Spring 1990): 158.

34. Corbett and Connors, *Classical Rhetoric for the Modern Student*, 25.

35. Corbett and Connors, *Classical Rhetoric for the Modern Student*, 62–71.

36. Merriam-Webster's online dictionary definition of eloquence: https://www.merriam-webster.com/dictionary/eloquence.

37. Robert C. Elliott, Satire, https://www.britannica.com/art/satire/Satirical-media.

38. Todd Nathan Thompson, *The National Joker: Abraham Lincoln and the Politics of Satire* (Carbondale: Southern Illinois University Press, 2015), 1. Biographers observe that among the writers Lincoln read in his youth were William Shakespeare and Lord Byron, and their verse included satire. Richard Carwardine notes that while riding the judicial circuit, Lincoln carried the works of satirists with him. *Lincoln's Sense of Humor* (Carbondale: Southern Illinois University Press, 2017), 18.

39. Miller, *Lincoln's Virtues*, 106–7.

40. Louise Stevenson, *Scholarly Means to Evangelical Ends: The New Haven Scholars and the Transformation of Higher Learning in America* (Baltimore: Johns Hopkins University Press, 1986), 5–6, quoted in Daniel Walker Howe, "Why Abraham Lincoln Was a Whig," *Journal of the Abraham Lincoln Association* 16, no. 1 (Winter 1995), https://quod.lib.umich.edu/j/jala/2629860.0016.105?view=text;rgn=main.

41. Robert Kelley, "Ideology and Political Culture from Jefferson to Nixon," *American Historical Review* 82 (June 1977): 545, in Stevenson, *Scholarly Means to Evangelical Ends*.

42. David Herbert Donald, *Lincoln* (New York: Simon and Schuster, 1996), 110.

43. Donald, *Lincoln*, 109–10.

44. Joel H. Silbey, "Always a Whig in Politics,' The Partisan Life of Abraham Lincoln," *Journal of the Abraham Lincoln Association* 8, no. 1 (1986), https://quod.lib.umich.edu/j/jala/2629860.0008.105?view=text;rgn=main.

Chapter 1. Entering the Illinois Political Arena and Confronting Stephen A. Douglas

1. Michael Burlingame, *Abraham Lincoln: A Life*, 2 vols. (Baltimore: Johns Hopkins University Press, 2008), 1:40.

2. Kunigunde Duncan and D.H. Nickols, *Mentor Graham: The Man Who Taught Lincoln* (Chicago: University of Chicago Press, 1944), 132.

3. Burlingame, *Lincoln: A Life*, 1:40.

4. For details about the resolutions and bills Lincoln composed while in the Illinois legislature, see Paul Simon, *Lincoln's Preparation for Greatness: The Illinois Legislative Years* (Urbana: University of Illinois Press, 1971) and Ron J. Keller, *Lincoln in the Illinois Legislature* (Carbondale: Southern Illinois University Press, 2019).

5. Burlingame, *Lincoln: A Life*, 1:166.

6. Lincoln, To Jesse W. Fell, Enclosing Autobiography, December 20, 1859, in *The Collected Works of Abraham Lincoln,* ed. Roy P. Basler et al., 9 vols. (New Brunswick, NJ: Rutgers University Press, 1953), 3:512. Hereafter cited as *CW*. Quotations from *CW* retain italics denoting emphasis. For a leading monograph on the Whig Party, see Michael F. Holt, *The Rise and Fall of the American Whig Party: Jacksonian Politics and the Onset of the Civil War* (New York: Oxford University Press, 2003). For a discussion of Lincoln's Whig beliefs and activities, see Joel H. Silbey, "'Always a Whig in Politics': The Partisan Life of Abraham Lincoln," *Journal of the Abraham Lincoln Association* 8, no. 1 (1986): 21–42. Whigs and Democrats somewhat agreed on the need for internal improvements legislation in Illinois, but unlike the Whigs, Democrats did not believe that federal funds should be used for internal improvements.

7. Lincoln, "Communication to the People of Sangamo County," March 9, 1832, *CW* 1:8.

8. Duncan and Nickols, *Mentor Graham*, 132. John McNeil (McNamar) was the man allegedly engaged to Ann Rutledge before he returned to the East, in legend being succeeded by Lincoln as Ann's suitor. Legend also has it that Lincoln and she studied Kirkham's *Grammar* together.

9. Duncan and Nickols, *Mentor Graham*, 132.

10. Lincoln, *Illinois State Journal* (Springfield), Nov. 5, 1864, quoted in Burlingame, *Lincoln: A Life*, 1:73.

11. Burlingame, *Lincoln: A Life*, 1:82. For a classification of Lincoln's funny stories and jokes, including examples used for various purposes, see Richard Carwardine, *Lincoln's Sense of Humor* (Carbondale: Southern Illinois University Press, 2017).

12. Simon, *Lincoln's Preparation for Greatness*, 17.

13. For a detailed account of Douglas's conspiracy with Wyatt to depose Hardin as well as accounts of Douglas's other self-serving chicanery of this period, see Reg Ankrom, *Stephen A. Douglas: The Political Apprenticeship, 1833–1843* (Jefferson, NC: McFarland and Company, Publishers, 2015), 43–52. For another account of Douglas's anti-Hardin plot, see Roy Morris Jr., *The Long Pursuit: Abraham Lincoln's Thirty-Year Struggle with Stephen Douglas for the Heart and Soul of America* (New York: HarperCollins Publishers, 2008), 15.

14. Burlingame, *Lincoln: A Life*, 1:96.

15. For a discussion of Lincoln's political sarcasm, see Robert Bray, "'The Power to Hurt,' Lincoln's Early Use of Satire and Invective," *Journal of the Abraham Lincoln Association* 16, no. 1 (Winter 1995): 39–58. From its origins in Greek and Roman literature, satire has been described as a way to bring about improvement in individuals and society. A rationale for satire is that individuals and groups are likely to reform when their weaknesses and culpability are exposed through humor. Thus, satire has an idealistic, moral purpose. One of the poets Lincoln enjoyed beginning

in his youth and whose satire must have influenced him was Robert Burns, but Bray's "'The Power to Hurt'" makes no reference to Burns. Bray elsewhere discusses in detail Burns's satirical methods that Lincoln also used, including mock-rustic dialect and such targets as pretense and hypocrisy. Robert Bray, *Reading with Lincoln* (Carbondale: Southern Illinois University Press, 2020), 92–121.

16. Burlingame, *Lincoln: A Life*, 1:156.

17. Burlingame, *Lincoln: A Life*, 1:158.

18. For details about Lincoln's 1836 pseudonymous campaign letters attacking Democrats, see Burlingame, *Lincoln: A Life*, 1:107–11.

19. Joshua F. Speed to William H. Herndon, 1882, in *Herndon's Informants: Letters, Interviews, and Statements about Abraham Lincoln*, ed. Douglas L. Wilson and Rodney O. Davis (Urbana: University of Illinois Press, 1998), 589.

20. Lincoln, *Sangamo Journal*, 4 June 1836, quoted in Burlingame, *Lincoln: A Life*, 1:109.

21. Burlingame, *Lincoln: A Life*, 1:108.

22. Burlingame, *Lincoln: A Life*, 1:110.

23. David Herbert Donald, *Lincoln* (New York: Simon and Schuster, 1996), 62.

24. Simon, *Lincoln's Preparation for Greatness*, 64.

25. Donald, *Lincoln*, 62–63.

26. Burlingame, *Lincoln: A Life*, 1:114.

27. Olivier Fraysse, *Lincoln, Land, and Labor, 1809–60* (Urbana and Chicago: University of Illinois Press, 1988), 72.

28. Lincoln, Speech in the Illinois Legislature Concerning the State Bank, January 11, 1837, *CW* 1:62.

29. Contemporary scholars of classical rhetoric, Edward P.J. Corbett and Robert J. Connors explain forecasting as a technique to gain coherence: "We want the parts of our discourse to 'hang together,' and while we would like the sutures to be as unobtrusive as possible, we nevertheless want our readers to be aware that they are passing over into another division of the discourse. Aristotle himself, that great master of exposition, is not at all hesitant about marking his transitions explicitly." *Classical Rhetoric for the Modern Student*, 4th ed. (New York: Oxford University Press, 1999), 269.

30. Lincoln, Speech in the Illinois Legislature, January 11, 1837, *CW* 1:65.

31. Lincoln, Speech in the Illinois Legislature, January 11, 1837, *CW* 1:66.

32. Simon, *Lincoln's Preparation for Greatness*, 64–65.

33. For a discussion of the context, purpose, structure, language, and implications of the Lincoln-Stone protest, see William Lee Miller, *Lincoln's Virtues: An Ethical Biography* (New York: Vintage Books, 2002), 121–25.

34. Lincoln, Protest in the Illinois Legislature on Slavery, March 3, 1837, *CW* 1:74–75.

35. For Lincoln's relationship to the founders, in chronological order, see Don E. Fehrenbacher, *Prelude to Greatness: Lincoln in the 1850s* (Stanford, CA: Stanford University Press, 1962), 107; Drew R. McCoy, "Lincoln and the Founding Fathers: A Reconsideration," *Journal of the Abraham Lincoln Association* 16, no. 1 (Winter 1995): 1–13; William C. Harris, *Lincoln's Rise to the Presidency* (Lawrence: University

Press of Kansas, 2007), 69, 86, 135, 168, 184, 187–88; Richard Brookhiser, *Founders' Son: A Life of Abraham Lincoln* (New York: Basic Books, 2014); Graham A. Peck, *Making an Antislavery Nation: Lincoln, Douglas, and the Battle over Freedom* (Urbana: University of Illinois Press, 2017), 160–61, 170–71, 173, 175, 176–78; Sean Wilenz, *No Property in Man: Slavery and Antislavery at the Nation's Founding* (Cambridge, MA: Harvard University Press, 2018); James Oakes, *The Crooked Path to Abolition: Abraham Lincoln and the Anti-Slavery Constitution* (New York: W.W. Norton & Company, 2021).

36. Lincoln, To William Minshall, December 7, 1837, *CW* 1:107.

37. Stephen A. Douglas, quoted in Burlingame, *Lincoln: A Life*, 1:139.

38. Various Lincoln studies include commentary on the logrolling controversy; especially see the works cited in this chapter that deal specifically with Lincoln's time in the Illinois legislature: Simon, *Lincoln's Preparation for Greatness*, 76–105; Keller, *Lincoln in the Illinois Legislature*, 29, 59.

39. Ankrom, *Stephen A. Douglas*, 119.

40. Simon, *Lincoln's Preparation for Greatness*, 156.

41. Lincoln, Remarks in Illinois Legislature Concerning Resolutions in Relation to Fugitive Slaves, January 5, 1839, *CW* 1:126.

42. Burlingame, *Lincoln: A Life*, 1:150.

43. Burlingame, *Lincoln: A Life*, 1:152.

44. Wilson, *Lincoln's Sword*, 28.

45. Simon, *Lincoln's Preparation for Greatness*, 193–94.

46. Sources cited by Lincoln in the Subtreasury speech showing his extensive research are a speech by Van Buren arguing for the subtreasury, speeches by Stephen A. Douglas and other congressmen, "annual reports, made by all the Secretaries of the Treasury from the establishment of the Government down to the close of the year 1838," "Senate Documents of 1833–34, Vol. 5, Doc. 422," and "Senate Documents, of the session of 1838–39." Lincoln, Speech on the Subtreasury, December 26, 1839, *CW* 1:159–79. For an account of the establishment of the Illinois State Library, its location in the Vandalia and Springfield capitols, size, and other details, see Mark W. Sorensen, "The Illinois State Library: 1818–1870," *Illinois Libraries* 81, no. 1 (Winter 1999): 33–38. No record of this library's holdings in its earliest years has been located.

47. Melvyn Dubofsky, "Daniel Webster and the Whig Theory of Economic Growth, 1828–1848," *The New England Quarterly* 42, no. 4 (December 1969): 553.

48. Lincoln, To John T. Stuart, January 20, 1840 *CW* 1:184.

49. Corbett and Connors, *Classical Rhetoric for the Modern Student*, 20, 256–92.

50. Lincoln, Speech on the Subtreasury, December 26, 1839, *CW* 1:160.

51. Lincoln, Speech on the Subtreasury, December 26, 1839, *CW* 1:164.

52. Lincoln, Speech on the Subtreasury, December 26, 1839, *CW* 1:170.

53. Lincoln, Speech on the Subtreasury, December 26, 1839, *CW* 1:177.

54. Lincoln, Speech on the Subtreasury, December 26, 1839, *CW* 1:178–79.

55. Roy P. Basler, Annotation #1, December 26, 1839, *CW* 1:179.

56. Brian R. Dirck, *Lincoln and the Constitution* (Carbondale: Southern Illinois University Press, 2012), 9–10.

57. Dirck, *Lincoln and the Constitution*, 12.

58. Lincoln, To John T. Stuart, January 20, 1840, *CW* 1:184.

59. Burlingame, *Lincoln: A Life*, 1:156. This work includes accounts of many of Lincoln's stump speeches of the 1840 presidential campaign.

60. Burlingame, *Lincoln: A Life*, 1:154.

61. Burlingame, *Lincoln: A Life*, 1:154–55.

62. Douglas L. Wilson, *Honor's Voice: The Transformation of Abraham Lincoln* (New York: Vintage Books, 1998), 195.

63. Burlingame, *Lincoln: A Life*, 1:140–42.

64. Harry V. Jaffa, *Crisis of the House Divided: An Interpretation of the Issues in the Lincoln-Douglas Debates* (Chicago: University of Chicago Press, 1982), 198.

65. John Channing Briggs, *Lincoln's Speeches Reconsidered* (Baltimore: Johns Hopkins University Press, 2005), 29–37. See also Diana Schaub, *His Greatest Speeches: How Lincoln Moved the Nation* (New York: St. Martin's Press, 2021).

66. Burlingame, *Lincoln: A Life*, 1:140.

67. Lincoln, Address before the Young Men's Lyceum of Springfield, Illinois, January 27, 1838, *CW* 1:115.

68. Jaffa, *Crisis of the House Divided*, 198–99.

69. For a discussion of Lincoln's ambition relating to the Lyceum address, see Michael Burlingame, *The Inner World of Abraham Lincoln* (Urbana: University of Illinois Press, 1997), 253–54.

70. Edmund Wilson, *Patriotic Gore: Studies in the Literature of the American Civil War* (New York: W.W. Norton and Company, 1994), 108.

71. Jaffa, *Crisis of the House Divided*, 184.

72. Burlingame, *Lincoln: A Life*, 1:140.

73. Burlingame, *Lincoln: A Life*, 1:141.

74. Wilson, *Lincoln's Sword*, 27.

75. Burlingame, *Lincoln: A Life*, 1:141.

76. Lincoln, Address before the Young Men's Lyceum, January 27, 1838, *CW* 1:110.

77. Ankrom, *Stephen A. Douglas*, 117.

78. Lincoln, Temperance Address, February 22, 1842, *CW* 1:273.

79. Burlingame, *Lincoln: A Life*, 1:216.

80. Wilson, *Honor's Voice*, 261. For a discussion of the idea that Lincoln's temperance address included an appeal for rational discourse to replace the inflammatory rhetoric of radical abolitionists, see Susan Zaesky, "Hearing the Silences in Lincoln's Temperance Address: Whig Masculinity as an Ethic of Rhetorical Civility," *Rhetoric & Public Affairs* 13, no. 3 (Fall 2010): 389–419.

Chapter 2. Writing Himself into Congress

1. Lincoln, Resolutions at a Whig Meeting, March 1, 1843, Roy P. Basler, et al., eds., *The Collected Works of Abraham Lincoln*, 9 vols. (New Brunswick, NJ: Rutgers University Press, 1953), 1:307. Hereafter cited as *CW*. Quotations from *CW* retain italics denoting emphasis.

2. For an explanation of Clay's distribution bill, see Lincoln, Resolutions at a Whig Meeting, March 1, 1843, *CW* 1:308, footnote #2.

3. Lincoln, Address to the People of Illinois, March 4, 1843, *CW* 1:314.

4. Lincoln, Address to the People of Illinois, March 4, 1843, *CW* 1:314.

5. Lincoln, Speech at Sugar Creek, Illinois, March 1, 1844, *CW* 1:334.

6. Debates with John Calhoun and Alfred W. Cavalry in Springfield, Illinois, March 20–25, 1844, *CW* 1:334.

7. Debates with Calhoun and Cavalry, March 20–25, 1844, *CW* 1:335.

8. Burlingame, *Lincoln: A Life*, 1:227.

9. Lincoln, Speech and Resolutions Concerning Philadelphia Riots, June 12, 1844, *CW* 1:337–38.

10. Burlingame, *Lincoln: A Life*, 1:226.

11. An anonymous reviewer has kindly provided this clarification.

12. Lincoln, To Williamson Durley, October 3, 1845, *CW* 1:347.

13. Lincoln, To Robert Boal, January 7, 1846, *CW* 1:353.

14. Lincoln, To Benjamin F. James, February 9, 1846, *CW* 1:366.

15. Lincoln, To John J. Hardin, January 19, 1846, *CW* 1:358, note #4.

16. Lincoln, To John J. Hardin, January 19, 1846, *CW* 1:357.

17. Lincoln, To John J. Hardin, February 7, 1846, *CW* 1:361.

18. Lincoln, To John J. Hardin, February 7, 1846, *CW* 1:364.

19. Lincoln, To John J. Hardin, February 7, 1846, *CW* 1:365.

20. Lincoln, To James Berdan, April 26, 1846, *CW* 1:380.

21. Lincoln, Speech at Lacon, Illinois, July 18, 1846, *CW* 381–82.

22. Lincoln, Handbill Replying to Charges of Infidelity, July 31, 1846, *CW* 1:382.

23. Richard Carwardine, *Lincoln: A Life of Purpose and Power* (New York: Vintage Books, 2006), 57.

24. William C. Harris, *Lincoln's Rise to the Presidency* (Lawrence: University Press of Kansas, 2007), 39.

25. Allen C. Guelzo, *Abraham Lincoln as a Man of Ideas* (Carbondale: Southern Illinois University Press, 2009), 33.

26. Burlingame, *Lincoln: A Life*, 1:239.

27. Lincoln, To Allen N. Ford, August 11, 1846, *CW* 1:384.

28. Lincoln, Open Letter on Springfield and Alton Railroad, June 30, 1847, *CW* 1:395.

29. Lincoln, Open Letter, June 30, 1847, *CW* 1:397.

30. Lincoln, Report on Alton and Springfield Railroad, August 5, 1847, *CW* 1:398–405.

31. Lincoln, Fragments of a Tariff Discussion, December 1, 1847(?), *CW* 1:408–16. Basler suggests the tariff fragments were composed "between [Lincoln's] election to Congress in 1846 and taking his seat in Dec. 1847." Dec. 1, 1847(?), *CW* 1:416.

32. Gabor S. Boritt, *Lincoln and the Economics of the American Dream* (Memphis: Memphis State University Press, 1978), 127. For another discussion of Lincoln's views on the tariff, see Olivier Fraysse, *Lincoln, Land, and Labor, 1809–60*, trans. Sylvia Neely (Urbana: University of Illinois Press, 1994), 99–104.

33. Fred Kaplan, *Lincoln: The Biography of a Writer* (New York: HarperCollins Publishers, 2008), 172.

34. Kaplan, *Lincoln*, 173.

35. Lincoln, Fragments of a Tariff Discussion, December 1, 1847(?), *CW* 1:412.

36. Lincoln, Fragments of a Tariff Discussion, December 1, 1847(?), *CW* 1:415.

Chapter 3. Writing and Speaking to Gain Distinction in Congress

1. Michael Burlingame, *Abraham Lincoln: A Life*, 2 vols. (Baltimore: Johns Hopkins University Press, 2008), 1:264.

2. David Herbert Donald, *Lincoln* (New York: Simon and Schuster, 1995), 123.

3. Abraham Lincoln, "Spot" Resolutions in the United States House of Representatives, December 22, 1847, Roy P. Basler et al., eds., *The Collected Works of Abraham Lincoln*, 9 vols. (New Brunswick, NJ: Rutgers University Press, 1953–55), 1:421. Hereafter referred to as *CW*. Quotations from *CW* retain italics denoting emphasis.

4. Lincoln, "Spot" Resolutions, December 22, 1847, *CW* 1:423.

5. Burlingame, *Lincoln: A Life*, 1:264.

6. Lincoln, To William H. Herndon, January 8, 1848, *CW* 1:430.

7. Lincoln, Remarks in the United States House of Representatives Concerning Postal Contracts, January 5, 1848, *CW* 1:427.

8. Criticisms of Lincoln's Mexican War speech are diverse and conflicting. For example, in chronological order: William H. Herndon (1889) offered a mixed review, beginning with a favorable description and interpretation of Lincoln's purpose. The speech, Herndon writes, was "carefully prepared and well arranged . . . a severe arraignment of President Polk and justified the pertinence and propriety of the inquiries he [Lincoln] had a few days before addressed to him [the "spot" resolutions]. . . . It was constructed much after the manner of a legal argument. Reviewing the evidence furnished by the President in his various messages, he undertook to 'smoke him out.'" Regardless, Herndon wrote to Lincoln to express agreement with the many Illinois Whigs who were offended by the speech. William H. Herndon and Jesse W. Weik, *Herndon's Lincoln*, ed. Douglas L. Wilson and Rodney O. Davis (Galesburg, IL: Lincoln Studies Center, Knox College; Champaign: University of Illinois Press, 2006), 175. Lord Charnwood offers only one sentence about this speech: "The subject [the war] was by that time so stale that his speech could hardly make much impression, but it appears to-day [1917] [as] an extraordinarily clear, strong, upright presentment of the complex and unpopular case against the war." Lord Charnwood, *Abraham Lincoln* (New York: Henry Holt and Company, 1917), 93. Albert J. Beveridge notes that when Lincoln revised his speech for publication in the *Congressional Globe* and elsewhere, he omitted some of the inflammatory language that witnesses of the speech had objected to. Albert J. Beveridge, *Abraham Lincoln, 1809–1858*, vol. 1 (New York: Harcourt, Brace and Co., 1928), 430. Edgar Lee Masters (1931) insinuates that Lincoln was hypocritical because he condemned President Polk for invading Mexican territory but later, as commander in chief, Lincoln authorized the invasion of the Confederacy, which cost "billions of treasure and the lives of myriads of men." Edgar Lee Masters, *Lincoln: The Man* (Columbia, SC: The Foundation for American Education, 1997), 98. Roy P. Basler notes the

political trouble Lincoln brought on himself because of the Mexican War speech, but unlike other Lincolnists, Basler offers high praise for its rhetoric: "As exposition it is one of the ablest speeches Lincoln ever delivered and deserves to rank with the best of his later expository writing, though the unpopularity of its theme may make it as difficult of appreciation for some students of his works as it was for his contemporaries." Basler points out the speech's "vigorous diction and strong figures in which he condemned Polk's action and defended the Whig position." Roy P. Basler, "Lincoln's Development as a Writer," in *A Touchstone for Greatness: Essays, Addresses, and Occasional Pieces about Abraham Lincoln* (Westport, CT: Greenwood Press, 1973), 67. John Channing Briggs notes that Lincoln strategically limited the scope of his accusations and applied his considerable skill in legalistic argumentation: "Lincoln restricts his conclusions to what he admits is limited evidence that needs Polk's reply so that Lincoln's charges can be confirmed or denied. Sarcasm and prosecutorial logic force the issue, and yet they are regularly subordinated to the desire to enlarge the deliberative grounds of the debate." Briggs contends that Lincoln was taking much risk by indicting the president, with rhetoric so overblown as to reach "questionable and gallery-reaching dimensions . . . embellishments of the theme that Polk is a Shakespearean tyrant." Briggs maintains that Lincoln interprets Polk as having the qualities of a Claudius and a Macbeth. John Channing Briggs, *Lincoln's Speeches Reconsidered* (Baltimore, MD: Johns Hopkins University Press, 2005), 93–94. Note: Lincoln was familiar with *Hamlet* and *Macbeth* but makes no explicit allusion to those plays in the Mexican War speech, as he does in later speeches. William C. Harris speculates that Lincoln knew an antiwar speech would trouble his Illinois constituents, but partisan zeal and ambition motivated him to take a political risk: "The young congressman believed that unless the party's majority rallied around an antiwar and anti-expansion policy, radical Whigs would again bolt the party and cost it the 1848 presidential election." William C. Harris, *Lincoln's Rise to the Presidency* (Lawrence: University Press of Kansas, 2007), 41–42. Michael Burlingame suggests that "Lincoln may have denounced Polk's action because he came to realize that the war might expand the realm of slavery." Burlingame, *Lincoln: A Life*, 1:270. Sidney Blumenthal also finds implicit allusions to *Macbeth* in the Mexican War speech owing to its four uses of "the first blood of the war was shed" and other imagery: "Lincoln's maiden speech dripped with 'blood' and themes of murder and guilt, drawing inspiration from Shakespeare's *Macbeth*, his favorite Shakespearean play. . . ." Blumenthal writes that Polk as a profoundly troubled figure is Lincoln's tyrannical, conflicted Macbeth. Sidney Blumenthal, *A Self-Made Man: The Political Life of Abraham Lincoln, 1809–1849* (New York: Simon and Schuster, 2016), 361.

9. Beveridge, *Abraham Lincoln*, 425.

10. William Lee Miller acknowledges the Mexican War speech's blend of legalistic method and moral courage, with the qualification that "one should not put Congressman Lincoln's speeches on Polk and the war on the same plane with Republican leader Lincoln's speeches and actions on slavery, or those of President Lincoln. . . . Congressman Lincoln did not think deeply and express all the considerations respectfully and carefully on the Mexican War. He rushed in, and overdid his attack

on Polk personally." William Lee Miller, *Lincoln's Virtues* (New York: Vintage Books, 2002), 182–83.

11. Lincoln, Speech in United States House of Representatives: The War with Mexico, January 12, 1848, *CW* 1:432. An anonymous review of this book's manuscript observes that "Lincoln took pains in 1861 to distinguish between the right to revolution and what he regarded as spurious attempts to justify 'peaceable secession.' His attention to the distinction may have been required by his defense of the right to revolution in his 1848 Mexican War speech."

12. Burlingame, *Lincoln: A Life*, 1:267. For further discussion of the implications of Lincoln's views on revolution relating to the Union and the Confederacy, see Briggs, *Lincoln's Speeches Reconsidered*, 100–102.

13. Lincoln, Speech in United States House of Representatives, January 12, 1848, *CW* 1:439.

14. Lincoln, Speech in United States House of Representatives, January 12, 1848, *CW* 1:440.

15. Lincoln, Speech in United States House of Representatives, January 12, 1848, *CW* 1:440.

16. Lincoln, Speech in United States House of Representatives, January 12, 1848, *CW* 1:441.

17. Lincoln, To William H. Herndon, February 1, 1848, *CW* 1:448.

18. Lincoln, To Horace Greeley, June 27, 1848, *CW* 1:493–94.

19. Reg Ankrom, *Stephen A. Douglas, Western Man: The Early Years in Congress, 1844–1850* (Jefferson, NC: McFarland and Company, Publishers, 2021), 235.

20. Robert W. Johannsen, *Stephen A. Douglas* (New York: Oxford University Press, 1973), 214.

21. Johannsen, *Stephen A. Douglas*, 215.

22. Johannsen, *Stephen A. Douglas*, 215.

23. Unlike Johannsen, Allen Johnson faulted Douglas's evidence defending Polk's argument that Mexico had attacked on US soil: "It goes without saying that Douglas's mental attitude was the opposite of the scientific and historic spirit. Having a proposition to establish, he cared only for pertinent evidence. He rarely inquired into the character of the authorities from which he culled his data. That this attitude of mind and these unscholarly habits often were his undoing, was inevitable. He was often betrayed by fallacies and hasty inferences. The speech before us [on February 1, 1848] illustrates this lamentable mental defect." Allen Johnson, *Stephen A. Douglas: A Study in American Politics* (New York: The Macmillan Company, 1908), 121–23.

24. Lincoln, Fragment: What General Taylor Ought to Say, March(?) 1848, *CW* 1:454.

25. Donald, *Lincoln*, 127.

26. Lincoln, Fragment, March(?), 1848, *CW* 1:454.

27. Lincoln, Speech at Wilmington, Delaware, June 10, 1848, *CW* 1:476.

28. Donald, *Lincoln*, 128.

29. Burlingame, *Lincoln: A Life*, 1:277.

30. Fred Kaplan, *Lincoln: The Biography of a Writer* (New York: HarperCollins Publishers, 2008), 180–82.

31. Harris, *Lincoln's Rise to the Presidency*, 48.

32. Miller, *Lincoln's Virtues*, 197–99.

33. Lincoln, Speech in the United States House of Representatives on Internal Improvements, June 20, 1848, *CW* 1:481.

34. Lincoln, Speech on Internal Improvements, June 20, 1848, *CW* 1:484.

35. Lincoln, Speech on Internal Improvements, June 20, 1848, *CW* 1:484.

36. Lincoln, Speech on Internal Improvements, June 20, 1848, *CW* 1:489.

37. Lincoln, Speech on Internal Improvements, June 20, 1848, *CW* 1:489.

38. Lincoln, Speech on Internal Improvements, June 20, 1848, *CW* 1:490.

39. William Lee Miller (2003) provides a one-page summary of the Presidential Question speech with limited critical commentary on its rhetorical methods. He concludes that in this speech Lincoln applies his moral principle of choosing the lesser of two evils. As president, Taylor might veto the Wilmot Proviso—prohibiting slavery in new territories—but Cass would likely allow slavery to extend into them: "Once more this responsible realist [Lincoln] is insisting that the actual alternative be faced, and the probable consequences of each alternative be measured, and a decision made on a realistic basis: which (of the two results, one of which will certainly come) is predictable?" Miller, *Lincoln's Virtues*, 202–3. William C. Harris (2007) writes that Lincoln's 1848 Speech on the Presidential Question "sounded more like a Lincoln stump speech in Illinois than an address on the floor of Congress." Harris, *Lincoln's Rise to the Presidency*, 48. Fred Kaplan (2008) observes this speech was "less formal" than Lincoln's Mexican War speech: "more conversational, more structurally casual. . . . Lincoln moved his language and argument through its appropriate paces, with humor and satiric deprecation rather than iron logic." Kaplan, *Lincoln: The Biography of a Writer*, 179. Michael Burlingame, too, refers to it as a stump speech, describing it as "idiosyncratic." Burlingame, *Lincoln: A Life*, 1:279. Sidney Blumenthal (2016) provides a three-page discussion of this speech, mostly summary but including almost a page of background on Cass. Blumenthal observes that Lincoln's criticism of Cass features personal attack: "In taking down Cass, Lincoln resumed his role as 'slasher,' deploying the techniques of sarcasm, belittlement, and ridicule he had honed against opponents in Illinois, with particular denigration of Cass's military record." Blumenthal also notes that in this speech Lincoln addressed Democrats to remind them (and his Illinois constituents) that he voted for legislation that supported US troops in the Mexican War. Blumenthal, *A Self-Made Man*, 388–89.

40. Lincoln, Speech in United States House of Representatives on the Presidential Question, July 27, 1848, *CW* 1:508.

41. Lincoln, Speech on the Presidential Question, July 27, 1848, *CW* 1:509.

42. Lincoln, Speech on the Presidential Question, July 27, 1848, *CW* 1:503–4.

43. Lincoln, Speech on the Presidential Question, July 27, 1848, *CW* 1:512.

44. Lincoln, Speech on the Presidential Question, July 27, 1848, *CW* 1:514.

45. Lincoln, Speech on the Presidential Question, July 27, 1848, *CW* 1:516.

46. Burlingame, *Lincoln: A Life*, 1:279.

47. Lincoln, To William Schouler, August 28, 1848, *CW* 1:518.

48. Lincoln, Speech at Worcester, Massachusetts, September 12, 1848, *CW* 2:2–3.

49. Lincoln, Speech at Worcester, September 12, 1848, *CW* 2:4–5.

50. Lincoln, Speech at Taunton, Massachusetts, September 21(?), 1848, *CW* 2:6–7.

51. Burlingame, *Lincoln: A Life*, 1:282.

52. Lincoln, Speech at Taunton, September 21(?), 1848, *CW* 2:8. An anonymous reviewer of this book's manuscript notes: "The United Party of the North did not become known as the Republican Party until the mid-1850s."

53. Lincoln, Speech at Taunton, September 21(?), 1848, *CW* 2:9.

54. Lincoln, Debate at Jacksonville, Illinois, October 21, 1848, *CW* 2:12–13.

55. Lincoln, Speech at Lacon, Illinois, November 1, 1848, *CW* 2:14.

56. Burlingame, *Lincoln: A Life*, 1:284.

57. Lincoln, Remarks and Resolution Introduced in United States House of Representatives Concerning Abolition of Slavery in the District of Columbia, January 10, 1849, *CW* 2:20.

58. James Q. Howard's notes of an interview with Lincoln (June 1860), *Abraham Lincoln Papers in the Library of Congress*, https://tile.loc.gov/storage-services/service/mss/mal/029/0297401/0297401.pdf.

59. Olivier Fraysse, *Lincoln, Land, and Labor, 1809–60*, trans. Sylvia Neely (Urbana: University of Illinois Press, 1994), 117.

60. Benjamin P. Thomas, *Abraham Lincoln* (New York: Alfred A. Knopf, 1952), 128.

61. Thomas, *Abraham Lincoln*, 129.

62. Burlingame, *Lincoln: A Life*, 1:303.

63. For assessments of Lincoln's congressional career and his life between 1849 and 1854, see Joel H. Silbey, "'Always a Whig in Politics': The Partisan Life of Abraham Lincoln," *Journal of the Abraham Lincoln Association* 8, no.1 (1986), http://hdl.handle.net/2027/spo.2629860.0008.105. Michael Burlingame, *The Inner World of Abraham Lincoln* (Urbana: University of Illinois Press, 1997), 1–2; Burlingame, *Lincoln: A Life*, 1:257. Lincoln's congressional speeches and other remarks have been preserved in the *Congressional Globe* not as texts but as reports about them. During this period texts also exist for his private and public political letters, "fragments" (exploratory writing), and newspaper reports on his speeches in the 1848 campaign.

64. Burlingame, *Lincoln: A Life*, 1:362.

Chapter 4. Introducing Arguments against Slavery and Douglas

Chapter 4 is an adaptation of D. Leigh Henson, "Classical Rhetoric as a Lens for Reading the Key Speeches of Abraham Lincoln's Political Rise, 1852–56," *Journal of the Abraham Lincoln Association* 35, no. 1 (Winter 2014): 1–25. Reprinted here with permission from the Board of Trustees of the University of Illinois.

1. Michael Burlingame, *Abraham Lincoln: A Life*, 2 vols. (Baltimore: Johns Hopkins University Press, 2008), 1:303.

2. For an account of how ideas in Lincoln's Peoria speech reappear in his other speeches and writings throughout his second political career and presidency, see Lewis E. Lehrman, *Lincoln at Peoria: The Turning Point* (Mechanicsburg, PA: Stackpole, 2008), 153–255.

3. Abraham Lincoln, Eulogy on Zachary Taylor, July 25, 1850, Roy P. Basler et al., eds., *The Collected Works of Abraham Lincoln*, 9 vols. (New Brunswick, NJ: Rutgers University Press, 1953–55), 2:87–88. Hereafter referred to as *CW*. Quotations from *CW* retain italics denoting emphasis.

4. Lincoln, Resolutions in Behalf of Hungarian Freedom, January 9, 1852, *CW* 2:116.

5. Lincoln, Eulogy on Henry Clay, July 6, 1852, *CW* 2:126.

6. These sources are in the order of their citations in the chapter: Ward Hill Lamon and Chauncey F. Black, *The Life of Abraham Lincoln: From His Birth to His Inauguration as President* (Boston: James R. Osgood and Company, 1872), 2:340; Don E. Fehrenbacher, *Prelude to Greatness* (Stanford, CA: Stanford University Press, 1962), 18; Roy Morris Jr., *The Long Pursuit: Abraham Lincoln's Thirty-Year Struggle with Stephen Douglas for the Heart and Soul of America* (New York: HarperCollins, 2008), 63; William Lee Miller, *Lincoln's Virtues: An Ethical Biography* (New York: Vintage, 2003), 327.

7. Burlingame, *Lincoln: A Life,* 1:357.

8. Fred Kaplan, *Lincoln: The Biography of a Writer* (New York: HarperCollins, 2008), 229.

9. Lincoln, Speech to the Springfield Scott Club, August 14, 26, 1852, *CW* 2:136. The printed versions of Douglas's speech at Richmond and Lincoln's rebuttal of it in the Scott Club speech have paragraphs ranging from one sentence to a dozen or more. Lincoln's speech is several paragraphs longer than its target.

10. Lincoln, Speech to the Springfield Scott Club, August 14, 26, 1852, *CW* 2:136.

11. Lincoln, Speech to the Springfield Scott Club, August 14, 26, 1852, *CW,* 2:152.

12. Lincoln, Speech at Peoria, Illinois, September 17, 1852, *CW* 2:158–59.

13. Robert W. Johannsen, *Stephen A. Douglas* (New York: Oxford University Press, 1973), 279.

14. Douglas felt the combination of the Compromise of 1850 and popular sovereignty in the unorganized territory would end slavery agitation for the most part so that the country could get on with the business of developing the West, and he was shocked at the intensity and duration of the backlash. Johannsen, *Stephen A. Douglas*, 439–56.

15. *The Lincoln Log*, July 10, 1854, https://www.thelincolnlog.org/Results.aspx?type=CalendarMonth&year=1854&month=7#.

16. Lincoln, Editorial on the Kansas-Nebraska Act, September 11, 1854, *CW* 2:230. During this period Lincoln may have written other anti-Nebraska editorials, but the Calhoun editorial is the only unsigned editorial from this period attributed to him. Lincoln surely also read editorials in the *Illinois Journal,* for example, "Political Power in Negroes," published there on September 23, 1854. This six-paragraph, unattributed editorial emphasizes the political advantage southern states had because of the constitutional provision counting three-fifths of the slave population in the total population, thus giving those states additional votes in the House of Representatives and the Electoral College. Lincoln cited the three-fifths provision as an advantage for the South in two places in his Peoria speech.

17. In different places in *Lincoln at Peoria*, Lehrman briefly cites ideas in the Eulogy on Henry Clay that appear in the Peoria speech, but Lehrman does not discuss other rhetorical qualities of this eulogy and does not reference the Scott Club speech. Lehrman does not compare and contrast the rhetorical qualities of Lincoln's 1852–56 political speeches. Neither do other books that treat Lincoln's rhetoric of the 1850s, such as John Channing Briggs, *Lincoln's Speeches Reconsidered* (Baltimore: Johns Hopkins University Press, 2005).

18. Lincoln, Speech at Bloomington, Illinois, September 12, 1854, *CW* 2:231.

19. Lincoln, Speech at Bloomington, September 26, 1854, *CW* 2:237.

20. Lincoln, Speech at Bloomington, September 26, 1854, *CW* 2:239.

21. For contemporaneous and reminiscent accounts of the culture of Peoria in 1854, Douglas's and Lincoln's speeches there, and photostatic copies of pertinent correspondence, including Lincoln's, see B.C. Bryner, *Abraham Lincoln in Peoria, Illinois* (reprint, 2001; Peoria, IL: Lincoln Historical Publishing, 1926).

22. Lincoln, Speech at Peoria, October 16, 1854, *CW* 2:247–48. Various other quotations from the speech at Peoria are from *CW* 2:247–83.

23. For Douglas's and Lincoln's treatment of morality in 1854, see John Burt, "Lincoln's Peoria Speech of 1854," *Social Research* 66, no. 2 (1999): 679–707. For a bibliographical essay on critical commentaries of the Peoria speech, see Lehrman (2008), *Lincoln at Peoria*, 269–87. For a study of Lincoln's argumentation in the Peoria speech, see Cindy Koenig Richards, "'To Restore the National Faith': Abraham Lincoln's 1854 Peoria Address and the Paradox of Moral Politics," *Southern Communication Journal* 76, no. 5 (November-December 2011): 401–23.

24. Mark E. Neely Jr., *The Last Best Hope of Earth: Abraham Lincoln and the Promise of America* (Cambridge: Harvard University Press, 1993), 39–41.

25. *Illinois Journal*, October 5, 1854, p. 1, col. 1.

26. Noah Brooks, quoted in Lehrman, *Lincoln at Peoria*, 271.

27. John S. Wright, quoted in Lehrman, *Lincoln at Peoria*, 281.

28. Wright, quoted in Lehrman, *Lincoln at Peoria*, 281.

29. Kaplan, *Lincoln: The Biography of a Writer*, 252.

30. Graham A. Peck, "New Records of the Lincoln-Douglas Debate at the 1854 Illinois State Fair: The *Missouri Republican* and the *Missouri Democrat* Report from Springfield," *Journal of the Abraham Lincoln Association* 30, no. 2 (Summer 2009): 38.

31. Douglas, quoted in John A. Corry, *The First Lincoln-Douglas Debates, October 1854* (Bloomington, IN: Xlibris, 2008), 75. For the full text of Douglas's Chicago speech on November 9, 1854, in defense of the Kansas-Nebraska Act, reprinted in the December 2, 1854, issue of the *National Intelligencer*, see Corry, 153–78.

32. Linda Ferreira-Buckley and S. Michael Halloran, eds., Hugh Blair, *Lectures on Rhetoric and Belles Lettres* (Carbondale: Southern Illinois University Press, 2005), 344–67.

33. Lincoln, Speech to the Springfield Scott Club, August 14, 26, 1852, *CW* 2:154; Lincoln, Autobiography Written for John L. Scripps, c. June 1860, *CW* 4:66.

34. For the text of Webster's 1850 Seventh of March Address, see Smith, *Defender of the Union: The Oratory of Daniel Webster* (New York: Greenwood Press, 1989), 167–74. This eighteen-paragraph speech reveals Webster's attempt to provide an

even-handed account of the history and implications of slavery agitation and to call for peaceful, legal measures in dealing with this problem.

35. Corbett and Connors, *Classical Rhetoric for the Modern Student*, 277.

36. Lincoln, Speech at Peoria, October 16, 1854, *CW* 2:255.

37. Lincoln, Speech at Peoria, October 16, 1854, *CW* 2:258.

38. Lincoln, Speech at Peoria, October 16, 1854, *CW* 2:266.

39. Lincoln, Speech at Peoria, October 16, 1854, *CW* 2:266.

40. Lincoln, Speech at Peoria, October 16, 1854, *CW* 2:271.

41. Lincoln, Speech at Peoria, October 16, 1854, *CW* 2:276.

42. Lincoln, Speech at Peoria, October 16, 1854, *CW* 2:276.

43. Peck, "New Records," 37. Given Lincoln's pressing court schedule at Pekin the week before his speech at Peoria, he was shrewd in using his time to compose the rebuttal to Douglas's response to his speech at Springfield and closing the Peoria speech with it for a strategic effect on his opponent rather than trying to incorporate those rebuttal points through an extensive revision of his speech at Springfield.

44. In rejecting Douglas's denial that the Nebraska Bill was conceived as an instrument to extend slavery, Lincoln employs a Shakespearean allusion, and this device suggests he had the well-educated members of his audience in mind: "Like the 'bloody hand' you may wash it, and wash it, the red witness of guilt still sticks, and stares horribly at you." This simile compares the Kansas-Nebraska Act to a bloody hand, which symbolizes the undeniable facts that Macbeth is haunted by a guilty conscience for murdering the good King Duncan and that the Kansas-Nebraska Act will allow slavery to enter those new territories. In an 1863 letter Lincoln wrote, "I think nothing equals Macbeth. It is wonderful." Lincoln, To James H. Hackett, August 17, 1863, *CW* 6:392.

45. Throughout the Peoria speech Lincoln draws heavily on his own research and knowledge of history, and at the end of his statement-of-facts section, he offers a disqualifier to offset any quibbling over his own use of facts: "The foregoing history [of the repeal of the Missouri Compromise] may not be precisely accurate in every particular; but I am sure it is sufficiently so, for all the uses I shall attempt to make of it." Lincoln, Speech at Peoria, October 16, 1854, *CW* 2:254.

46. Lincoln, Speech at Peoria, October 16, 1854, *CW* 2:283.

47. Corbett and Connors, *Classical Rhetoric for the Modern Student*, 280–82.

48. Lincoln, Speech at Peoria, October 16, 1854, *CW* 2:250, 262.

49. Gabor S. Boritt, *Lincoln and the Economics of the American Dream* (Urbana: University of Illinois Press, 1978), 155–56.

50. According to *The Lincoln Log*, after his speech at Peoria of October 16, 1854, Lincoln delivered speeches at Urbana (October 24), Chicago (October 27), Quincy (November 1), possibly at Naples (November 2), and possibly at Carlinville (November 4), http://www.thelincolnlog.org/CalendarYear.aspx?year=1854&r=L 0NhbGVuZGFyLmFzcHg=.

51. Lincoln, Speech at Chicago, Illinois, October 27, 1854, *CW* 2:283.

52. For information about Lincoln's role in the formation of the Illinois Republican Party, see Don E. Fehrenbacher, *Prelude to Greatness: Lincoln in the 1850s* (Stanford, CA: Stanford University Press, 1962), 19–47; Burlingame, *Lincoln: A Life*, 1:407–42.

53. Burlingame, *Lincoln: A Life*, 1:418–20.

54. Lincoln, Editorial on the Right of Foreigners to Vote, July 23, 1856, *CW* 2:355–56.

55. According to *The Lincoln Log*, after his Lost speech at Bloomington of May 29, 1856, Lincoln frequently spoke from June through November 1. Lincoln's July speeches were in northern Illinois, where there were more abolitionists than in other sections of the state; but he eventually and often spoke in them, too, http://www.thelincolnlog.org/CalendarYear.aspx?year=1856&r=L0NhbGVuZGFyLmFzcHg=.

56. Burlingame, *Lincoln: A Life*, 1:430–33.

57. Lincoln, Speech at Kalamazoo, Michigan, August 27, 1856, *CW* 2:361–66.

58. Lincoln, Speech at Kalamazoo, August 27, 1856, *CW* 2:364.

59. For Lincoln's allusions to Clay and Webster, see Lincoln, Speech at Jacksonville, Illinois, September 6, 1856, *CW* 2:370–73; to Washington and Jefferson, see Lincoln, Speech at Olney, Illinois, September 20, 1856, *CW* 2:378.

60. Lincoln, Speech at Vandalia, Illinois, September 23, 1856, *CW* 2:377.

61. Lincoln, Speech at Belleville, Illinois, October 18, 1856, *CW* 2:379.

62. Lincoln, Speech at a Republican Banquet, Chicago, Illinois, December 10, 1856, *CW* 2:385.

63. Lincoln, Speech at a Republican Banquet, December 10, 1856, *CW* 2:385.

64. Burlingame, *Lincoln: A Life*, 1:434.

65. Burlingame, *Lincoln: A Life*, 1:376.

66. Lincoln, Fragment on Stephen A. Douglas, December 1856(?), *CW* 2:382–83.

Chapter 5. Pursuing the Case against Slavery and Douglas for the US Senate

1. Stephen A. Douglas, "Remarks of the Hon. Stephen A. Douglas, on Kansas, Utah, and the *Dred Scott* Decision, Delivered at Springfield, Illinois, June 12, 1857," the Library of Congress, http://www.archive.org/details/remarksofhonstep00doug.

2. For an argument that Douglas's portrayal of Republicans as abolitionists was sincere and not demagogic, see Forest L. Whan, "Stephen A. Douglas," in *A History and Criticism of American Public Address,* ed. William Norwood Brigance (New York: McGraw-Hill Book Co., 1943), 798.

3. Lincolnists have mainly praised Lincoln's Dred Scott speech. For example, see David Herbert Donald, *Lincoln* (New York: Simon and Schuster, 1996), 202; Michael Burlingame, *Abraham Lincoln: A Life*, 2 vols. (Baltimore: Johns Hopkins University Press, 2008), 1:438; Ronald C. White Jr., *A. Lincoln: A Biography* (New York: Random House, 2009), 238.

4. Abraham Lincoln, Speech at Springfield, Illinois, June 26, 1857, Roy P. Basler et al., eds., *Collected Works of Abraham Lincoln*, 9 vols. (New Brunswick, NJ: Rutgers University Press, 1953–55), 2:398–410. Hereafter cited as *CW*. Quotations from *CW* retain italics denoting emphasis.

5. Lincoln, Speech at Springfield, June 26, 1857, *CW* 2:404.

6. Michael Burlingame, review of this book's manuscript, July 2022.

7. Lincoln, Speech at Springfield, June 26, 1857, *CW* 2:405.

8. Lincoln, Speech at Springfield, June 26, 1857, *CW* 2:406.

9. Lincoln, Speech at Springfield, June 26, 1857, *CW* 2:409.

10. Lincoln to Lyman Trumbull, Nov. 30, 1857, *CW* 2:427; Dec. 28, 1857, *CW* 2:430.

11. Lincoln, Fragment of a Speech, c. December 28, 1857, *CW* 2:452.

12. William H. Herndon and Jesse W. Weik, *Herndon's Lincoln*, ed. Douglas L. Wilson and Rodney O. Davis (Galesburg, IL: Lincoln Studies Center, Knox College; Champaign: University of Illinois Press, 2006), 243.

13. Don E. Fehrenbacher, "The Origins and Purpose of Lincoln's 'House-Divided' Speech," *The Mississippi Valley Historical Review* 46, no. 4 (March 1960): 637–41.

14. For an account of the advice Lincoln's friends gave him not to deliver the House Divided speech, see John Channing Briggs, *Lincoln's Speeches Reconsidered* (Baltimore: Johns Hopkins University Press, 2005), 166–67.

15. For discussion of the likelihood of slavery becoming national, see Allan Nevins, *The Emergence of Lincoln: Douglas, Buchanan, and Party Chaos, 1857–1859* (New York: Charles Scribner's Sons, 1950), 162–3; Harry V. Jaffa, *Crisis of the House Divided: An Interpretation of the Issues in the Lincoln-Douglas Debates* (Chicago: University of Chicago Press, 1959), 289–93; Fehrenbacher, "Origins and Purpose," 629; William C. Harris, *Lincoln's Rise to the Presidency* (Lawrence: University Press of Kansas, 2007), 169; Michael Burlingame, *Lincoln: A Life*, 1:464.

16. Burlingame, *Lincoln: A Life*, 1:458.

17. Lincoln, "A House Divided": Speech at Springfield, Illinois, June 16, 1858, *CW* 2:461.

18. Fehrenbacher, "Origins and Purpose," 628.

19. David Zarefsky, "Lincoln and the House Divided: Launching a National Political Career," *Rhetoric & Public Affairs* 13, no. 3 (2010): 448.

20. Edward P.J. Corbett and Robert J. Connors, *Classical Rhetoric for the Modern Student*, 4th ed. (New York: Oxford University Press, 1999), 69.

21. Jason H. Silverman, "Lincoln's Magician: The Saga of Captain Horatio G. 'Harry' Cooke," *Lincoln Lore* 1921 (Spring 2019): 22–27.

22. For use of rhetorical *sleight of hand* in relation to the Cooper Union address, see Graham A. Peck, *Making an Antislavery Nation: Lincoln, Douglas, and the Battle over Freedom* (Urbana: University of Illinois Press, 2017), 176. For use of rhetorical *sleight of hand* relating to the First Inaugural Address, see Michael Knox Beran, "Lincoln, *Macbeth*, and the Moral Imagination," *Humanitas* XI, no. 2 (1998), http://www.nhinet.org/beran.htm. For use of rhetorical *sleight of hand* in the Gettysburg address, see Garry Wills, *Lincoln at Gettysburg: The Words That Remade America* (New York: Simon and Schuster, 1992), 38.

23. Lincoln, "A House Divided," June 16, 1858, *CW* 2:465.

24. Burlingame, *Lincoln: A Life*, 1:464.

25. Lincoln, "A House Divided," June 16, 1858, *CW* 2:465–66. The construction analogy featuring timbers is one example of Lincoln's rhetorical use of subjects relating to nature. For a discussion of this technique, see David S. Reynolds, *Abe: Abraham Lincoln in His Times* (New York: Penguin Books, 2020), 145–46. Reynolds's book won the 2021 Lincoln Prize.

26. Allan Nevins, *The Emergence of Lincoln* (New York: Charles Scribner's Sons, 1950), 350.

27. Burlingame, *Lincoln: A Life*, 1:447.

28. Lincoln, "A House Divided," June 16, 1858, *CW* 2:467.

29. Burlingame, *Lincoln: A Life*, 1:463.

30. Lincoln, "A House Divided," June 16, 1858, *CW* 2:468–69.

31. Horace White, quoted in Burlingame, *Lincoln: A Life*, 1:481.

32. Lincoln, Speech at Chicago, July 10, 1858, *CW* 2:484.

33. For Burlingame's praise of Lincoln's Chicago speech of July 10, 1858, see *Lincoln: A Life*, 1:471. William Lee Miller quotes notable passages from this speech, with the only commentary being that one passage suggests Lincoln accepted racial equality, *Lincoln's Virtues: An Ethical Biography* (New York: Vintage Books, 2003), 342–44.

34. Lincoln, Speech at Chicago, July 10, 1858, *CW* 2:491.

35. For Lincoln's political use of the US Constitution related to slavery, see Brian R. Dirck, *Lincoln and the Constitution* (Carbondale: Southern Illinois University Press, 2012); Lucas E. Morel, *Lincoln and the American Founding* (Carbondale: Southern Illinois University Press, 2020); James Oakes, *The Crooked Path to Abolition: Abraham Lincoln and the Antislavery Constitution* (New York: W.W. Norton and Company, 2021).

36. Lincoln, Speech at Chicago, July 10, 1858, *CW* 2:499–500.

37. Lincoln, Speech at Chicago, July 10, 1858, *CW* 2:500.

38. Lincoln, Speech at Chicago, July 10, 1858, *CW* 2:501.

39. Lincoln, Speech at Chicago, July 10, 1858, *CW* 2:501–2.

40. In a reminiscent account published in *Century Magazine*, December 1881, sculptor Leonard Volk wrote that he was on the train that took Douglas from Chicago to Springfield with a stop in Bloomington, where Douglas spoke on the evening of July 16. Volk said Lincoln was in Bloomington to witness that speech. Volk then wrote, "The next day we all stopped at the town of Lincoln, where short speeches were made by the contestants, and dinner was served at the [Lincoln] Hotel, after which and as Mr. Lincoln came out on the plank walk in front, I was formally presented to him." Volk wrote that he asked Lincoln to sit for a bust sometime in Chicago, and Lincoln agreed. The first sitting took place in Chicago in April 1860. Leonard Volk, "The Lincoln Life-Mask and How It Was Made," *Journal of the Illinois State Historical Society* 8, no. 2 (July 1915), 239.

41. Burlingame, *Lincoln: A Life*, 1:474.

42. Burlingame, *Lincoln: A Life*, 1:475.

43. For contemporaneous reactions to Lincoln's Springfield speech of July 17, 1858, see Burlingame, *Lincoln: A Life*, 1:475. For one of the few contemporary commentaries on this speech, see Miller, *Lincoln's Virtues*, 334–35.

44. Lincoln, Speech at Springfield, Illinois, July 17, 1858, *CW* 2:506.

45. Lincoln, Speech at Springfield, July 17, 1858, *CW* 2:514.

46. Lincoln, Speech at Springfield, July 17, 1858, *CW* 2:519.

47. Lincoln, Speech at Springfield, July 17, 1858, *CW* 2:520.

48. Don E. Fehrenbacher, *Prelude to Greatness: Lincoln in the 1850s* (Stanford, CA: Stanford University Press, 1962), 16.

49. Lincoln, Speech at Monticello, Illinois, July 29, 1858, *CW* 2:527.

50. Burlingame, *Lincoln: A Life*, 1:477.

51. For testimony from those who witnessed Douglas's excessive drinking during the 1858 Senate race, see Burlingame, *Lincoln: A Life*, 1:478–79.

52. Whan, "Stephen A. Douglas," 799.

53. Isaac N. Arnold, *The Life of Abraham Lincoln* (Chicago: Jansen, McClurg, and Company, 1885), 145.

54. For a discussion of Douglas and Lincoln's rivalry to claim the political legacy of Henry Clay, see Dan Monroe, "Henry Clay and the Political Courtship of the Old Whigs of Illinois," *Journal of Illinois History* 5, no. 1 (Spring 2002): 2–18.

55. Lincoln, Speech at Lewistown, Illinois, August 17, 1858, *CW* 2:545.

56. Lincoln, Speech at Lewistown, August 17, 1858, *CW* 2:547.

57. Richard Carwardine, *Lincoln: A Life of Purpose and Power* (New York: Vintage Books), 86–87.

Chapter 6. Sparring with Douglas over Credibility during Their First Four Debates

1. Untold numbers of biographies and histories have treated the debates in their chronological order, discussing such various factors as their historical background; their political and social contexts; the speakers' motives, arguments, physical appearance, and behavior; the debate settings; audience reactions; and coverage in newspapers. For brief discussions of the significance of the Lincoln-Douglas debates, including evaluation of historians' positions, see Don E. Fehrenbacher, "A New Look at the Great Debates," *Prelude to Greatness: Lincoln in the 1850s* (Stanford, CA: Stanford University Press, 1962), 96–120; Harold Holzer, ed., Introduction, *The Lincoln-Douglas Debates: The First Complete, Unexpurgated Text* (New York: Fordham University Press, 2004), 1–33; Rodney O. Davis and Douglas L. Wilson, eds., General Introduction, *The Lincoln-Douglas Debates* (Galesburg, IL: Lincoln Studies Center Edition, Knox College; Urbana: University of Illinois Press, 2008), ix–xxv. Monographs on the Lincoln-Douglas Debates: Harry V. Jaffa, *Crisis of the House Divided: An Interpretation of the Issues in the Lincoln-Douglas Debates* (Chicago: University of Chicago Press, 1959). Jaffa explicates the historical/philosophical roots of Lincoln's and Douglas's central arguments, finding in favor of Lincoln's argument that the natural rights of African Americans derived from the Declaration of Independence. In another major twentieth-century study, rhetorician David Zarefsky takes a different approach: in *Lincoln, Douglas, and Slavery: In the Crucible of Public Debate* (Chicago: University of Chicago Press, 1990), he discusses four types of arguments in the debates: conspiracy, legal, historical, and moral. Debate by debate, historian Allen C. Guelzo in *Lincoln and Douglas: The Debates That Defined America* (New York: Simon and Schuster, 2008) provides tables listing the sequential subjects of each candidate's speech. Also for debate-by-debate accounts, see Michael Burlingame, *Abraham Lincoln: A Life*, 2 vols. (Baltimore: Johns Hopkins University Press, 2008), 1:466–577. In *Lincoln's Tragic Pragmatism: Lincoln, Douglas, and Moral Conflict* (Cambridge: Harvard University Press, 2013), John Burt offers a critical explication of the underlying assumptions and consequences of Douglas's and Lincoln's approaches to the problems of slavery and race.

2. For accounts of the pageantry and excitement of the Lincoln-Douglas debates, see Guelzo, *Lincoln and Douglas: The Debates That Defined America*.

3. Guelzo, *Lincoln and Douglas*, 124–25.

4. Douglas's Opening Speech, First Debate with Stephen A. Douglas at Ottawa, Illinois, October 21, 1858, Roy P. Basler et al., eds., *Collected Works of Abraham Lincoln*, 9 vols. (New Brunswick, N.J.: Rutgers University Press, 1953–1955), 3:1–37. Hereafter cited as *CW*. Quotations from *CW* retain italics denoting emphasis.

5. For a thorough account of Douglas's accusation that in 1854 Lincoln contributed to a Republican abolitionist platform at Springfield and the complex repercussions of that accusation, see Burlingame, *Lincoln: A Life*, 1:490–91.

6. Lincoln's Reply, First Debate, October 21, 1858, *CW* 3:18.

7. Lincoln's Reply, First Debate, October 21, 1858, *CW* 3:23

8. Lincoln's Reply, First Debate, October 21, 1858, *CW* 3:27.

9. Lincoln's Reply, First Debate, October 21, 1858, *CW* 3:28–29.

10. Lincoln's Reply, First Debate, October 21, 1858, *CW* 3:29.

11. Burlingame, *Lincoln; A Life*, 1:492.

12. Davis, Introduction, *The Lincoln-Douglas Debates*, 3.

13. Douglas's Reply, First Debate, October 21, 1858, *CW* 3:35.

14. Lincoln's Opening Speech, Second Debate with Stephen A. Douglas at Freeport, Illinois, August 27, 1858, *CW* 3:44.

15. For a discussion of the Chase amendment in the Lincoln-Douglas debates, see David Zarefsky, *Lincoln, Douglas, and Slavery: In the Crucible of Public Debate* (Chicago: University of Chicago Press, 1990), 88–89.

16. Douglas's Reply, Second Debate, August 27, 1858, *CW*, 3:52.

17. Burlingame, *Lincoln: A Life*, 1:457.

18. Lincoln, Speech at Carlinville, Illinois, August 31, 1858, *CW* 3:78–79.

19. Lincoln, Speech at Clinton, Illinois, September 2, 1858, *CW* 3:84.

20. Lincoln, Speech at Paris, Illinois, September 7, 1858, *CW* 3:91.

21. Lincoln, Speech at Edwardsville, Illinois, September 11, 1858, *CW* 3:92–93.

22. Lincoln, Speech at Edwardsville, September 11, 1858, *CW* 3:93.

23. Lincoln, Speech at Edwardsville, September 11, 1858, *CW* 3:95–96.

24. Douglas's Speech, Third Debate with Stephen A. Douglas at Jonesboro, Illinois, September 15, 1858, *CW* 3:116.

25. Lincoln's Reply, Third Debate, September 15, 1858, *CW* 3:131.

26. Burlingame, *Lincoln: A Life*, 1:514.

27. Lincoln's Reply, Third Debate, September 15, 1858, *CW* 3:133. An anonymous reviewer explains that "Douglas was technically correct: The Supreme Court had not ruled on the ability of a territorial legislature to outlaw slavery, but since the territorial legislature is the creature of the Congress (which was so enjoined), the conclusion follows by inference."

28. Lincoln's Reply, Third Debate, September 15, 1858, *CW* 3:135.

29. Douglas's Reply, Third Debate, September 15, 1858, *CW* 3:141–42.

30. Burlingame, *Lincoln: A Life*, 1:515.

31. Davis, *The Lincoln-Douglas Debates*, 127.

32. Guelzo, *Lincoln and Douglas*, 186.

33. James Oakes, *The Crooked Path to Abolition: Abraham Lincoln and the Anti-slavery Constitution* (New York: W.W. Norton & Co., 2021), 116. For Oakes's discussion of Lincoln's views on race, the limits of natural equality, and the question of citizenship for black people, see pp. 99–133.

34. Allan Nevins, *The Emergence of Lincoln: Douglas, Buchanan, and Party Chaos, 1857–1859* (New York: Charles Scribner's Sons, 1950), 395.

35. Lincoln's Speech, Fourth Debate with Stephen A. Douglas, September 18, 1858, *CW* 3:157.

36. Guelzo, *Lincoln and Douglas*, 196.

37. Douglas's Speech, Fourth Debate, September 18, 1858, *CW* 3:173.

38. Lincoln's Reply, Fourth Debate, September 18, 1858, *CW* 3:182.

Chapter 7. Concluding the Senate Race and Gaining National Distinction

1. Abraham Lincoln, Fragment on Proslavery Theology, October 1, 1858, and Fragment: Notes for Speeches, October 1, 1858, Roy P. Basler et al., eds., *The Collected Works of Abraham Lincoln*, 9 vols. (New Brunswick, NJ: Rutgers University Press, 1953–1955), 3:204–5. Hereafter cited as *CW*. Quotations from *CW* retain italics denoting emphasis.

2. Ronald C. White, *Lincoln in Private: What His Most Personal Reflections Tell Us about Our Greatest President* (New York: Random House, 2021), 106. White claims that Lincoln's Fragment on Pro-slavery Theology reflects the influence of Presbyterian minister Frederick A. Ross's popular 1857 *Slavery Ordained of God,* which White speculates Lincoln read in the nearly three weeks between the fourth and fifth debates.

3. Lincoln, Fragment: Notes for Speeches, October 1, 1858(?), *CW* 3:205.

4. Lincoln, Fragment on Pro-slavery Theology, October 1, 1858(?), *CW* 3:204.

5. Douglas's Speech, Fifth Debate, Galesburg, Illinois, October 7, 1858, *CW* 3:216.

6. Douglas's Speech, Fifth Debate, October 7, 1858, *CW* 3:219.

7. Lincoln's Rejoinder, Sixth Debate, Quincy, Illinois, October 13, 1858, *CW* 3:276.

8. Lincoln's Rejoinder, Sixth Debate, October 13, 1858, *CW* 3:277.

9. Douglas's Speech, Seventh Debate, Alton, Illinois, October 15, 1858, *CW* 3:296–97.

10. Rodney O. Davis and Douglas L. Wilson, eds., *The Lincoln-Douglas Debates* (Galesburg, IL: Lincoln Studies Center Edition, Knox College; Urbana: University of Illinois Press, 2008), 13, note #14.

11. Lincoln's Reply, Seventh Debate, October 15, 1858, *CW* 3:301.

12. Lincoln's Reply, Seventh Debate, October 15, 1858, *CW* 3:302.

13. Lincoln's Reply, Seventh Debate, October 15, 1858, *CW* 3:304.

14. Lincoln's Reply, Seventh Debate, October 15, 1858, *CW* 3:307.

15. Douglas's Reply, Seventh Debate, October 15, 1858, *CW* 3:322–23.

16. Lincoln's Reply, Fifth Debate, October 7, 1858, *CW* 3:226.

17. Lincoln's Reply, Fifth Debate, October 7, 1858, *CW* 3:226.
18. Lincoln's Reply, Fifth Debate, October 7, 1858, *CW* 3:233.
19. Lincoln's Speech, Sixth Debate, October 13, 1858, *CW* 3:255.
20. Lincoln's Speech, Sixth Debate, October 13, 1858, *CW* 3:256.
21. Douglas's Reply, Sixth Debate, October 13, 1858, *CW* 3:274.
22. Douglas's Reply, Sixth Debate, October 13, 1858, *CW* 3:274–75.
23. Douglas's Reply, Sixth Debate, October 13, 1858, *CW* 3:275.
24. Lincoln's Reply, Seventh Debate, October 15, 1858, *CW* 3:311.
25. Lincoln's Reply, Seventh Debate, October 15, 1858, *CW* 3:312.
26. Lincoln's Reply, Seventh Debate, October 15, 1858, *CW* 3:313.
27. Lincoln's Reply, Seventh Debate, October 15, 1858, *CW* 3:315.
28. Douglas's Reply, Seventh Debate, October 15, 1858, *CW* 3:323–24.
29. Douglas's Reply, Seventh Debate, October 15, 1858, *CW* 3:324.
30. Douglas's Speech, Fifth Debate, October 7, 1858, *CW* 3:207.
31. Lincoln's Reply, Fifth Debate, October 7, 1858, *CW* 3:232.
32. Lincoln's Rejoinder, Sixth Debate, October 13, 1858, *CW* 3:279.
33. Douglas's Speech, Seventh Debate, October 15, 1858, *CW* 3:288.
34. Lincoln's Reply, Seventh Debate, October 15, 1858, *CW* 3:317.
35. Lincoln's Reply, Seventh Debate, October 15, 1858, *CW* 3:318.
36. Burlingame, *Lincoln: A Life*, 1:540.
37. Douglas's Speech, Seventh Debate, October 15, 1858, *CW* 3:318.
38. Lincoln's Reply, Fifth Debate, October 7, 1858, *CW* 3:228.
39. Douglas's Reply, Fifth Debate, October 7, 1858, *CW* 3:240.
40. Douglas's Reply, Fifth Debate, October 7, 1858, *CW* 3:238.
41. Lincoln's Reply, Fifth Debate, October 7, 1858, *CW* 3:222.
42. Lincoln's Speech, Sixth Debate, October 13, 1858, *CW* 3:252–53.
43. Lincoln's Speech, Sixth Debate, October 13, 1858, *CW* 3:254.
44. Robert W. Johannsen, *Stephen A. Douglas* (Urbana: University of Illinois Press, 1997), 34.
45. Douglas's Reply, Sixth Debate, October 13, 1858, *CW* 3:260.
46. "Mass Meeting at Lincoln," Bloomington *Pantagraph*, October 18, 1858: 1. On October 16, 2008, the Abraham Lincoln Bicentennial Commission of Lincoln, Illinois, reenacted this "monster" Republican rally, including a creative, condensed rendition of Abraham Lincoln's two-hour stemwinder, based on this author's research-based playscript. D. Leigh Henson, "Lincoln at Lincoln: Abraham Lincoln Rallies Logan County, Illinois, in His First Namesake Town on October 16, 1858," *Journal of the Illinois State Historical Society* 101, nos. 3–4 (Fall/Winter, 2009): 356–92.
47. Lincoln, Fragment: Last Speech of the Campaign at Springfield, Illinois, October 30, 1858, *CW* 3:334.
48. Lincoln's Speech, Third Debate, Jonesboro, Illinois, September 15, 1858, *CW* 3:116.
49. Lincoln's Speech, Seventh Debate, October 15, 1858, *CW* 3:301.
50. Lincoln's scrapbook collection of the Lincoln-Douglas debates was first published in the spring of 1860, just before his Republican presidential nomination.

The texts of Lincoln's speeches were from the pro-Republican *Chicago Press and Tribune*, and Douglas's speech texts came from the pro-Democratic *Chicago Times*. More than three dozen editions of the Lincoln-Douglas debates have been published. For discussions of the Lincoln-Douglas speech texts in various editions, see Edwin Erle Sparks, ed., Preface, *The Lincoln-Douglas Debates of 1858*, Collections of the Illinois State Historical Library vol. III, Lincoln Series vol. I (Springfield: Illinois State Journal Company, 1908), v–vii; Harold Holzer, ed., Preface to the Fordham University Press Edition, and Preface, *The Lincoln-Douglas Debates: The First Complete, Unexpurgated Text* (New York: Fordham University Press, 2004), xi-xxii; Rodney O. Davis and Douglas L. Wilson, eds., General Introduction, *The Lincoln-Douglas Debates* (Galesburg, IL: Lincoln Studies Center Edition, Knox College; Urbana: University of Illinois Press, 2008), xxv.

Chapter 8. Expanding Arguments against Slavery and Douglas

1. Michael Burlingame, *Abraham Lincoln: A Life*, 2 vols. (Baltimore: Johns Hopkins University Press, 2008), 1:559.

2. Abraham Lincoln, To Salmon P. Chase, April 30, 1859, Roy P. Basler et al., eds., *The Collected Works of Abraham Lincoln*, 9 vols. (New Brunswick, NJ: Rutgers University Press, 1953–1955), 3:378. Hereafter cited as *CW*. Quotations from *CW* retain italics denoting emphasis.

3. Lincoln, To Salmon P. Chase, June 9, 1859, *CW* 3:384.

4. Lincoln, To Nathan Sargent, June 23, 1859, *CW* 3:388.

5. Lincoln, To the Editor of the *Central Transcript*, July 3, 1859, *CW* 3:389–90.

6. Lincoln, To Samuel Galloway, July 28, 1859, *CW* 3:395.

7. Lincoln, To Salmon P. Chase, September 21, 1859, *CW* 3:471. Besides Chase, another potential rival for the 1860 Republican nomination was Senator Simon Cameron of Pennsylvania, and in the fall of 1859 when a citizen of that state asked Lincoln to endorse Cameron for that nomination, Lincoln tactfully said he wanted to keep his options open. Lincoln, To William E. Frazier, November 1, 1859, *CW* 3:491.

8. Robert W. Johannsen, *Stephen A. Douglas* (New York: Oxford University Press, 1973), 344–46. For an extensive treatment of the reform movement known as Young America, see Mark A. Lause, *Young America: Land, Labor, and the Republican Community* (Urbana: University of Illinois Press, 2005).

9. David S. Reynolds, *Abe: Abraham Lincoln in His Times* (New York: Penguin Books, 2020), 496–97.

10. Burlingame, *Lincoln: A Life*, 1:443.

11. Burlingame, *Lincoln: A Life*, 1:443–44.

12. Lincoln, Second Lecture on Discoveries and Inventions, February 11, 1859, *CW* 3:357.

13. David Herbert Donald, *Lincoln* (New York: Simon and Schuster, 1995), 146.

14. Lincoln, Second Lecture, February 11, 1859, *CW* 3:358–59.

15. Lincoln, Speech at Chicago, Illinois, March 1, 1859, *CW* 3:366.

16. Lincoln, Speech at Chicago, March 1, 1859, *CW* 3:369–70.

17. Lincoln, Speech at Chicago, March 1, 1859, *CW* 3:370.

18. Earl W. Wiley, "Behind Lincoln's Visit to Ohio in 1859," *Ohio State Archaeological and Historical Quarterly* 60, no. 1 (1951): 30.

19. Wiley, "Behind Lincoln's Visit," 31.

20. William C. Harris, *Lincoln's Rise to the Presidency* (Lawrence: University Press of Kansas, 2007), 167.

21. Wiley, "Behind Lincoln's Visit," 28.

22. Robert W. Johannsen, *Stephen A. Douglas* (New York: Oxford University Press, 1973), 707.

23. Burlingame, *Lincoln: A Life*, 1:565.

24. Johannsen, *Stephen A. Douglas*, 709.

25. Lincoln, Speech at Columbus, Ohio, September 16, 1859, *CW* 3:409.

26. Lincoln, Speech at Columbus, September 16, 1859, *CW* 3:417.

27. Lincoln, Speech at Columbus, September 16, 1859, *CW* 3:418.

28. Lincoln, Speech at Columbus, September 16, 1859, *CW* 3:424.

29. Johannsen, *Stephen A. Douglas*, 710–11.

30. Lincoln, Speech at Cincinnati, Ohio, September 17, 1859, *CW* 3:443.

31. Lincoln, Speech at Cincinnati, September 17, 1859, *CW* 3:453.

32. Gary Ecelbarger, "Before Cooper Union: Abraham Lincoln's 1859 Cincinnati Speech and Its Impact on His Nomination, *Journal of the Abraham Lincoln Association* 30, no. 1 (Winter 2009), http://hdl.handle.net/2027/spo.2629860.0030.103.

33. Burlingame, *Lincoln: A Life*, 570.

34. "Lincoln's 1859 Address at Milwaukee," *The Wisconsin Magazine of History* 10, no. 3 (March 1927): 243, http://www.jstor.org/stable/4630667.

35. Charles Caverno, "A Day with Lincoln," *The Magazine of History* (March 1916): 95.

36. Daniel Kilham Dodge, "Lincoln's Only Speech on Farming," *The Country Gentleman* (February 7, 1925): 30. Dodge, an English professor at the University of Illinois, had published an early monograph on Lincoln's "literary style," but Dodge's treatment of Lincoln's Milwaukee lecture focuses on its content and says nothing about its other rhetorical qualities.

37. Lincoln, Address before the Wisconsin State Agricultural Society, Milwaukee, Wisconsin, September 30, 1859, *CW* 3:474.

38. Lincoln, Address before the Wisconsin State Agricultural Society, September 30, 1859, *CW* 3:476. Perhaps one of these "mammoth farms" was the estate of Irish immigrant and absentee landlord William Scully, who in the 1850s offered tens of thousands of acres in Illinois for sale out of frustration. Lincoln may have known about these conditions because Scully's agents had their land office in Springfield. Paul Beaver, *William Scully and the Scully Estates of Logan County, Illinois* (privately published, 2003), 10.

39. Lincoln obtained a patent on a device to free vessels from being stranded on gravel bars in streams and is the only president to hold a patent. Ian de Silva, "Evaluating Lincoln's Patented Invention," *Journal of the Abraham Lincoln Association* 39, no. 2 (Summer 2018): 1–28.

40. Stewart Winger, "Lincoln's Economics and the American Dream," *Journal of the Abraham Lincoln Association* 22, no. 1 (Winter 2001), http://hdl.handle.net/2027/spo.2629860.0022.106.

41. Lincoln, Address before the Wisconsin State Agricultural Society, September 30, 1859, *CW* 3:480.

42. Lincoln, Address before the Wisconsin State Agricultural Society, September 30, 1859, *CW* 3:480.

43. For a discussion of whether Lincoln had read *Leaves of Grass*, see Robert Bray, *Reading with Lincoln* (Carbondale: Southern Illinois Press, 2010), 136–38.

44. Olivier Fraysse, *Lincoln, Land, and Labor, 1809–60*, translated by Sylvia Neely (Urbana: University of Illinois Press, 1988), 173–75. Fraysse critiques Lincoln's rejection of large-scale farming by pointing out that some large-scale farms were successful, including that of Lincoln's friend Judge David Davis, and some large-scale farms failed not owing to lack of mechanization but to problems with labor availability and management.

45. Lincoln, Address before the Wisconsin State Agricultural Society, September 30, 1859, *CW* 3:482.

46. Caverno, "A Day with Lincoln," 98.

47. Harold Holzer, *Lincoln at Cooper Union: The Speech That Made Abraham Lincoln President* (New York: Simon and Schuster Paperbacks, 2004), 7–8.

48. Lincoln, Speech at Beloit, Wisconsin, October 1, 1859, *CW* 3:482.

49. Lincoln, Speech at Clinton, Illinois, October 14, 1859, *CW* 3:488.

50. Burlingame, *Lincoln: A Life*, 1:577.

51. Lincoln, Speech at Elwood, Kansas, December 1 [November 30?], 1859, *CW* 3:497. Basler notes that the Elwood speech apparently included Lincoln's first public reference to John Brown, who was executed the day after this speech.

52. "When Abraham Lincoln Spoke in Leavenworth," *Kansas Historical Quarterly* 20, no. 7 (August 1953): 530.

53. In 1859 Kansan John James Ingalls wrote: "It is estimated that there are five hundred slaves in the territory today by virtue of the *Dred Scott* decision." John James Ingalls, To Elias T. Ingalls, June 10, 1859, https://www.kshs.org/km/items/view/2966.

54. Lincoln, Speech at Leavenworth, Kansas, December 3, 1859, *CW* 3:501.

55. Lincoln, Speech at Leavenworth, December 3, 1859, *CW* 3:502.

56. Lincoln, Second Speech at Leavenworth, December 5, 1859, *CW* 3:503.

57. Lincoln, Second Speech at Leavenworth, December 5, 1859, *CW* 3:504.

58. For details about the Illinois intra–Republican Party dispute between Norman B. Judd and John ("Long John") Wentworth and Lincoln's efforts to mediate it, see Burlingame, *Lincoln: A Life*, 1:578–79.

59. Lincoln, To Jesse W. Fell, Enclosing Autobiography, December 20, 1859, *CW* 3:511–12.

60. Lincoln, To Norman B. Judd, February 9, 1860, *CW* 3:517.

61. Lincoln, To Oliver P. Hall, Jacob N. Fullinwider, and William F. Correll, February 14, 1860, *CW* 3:520.

62. See John A. Corry, *Lincoln at Cooper Union: The Speech That Made Him President* (Xlibris, 2003); Holzer, *Lincoln at Cooper Union*.

63. Holzer, *Lincoln at Cooper Union*, xix.

64. Calculation for the worth of an 1860 dollar in 2023, https://www.officialdata
.org/us/inflation/1860?amount=200.

65. Wil Linkugel, "Lincoln, Kansas and Cooper Union," *Speech Monographs* 37,
no. 3 (1970): 172–79; Michael Leff and Gerald Mohrmann, "Lincoln at Cooper
Union: A Rhetorical Analysis of the Text," *Quarterly Journal of Speech* 60, no. 3
(1974): 346–58; Michael Leff, "Lincoln at Cooper Union: Neo-Classical Criticism
Revisited," *Western Journal of Communication* 65, no. 3 (2001): 232–48; Corry,
Lincoln at Cooper Union; Holzer, *Lincoln at Cooper Union*; John Channing Briggs,
"The Cooper Union Address," in *Lincoln's Speeches Reconsidered* (Baltimore: Johns
Hopkins University Press, 2005), 237–56.

66. Holzer, *Lincoln at Cooper Union*, 3.

67. Burlingame, *Lincoln: A Life*, 1:587.

68. Graham A. Peck, *Making an Antislavery Nation: Lincoln, Douglas, and the
Battle over Freedom* (Urbana: University of Illinois Press, 2017), 176.

69. Briggs, *Lincoln's Speeches Reconsidered*, 246–47.

70. Lincoln, Address at Cooper Institute, New York City, February 27, 1860,
CW 3:532.

71. Lincoln, Address at Cooper Institute, February 27, 1860, *CW* 3:535.

72. Lincoln, Address at Cooper Institute, February 27, 1860, *CW* 3:535.

73. Lincoln, Address at Cooper Institute, February 27, 1860, *CW* 3:537.

74. Lincoln, Address at Cooper Institute, February 27, 1860, *CW* 3:546–47.

75. Lincoln, Address at Cooper Institute, February 27, 1860, *CW* 3:548–49.

76. For contemporaneous reactions to the Cooper Union address, see Holzer,
Lincoln at Cooper Union, 149–74; Burlingame, *Lincoln: A Life*, 1:587–88; Corry,
Lincoln at Cooper Union, 151–61. Of these three sources, Corry provides the lengthi-
est quotations from the contemporaneous press.

77. Holzer, *Lincoln at Cooper Union*, 139.

78. Burlingame, back cover, Peck, *Making an Antislavery Nation*. See also Reynolds, *Abe*, 924.

79. Holzer, *Lincoln at Cooper Union*, 207–8.

Conclusions

1. Key speeches of Lincoln's first political career: 1838 Lyceum address, 1839
Subtreasury speech, 1848 Mexican War speech, 1848 Internal Improvements speech,
1848 Presidential Question speech. Political careers interim speech: 1852 Eulogy on
Henry Clay. Key speeches of his second political career: 1854 Peoria speech, 1857
Dred Scott speech, 1858 House Divided speech, 1858 final speech of the Lincoln-
Douglas debates (Alton), 1859 Columbus speech, 1859 Cincinnati speech, 1860
Cooper Union address. Lincoln's Chicago speech of July 10, 1858, could be added
to this list.

2. Abraham Lincoln, Fragment on the Constitution and the Union, c. January
1861, Roy P. Basler et al., eds., *The Collected Works of Abraham Lincoln*, 9 vols. (New
Brunswick, NJ: Rutgers University Press, 1953–1955), 4:169. Quotations from *CW*
retain italics denoting emphasis.

Bibliography

Ankrom, Reg. *Stephen A. Douglas: The Political Apprenticeship, 1833–1843*. Jefferson, NC: McFarland and Co., 2015.

Ankrom, Reg. *Stephen A. Douglas, Western Man: The Early Years in Congress, 1844–1850*. Jefferson, NC: McFarland and Co., 2021.

Arnold, Isaac N. *The Life of Abraham Lincoln*. Chicago: Jansen, McClurg, and Co., 1885.

Barr, John McKee. *Loathing Lincoln: An American Tradition from the Civil War to the Present*. Baton Rouge: Louisiana State University Press, 2014.

Barrett, Joseph H. *Life of Abraham Lincoln*. New York: Moore, Wilstach and Baldwin, 1865 (repr., Mechanicsburg, PA: Stackpole Books, 2006).

Barzun, Jacques. "Lincoln the Writer." In *On Writing, Editing, and Publishing: Essays Explicative and Hortatory*. Chicago: University of Chicago Press, 1971.

Basler, Roy P. "Abraham Lincoln's Rhetoric." *American Literature* 11, no. 2 (May 1939): 167–82.

Basler, Roy P. "Lincoln's Development as a Writer." In *A Touchstone for Greatness: Essays, Addresses, and Occasional Pieces about Abraham Lincoln*, 53–99. Westport, CT: Greenwood Press, 1973.

Berry, Mildred Freburg. "Abraham Lincoln: His Development in the Skills of the Platform." Vol. II, *A History and Criticism of American Public Address*. Edited by William Norwood Brigance, 828–58. New York: McGraw-Hill Book Co., 1943.

Berry, Mildred Freburg. "Lincoln—The Speaker," Part I. *Quarterly Journal of Speech* 17, no. 1 (February 1931): 25–40.

Berry, Mildred Freburg. "Lincoln—The Speaker," Part II. *Quarterly Journal of Speech* 17, no. 2 (April 1931): 177–90.

Beveridge, Albert J. Vol. 1, *Abraham Lincoln, 1809–1858*. New York: Harcourt, Brace and Co., 1928.

Black, Edwin. "The Ultimate Voice of Lincoln." *Rhetoric & Public Affairs* 3, no. 1 (Spring 2000): 49–57.

Blair, Hugh. *Lectures on Rhetoric and Belles Lettres.* Edited by Linda Ferreira-Buckley and S. Michael Halloran. Carbondale: Southern Illinois Press, 2005.

Blumenthal, Sidney. *A Self-Made Man: The Political Life of Abraham Lincoln, Vol. 1, 1809–1849.* New York: Simon and Schuster, 2016.

Blumenthal, Sidney. *All the Powers of Earth: The Political Life of Abraham Lincoln, Vol. III, 1856–1860.* New York: Simon and Schuster, 2019.

Blumenthal, Sidney. *Wrestling with His Angel: The Political Life of Abraham Lincoln, Vol. II, 1849–1856.* New York: Simon and Schuster, 2017.

Boritt, Gabor S. *Lincoln and the Economics of the American Dream.* Memphis: Memphis State University Press, 1978.

Bray, Robert. *Reading with Lincoln.* Carbondale: Southern Illinois University Press, 2010.

Bray, Robert. "'The Power to Hurt,' Lincoln's Early Use of Satire and Invective." *Journal of the Abraham Lincoln Association* 16, no. 1 (Winter 1995): 39–58.

Bray, Robert. "What Abraham Lincoln Read—An Evaluative and Annotated List." *Journal of the Abraham Lincoln Association* 28, no. 2 (Summer 2007): 28–81.

Brice, Marshall M. "Lincoln and Rhetoric." *College Composition and Communication* 17, no. 1 (February 1966): 12–14.

Briggs, John Channing. *Lincoln's Speeches Reconsidered.* Baltimore: Johns Hopkins University Press, 2005.

Brookhiser, Richard. *Founders' Son: A Life of Abraham Lincoln.* New York: Basic Books, 2014.

Bryner, B.C. *Abraham Lincoln in Peoria, Illinois.* Peoria, IL: Lincoln Historical Publishing, 1926 (repr., Henry, IL: M and D Printing, 2001).

Burlingame, Michael. *Abraham Lincoln: A Life.* 2 vols. Baltimore: Johns Hopkins University Press, 2008.

Burlingame, Michael. *The Inner World of Abraham Lincoln.* Urbana: University of Illinois Press, 1997.

Burlingame, Michael. *Lincoln's Tragic Pragmatism: Lincoln, Douglas, and Moral Conflict.* Cambridge: Harvard University Press, 2013.

Burt, John. "Lincoln's Peoria Speech of 1854." *Social Research* 66, no. 2 (1999): 679–707.

Carwardine, Richard. *Lincoln: A Life of Purpose and Power.* New York: Vintage Books, 2006.

Carwardine, Richard. *Lincoln's Sense of Humor.* Carbondale: Southern Illinois University Press, 2017.

Caverno, Charles. "A Day with Lincoln." *The Magazine of History* 22 (March 1916): 94–99.

Corbett, Edward P.J., and Robert J. Connors. *Classical Rhetoric for the Modern Student.* New York: Oxford University Press, 1999.

Corry, John A. *Lincoln at Cooper Union: The Speech That Made Him President.* Philadelphia: Xlibris, 2003.

Corry, John A. *The First Lincoln-Douglas Debates, October 1854.* Bloomington, IN: Xlibris, 2008.

Current, Richard N. "Lincoln and Daniel Webster." *Journal of the Illinois State Historical Society* 48, no. 3 (Autumn 1955): 307–21.

Davis, Rodney O., and Douglas L. Wilson, eds. *The Lincoln-Douglas Debates*. Galesburg, IL: Lincoln Studies Center Edition, Knox College. Urbana: University of Illinois Press, 2008.

Dirck, Brian R. *Lincoln and the Constitution*. Carbondale: Southern Illinois University Press, 2012.

Dodge, Daniel Kilham. *Abraham Lincoln: The Evolution of His Literary Style*. Urbana: University of Illinois Press, 1900 (repr., Urbana: University of Illinois Press, 2000).

Dodge, Daniel Kilham. "Lincoln's Only Speech on Farming." *The Country Gentleman* (February 7, 1925): 5, 30.

Donald, David Herbert. *Lincoln*. New York: Simon and Schuster, 1996.

Douglas, Stephen A. "Remarks of the Hon. Stephen A. Douglas, on Kansas, Utah, and the *Dred Scott* Decision, Delivered at Springfield, Illinois, June 12th 1857," The Library of Congress, http://www.archive.org/details/remarksofhonstep00doug.

Dubofsky, Melvyn. "Daniel Webster and the Whig Theory of Economic Growth, 1828–1848." *The New England Quarterly* 42, no. 4 (Dec. 1969): 551–72.

Duncan, Kunigunde, and D.H. Nickols. *Mentor Graham: The Man Who Taught Lincoln*. Chicago: University of Chicago Press, 1944.

Ecelbarger, Gary. "Before Cooper Union: Abraham Lincoln's 1859 Cincinnati Speech and Its Impact on His Nomination." *Journal of the Abraham Lincoln Association* 30, no. 1 (Winter 2009): 1–17.

Edwards, Herbert J., and John E. Hankins. *Lincoln the Writer: The Development of His Literary Style*. University of Maine Studies, Second Series, No. 76. Orono: University of Maine Press, 1962.

Enos, Theresa, ed. *Encyclopedia of Rhetoric and Composition: Communication from Ancient Times to the Information Age*. London: Routledge, 2013.

Fehrenbacher, Don E., ed. *Abraham Lincoln: A Documentary Portrait through His Speeches and Writings*. Stanford, CA: Stanford University Press, 1964.

Fehrenbacher, Don E. *Lincoln in Text and Context: Collected Essays*. Stanford, CA: Stanford University Press, 1987.

Fehrenbacher, Don E. *Prelude to Greatness: Lincoln in the 1850s*. Stanford, CA: Stanford University Press, 1962.

Fehrenbacher, Don E. "The Anti-Lincoln Tradition." *Journal of the Abraham Lincoln Association* 4, no. 1 (1982): 6–28.

Fehrenbacher, Don E. "The Origins and Purpose of Lincoln's 'House-Divided' Speech." *The Mississippi Valley Historical Review* 46, no. 4 (March 1960): 637–41.

Frayssé, Olivier. *Lincoln, Land, and Labor, 1809–60*. Urbana: University of Illinois Press, 1988.

Gross, Alan G. "Lincoln's Use of Constitutive Metaphors." *Rhetoric & Public Affairs* 7, no. 2 (2004): 173–90.

Guelzo, Allen C. *Abraham Lincoln as a Man of Ideas*. Carbondale: Southern Illinois University Press, 2009.

Guelzo, Allen C. *Lincoln and Douglas: The Debates That Defined America*. New York: Simon and Schuster, 2008.

Gustainis, J. Justin. "Demagoguery and Political Rhetoric: A Review of the Literature." *Rhetoric Society Quarterly* 20, no. 2 (Spring 1990): 155–61.

Harris, William C. *Lincoln's Rise to the Presidency*. Lawrence: University Press of Kansas, 2007.

Henson, D. Leigh. *Inventing Lincoln: Approaches to His Rhetoric*. CreateSpace/Amazon, 2017.

Herndon, William H., and Jesse W. Weik. *Herndon's Lincoln*. Edited by Rodney O. Davis and Douglas L. Wilson. Galesburg, IL: Lincoln Studies Center, Knox College; Champaign: University of Illinois Press, 2006.

Hickey, James T. "Three R's in Lincoln's Education: Rogers, Riggin and Rankin." In *The Collected Writings of James T. Hickey*, 5–13. Springfield: The Illinois State Historical Society, 1990.

Hirsch, David, and Dan Van Haften. *Abraham Lincoln and the Structure of Reason*. New York: Savas Beatie, 2010.

Holt, Michael F. *The Rise and Fall of the American Whig Party: Jacksonian Politics and the Onset of the Civil War*. New York: Oxford University Press, 2003.

Holzer, Harold. *Lincoln at Cooper Union: The Speech That Made Abraham Lincoln President*. New York: Simon and Schuster Paperbacks, 2004.

Holzer, Harold, ed. *The Lincoln-Douglas Debates: The First Complete, Unexpurgated Text*. New York: Fordham University Press, 2004.

Howe, Daniel Walker. "Why Abraham Lincoln Was a Whig." *Journal of the Abraham Lincoln Association* 16, no. 1 (Winter 1995): 27–38.

Hurt, James. "All the Living and the Dead: Lincoln's Imagery." *American Literature* 52, no. 3 (November 1980): 351–80.

Jaffa, Harry V. *Crisis of the House Divided: An Interpretation of the Issues in the Lincoln-Douglas Debates*. Chicago: University of Chicago Press, 1982.

Jaffa, Harry V. "The Speech That Changed the World." *Interpretation* 24, no. 3 (Spring 1997): 363–70.

Johannsen, Robert W. *Stephen A. Douglas*. New York: Oxford University Press, 1973.

Johnson, Allen. *Stephen A. Douglas: A Study in American Politics*. New York: The Macmillan Company, 1908.

Johnson, Nan. Introduction to "A Profile of Nineteenth-Century Rhetoric." *Nineteenth-Century Rhetoric in North America*, 3–17. Carbondale: Southern Illinois University Press, 1991.

Kaplan, Fred. *Lincoln: The Biography of a Writer*. New York: Harper, 2008.

Kateb, George. "Lincoln as a Writer." In *Lincoln's Political Thought*, 36–52. Cambridge: Harvard University Press, 2015.

Keller, Ron J. *Lincoln in the Illinois Legislature*. Carbondale: Southern Illinois University Press, 2019.

Kelley, Robert. "Ideology and Political Culture from Jefferson to Nixon." *American Historical Review* 82, no. 3 (June 1977): 531–62.

King, Andrew, and Jim A. Kuypers. *Twentieth-Century Roots of Rhetorical Studies.* Westport, CT: Praeger Publishers, 2001.

Krannawitter, Thomas L. *Vindicating Lincoln: Defending the Politics of Our Greatest President.* New York: Rowman and Littlefield Publishers, 2008.

LaFantasie, Glenn W. "Lincoln, Euclid, and the Satisfaction of Success." *Journal of the Abraham Lincoln Association* 41, no. 1 (Winter 2020): 24–46.

Lamon, Ward Hill, and Chauncey F. Black. *The Life of Abraham Lincoln: From His Birth to His Inauguration as President.* Boston: James R. Osgood and Company, 1872.

Leff, Michael C., and G. P. Mohrmann, "Lincoln at Cooper Union: A Rationale for Neo-Classical Criticism," *Quarterly Journal of Speech* 60, no. 1 (December 1974): 459–67.

Leff, Michael C., and G. P. Mohrmann. "Lincoln at Cooper Union: A Rhetorical Analysis of the Text." *Quarterly Journal of Speech* 60, no. 3 (October 1974): 346–58.

Leff, Michael C., and Jean Goodwin. "Dialogic Figures and Dialectical Argument in Lincoln's Rhetoric." *Rhetoric & Public Affairs* 3, no. 1 (Spring 2000): 59–69.

Leff, Michael. "Lincoln at Cooper Union: Neo-Classical Criticism Revisited." *Western Journal of Communication* 65, no. 3 (Summer 2001): 232–48.

Leff, Michael. "Rhetorical Timing in Lincoln's 'House Divided' Speech." Evanston: Northwestern University Press, 1984.

Lehrman, Lewis E. *Lincoln at Peoria: The Turning Point.* Mechanicsburg, PA: Stackpole, 2008.

Lincoln, Abraham. *The Collected Works of Abraham Lincoln,* 9 vols. Edited by Roy P. Basler et al. New Brunswick, NJ: Rutgers University Press, 1953.

Linkugel, Wil. "Lincoln, Kansas, and Cooper Union." *Speech Monographs* 37, no. 3 (1970): 172–79.

Lord Charnwood. *Abraham Lincoln.* New York: Henry Holt and Company, 1917.

Luthin, Reinhard H. *American Demagogues.* Boston: Beacon Press, 1954.

Miller, William Lee. *Lincoln's Virtues: An Ethical Biography.* New York: Vintage Books, 2002.

Mills, Glen E. "Daniel Webster's Principles of Rhetoric." *Speech Monographs* 9, no. 1 (1942): 124–40.

Morris, Roy, Jr. *The Long Pursuit: Abraham Lincoln's Thirty-Year Struggle with Stephen Douglas for the Heart and Soul of America.* New York: HarperCollins Publishers, 2008.

Myers, Marshall. "'Rugged Grandeur': A Study of the Influences on the Writing Style of Abraham Lincoln and a Brief Study of His Writing Habits." *Rhetoric Review* 23, no. 4 (2004): 350–67.

Neely, Mark E., Jr. *The Last Best Hope of Earth: Abraham Lincoln and the Promise of America.* Cambridge: Harvard University Press, 1993.

Nevins, Allan. *The Emergence of Lincoln.* New York: Charles Scribner's Sons, 1950.

Nicolay, John G., and John Hay. *Abraham Lincoln: A History.* 10 vols. New York: The Century Co., 1890.

Oakes, James. *The Crooked Path to Abolition: Abraham Lincoln and the Antislavery Constitution*. New York: W.W. Norton and Company, 2021.

Peck, Graham A. "New Records of the Lincoln-Douglas Debate at the 1854 Illinois State Fair: The *Missouri Republican* and the *Missouri Democrat* Report from Springfield." *Journal of the Abraham Lincoln Association* 30, no. 2 (Summer 2009): 25–80.

Ray, Angela G. "Learning Leadership: Lincoln at the Lyceum, 1838." *Rhetoric & Public Affairs* 13, no. 3 (2010): 349–86.

Remini, Robert V. *Henry Clay: Statesman for the Union*. New York: W.W. Norton and Company, 1991.

Reynolds, David S. *Abe: Abraham Lincoln in His Times*. New York: Penguin Books, 2020.

Richards, Cindy Koenig. "'To Restore the National Faith': Abraham Lincoln's 1854 Peoria Address and the Paradox of Moral Politics." *Southern Communication Journal* 76, no. 5 (November-December 2011): 401–23.

Robinson, Luther Emerson. *Abraham Lincoln as a Man of Letters*. Chicago: Reilly and Britton, 1918.

Schaub, Diana. *His Greatest Speeches: How Lincoln Moved the Nation*. New York: St. Martin's Press, 2021.

Silbey, Joel H. "'Always a Whig in Politics': The Partisan Life of Abraham Lincoln," *Journal of the Abraham Lincoln Association* 8, no. 1 (1986): 21–42.

Simon, Paul. *Lincoln's Greatness: The Illinois Legislative Years*. Urbana: University of Illinois Press, 1971.

Smith, Craig R. *Defender of the Union: The Oratory of Daniel Webster*. New York: Greenwood Press, 1989.

Sorensen, Mark W. "The Illinois State Library: 1818–1870." *Illinois Libraries* 81, no. 1 (Winter 1999): 33–38.

Sparks, Edwin Erle, ed. *The Lincoln-Douglas Debates of 1858*. Vol. I, Collections of the Illinois State Historical Library, Lincoln Series. Springfield: Illinois State Journal Company, 1908.

Stevenson, Louise. *Scholarly Means to Evangelical Ends: The New Haven Scholars and the Transformation of Higher Learning in America*. Baltimore: Johns Hopkins University Press, 1986.

Thomas, Benjamin P. *Abraham Lincoln: A Biography*. New York: Alfred A. Knopf, 1952.

Thomas, Benjamin P. *Lincoln's New Salem*. Chicago and New Salem: Lincoln's New Salem Enterprises, 1934.

Thompson, Todd Nathan. *The National Joker: Abraham Lincoln and the Politics of Satire*. Carbondale: Southern Illinois University Press, 2015.

Volk, Leonard. "The Lincoln Life-Mask and How It Was Made." *Journal of the Illinois State Historical Society* 8, no. 2 (July 1915), https://www.jstor.org/stable/i40006219.

Watson, Martha. "Ordeal by Fire: The Transformative Rhetoric of Abraham Lincoln." *Rhetoric & Public Affairs* 3, no. 1 (Spring 2000): 33–49.

Weaver, Richard M. "Abraham Lincoln and the Argument from Definition." In *The Ethics of Rhetoric*, 85–114. Chicago: Henry Regnery Company, 1953.

Webster, Daniel. Selected 1830s speeches, https://www.loc.gov/rr/program/bib/webster/index.html.

Whan, Forest L. "Stephen A. Douglas." Vol. II, *A History and Criticism of American Public Address*. Edited by William Norwood Brigance, 807–10. New York: McGraw-Hill Book Co., 1943.

White, Horace. *The Lincoln and Douglas Debates: An Address Before the Chicago Historical Society, February 17, 1914*. Chicago: University of Chicago Press, 1914.

White, Ronald C., Jr. *A. Lincoln: A Biography*. New York: Random House, 2009.

White, Ronald C., Jr. *The Eloquent President: A Portrait of Lincoln through His Words*. New York: Random House, 2005.

Wilenz, Sean. *No Property in Man: Slavery and Antislavery at the Nation's Founding*. Cambridge, MA: Harvard University Press, 2018.

Wiley, Earl W. "Abraham Lincoln: His Emergence as the Voice of the People." Vol. II, *A History and Criticism of American Public Address*. Edited by William Norwood Brigance, 859–77. New York: McGraw-Hill Book Company, 1943.

Wiley, Earl W. "Behind Lincoln's Visit to Ohio in 1859." *Ohio State Archaeological and Historical Quarterly* 60, no. 1 (January 1951): 28–47.

Wilson, Douglas L., and Rodney O. Davis, eds. *Herndon's Informants: Letters, Interviews, and Statements about Abraham Lincoln*. Urbana: University of Illinois Press, 1998.

Wilson, Douglas L. *Honor's Voice: The Transformation of Abraham Lincoln*. New York: Vintage Books, 1998.

Wilson, Douglas L. "Lincoln's Rhetoric." *Journal of the Abraham Lincoln Association* 34, no. 1 (Winter 2013): 1–17.

Wilson, Douglas L. *Lincoln's Sword*. New York: Alfred A. Knopf, 2006.

Wilson, Edmund. *Patriotic Gore: Studies in the Literature of the American Civil War*. New York: W.W. Norton and Company, 1994.

Wilson, Kirt H. "The Paradox of Lincoln's Rhetorical Leadership." *Rhetoric & Public Affairs* 3, no. 1 (Spring 2000): 15–32.

Zaesky, Susan. "Hearing the Silences in Lincoln's Temperance Address: Whig Masculinity as an Ethic of Rhetorical Civility." *Rhetoric & Public Affairs* 13, no. 3 (Fall 2010): 389–419.

Zarefsky, David. "Lincoln and the House Divided: Launching a National Political Career." *Rhetoric & Public Affairs* 13, no. 3 (Fall 2010): 421–54.

Zarefsky, David. *Lincoln, Douglas, and Slavery: In the Crucible of Public Debate*. Chicago: University of Chicago Press, 1990.

Zarefsky, David. "Rhetoric in Lincoln's Time." *Lincoln Lore* (Fall 2008): 24–30.

Index

classical rhetoric: AL's rhetorical growth, 3–7, 16–17; antithesis, 100; Blair's *Lectures*, 5, 93; Blair's theory, 245n8; building toward most significant point, 95; "Classical Rhetoric as a Lens . . . ," 257; Clay eulogy, 106; confirmation, 28; Dred Scott speech, 109; ethics, 3; flowery language, 31; forecasting, 23, 94, 249n29; Internal Improvements speech, 65; introduction, 94; irony, 100; *Lessons in Elocution*, 3; logical organization, 65; maxim, 51; oratory, 2; overview, 2–3; pedagogy, 4; Peoria speech, 6, 92–95, 100, 106, 228; plain language, 31; refutation, 28, 229; State Bank speech, 23; structural design, 2, 109, 228; structural parallelism, 100; John T. Stuart, 6, 16; style, 2; Subtreasury speech, 5, 28, 32, 38, 106, 228; tariff fragments, 53; Webster, 5–6, 246n22, 246n28. *See also* rhetoric

Clay, Henry: AL claims alignment with, 5, 9, 103, 127, 131, 141, 148, 166–67, 182, 184–86, 227, 261n59; AL's 1844 support for as president, 43–44; AL's eulogy for, 6, 84–85, 105–6, 123, 227, 259n17; AL's support for Taylor over Clay as president, 63–64, 184–88; American System, 9–10; Clay's bill, 40; Clay's rhetoric, 5–6; colonization proponent, 109; Compromise of 1850, 86, 178; condemned slavery, 167, 182, 186; Kentuckian, 10; Land Bill, 41; lover of liberty, 170; Missouri Compromise of 1820, 85; moral lights, 170, 234; opposed to slavery extension, 201; presidential election loss to Polk, 44–45; SD's claims of alignment with, 131–32, 264n54

colonization, 109, 112

communicative purpose, 2–3, 19, 28, 208, 245n3

Compromise of 1850: Clay eulogy, 85; SD, 8; LDD, 149, 164, 175, 178, 258n14; Peoria speech, 93, 95–96, 99

conclusion (rhetorical), 3, 28, 31–32, 93

confirmation (rhetorical), 3, 28, 93–94, 102

confutation, 3, 28

connotation, 68, 98, 198, 232

Constitution: AL's criticism of SD's use of, 151, 167–68, 179, 203–4; AL's proportionate use, Constitution vs. Declaration of Independence, 229–30; authorized slavery, 90, 122, 126–28, 148, 167–68, 185; Chicago speech (July 10, 1858), 120–22, 126, 128; Cincinnati speech, 203–6, 235; Cooper Union address, 217–20; *Dred Scott* decision, 110, 157, 176–77, 234; founders, 128, 204; Fragment on the Constitution, 229, 271n2; Fugitive Slave Law, 151, 191; internal improvements, 65–66; a key AL nonartistic proof, 2, 32–33, 122, 227–28; Lincoln-Stone protest, 25; Lyceum address, 35–36; national bank, 30, 127; Northwest Ordinance of 1787, 204; picture of silver, 229; polygamy, 110, 239; Republican Party, 102, 104; responsibility of Congress to apply, 6, 25, 30; SD's use of, 166, 169–71, 174–75, 195–97, 200, 204; slave trade, 120, 167–68, 200; Subtreasury speech, 32–33; Roger B. Taney, 110; Zachary Taylor, 69; territories becoming states, 197–98, 240; ultimate extinction of slavery, 120, 160, 218; Wilmot Proviso, 74

Declaration of Independence: AL's apple of gold comparison, 229; AL's foundational proposition source, 2, 25, 228–29, 238; AL's stump speech use of, 129, 132–33; AL's use of in LDD, 139, 141, 166–67, 181, 184–85, 188; Chicago speech (July 10, 1858), 121–23; Cincinnati speech, 203; cited in turnabout is fair play argument, 237; Columbus speech, 201; Cooper Union address, absence of reference to, 230, 235; Dred Scott speech, 111–12, 134, 232; Hume's influence on, 3; natural rights/equality principle, 99, 139, 147, 149, 162–64, 181, 184, 201, 238, 264n1; Peoria speech, 98–100, 134; proslavery fragment,

162; Republican robe soiled, 238; SD's use of, 111, 149, 163–65, 181; Subtreasury speech, 32; Taney, 110–11
deliberative discourse, 5, 28, 92, 109, 253–54n8
delivery (rhetorical), 2, 74, 92
demagoguery: AL's demagogic techniques, 38, 136, 160, 225–26, 228, 236–37, 239; AL/SD's mutual accusations of, 136, 179, 187; AL's problems with SD's use of, 9, 31, 79, 90–91, 107, 134, 144–45, 152; audience/readers' reaction to, 34, 38; 1858 US senate race, 134, 136–37, 144, 160, 187; factor in political rhetoric, 244nn6–7, 247n33; Handbill on Infidelity, 55; House Divided speech, 115; Lost speech, 236; Mexican War speech, 59; mixed with other qualities in AL's rhetoric, 7, 17, 32, 38, 55, 115, 237, 239, 241; nineteenth-century political/rhetorical culture, 21, 235; Pekin Agreement, 55; Peoria speech, 100, 238; SD's demagogic techniques, 31, 37, 134, 144–45, 160, 239, 241; Springfield speech (July 17, 1858), 123–26; State bank speech, 22; Trumbull attacked by SD for it, 138
Democratic Party: antislavery contingent, 150, 240; Buchanan candidacy, 102; compliments, 103; convention system, 47; criticism of, 22, 34, 57, 72, 186; *Dred Scott* case, 166; free soil wing, 75; House Divided speech, 114; policies/positions, 10, 17, 113, 164, 174; satire, 68, 78, 236; SD, 145–46, 149, 168, 170, 174, 223; slavery question, 153, 178, 189, 191, 202; turnabout is fair play, 87
desideratum, 42, 209
division (political and rhetorical): AL's claim of it lacking in founders' approach to slavery, 220; conflicts between political parties, 154, 202; forecasting for coherence, 249n29; intra-political party, 149–50, 181, 202; local vs. federal control of slavery, 218–19; national disagreement over slavery, 139, 171; rhetorical design

element, 2–3, 28–29; Subtreasury speech, 29
Doctrine of Necessity, 50
Douglas, Stephen A.: accusations against AL, 109, 118, 135–38, 143, 160, 265n5; alcohol use, 130–31, 153, 264n51; AL faults SD's moral character and rhetorical abuses, 25, 79, 86–87, 90–91, 100, 110–11, 114, 119, 132, 134; AL rejects SD's alignment with Clay, 128, 131–32; AL's first impression of, 19–20; AL's main rival, 9, 17, 19–20; American blood on American soil, 62; ancestry distortion, 37; Bank of the US, 27; Black Republican Party, 90; "caged and toothless lion," 233; Chicago Doctrine, 181, 186; Chicago speech (July 9, 1858), 119–22; Cincinnati speech, 201–6, 226, 235, 240; claims AL to be most dangerous opponent, 89; Clay eulogy, 237; Clay mantle, 131–32, 264n54; Clinton speeches, 129, 147; Columbus speech, 195, 222, 233–34; conspiracy with Wyatt, 248n13; Cooper Union address, 218–20; Declaration of Independence, 111–12, 121; defends popular sovereignty, 8; demagoguery, 31, 79, 91, 100, 126; denies AL's accusation of proslavery conspiracy, 130; *Dred Scott* decision, 108–10, 199; Dred Scott speech, 134, 238; elected to US House, 34; eloquence, 187, 241; faults in SD's rhetoric charged by AL, 86–87, 90–91, 110–11, 119, 134, 187, 198; fearmongering, 187, 237; Fillmore, 87; first speech as US senator, 62–63; Freeport Doctrine, 145, 153, 160, 178, 199; *Harper's* essay, 195–99, 232, 237; Holland's biography, 33; homecoming speech, Chicago (July 9, 1858), 118, 259n31; House Divided speech, 115–17; insanity accusation by AL, 61; Kansas-Nebraska Act, 88, 90–91, 99, 204; LDD terms/conditions, 129, 136; LeCompton Constitution, 8, 113; Lincoln-Stone protest, 25; Lyceum address, 34; Mary Todd, 38; misrepresentation of AL's views,

117, 226, 232; factor in nineteenth-century demagoguery, 235, 237; in AL's criticism of opposing politicians and policies, 61, 127, 226, 238; in conclusions of AL's compositions, 217, 220; SD's use of, 63, 150, 156

enthymeme, 245n5

epiphora, 31

ethical appeal (ethos, rhetor's credibility), 2, 7, 38, 203; central to AL and SD's rivalry, 87, 160, 239; combined with rational and emotional appeals, 51, 95, 225, 230; expressed in AL's personal political letters, 46, 51; expressed in AL's speeches, 32, 87, 95, 160, 239; most important of the three appeals, 7

Euclid, 6, 159, 199, 247n30

exordium, 2, 28, 93

fallacy, 111, 116, 172, 175, 203, 239

fearmongering: AL's use of, 24, 237; SD's use of, 118, 176, 178, 187, 237

Fell, Jesse W., 89, 215, 248n6, 270n59

figurative language, 125, 132, 215; AL's and Webster's use of, 6; AL's use relating to common life, 2; associated with plain language, 106, 217; attacking slavery, 198, 237, 240; Cooper Union address, 217, 220; founders, 132; House Divided speech, 115–17; Lewistown speech, 132; Peoria speech, 106; personal attacks, 141, 150, 198, 226, 232–35; State Bank speech, 23–24. *See also* metaphor/metaphoric

Fillmore, Millard, 87–88, 102, 104, 147

forecasting: clarity, 23; coherence, 41, 249n29; Mexican War speech, 59; Peoria speech, 94, 99; tariff fragments, 54

forensic, 109

fragments: AL's private brainstorming/exploratory writing, 113; General Taylor, 63–64; tariff, 53–55, 252n31, 253nn35–36. *See also* Lincoln, Abraham: notable prepresidential compositions

Freeport Doctrine, 150–51, 175; Chicago Doctrine, 181; *Dred Scott*, 177–78,

199; *Harper's* essay, 195; Jefferson Davis, 178; southern rejection, 186; SD's defense, 153, 160; slavery, 145

Free Soil Democrats, 63, 202

Free Soil Party, 64, 67, 73, 75

Fugitive Slave Law: AL's position on, 90, 142–43; Chase, 190; Constitution, 151; final LDD, 179; history, 148; Ohio Republicans, 192; Peoria speech, 98, 230; Pierce, 88; Republican platform, 191; SD, 138

full induction, 245n5

Gettysburg address, 241, 262n22

Graham, Mentor, 16, 19, 248n8

Greeley, Horace, 62, 76, 208

Hardin, John J.: AL's dispute about congressional nomination, 45–49, 237, 252nn15–19; convention system, 47; former Democrat, 20; killed in Mexican War, memorialized by Congressman AL, 50; Pekin Agreement, 45, 55; SD's conspiracy to depose Hardin, 248n13; US congressman, 42

Herndon, William H.: AL influenced by *The English Reader*, 3, and *Elements of Geometry*, 6; AL's Mexican War speech, 62, 253n8, 255n17; AL's Postal Contracts speech, 58; AL's speech delivery, 243n1; Herndon-Weik on Lincoln's rhetoric, 243n3; House Divided speech, 113

historical argumentation. *See* moral argumentation

Horatian (light) satire, 8

hyperbole: AL's attack on Polk, 78; AL's Democratic conspiracy accusation, 114; Lewistown speech, 133; Lyceum address, 36–37; Mexican War speech, 60; Peoria speech, 100; Presidential question speech, 70; Scott club speech, 86; SD's last LDD speech, 168; Springfield speech (July 17, 1858), 125–26; State Bank speech, 24; Whig campaign circular, 41–42

Illinois Republican Party: AL as 1858 US Senate nominee, 108, 113; AL's role in

Illinois Republican Party (*continued*)
forming, 89, 106, 260n52; AL's "spot" resolutions, 145; intra-party feud, 215; opposition to slavery extension, 101; Trumbull, 137, 157
Illinois State Library, 28, 216, 250n46
Illinois Supreme Court, 23, 141
internal improvements: AL's congressional speech on, 64–67, 229; AL's first campaign announcement, 17, 20; AL's public letter on Springfield railroad, 52; central Whig policy, 10, 51; Illinois overspending on, 66–67; Illinois State Bank, 22; moral argumentation implied in, 227; presidential question speech, 69–70; SD's support for, 171; Whig/Democratic positions on, 248n6
invention: AL's US patent, 269n39; cotton gin, 165, 169; Milwaukee address, 208–9; no invention enables slaves to escape, 111, 233; rhetorical term for creativity, 2; Second Lecture on Discoveries and Inventions, 192–94, 221, 240, 268n12

Jackson, Andrew: AL's criticism of Jackson Democrats/administration, 9, 22, 31, 34, 70; AL's criticism of SD for supporting, 110, 120; Whig opposition to, 9
James, Benjamin F., 40, 46–47
Jefferson, Thomas: Cincinnati speech, 205; cited by AL to support his arguments, 1856 presidential campaign speeches, 103; cited by SD to support his arguments, 163; Columbus speech, 198; Cooper Union address, 220; fifth LDD, 164; helped establish Northwest Ordinance of 1787, 95; Lewistown speech, 133; Presidential question speech, 69; Springfield speech (July 17, 1858), 127
Jesus, 113
Judd, Norman B.: AL's political friend, 215–16, 270n58
Juvenalian (heavy, sarcastic) satire, 8

Kansas-Nebraska Act (Nebraska bill): AL's Democratic conspiracy

accusation, 114; AL's 1854 motivation to reenter national politics, 236; AL's first criticism of, 89–90; Beardstown speech, 131; Columbus speech, 196, 232; editorial, 258n16; first four LDD, 136; first LDD, 167; House Divided speech, 231; Kalamazoo speech, 102; last LDD, 167; machinery/construction analogy, 115, 233; Missouri Compromise of 1820, 204; Peoria speech, 95–100; Pierce signed, 88; popular sovereignty, 88, 116, 147, 174; SD's role in passing, 8, 99, 136, 144, 153, 178, 187, 259n31; second LDD, 144; Shakespearean allusion, 260n44; Springfield speech (July 17, 1858), 126; third LDD, 149
Know-Nothing Party: AL faults, 89; courts members to "fuse" with Republicans, 102

Lecompton Constitution: AL's admonition to Republicans on, 117, 119–20; AL's criticism of SD's opposition to, 124–25, 146; Buchanan's support for, 116, 119; SD's conflict with Buchanan over, 113, 116, 146; SD's opposition to, 8, 113, 149, 179
lectures, 17, 217, 221, 227
legalistic argumentation: Beardstown speech, 130–31; combined with AL's historical, moral argumentation, 8, 78, 238, 241; Dred Scott speech, 109, 112; featured in refutations, 23, 69; final LDD, 179; legal terms and phrasing, 48, 58; Lincoln-Stone protest, 25, 227; Mexican War speech, 59–61, 78, 254n10; Peoria speech, 93, 238; Postal Contracts speech, 58; Presidential question speech, 69; Remarks and Resolutions Concerning Abolition of Slavery in the District of Columbia, 76; Scott Club speech, 86; Subtreasury speech, 31; Taunton speech, 74; third LDD, 150; vital rhetorical strategy, 225, 228, 241, 254n8, 254n10
Lincoln, Abraham (chronology): reading, writing, and speaking in Indiana, 3, 9, 15; at New Salem, 4,

Lincoln, Abraham: notable prepresidential compositions (*continued*)
—Communication to the People of Sangamo County (first campaign announcement) (March 9, 1832), 9, 17–19, 78, 226–27
—Debate at Jacksonville, Illinois (October 21, 1848), 75, 257n54
—Eulogy on Henry Clay (July 6, 1852), 6, 84–85, 105–6, 123, 227–28, 237, 246n29, 258n5, 259n17, 271n1
—Eulogy on Zachary Taylor (July 25, 1850), 83–84, 227, 258n3
—First speech at Leavenworth, Kansas (December 3, 1859), 213–14, 270n52
—Fragment on SD (December 1856[?]), 106, 262n66
—Handbill Replying to Charges of Infidelity (July 31, 1846), 50, 55, 252n22
—Last speech (April 11, 1865), 228, 241
—LDD, Conclusion to the final three debates, 186–88
—LDD, Conclusion to the first four debates, 159–60
—LDD, final three debates: disputing founding principles related to slavery, 163–69; disputing moral perspectives on slavery and related policies, 169–79; disputing rhetorical methods, 179–186
—LDD, fragments allegedly composed between fourth and fifth debates: Fragment on Proslavery Theology (October 1, 1858[?]), 162; Fragment: Notes for Speeches (October 1, 1858[?]), 162, 266n3
—LDD, opening speeches: second debate, 142–44; fourth debate, 154–55
—LDD, rejoinders: second debate, 146; fourth debate, 158–59
—LDD, replies: first debate, 138–42; third debate, 150–52
—LDD, stump speeches between second and third debates: Carlinville, 147; Clinton, 147; Edwardsville, 147–49
—Lost Speech, Bloomington, Illinois (May 29, 1856), 6, 101, 113, 236, 261n55
—Protest in the Illinois Legislature on Slavery (March 3, 1837), 22, 25, 38, 227, 249n34
—Remarks and Resolution Introduced in United States House of Representatives Concerning Abolition of Slavery in the District of Columbia (January 10, 1849), 76–77, 79, 257n57
—Remarks in the United States House of Representatives Concerning Postal Contracts (January 5, 1848), 58–59, 253n7
—Resolutions in Behalf of Hungarian Freedom (January 9, 1852), 77–78, 258n4
—Second Lecture on Discoveries and Inventions (February 11, 1859), 192–94, 221, 240
—Second speech at Leavenworth, Kansas (December 5, 1859), 214–15
—Speech at Belleville, Illinois (October 18, 1856), 34, 104, 261n61
—Speech at Beloit, Wisconsin (October 1, 1859), 211
—Speech at Bloomington, Illinois (September 12, 1854), 90, 96, 259n18
—Speech at Bloomington, Illinois (September 26, 1854), 90–91, 259n19
—Speech at Chicago, Illinois (July 10, 1858), 119–23, 173, 187, 217; AL's defense of, 129, 185; SD's criticism of, 181, 183–84
—Speech at Chicago, Illinois (March 1, 1859), 194
—Speech at Chicago, Illinois (October 27, 1854), 101, 260n50
—Speech at Cincinnati, Ohio (September 17, 1858), 201–7; addressing Kentuckians, 201–5, 235; addressing Ohioans, 206; Constitution, 230; extended irony to satirize SD, 222, 226, 235; free labor, 201; slavery, 202; 269n32; 271n1
—Speech at Clinton, Illinois (July 27, 1858), 129
—Speech at Clinton, Illinois (October 14, 1859), 212
—Speech at Columbus, Ohio (September 16, 1859), 195–201; critiquing popular sovereignty, 197, 200,

222; critiquing SD's Harper's essay, 197–99; critiquing SD's view of Dred Scott, 199–201

—Speech at Havana, Illinois (August 14, 1858), 130–31

—Speech at Kalamazoo, Michigan (August 27, 1856), 102–3, 105, 261nn57–58

—Speech at Lewistown, Illinois (August 17, 1858), 130–34

—Speech at Monticello, Illinois (July 29, 1858), 123, 129

—Speech at Peoria, Illinois (October 16, 1854), 6, 83, 88, 91–102, 105–6, 154; comparisons, 109, 119, 134, 216–17, 257n2, 259n17; Constitution, 218–19, 230; eloquent, 241; foundational speech, 135, 271n1; lecture aspect, 217; longest speech, 216; Missouri Compromise, 92, 94–98, 230; moral argumentation, 160, 217, 237; Nebraska bill, 95–100; newspaper publication, 91; organization, 92–94; patriotism, 238; political rhetoric, 89; political/social equality, 139, 156; read from in LDD, 182; refutation, 91, 93–94, 98–100, 260n43; republican robe soiled, 98, 238; SD's indifference to slavery, 237; second political career, 83, 228; sentence structural parallelism, 100; slavery as a disease, 232; statement of facts, 260n45; statesman, 221; three-fifths provision, 258n16

—Speech at Peoria, Illinois (September 17, 1852), 88, 258n12

—Speech at Republican Banquet, Chicago (December 10, 1856), 104–5, 261n62

—Speech at Springfield, Illinois (July 17, 1858), 123–29, 263n43

—Speech at Springfield, Illinois (June 26, 1857) (Dred Scott speech), 109–13; Constitution, 229–30; Declaration of Independence, 166, 229–30, 232, 238; natural rights, 134; praised, 261n3; rhetorical sleight of hand, 115, 226; SD's speech, 109, 134, 261n1; speech organization, 109; 271n1

—Speech at Springfield, Illinois (October 4, 1854), 91, 93

—Speech at Taunton, Massachusetts (September 21[?], 1848), 74–75, 257n50

—Speech at Vandalia, Illinois (September 23, 1856), 104, 261n60

—Speech at Worcester, Massachusetts (September 12, 1848), 73–74, 256nn48–49

—Speech in the Illinois Legislature Concerning the State Bank (January 11, 1837), 22–25, 27–28, 232, 249n28

—Speech in the United States House of Representatives on Internal Improvements (June 20, 1848), 64–67, 78, 229, 240, 271n1

—Speech in the United States House of Representatives on the Presidential Question (July 27, 1848), 57, 67–72, 86, 229, 232, 238, 256nn39–40, 271n1

—Speech in the United States House of Representatives, The War with Mexico (January 12, 1848), 59–63, 73, 78; critical commentary, 253–54nn8–10; personal attacks, 106, 227, 232, 238; 271n1

—Speech on the Subtreasury (December 26, 1839), 5, 27–32; classical rhetoric, 38, 92–93, 102, 106, 228; Constitution, 229; criticized SD, 236; Declaration of Independence, 229; humility, 240; 250nn46–50, 271n1

—Speech to the Springfield Scott Club (August 14, 26, 1852), 84–88, 92, 101–2, 105, 113, 236, 238, 258nn9–10, 259n17, 259n33

— "Spot" Resolutions in the United States House of Representatives (December 22, 1847), 58, 253n3

—Temperance Address (February 22, 1842), 4, 37–38, 251n78, 251n80

Linder, Usher F., 22–24, 38, 78, 232

logic/logical (logos, rational appeal): accusations of AL's faulty use, 50, 74; AL's accusation of faulty use by Polk, 66, 254n8; by SD, 87, 111, 121, 151, 169–70, 198, 203–4; founders' use of, 122; in AL's argumentation, 32–33, 44, 54, 117, 148, 160, 177; in AL's composition structure, 35, 41, 44,

logic/logical (logos, rational appeal)
(*continued*)
59, 61, 65, 68, 76, 92–93, 114, 208;
in AL's study of Euclid, 6; integrated
with ethos and pathos, 2; interrelated with grammar and rhetoric, 4,
175–76; SD's claim to use of, 178
Logan, Stephen T., 16, 38, 243n3
logos, 2, 7. *See also* logic/logical
Lovejoy, Elijah, 35, 163

Madison, James, 205, 228
maxim, 51, 111, 148, 166
memory (rhetorical factor), 2, 126
metaphor/metaphoric: AL's comparisons
using legal terms, 48, 130; AL's criticism of Democratic Party, 70, 98, 111,
115–16, 201, 214; AL's criticism of SD,
35, 124–25, 159, 168, 173, 180, 233;
AL's ennobling expressions, 121, 133,
165–66, 229, 235; AL's self-denigration, 233; biblical, 42, 60; mixed, 232
Missouri Compromise of 1820: AL's
renewed interest in politics, 215, 236;
Bloomington speeches (September 12,
26, 1854), 93; brief history of, 90, 94;
Clay, 85; House Divided speech, 115,
128; LDD, 160; Peoria speech, 92–98,
230, 232, 260n45; SD, 91, 199,
204; repealed, 88; Springfield speech
(October 30, 1858), 186; Supreme
Court, 109; third LDD, 150
moral argumentation: AL's allegations
of SD's moral deficiency, 108, 111,
222; in AL's compositions, first political career, 2, 4, 17–18, 32, 36–37,
57, 76; in AL's compositions, second
political career, 106, 114, 117–18,
148, 160, 217–18, 228, 237, 259n23;
non-personal sources of possible
moral influence on AL, 3, 38, 57, 85,
249n15; related to AL's other modes
of argumentation, 9, 38, 225, 228,
238–39; related to AL's satire, 8, 227,
235–36, 248n15; related to turnabout
is fair play, 237; SD's rhetoric, 171,
186–87, 241; vital to AL's eloquence,
8, 228–29. *See also* Constitution;
Declaration of Independence

mud-sill theory, 209
Murray, Lindley, 3–5, 93, 245n8

narration, 2, 28
Nebraska Act, Nebraska bill, Nebraska.
See Kansas-Nebraska Act
Nebraska doctrine, 115
nonartistic proofs: definition, contribution to rational appeal/logic, 2. *See
also* Constitution; Declaration of
Independence
nullification, 168

oratory: camp meeting speeches, 133;
classical rhetoric, 2, 5; florid style
of nineteenth-century political discourse, 206, 217; Webster, 246n22,
259n34

pathos, 2, 7. *See also* emotional appeal
peroration/conclusion: classical rhetoric,
3; Cooper Union address, 194; Lincoln's and Webster's flowery language,
6; Lyceum address, 35; Peoria speech,
93; Springfield speech (October 4,
1854), 93–94; Subtreasury speech,
28, 31
Pierce, Franklin: AL's accusation of participation in Democratic proslavery
conspiracy, 115–16, 129, 180, 233; AL's
criticism of Democrats for supporting, 87–88; AL's criticism of SD for
supporting, 85; AL's racist slur on, 88;
elected president, 90; SD denied conspiracy with, 129, 180; signed Kansas-
Nebraska Act, 88
Polk, James: AL's accusation of New
York abolitionists causing Clay's
presidential loss to Polk, 45, 75; AL's
accusation of Polk starting an unjustified war with Mexico, 58–61, 64, 227,
253–54n8, 255n23; AL's challenge
to Polk to justify Mexican War, 58,
60; AL's criticism of Free Soilers for
supporting Polk on Mexican War, 73;
AL's criticism of Polk's position/policy
on internal improvements, 65–66, 70;
AL's personal attacks on Polk, 59, 61,
78, 106, 232, 236, 238; SD's defense

of Polk, 62; structure of AL's Mexican War speech, 59; Walker Tariff, 53

popular sovereignty (local control of slavery): AL's objection to as factor in his return to national politics, 88; Beloit speech, 211; Cass alleged originator, 63; Chicago speech (July 10, 1858), 119; Cincinnati speech, 204, 206, 240; Columbus speech, 196–200, 222; Compromise of 1850, 96, 175, 258n14; consideration of slaves as property or human, 91; Constitution, 230; Cooper Union address, 220–21, 235; defined, 63; *Dred Scott* decision, 109, 231, 234; Dred Scott speech, 110, 239; Elwood speech, 213–14; first LDD, 138–40; *Harper's* essay, 195; Janesville speech, 211; Kalamazoo speech, 102; Kansas-Nebraska Act, 8; Leavenworth speech, 214; letter to Sangamon County farmers, 216; machinery analogy, 115; Missouri Compromise of 1820, 88; moral defense, 241; natural rights, 187; Ohio Republicans, 192; Peoria speech, 93; SD's cannon named, 123; SD's Chicago homecoming speech (July 9, 1858), 118; SD's positions on, 110, 160, 174, 186, 189; sixth LDD, 177; Springfield speech (July 17, 1858), 124–25, 128; "squatter sovereignty," AL's derogatory name for, 233; stump speeches, 147; third LDD, 149

procatalepsis, 29, 99, 151, 162

prolepsis, 29

prosopoeia, 201, 218

race-baiting, 21, 33, 145, 149, 236

Rebecca letter, 39, 236

reductio ad absurdum, 177

refutation: AL's extraordinary use of, 235; Columbus speech, 196, 201, 222; Cooper Union address, 218–20; criticism of SD and others, 9, 227; design element, 3; Dred Scott speech, 109–10; fact-based, 160; fallacies, 245n5; fourth LDD, 158; Hardin's letter, 48; Internal Improvements speech, 65; Kalamazoo speech, 102–3;

lawyerly/legalistic, 9, 38, 69; letter to Sangamon County farmers, 216; Mexican War speech, 59–60, 71; Peoria speech, 91, 93–94, 98, 100, 228; Republican banquet speech, 104; satire, 8; Scott Club speech, 86–87; second LDD, 142, 146; sixth LDD, 182; Springfield speech (July 17, 1858), 124, 126–28; State Bank speech, 23; John T. Stuart, 16; stump speeches, 147; Subtreasury speech, 5, 28–30; Taunton speech, 74; tu quoque, 179; Worcester speech, 73

Republican Party: AL's help in developing, 11, 63, 89, 260n52; AL, spokesman for Illinois Republican Party, 101, 189; AL, strategist for Illinois Republican Party, 106; AL's US senate nomination, 108, 113; antislavery, 133, 148, 186; "Black Republican" Party, 90; Columbus speech, 197; Cooper Union address, 217–19; disunion, 8; Edwardsville speech, 148; fifth LDD, 175; founding fathers, 102; Frémont, 2; House Divided speech, 114, 134, 233; Illinois Republican Party, 145, 215, 270n58; Ohio republicans, 190; opposing *Dred Scott*, 170; popular sovereignty, 200; SD, 157, 166, 175–76; sectional criticism, 207; slave trade, 191; third LDD, 149; Trumbull, 137, 157; United Party of the North, 75, 257n52; Young America, 192. *See also* Illinois Republican Party

rhetoric/rhetorical: AL's composition targets, 9; AL's confidence in his rhetorical ability, 101; AL's defense of attacks on SD's rhetoric 108; AL's greater good, 225; AL's rhetorical achievement and growth, 1, 9–10, 17, 20, 105, 221, 243nn2–3, 244n12; AL's satire, 8, 20, 236, 240; Aristotle, 4; basic subject in nineteenth-century American education, 4; Basler, 246n18, 254n8; Blair's *Lectures*, 3, 246n21, 259n32; cherry-picking, 185, 239; Chicago banquet speech, 104; Chicago speech (July 10, 1858), 101, 120, 124–26; Cincinnati speech,

rhetoric/rhetorical (*continued*)
201–4, 222, 226; classical, 2–6; "Classical Rhetoric as a Lens . . . ," 257; Clay, 6; Clay eulogy, 106; Columbus speech, 195–96, 199; Cooper Union address, 218; demagoguery, 7, 241, 244nn6–7, 247n33; Dred Scott speech, 109; eloquence/eloquent, 7–8, 160; emotional appeal, 176; encyclopedia of, 245n3; *English Reader*, 3, 5; ethical political rhetoric, 226; ethics, 3, 79, 160, 182; ethos, 7; fairness, 40; fearmongering, 187; figurative language, 232; forecasting, 94, 249n29; founders, 218; genre hybrids, 227; high flown, 244n3; House Divided speech, 108, 117, 134; humor, 16; Internal Improvements speech, 64–65, 67; lawyerly refutation, 38, 228; letter to Ford, 51; letter to Hardin; 49; logic, 176; logos, 7; Lyceum's prohibition of political rhetoric, 34; main political weapon of AL and SD, 8; Mexican War speech, 61; moral aspects, 17, 76, 78; natural rights, 165; nineteenth-century rhetoric, 2; nonartistic proofs, 117, 245n5; pathos, 7; patriotism, 237; pejorative stigma, 1; Peoria speech, 6, 91–95, 100, 228; personal attacks, 124, 236–37; political advancement, 38; Presidential Question speech, 256n39; rhetorical sleight of hand, 112, 115, 218, 226, 262n22; rhetorical tension, 15; Scott Club speech, 86; SD and alcohol, 152; SD's demagoguery, 37, 90, 107, 120, 125–26, 144, 238; SD's effort to regain party status, 146; SD's ethical failure, 138, 158, 183; SD's indifference to slavery, 195, 222; SD's moral character, 188; SD's obfuscation, 173, 233; second *Dred Scott* decision, 148; Shakespearean tyrant, 254n8; shaping Whig and Republican positions, 227; sixth LDD, 165, 183; slavery question, 63; State Bank speech, 22–24, 27–28; structural elements, 109, 245n6; Stuart, 6; stump speeches, 67; stylistic techniques, 104, 244n4; Subtreasury speech, 5, 28, 30, 228; tariff fragments, 53; teaching of rhetoric, 245n7; Temperance address, 4, 251n80; turnabout is fair play, 184, 186–87, 239; turning the tables, 87; vital to AL's political purposes, 2; Webster, 5–6, 93, 246n22; what AL read, 3, 245n8; Zarefsky, 246nn19–20. *See also* classical rhetoric; refutation

rhetorical sleight of hand, 112, 115, 218, 226, 262n22

rhetorical/textual analysis, 1–2, 64, 135, 229

satire: AL's literary sources of influence, 249n15, 247n38; AL's stock-in-trade attack mode, 39, 79; Cincinnati speech, 9, 202, 222, 235; demagoguery, 7; Havana speech, 134; Horatian and Juvenalian satire defined, 8; House Divided speech, 134; literary genre adapted for political/rhetorical purposes, 8; Mexican War speech, 60, 78, 227; moral appeal, 8, 17, 248n15; Peoria speech, 100; Presidential Question speech, 67–68, 71, 86; Scott Club speech, 85–87, 236; Second Lecture on Discoveries and Inventions, 192–93, 221, 240; Senate race, 239

Shakespeare, 247n38, 254n8, 260n44

southern fire-eaters, 85

straw man fallacy, 172

structure (rhetorical organization): AL's Address to the People of Illinois, 41; AL's first candidacy announcement, 18; Chicago speech (July 17, 1858), 124; coherence, 2; Columbus speech, 196; Dred Scott speech, 109, 111; House Divided speech, 114, 117; Kalamazoo speech, 102; Lincoln-Stone protest, 25, 249n33; Lyceum address, 34–35; Mexican War speech, 59, 61; organization, 245n3; Peoria speech, 6, 91–93, 100, 106; rhetorical design element, 2–3, 5, 68, 228; Scott Club speech, 86; State Bank speech, 23; Subtreasury speech, 5, 27–28, 32, 38, 93; Webster's Speech on the Currency, 5 style (language techniques): AL's first candidacy announcement, 18; AL's letters to Stuart, 33; Cooper Union address, 221; importance of competent grammar and vocabulary, 2; language usage, 217, 245n3; Lyceum address, 36; Milwaukee address, 269n36; Peoria speech, 92, 100; plain writing, 3, 6, 37, 79, 246n28; rhetorical/textual analysis, 2; stylistic techniques, 244n4; Subtreasury speech, 27, 31; tariff fragments, 53–54; Webster, 28, 36; Worcester speech, 74. *See also* figurative language, metaphor/metaphoric

syllogism, 245n5

synecdoche, 201, 235

tu quoque, 179

turnabout is fair play (rhetorical strategy): AL's implied threat to use against SD, 126; AL's/SD's uses related to personal attacks, 160, 184–85; AL's use as ethical appeal in seeking congressional nomination, 40, 46–48; AL's use in LDD, 136, 142, 152, 186–87; AL's use, mildly demagogic, 55; AL's uses past LDD, 237; AL's use to protect self-esteem, 40; SD's use of in LDD, 157, 174, 181; summary of AL's use, 237

turning the tables (rhetorical strategy): AL against Democrats for attacking Winfield Scott, 87; AL against SD for accusing AL of being an abolitionist, 232; AL against SD for accusing Republicans of sectionalism, 175; AL against SD for claiming the founders understood slavery "as well as or better" than present-day politicians, 218, 222; AL against SD for conspiring with Republicans, 116; AL against SD for using nonartistic proofs in falsely associating AL with abolitionists, 150; AL's justification for retaliation against Hardin, 40

Turner, Jonathan B., 208

ultimate extinction (a part of AL's solution to slavery agitation): Chicago speech (July 10, 1858), 119–21, Cincinnati speech, 204, 206; Cooper Union address, 218; Edwardsville speech, 148; final LDD, 167; first LDD, 139; founders, 218; sixth LDD, 165; Springfield speech (July 17, 1858), 126

Washington, George: AL's allusions to, 60, 261n59; Cincinnati speech, 205; Cooper Union address, 219–20; Kalamazoo speech, 103; Leavenworth speech, 213; Lyceum address, 238; Subtreasury speech, 229

Webster, Daniel: AL's allusions to, 261n59; House Divided speech, 114, 117, 246n28; influenced AL, 5–6, 28, 36; instructed in classical rhetoric, 5–6, 246n22; Kalamazoo speech, 103; Lyceum address, 36; Nebraska bill, 99; Peoria speech, 6, 93; son, a Mexican War casualty, 71; speech texts available, 246n23; Whig theory of economic growth, 246n25, 250n47

Whig Party: AL's Address to the People of Illinois, 41; AL's congressional nomination, 55, 237; AL's state legislature nomination, 89; AL's withdrawal from, 11; Clay's "American system," 9; collapse of party, 154; convention system, 41, 47; federal patronage, 77; Illinois Whig platform, 40–41; influence on AL, 10, 17; internal improvements, 17, 51; Massachusetts convention, 73; party history, 248n6; slavery causing intra-party conflict, 67, 86; Subtreasury speech, 27; Webster, 28

D. LEIGH HENSON is an emeritus professor in the department of English at Missouri State University. He is the author of *The Town Abraham Lincoln Warned: The Living Namesake Heritage of Lincoln, Illinois* and *Inventing Lincoln: Approaches to His Rhetoric*. His articles have appeared in the *Journal of the Abraham Lincoln Association*, *The Lincoln Herald*, and *Lincoln Lore*.

The University of Illinois Press
is a founding member of the
Association of University Presses.

———————————————————

University of Illinois Press
1325 South Oak Street
Champaign, IL 61820-6903
www.press.uillinois.edu